This book demonstrates, in fascinating diversity, how musicians in the nineteenth century thought about and described music. The analysis of music took many forms (verbal, diagrammatic, tabular, notational, graphic), was pursued for many different purposes (educational, scholarly, theoretical, promotional) and embodied very different approaches. This, the first volume of two, is concerned with writing on fugue, form and questions of style in the music of Palestrina, Handel, Bach, Mozart, Beethoven and Wagner and presents analyses of complete works or movements by the most significant theorists and critics of the century. The analyses are newly translated into English and are introduced and thoroughly annotated by Ian Bent, making this a volume of enormous importance to our understanding of the nature of music reception in the nineteenth century.

CAMBRIDGE READINGS IN THE LITERATURE OF MUSIC

General Editors: John Stevens and Peter le Huray

Music Analysis in the Nineteenth Century
Volume I: Fugue, Form and Style

CAMBRIDGE READINGS IN THE LITERATURE OF MUSIC

Cambridge Readings in the Literature of Music is a series of source materials (original documents in English translation) for students of the history of music. Many of the quotations in the volumes will be substantial, and introductory material will place the passages in context. The period covered will be from antiquity to the present day, with particular emphasis on the nineteenth and twentieth centuries. The series is part of *Cambridge Studies in Music*.

Already published:

Andrew Barker: *Greek Musical Writings, Volume I: The Musician and His Art*
Andrew Barker: *Greek Musical Writings, Volume II: Harmonic and Acoustic Theory*
James W. McKinnon: *Music in Early Christian Literature*
Peter le Huray and James Day: *Music and Aesthetics in the Eighteenth and Early-Nineteenth Centuries*
Bojan Bujić: *Music in European Thought 1851–1912*

Music Analysis in the Nineteenth Century

Volume I
Fugue, Form and Style

Edited by

Ian Bent
Columbia University, New York

CAMBRIDGE
UNIVERSITY PRESS

Published by the Press Syndicate of the University of Cambridge
The Pitt Building, Trumpington Street, Cambridge CB2 1RP
40 West 20th Street, New York, NY 10011-4211, USA
10 Stamford Road, Oakleigh, Melbourne 3166, Australia

First published in 1994

Printed in Great Britain at the University Press, Cambridge

A catalogue record for this book is available from the British Library

Library of Congress cataloguing in publication data

Music Analysis in the Nineteenth Century / edited by Ian Bent.
   p.   cm. – (Cambridge readings in the literature of music)
Includes bibliographical references and index.
Contents: v. 1. Fugue, form and style.
ISBN 0 521 25969 X (v. 1 : hardback)
1. Musical analysis – 19th century.   2. Music – History and criticism..
I. Bent, Ian.   II. Title: Music Analysis in the Nineteenth Century.   III. Series.
MT90.M88 1993 781'.09'034–dc20   93–12313 CIP MN

ISBN 0 521 25969 X hardback

In memory of Ailsa Coverdale,
who revered words

Contents

Part III: The classification of personal style

Preface to volumes I and II

'Never confuse analysis with mere description!', Hans Keller used waggishly to say, chastising unfortunate speakers at conferences. To Keller, most so-called 'criticism' and 'analysis' was an amalgam of the descriptive and the metaphorical: 'The descriptive is senseless, the metaphorical usually nonsense.' Most analytical writings boiled down to 'mere tautological descriptions'. Not even Tovey was beyond reproach: 'his "analyses" are misnomers', Keller remarked; they were in his view 'faultless descriptions' with 'occasional flashes of profound analytical insight'; otherwise they contained 'much eminently professional tautology'.[1] More recently, V. Kofi Agawu has taken one analyst to task for failing to observe 'the distinction between description and analysis, between a critical, necessarily impressionistic commentary and a rigorous interpretative exercise . . .'[2]

With censure such as this, what justification is there for entitling the contents of these two volumes 'Music *Analysis* in the Nineteenth Century'? There are in fact two justifications, one intentional, the other actual.

First, it is upon 'analysis' that most of the authors represented in these volumes considered they were engaged. Thus, analysing is what Berlioz thought he was doing when he wrote about Beethoven's nine symphonies in 1838 ('Nous allons essayer l'analyse des symphonies de ce grand maître'), and when he reviewed the first performance of Meyerbeer's *Les Huguenots* on 6 March 1836, and later its score. 'Analysis' is what Momigny set out to do with the first movement of Mozart's D minor string quartet ('Analyse du beau Quatuor en ré mineur du célèbre Mozart') and Haydn's 'Drumroll' Symphony; it is what Reicha sought to do with harmonic, melodic and contrapuntal models in all three of his major treatises; what Fétis claimed to have done with the late string quartets of Beethoven, and what von Lenz promised his readers in his treatment of Beethoven's sonatas for piano. Basevi claimed to have 'analysed' the operas of Verdi in 1859 (he called the process 'critica analitica'), and Beethoven's string quartets Op. 18 in 1874 ('analisi dei sei quartetti'). So too did Sechter in his examination of Mozart's 'Jupiter' Finale in 1843 ('Analyse der Mozartschen Instrumentalfuge'), Dehn in his studies of three fugues from Bach's *Well-tempered Clavier* in 1858 ('zu analysiren und in Betracht ihres Baues kritisch zu beleuchten'[3]), Lobe in 1850 and Helm in 1885 in their

---

1 Quoted from Hans Keller, 'K.503: The Unity of Contrasting Themes and Movements – I', *Music Review*, 17 (1956), 48–9; these views, always trenchantly put, are widespread in his writings.
2 *Music Analysis*, 7 (1988), 99: review of W. Frisch, *Brahms and the Principle of Developing Variation* (Berkeley: University of California Press, 1984).
3 'to analyse and illuminate critically in regard to their construction': the editor (Foreword) reporting Dehn's intentions before he died.

studies of works by Beethoven, and Kretzschmar in his 'analytische Bestrebungen'.[4]

Nor was this corporate expression of purpose limited to cognate forms of the Greek word *Analysis*. A multitude of terms existed in the eighteenth and nineteenth centuries by means of which those who subjected musical fabrics, configurations, structures and styles to close scrutiny might designate what they were doing: in French, *décomposer, dégager, expliquer*; in German, *auffassen, betrachten, beurtheilen, entdecken, enträthseln, erklären, erläutern, phrasiren, zergliedern, zerlegen* – to mention only a few. Each of these terms had its own special implication, each formed part of a terminological network, each belonged to a particular array of time and space. The principal terms will be discussed at strategic points in the introductions and editorial material below.

Most of the writers represented in the present volumes characterize their work in some such terms. Surprisingly, A. B. Marx (vol. II, Analysis 12) is an exception. His minutely detailed descriptions of musical formations, in his manual of composition as well as his volumes on Beethoven's works, are couched in synthetic rather than analytic terms – they are phrased constructively rather than deconstructively. (Where he used the German term *Analyse*, it was in reference to the work of others not himself, specifically that of Berlioz and Ulïbïshev.[5]) His case demonstrates that the absence of such defining terms by no means necessarily signals absence of analytical material. Nor does it for that matter imply a desire to avoid self-characterization. In the case of E. T. A. Hoffmann, for example (vol. II, Analysis 9), whose descriptions are at times highly detailed and technical, it reflects perhaps a mastery of language and a lack of self-consciousness about what he is doing.

None of this would, of course, have mollified Hans Keller, who saw the confusion as lying not in the realm of public perception, but in the mind of each deluded would-be analyst. But to return for a moment to Berlioz: when, confronted by 'bold and imposing' effects in the Act V trio of *Les Huguenots*, Berlioz pleads for 'time to reflect on my impressions', who are we to disparage his intention, which is 'to *analyse* them and *discover their causes*' (my italics)? To be sure, he was not seeking 'the latent elements of the unity of manifest contrasts' (Keller), or 'a precise formulation of norms of dimensional behaviour against which we can evaluate [the composer's] practice' (Kofi Agawu). But he *was* seeking, from an examination of Meyerbeer's complex deployment of forces in the massacre scene of this trio (three soloists and two separate on-stage choruses, with markedly conflicting gestural and emotional characters and contrasting musical styles, orchestra in the pit and brass chorus outside the auditorium) and from study of Meyerbeer's treatment of tonality here (minor key, but with the sixth degree frequently and obdurately raised), to determine precisely how the terrifying and blood-curdling effect that he had observed came about. To take apart, and uncover the prime causes – is that not a type of analytical procedure?

4 'analytical endeavours': 'Anregungen zur Förderung musikalischer Hermeneutik', *Jahrbuch der Musikbibliothek Peters für 1902*, 9 (1903), 47; later issued in *Gesammelte Aufsätze aus den Jahrbüchern der Musikbibliothek Peters* (Leipzig: Peters, 1911; reprint edn ibid 1973), p. 168.

5 Seemingly without disparagement (*Ludwig van Beethoven: Leben und Schaffen* (Berlin: Otto Janke, 1859), vol. I, p. 295 note). More likely, *Analyse* alludes to their being written in French. Marx occasionally used *zergliedern* and *Zergliederung* for what he himself did.

This, then, is the second justification for the entitling of the present volumes: that, irrespective of the name given to them, there were in the nineteenth century species of activity that meet the general criteria of the present day for analysis. Dunsby and Whittall say something of this latter sort in the following statement, while qualifying it with respect to purpose:[6]

> The kind of analysis we would nowadays recognize as 'technical' has been in practice for more than two centuries. Yet it came to be regarded as a discipline apart from compositional theory only at the turn of this century. Around this time, the relationship between traditional analysis and compositional theory ceased to be significantly reflexive.

Their first sentence, however, invokes technicality, and therefore makes a slightly different point from my own. Were we still in the 1960s or 1970s, then our two statements would perhaps be saying the same thing (intentionally or not); but in the world of the 1990s I believe they no longer do this. I shall return to this in a moment.

Consider the latter two sentences of the above quotation. Taken on their own terms, the thesis that they embody is factually disprovable: the analysis of J. S. Bach's *The Art of Fugue* in Analysis 3 below, dating from 1841 and as rigorous and technical as anything presented here, arose in the context not of compositional theory but of historical textuality. It formed the critical commentary to the *Art of Fugue* volume of a collected edition of Bach's keyboard works. Far from being prescriptive, it was an abstract engagement in contrapuntal process – written, as it was, by Moritz Hauptmann, one of the principal theorists of the century but a writer of 'pure' theory rather than compositionally instructional theory. Then again, the analysis of leitmotifs in *Tristan and Isolde* by Karl Mayrberger (Analysis 13), dating from 1881 and highly technical, was a contribution not to a composition manual but to a journal intended for amateur devotees of Wagner's music dramas, a contribution that was then turned into a small monograph indicatively titled *The Harmonic Style of Richard Wagner*.

Not that the above disproof invalidates Dunsby's and Whittall's argument. The bulk of technical analysis in the nineteenth century probably did indeed reside within compositional theory. The analyses given below by Reicha, Sechter, Czerny and Lobe certainly did; and those by Vogler, Dehn, Marx and Riemann can be seen as outgrowths of composition manuals already written or edited by those authors. The effect of my disproof is perhaps no more than to set back earlier in time the moment at which the 'reflexivity' between analysis and theory began to break down. Indeed, the continuation of Dunsby's and Whittall's statement invites this very suggestion:

> Analysis became the technical or systematic study, either of the kind of familiar tonal style few composers felt to be current any longer, or of new music that the wider public found profoundly hard to understand, and the challenges of which seemed to focus on the question of whether tonal comprehensibility was present at all.

Hauptmann's analysis of *The Art of Fugue* perfectly exemplifies the former, itself an early manifestation of the Bach revival and its author a figure later associated with that movement; and Mayrberger's exemplifies the latter, since it was one of the earliest attempts to tackle the apparent incomprehensibility of Wagner's

6 J. Dunsby and A. Whittall, *Music Analysis in Theory and Practice* (London: Faber, 1988), p. 62.

harmonic idiom, and its author was hailed as the seer who would unlock the technical mysteries of that idiom.

How far back might that moment of break-down then be set? Noting that Gottfried Weber's analysis of the opening of Mozart's 'Dissonance' Quartet was probably submitted first to his own journal, *Caecilia*, and only subsequently incorporated into the third edition of his composition manual, at least as early as 1830.

But is not this chronological exercise ultimately futile? Perhaps we should address a deeper issue, namely: whether a theorist, when executing an analysis within the environment of a manual of compositional theory, might not temporarily operate as *analyst* rather than as *instructor* – might not, that is, abandon the educational mode of thought for one that is entirely analytical. Given the peculiarly absorbing, compelling, even obsessive nature of musical analysis, is it not possible that he might become drawn into the exhilarations, fascinations and frustrations of the purely analytical process, and forget the educational purpose that he was serving? Would we wish to assert that analysis became fascinating only in the twentieth century?–the question seems somehow absurd! The purpose of this long excursion is only to ask whether technical analysis might psychologically have been analysis *per se* long before it could be said to have cut any umbilical cord previously connecting it to compositional theory.

Dunsby's and Whittall's invocation of the 'technical', to which we can now at last return, was prefatory to a discussion of the work of Donald Francis Tovey (1875–1940). As they say, Tovey brought a modest technical element to his writings on music; nevertheless, he wrote for the musically untrained reader, for the music lover who hated jargon, for what he liked to think of as the 'naïve listener'. Tovey himself, though we tend to overlook the fact nowadays, was heir to a tradition – as were Schoenberg and Schenker to other traditions –: in his case, a tradition of writings for the nineteenth-century musical amateur. This is the unremarked obverse of Dunsby's and Whittall's technical tradition: a body of writings that was almost coeval with Romantic music criticism, and which was from the beginning completely independent of compositional theory. This 'elucidatory' tradition, as I have loosely styled it, sought to explain music in terms of content rather than of sonic fabric. It was Peter Kivy who in 1980 acknowledged the disesteem into which content-based music analysis has fallen in the twentieth century by virtue of its congenital subjectivity, and set himself the challenge of showing:[7]

> that a humanistic musical analysis could be reconstituted and made respectable once again in the form of the familiar emotive characterization of music – but only if two things were established: first, how it makes sense to apply expressive predicates to music (which answers the charge of unintelligibility); and, second, what the public, intersubjective criteria of application are (which answers the charge of subjectivity).

Since that time, others, some of them building on, or influenced by, Joseph Kerman's appeals from the mid-1960s on for a higher form of criticism,[8] have sought to

7   P. Kivy, *The Corded Shell: Reflections on Musical Expression* (Princeton: Princeton University Press, 1980), p. 132, also 9–11.
8   J. Kerman, 'A Profile for American Musicology', *JAMS*, 18 (1965), 61–9; *Musicology* (London: Fontana/Collins, 1985) also published as *Contemplating Music* (Cambridge, MA: Harvard University Press, 1985), chap. 3 and *passim*.

envisage such a 'humanistic' – in contrast to quasi-scientific – mode of analysis. Fred Everett Maus has propounded a type of analysis in which the distinctions between 'structural' and 'emotive', between 'technical' and 'non-technical', are lost; using a dramatic model, he interprets music in terms of 'actions' and 'agents'. The music's structure becomes a 'plot', and the analysis 'narrates' (in the fullest sense of that word) that plot.[9] Marion Guck has for some time been engaged in a systematic investigation of metaphor in analytic discourse about music with a view to locating new modes of description.[10] No longer will a statement such as the following (from vol. II, Analysis 4 of the present work) be greeted with universal scorn or discomfort:

> The movement begins with strident augmented sixths, like a sudden cry of anguish from the terrified soul. Passagework now follows, which, like some foaming mountain stream, plunges wildly into the chasm below, growls and grumbles in the depths, until at last a figure, tossing back and forth – the first principal theme – breaks away from the whirlpool, eddies up and down, then spouts up roaring in uncontrolled passion, undeterred by the wailing parallel thirds which themselves are dragged into the maelstrom.

These words, a mixture of technicality ('augmented sixths', 'passagework', and the like), simile ('like a sudden cry . . .'), metaphor ('plunges wildly into the chasm below') and partial personification ('roaring in uncontrolled passion'), map the motions of natural phenomena and the human psyche on to the motions of the music in an effort to exteriorize the interior life of that music. The words are by Ernst von Elterlein, a minor mid-nineteenth-century writer on music. Written in 1856, they depict the opening of the Finale of Beethoven's 'Appassionata' Sonata.

A significant group of thinkers is nowadays prepared to acknowledge that figurative writing containing these categories of language usage has a legitimate place in analytical discourse. Such vividly naturalistic images as the above, in such profusion, seem quintessentially Romantic, recalling (to take English examples) the paintings of John Martin or the poetry of Wordsworth and Tennyson (albeit in a debased and only semi-literary form). The 1990s have their own world of images upon which to draw for analytical purposes. The present volumes appear perhaps not inopportunely, displaying as they do a broad range of analytical types from the last century: technically theoretical, compositionally instructive, musicologically historical and metaphorically experiential.

These two volumes differ from others already published in the series *Cambridge Readings in the Literature of Music* not only in their concern with specifically

---

9 F. E. Maus, 'Music as Drama', *Music Theory Spectrum*, 10 (1988), 56–73. Maus's approach is informed by the work of Edward T. Cone, *The Composer's Voice* (Berkeley: University of California Press, 1974), and by recent literary theory and narratology, notably by T. Todorov, *Introduction to Poetics* (Minneapolis: University of Minnesota Press, 1981). The term 'plot' was first imported into musical discourse from historian Paul Veyne by Jean-Jacques Nattiez in 'The Concepts of Plot and Seriation Process in Music Analysis', *Music Analysis*, 4 (1985), 107–18.

10 M. A. Guck, e.g. 'Rehabilitating the Incorrigible', in *'Cognitive Communication' about Music*, ed. F. E. Maus and M. A. Guck (Princeton: Princeton University Press, forthcoming); see Guck's notes 19 and 23 for a survey of recent analyses by Cone, Lewin and Treitler that use figurative language, and by Newcombe that uses emotive descriptions. Tangentially, see remarks in my own 'History of Music Theory: Margin or Center?', *Theoria*, 6 (1993), 1–21.

musical rather than aesthetic, social and philosophical issues (something that they share only with vol. II of *Greek Musical Writing*s), but also, and most particularly, in the concern of each of the passages presented here with a single piece of music or repertory of pieces. In almost every case, the integrity of the piece or repertory under discussion demanded entire and uncut discussion. The only exceptions are Hans von Wolzogen's thematic guide to Wagner's *Parsifal* (vol. II, Analysis 6), the sheer length of which demanded selection of an excerpt, Lobe's discussion of Beethoven's Quartet Op. 18 no. 2, which necessitated the excision of much inter-woven educational material, and one or two cases in which I have omitted an author's general introduction or a non-analytical interpolation, where these were not essential to the complete discourse.

The result is a pair of volumes with fewer and for the most part longer excerpts than in other volumes of the series. In two cases, what is presented is an entire monograph; in others, an entire chapter or section of a book. Only in the cases of the discussions of Beethoven's three periods by Fétis and Ulïbïshev have I excerpted brief passages in the manner of previous volumes. The two volumes in a sense serve as companions to two earlier ones: *Music and Aesthetics in the Eighteenth and Early-Nineteenth Centuries* by le Huray and Day, which was constructed around the concept of Romanticism, and *Music in European Thought 1851–1912* by Bujić, which delineated a number of themes and issues. In turn, those two volumes provide a wonderful aesthetic backdrop to the present ones that I urge the reader to explore. The four volumes can be viewed together as a subset of the series.

Every effort has been made to provide high-quality texts. Where several primary texts exist, I have usually taken the earliest, consulting first editions if possible and reporting notable differences wherever I also had access to later ones. Where two significantly divergent texts exist, I have again usually adopted the earlier, as in the case of Schumann's analysis of Berlioz's *Symphonie fantastique* (vol. II, Analysis 10), where I have presented the original article from the *Neue Zeitschrift für Musik* of 1835 rather than Schumann's own curtailed text in his collected works of 1854, and the case of Fétis's discussion of the three periods of Beethoven's music, where preservation of the interchange between Fétis and Ulïbïshev dictated my presenting the first edition of the *Biographie universelle*. I have taken a later reading only for a good reason, as in the case of Gottfried Weber's discussion of Mozart's 'Dissonance' Quartet and Mayrberger's of Wagner's *Tristan and Isolde*, where the second version in each case significantly expands the first. Of von Elterlein I had no choice but to take a later edition, since the first was not accessible to me.

Of the analyses presented here, five originally incorporated the entire text of the music under discussion. In two of those cases, the music is nowadays readily available to non-specialist readers, and has not been included: the first movement of Haydn's 'Drumroll' Symphony, and the Finale of Mozart's 'Jupiter' Symphony; information supplied by the analyst on the score has been incorporated editorially into the analytical text. In the three remaining cases, the music has been supplied in the Appendix: (a) the fugue from Handel's Harpsichord Suite No. 6 in F♯

minor; (b) the Prelude No. 8 in D minor from Vogler's *Thirty-two Preludes for Organ and Fortepiano*; and (c) the Andante for Wind Quintet by Reicha.

It is the translator's duty to be faithful to the original-language text throughout. A literal rendering, however, can produce a translated text that is lifeless. At worst, it can lead to a linguistic no-man's land devoid of idiom, character or rhetoric, in which the reader has to infer the original in order to understand the translation. I have sought to catch the spirit of the original as well as its narrow meaning, and at the same time to make my renderings vivid, immediate and enjoyable. I have used footnotes and square-bracketed original words to signal liberties taken, and to alert the reader to the presence of terminological problems. I have also interpolated page numbers so as to facilitate reference to the original.

While never attempting to produce counterfeit Victorian prose, I have tried to avoid anachronistic twentieth-century terms and expressions. The volume in this series edited by Bojan Bujić was criticized by one reviewer for failing to use contemporary translations where they exist.[11] I take the contrary view. Many nineteenth-century translations of music theory were without literary merit; they were frequently guilty of excessive literalness (the use of 'clang-tone' for the German *Klangton* is a notorious example); moreover, they used technical terms that were current in their own day but now mean little or nothing. Consider the opening of John Bishop's translation of the essay by Weber included in this volume:

> [Bishop:] It now remains for me to fulfil the promise made at the end of §225 . . . , of presenting an analysis of the texture of the transitions, as well as of the modulatory course and other peculiarities, in the introduction of Mozart's violin-quartett in C . . .

> [Bent:] All that remains for me at the close of this volume is to discharge the duty that I gave myself at the end of §225 . . . of undertaking an analysis of the intricate web of passing notes, and at the same time of the tonal scheme and other unusual features of the introduction to the String Quartet in C by Mozart . . .

For a start, Bishop omits a phrase (*am Schlusse dieses Bandes*). Secondly, by translating *modulatorisch* as 'modulatory' he shows his insensitivity to the distinction between *Ausweichung* and *Modulation*, the former being the term for what in English meant, and means, 'modulation' (for 1832, my 'tonal scheme' for *modulatorischer Gang* is admittedly a shade modern, but it conveys the sense of a difficult phrase more accurately). Thirdly, Bishop's use of 'transition' (which is nowadays a structural-tonal term) for *Durchgang* places a veil between the modern reader and the original German text, as do to a lesser degree the now antiquated term 'violin-quartett', and the archaic usage of 'peculiarities'. It is for these reasons that I also rejected the nineteenth-century translations of Reicha's main treatises, Riemann's *Katechismus der Fugen-Komposition*, Wagner's programme for the Ninth Symphony of Beethoven, von Elterlein's *Beethoven's Clavier-Sonaten*, Spitta's Bach volume and Wolzogen's thematic guide to *Parsifal*. Contemporaneous

---

11 Leon Botstein, in *19th-Century Music*, 13 (1989/90), 168–78: 'By retranslating Hanslick and Wagner, we might gain in clarity from a philosophical or revisionist historical point of view. But by abandoning Cohen and Ellis, we would lose the opportunity to use the historical surfaces of semantics and language to illuminate the nature of perceived meanings in the past and to lay bare the historical distance of texts' (p. 174).

translations are not a satisfactory means by which to get to know nineteenth-century theoretical works; consider only how badly served has Moritz Hauptmann been with W. E. Heathcote's translation of his *Die Natur der Harmonik und Metrik*,[12] and the adverse effect that that unusable text has had on the understanding of Hauptmann's important theories in the English-speaking world.

There are only four exceptions to my rule of independent translation: the analysis by Czerny, for which the German original was unavailable to me, leaving the text by Merrick and Bishop as my only resort; that by E. T. A. Hoffmann, a translation of which by Martyn Clarke for Cambridge University Press was already underway, where to duplicate this would have been perverse (I greatly appreciate the licence he and his editor David Charlton gave me to make slight modifications to their finished text in the interests of consistency with the rest of my two volumes); and the two analyses in Italian, for which my linguistic abilities were wholly inadequate. I am grateful to Walter Grauberg and Jonathan Shiff for supplying such excellent translations of these, and also for allowing me ultimate control of the text.

My prime debt of gratitude is to the trustees of the Radcliffe Trust, who did me the honour of appointing me the first Radcliffe Fellow in Musicology, so providing me with the year's sabbatical leave, part of it spent at Harvard University, during which this project was conceived and initiated. Two Columbians and one Nottinghamian must be singled out for the special quality of help that they gave me over long periods of time: Thomas Mace, for brilliant detective work in Butler Library, and for bringing his formidable command of languages to bear on many of my translations; Robert Austerlitz, an inexhaustible fount of linguistic knowledge to me over the past five years; and Robert Pascall, my confederate on nineteenth-century matters for so many years. Numerous others have freely given advice, and have supplied me with materials and information. Such assistance is ultimately unaccountable; but where specific account is possible, I have given it in footnotes. Here, I can do no more than call an inevitably incomplete roll of generous-spirited scholars who have aided me: Milton Babbitt, David Bernstein, Jennifer Day, James Day, John Deathridge, Esther Dunsby, Keith Falconer, Cynthia Gessele, Jennifer Hughes, Peter le Huray, Wulf Liebeschuetz, Lewis Lockwood, C. P. McGill, Karen Painter, Roger Parker, Leeman Perkins, Harold S. Powers, Fritz Reckow, John Reed, Jerome Roche, Janna Saslaw, Desmond Shawe-Taylor, Hinrich Siefken, Elaine Sisman, Maynard Solomon, Richard Taruskin, Joanne Wright and James Zetzel.

Without the assistance of the librarians and staff of the following libraries, my work could not have been done: the Bibliothèque nationale, Paris; the British Library, London; Cambridge University Library (my wonderful summer work-haven!), and the Pendlebury Library, Cambridge University; Columbia University Avery, General and Music Libraries; the Eda Kuhn Loeb and Isham Memorial Libraries of Music, and Widener Library, Harvard University; the New York Public Library; The Nottingham University Arts and Music Libraries; the Österreichische Nationalbibliothek Musiksammlung, Vienna. These volumes are

---

12   (Leipzig: B&H, 1853; Eng. trans., London: Sonnenschein, 1884, 2/1893).

silent testimony to the toll that academic work is apt to take on home life; I thank my close family, all of whom have been affected in one way or another, and in particular Caroline and Jonathan, who bore the brunt, and gave nothing but love and support in return.

Abbreviations

AmZ	*Allgemeine musikalische Zeitung*
B&H	Breitkopf und Härtel
Bujić	Bojan Bujić: *Music in European Thought 1851–1912* (Cambridge: CUP, 1988)
HwMT	*Handwörterbuch der musikalischen Terminologie*, ed. H. H. Eggebrecht and others (Wiesbaden: Steiner, 1972–)
JAMS	*Journal of the American Musicological Society*
JMT	*Journal of Music Theory*
le Huray/Day	Peter le Huray and James Day: *Music and Aesthetics in the Eighteenth and Early-Nineteenth Centuries* (Cambridge: CUP, 1981)
MGG	*Die Musik in Geschichte und Gegenwart*, ed. F. Blume (Kassel and Basel: Bärenreiter, 1949–69)
NGDM	*The New Grove Dictionary of Music and Musicians*, ed. S. Sadie (London: Macmillan, 1980)
NZM	*Neue Zeitschrift für Musik*
OED	*Oxford English Dictionary*, 12 vols (Oxford: Clarendon Press, 1933)
64^2	the second beat of b. 64
$^3 17$	the third beat of the bar preceding b. 17

General introduction

§1 Music theory and music analysis

> . . . a *new theory*, established on the true interpretation of Nature, on meticulous analysis of good musical compositions . . .[1]

1803: Jérôme-Joseph de Momigny's ringing Preface to his *Complete Course in Harmony and Composition*. Like a fanfare for the newly dawning century and a repudiation of the old, it is a symbolic declaration.

Momigny, whose work is the earliest represented in the present volume and launches the series of extended analytical extracts given below, was admittedly a writer of minor significance to the advancement of music theory, but he remains nonetheless an intriguing and historically illuminating figure. This Introduction will take his declaration in its music-theoretical context, first as a charge against Rameau, which will in turn require a brief examination of Rameau's own theory, then as a statement of intent for its own age. To accomplish the latter will necessitate looking first at four models (other than Rameau's mathematical model) that the eighteenth century held out for musical structure: *rhetoric* (music as gesture and strategy) and *syntax* (music as language), which together furnish a quasi-scientific procedure for music analysis here called an 'agenda', which continues into the nineteenth century; physiological *anatomy* (music as a body with limbs) and *mechanism* (music as a system with functioning parts). Then it will trace a fifth model: that of *organism* (music as holistic and purposive structure). It will examine how this new model superseded previous ones, how it replaced the earlier aesthetic theory of unity and how the technical means were found for describing music as organism.

To return, now, to that ringing Preface quoted at the opening: Momigny qualifies his declaration by saying that his '*new theory*' is one that admits only two things:

> what is furnished by the resonance of the sonorous body, *correctly heard*, and what is at the same time sanctioned by the ear, and buttressed by the reason and authority of the greatest masters.

From these conditions, it is possible already to prognosticate the type of theory that is to come. 'Sonorous body' signals a theory founded on a natural acoustical phenomenon, the overtones of a single note – a theory that evidently derives from the work of that most influential of all French eighteenth-century music theorists,

---

1   *sur l'analyse réfléchie des bons ouvrages pratiques* (J. -J. de Momigny, *Cours complet d'harmonie et de composition, d'après une théorie nouvelle et générale de la musique*, vol. I (Paris: Momigny, 1803–05), p. iii).

Jean-Philippe Rameau – and '*correctly heard*' indicates a belief that Rameau's observation of that acoustical phenomenon was faulty. 'Sanctioned by the ear' introduces the human cognitive system as arbiter, whilst 'buttressed by . . . the greatest masters' heralds verification of theory by the analysis of the work of publicly ratified composers.

The 'greatest masters' – that is to say, the greatest of the great composers – are invoked here, Momigny says, not in a spirit of sycophancy, but in emulation of the man of enlightenment who:

> while admiring what is substantial and delightful in their masterpieces, does not on that account close his eyes to the faults that have crept into them, whether through ill-considered haste or through an excessively cerebral approach.[2]

This is an affirmation not so much of good taste as of the primacy of unbiased observation, of reliance on seeing things as they really are. Momigny invokes, through the French philosopher Étienne Condillac (1715–80), the principle of empirical sensationism articulated by the English thinker John Locke (1632–1704). Since, Momigny says, we have no innate ideas, since all that we have we acquire through sensation and reflection – that is, through the impressions that external objects make upon us via our senses, and through our capacity to compare and correlate those objects reflectively – the best method for the instruction of others is that method which we unconsciously use for instruction of ourselves, namely *analysis*. In contrast to synthesis, which dictates laws:[3]

> analysis, a more modest pursuit, involves the pupil in the work of the teacher. It is a reasoned examination, jointly conducted, its apparent purpose being to satisfy mutual curiosity, hence more a recreation than a labour.

Momigny believed in the affinity of music and natural language, and so characterized analysis as the separating out of the structural components of music as if they were the components of prose and poetry, governed by the rules of grammar, syntax and versification. Drawing presumably on the German music-theoretical tradition established by Riepel, Koch and Kirnberger in the mid- and late eighteenth century, and based in rhetoric and poetics, he understood that the task of analysis was 'to distinguish period from period, verse from verse, hemistiche from hemistiche, all the way down to the level of the proposition and its various members' (hemistiche being a division of a line of verse, proposition a statement comprising subject and predicate).

Though understating the scope and richness of his own analyses, Momigny does not misrepresent his reliance on analytical method: again and again he resorts directly to it, adducing rules and principles only afterwards, on the basis of observation. Nor does he misrepresent Rameau in suggesting that the latter's method is the opposite, proceeding as it does from rational argument in the confident belief that all of reality has an inherently rational structure. However, Momigny seems to insinuate more than this: that Rameau discounted altogether the empirical data of finished, artistic compositions, never using them to exemplify his theoretical assertions.

2   . . . *soit par préc[ip]itation, soit par esprit de système* (ibid, iii–iv).   3   ibid, 270–71.

§2 Rameau and music analysis

Momigny's charge is factually incorrect. Rameau introduced a complete composition into even his first published theoretical work, the *Treatise on Harmony* of *1722*, though it may have been written specially for the *Treatise* rather than having had an independent life in the performed repertory.[4] This, appearing at the end of Book III of the *Treatise*, was a five-part vocal fugue with instrumental accompaniment, *Laboravi clamans*, beneath the lowest part of which he placed a separate staff showing a series of conceptual bass notes from which he saw the harmonies deriving.

Four years later, in the *New System of Theoretical Music* of 1726, Rameau invoked two works that undoubtedly were independent: the Twelve Sonatas for Violin Solo Op. 5 (1700), of Corelli, and the monologue 'At last, he is in my power' from Act II Scene 5 of the opera *Armide* (1686) by Lully. To the former he devoted a whole chapter, quoting seventeen passages containing 'errors', signalling certain bass notes with letters of the alphabet, and then constructing chains of reasoning to expose internal inconsistencies.[5] The monologue by Lully was cited for the first time in the *New System*'s chapter 7, on modulation. Rameau then printed it entire in chapter 22, with voice and bass line in score and parallel staff beneath. This score, too, is marked with letters which refer to a page of commentary at the end delineating seven harmonic situations.[6]

Twenty-eight years later, in 1754, Rameau returned to Lully's monologue for a much more extended treatment in his *Observations on Our Instinct for Music*.[7] He discussed there another passage from Lully's *Armide*, and also took up again the monologue 'Sad Auguries' from his own opera *Castor and Pollux* (1737, revised 1754), which he had cited briefly in 1750 in his *Demonstration of the Principle of Harmony*.[8] Six years later he returned yet again to his own and Lully's monologues in his *Code of Musical Practice*.[9]

What was Rameau's purpose in engaging in these discussions, in particular those of his own fugue, and the operatic items by Lully and himself? To answer this will require a brief excursion to look at Rameau's extraordinarily significant theory, at the very heart of which lay the 'resonating body' (*corps sonore*), as

---

4 See Jean Duron, 'Le Grand Motet: Rameau face à ses contemporains', *Jean-Philippe Rameau: Colloque international organisé par la Société Rameau: Dijon 21–24 septembre 1983*, ed. J. de la Gorce (Paris and Geneva: Champion-Slatkine, 1987), pp. 331–2. J.-P. Rameau, *Traité d'harmonie* (Paris: Ballard, 1722), pp. 341–55; Eng. trans. P. Gossett (New York: Dover, 1971), pp. 357–66.

5 J.-P. Rameau, *Nouveau système de musique théorique . . .* (Paris: Ballard, 1726), pp. 94–106; Eng. trans. in Joel Lester, *Compositional Theory in The Eighteenth Century* (Cambridge, MA: Harvard University Press, 1992), pp. 305–19.

6 ibid, 41, 80–89, 89–90.

7 J.-P. Rameau, *Observations sur notre instinct pour la musique, et sur son principe . . .* (Paris: Prault, 1754), pp. 69–125 (Exx.B–G). The monologue had in the meantime become a *cause-célèbre* in the disputes over Italian and French opera: see C. Verba, 'The Development of Rameau's Thoughts on Modulation and Chromatics', *JAMS*, 26 (1973), 69–91.

8 ibid, 55–61 (Ex.A), 67; *Démonstration du principe de l'harmonie . . .* (Paris: Durand and Pissot, 1750), p. 97. The plates for both Lully extracts now lacked fundamental bass stave but had instead key-areas verbally designated beneath the score, giving them to the modern eye a more 'analytical' appearance.

9 J.-P. Rameau, *Code de musique pratique, ou Méthodes pour apprendre de la musique . . .* (Paris: Imprimerie Royale, 1760), pp. 168–9 (Ex.T).

presented in his *Treatise* of 1722. A string, or column of air in a pipe, Rameau observed, once set in vibration, gives out not a single pitch but a set of pitches related proportionally to one another (now commonly known as overtones, or collectively as the harmonic spectrum, although Rameau understood them in these terms only later in his career). From this observed acoustical phenomenon, according to Rameau, followed all the other principles of harmony: chords (triads and seventh chords), chord inversion, cadence, chord progression, function (tonic, dominant, subdominant), consonance and dissonance, key, mode and modulation.

Following Descartes' use of the verb 'to generate', Rameau in his *Treatise* spoke of the octave as *generated by* division of a given source pitch, the fifth as *generated by* division of that octave, the third as *generated by* the division of that fifth, the tone as *generated by* the division of that major third; then by extension, of chord types as *generated by* fundamental chords. This, then, is what the five-part fugue *Laboravi clamans* was intended to demonstrate. The additional staff with the series of conceptual bass notes (not unlike that seen in Analysis 2 below, though split there into staves 5, 6 and 7) was a device that Rameau had already used in the earlier music examples of the *Treatise*. It displayed notes that were implicit, but not always sounded in the actual bass line, and these were the source pitches that generated the intervals, hence harmonies, hence chord types, above them. Together these source pitches made up the foundational bass line that Rameau called the 'fundamental bass' (*basse fondamentale*). In effect, then, by adding this staff, he was conducting a harmonic analysis of the piece, one which showed that the piece conformed to his theory, and at the same time gave practical validation to that theory.

Only later in his career did Rameau widen this concept by speaking of *génération harmonique*. By 'harmonic generation', Rameau denoted not merely the generation of the triad from an initial source pitch, or fundamental, but the generation of a succession of fundamentals from the first, then in turn a succession of chords upon those fundamentals, hence linear progressions connecting those chords. In short, all the materials of French Baroque harmonic practice could be *generated from* the single tone; or, to put it another way, the single tone contained within itself the seeds of all harmonic practice – and that included melody and counterpoint, and even metre and rhythm, as well as harmony in the narrow sense. Thus, in invoking the monologue by Lully, Rameau sought at first to demonstrate that its tonal areas were correctly distributed and its movement from key to key was perfectly executed, and also to show how the implied fundamentals of a piece could be adduced, and what 'beautiful simplicity' existed between the actual bass line and the fundamental bass. When he returned to the piece in 1754, he had the larger aim of showing that the tonal distance traversed by a musical modulation could be used to match with precision the distance in sentiment between two adjacent phrases of libretto. Lully, he believed, had possessed a mastery of this process, despite knowing nothing of the scientific basis of his art. He had been led solely by feeling, by good taste and by instinct.[10] His era had been totally ignorant of the underlying principle of music. Thus, when the clear light of reason was directed on to his music – that

10   *Nouveau système*, p. 41; *Observations*, p. 76; *Code*, p. 168.

is, when the fundamental bass was adduced, and was compared with the sentiments of the text – a perfect homology was disclosed between the two, and a complete conformity of the fundamental bass itself to Rameau's rules.

If Momigny was factually wrong in insinuating that Rameau discounted artistic compositions as empirical data, he was surely right in spirit. Rameau's theory is a self-reliant edifice (or series of edifices, to be more correct): at no point does it depend on analysis of such data, as by contrast does that of Momigny. Analysis of extant compositions by known composers is one of the distinguishing features of Momigny's *Complete Course*, constituting a significant legacy for theorists and for historians of analysis today. The treatise contains many analyses of works (in part or whole) by C. P. E. Bach, J. S. Bach, Beethoven, Clementi, Handel, Haydn, Momigny himself and Mozart. Most notable among these are the extended analyses of the first movements of Mozart's String Quartet in D minor, K421/417*b*, and Haydn's 'Drumroll' Symphony, No. 103 in E♭.

§3 Rhetoric and syntax; analytical agendas

Music analysis, then, was by no means a nineteenth-century invention. Its ancestry is in fact easily traced back to the beginning of the seventeenth century, and analytical processes can be observed at work in music theory a whole millenium earlier. We have already glimpsed the harnessing of two non-musical models for music-analytical purposes: those of rhetoric and language. The application to music of both models extends back well into the Middle Ages. Thus, in what is widely regarded as the first surviving full-scale analysis of a piece of music, we can find traces of both: Joachim Burmeister's *Musica poetica* of 1606 contains a minutely detailed analysis of a five-part motet, *In me transierunt* by Orlando di Lasso, which diagnoses certain general technical characteristics, then breaks the piece into three rhetorical phases (*Exordium–Confirmatio–Epilogus*) and nine quasi-linguistic units (*periodos*), scanning each of these units for the presence of rhetorical devices, of which Burmeister has previously supplied a glossary of twenty-seven 'figures'. The purpose of the exercise is to exemplify the more general agenda with which Burmeister has equipped the analyst:[11]

> Analysis of a composition is the resolution of that composition into a particular mode and a particular species of counterpoint, and into its affections or periods . . . Analysis consists of five parts: determination of (1) mode, (2) species of tonality and (3) counterpoint, (4) consideration of quality and (5) resolution of the composition into affections, or periods.

Burmeister then enlarges on each of these categories in turn. It is interesting to juxtapose with the above a not dissimilar agenda provided nearly a century and a half later in 1737 by Johann Mattheson for the purpose of analysing purely instrumental pieces of music:[12]

11 Joachim Burmeister, *Musica poetica* (Rostock: Myliander, 1606; reprint edn Kassel and Basel: Bärenreiter, 1955), pp. 71–3, analysis 73–4. There are antecedents to this material in Burmeister's two earlier treatises of 1599 and 1601.

12 J. Mattheson, *Kern melodischer Wissenschaft* (Hamburg: Herold, 1737; reprint edn Hildesheim: Olms, 1976), §49, pp. 109–10; *Der vollkommene Capellmeister* (Hamburg: Herold, 1739; reprint edn Kassel: Bärenreiter, 1954), Eng. trans. E.C. Harriss (Ann Arbor, MI: UMI Research Press, 1954), §79, pp. 224–5.

one must identify (1) the affections intended to be expressed by the music alone, without words; (2) the [syntactic] subdivisions of the discourse, for which there are no words to show the way; (3) the accentuation, or emphasis; (4) the geometric proportion and (5) the arithmetic proportion. In even the shortest of pieces, all of this is to be found.

Mattheson's analysis, following Baroque affective doctrine, identifies an emotional state that characterizes the piece as a whole (e.g. 'moderate gaiety' for a typical minuet, 'jubilant delight' for a gavotte). His syntactic analysis successively breaks a piece down into paragraphs, sentences, clauses, subclauses and phrases, marking them off by paragraph signs, periods, colons, semicolons and commas, respectively. By accentuation is meant the piece's climactic stress points; by geometric proportion, its underlying, regular phrase structure (e.g. four-by-four bars) and by arithmetic proportion, the recurrence of specific rhythmic patterns (expressed as poetic feet, e.g. spondee, dactyl). Mattheson then restated this procedure as an eight-stage process whereby the total structure is segmented at four hierarchical levels, and periodicity and recurrent rhythmic configurations are observed. A basis for all of this in grammatical, rhetorical and poetic analysis had been given in an earlier chapter (as a pioneering venture: 'you won't find these terms in even the very latest music dictionaries'), under the general name *Diastolica*.[13]

At another point in his treatise, Mattheson provided a second analytical procedure, based entirely on the principles of rhetoric. In this, he set forth a six-phase schema for the structure of a piece of vocal music, then exemplified it with an analysis of an aria (otherwise unknown) by Benedetto Marcello.[14] These prescriptions have an optimism about them that perhaps makes them a product of their age, an optimism reflecting the positive spirit of an era of rapid scientific progress. They are like laboratory experiments conducted according to standardized procedures, the very prescriptive nature of which guarantees success. Their naïveté is exposed even in Mattheson's own implementation, for the Marcello analysis seems to lose its way hopelessly. It is hard to tell whether the six-phase schema applies once through the whole aria, or whether the aria passes several times through it, section by section. Mattheson's account is confident in tone, but vague in substance.

This kind of analytical prescription is to be found also in the nineteenth century. There are two overt examples in the present volume. Abbé Georg Joseph Vogler analyses his own Prelude No. 8 (1806: Analysis 7 below) against a three-stage agenda: 1) *rhetoric*, 2) *harmonic logic*, 3) *aesthetics*. Under rhetoric, he traces recurrences of the opening thematic material in almost semiotic detail; under harmonic logic, he charts the roots of all the vertical sonorities and performs a phrase segmentation that tracks tonal movement; and under aesthetics he answers seven questions designed to test whether the inner content of the piece matches its formal structure. Gottfried Weber analyses the opening of Mozart's 'Dissonance'

13   *Kern*, Part V, pp. 71–92, 'The Subdivisions of Musical Discourse', expanded as *Capellmeister*, Part II, chapter 9, pp. 180–95, 'The Sections and Subdivisions of Musical Discourse', the term *diastolica* only in *Capellmeister*. The eight-stage process is merely stated in *Kern*, §52, p. 110, but is itemized in *Capellmeister*, §84, p. 225.

14   *Kern*, Part VII, pp. 127–43, 'Disposition, Elaboration and Embellishment in Musical Composition', expanded as *Capellmeister*, Part II, chap. 14, pp. 235–44, 'The Disposition, Elaboration and Embellishment of a Piece of Music'.

Quartet (1831–2: Analysis 10 below) against a six-stage agenda of even greater technical detail: 1) *tonal scheme*, 2) *passing notes*, 3) *cross-relations*, 4) *parallel progressions*, 5) *grammatical construction*, 6) *rhetorical import*.[15] Under tonal scheme, Weber measures ambiguity as a property of the chords in this passage; under grammatical construction, he draws together the data of stages 1–4, reanimating the dynamics of the passage; under rhetorical import, he investigates the composer's intentions, and extracts from the passage its 'governing idea'. (We shall encounter a third user of prescription in volume II of the present work: rather surprisingly, Robert Schumann, who analyses Berlioz's *Symphonie fantastique* (1835: vol. II, Analysis 10) against a four-stage agenda: 1) *form*, 2) *techniques of composition*, 3) *idea*, 4) *governing spirit*.)

§4 Biological models for music analysis

Rhetoric and syntax were not the only non-musical models for music analysis in the eighteenth century. If we return for a moment to Mattheson's analytical method for instrumental pieces, from 1737, we find this statement immediately following the five-point agenda:

> Just as in the whole of nature and in all of Creation there is not a single bodily form that can be properly apprehended without dissection, so let me be the first ever to take apart a melody, and systematically to investigate its parts. For our experiment, a short Minuet will serve first, so that everyone may see how so small a thing is bodily constructed, unless it is a monstrosity, and so that one may learn from tiny objects how to pronounce sound judgment on more weighty ones.

In using words such as 'dissection' (*Zergliederung*) and 'take apart' (*zerlegen*), Mattheson was transferring the language of the natural sciences to the world of music theory. Strongly influenced himself by the ideas of Locke, and believing in the paramount importance of the senses, he was suggesting that the empirical methods of the scientific investigator (*Probe*: 'experiment') might be applied to the living forms of music.

The history of science in the sixteenth and seventeenth centuries had seen enormous advances with the growth of anatomy as a field, and of dissection as its primary technique, aided latterly by the microscope. Beginning with the revolutionary work of Vesalius (1514–64) and his followers in Padua, and continuing with that of others such as William Harvey (1578–1657), Regnier de Graaf (1641–73), Jan Swammerdam (1637–80) and Giovanni Borelli (1608–79), it had brought about a significant understanding of how the body worked as both a physical system comprising muscles, bones and the heart, and a chemical system involving blood, gland secretions and digestive processes. On the other hand, it presented the early eighteenth century with a dilemma that was to last for 150 years: whether the body could be explained purely as a physico-chemical system, as seventeenth-century

---

15 Cf. J. B. Logier, *A System of the Science of Music and Practical Composition* (London: Green, 1827), p. 295: '[1] The Key, whether major or minor. [2] The Time. [3] Fundamental Basses. [4] Modulation and Fundamental 7ths. [5] Dissonances. [6] Passing Notes, Auxiliary Notes, and Secondary Harmony. [7] Periods. [8] Sections and Imitation.'

thinkers had in the main sought to show, or whether it possessed some property exclusive to living organisms – a special vital principle.

In one sense, what follows the passage by Mattheson quoted above is purest musical anatomy. The parts into which the melody is dissected are its *Glieder*, 'limbs', or 'members', and their subordinate parts; to analyse is *zergliedern*, 'to dismember' (about which there will be more to say in the Introduction to Part I, below). But most striking is the aside 'unless it is a monstrosity'. The noun here is *Misgeburt*: literally, 'misbegotten', but really meaning 'born with a deformity', a 'monstrosity', a 'hideosity'. For eighteenth-century natural historians, children or animals born with parts of the body missing or superabundant, such as were commonly displayed at fairs and carnivals, were no mere objects of curiosity (any more than were children found to have been brought up by animals in the wild, or even the blind, the deaf and the dumb): they were valuable clues in the search for an understanding of how species reproduced and were regenerated – for what was to become the theory of heredity in the new nineteenth-century science of biology.[16] The principal discussions of *monstres* were those by Pierre de Maupertuis (1698–1759) in the 1740s and Charles Bonnet (1720–93) in the 1760s, especially concerning celebrated cases of albino Negros, and of families with a recurrence of six fingers and six toes; but the phenomenon of gross abnormality had already troubled seventeenth-century thinkers who believed that God had created all species as fixities, and also those who maintained that each new life-form was 'preformed' in the image of one or other of its parents.[17]

§5 Nature versus mind as organizing principle

The views of Rameau and Mattheson as to the origin of music were sharply at odds. According to Rameau, music's organizing principle lay in nature, the resonating body providing all the material of harmony; harmony preceded melody, and from it composition was generated via the succession of fundamentals. Mattheson, in a work provocatively entitled *Essence of the Science of Melody* (1737), disputed every one of these points:[18]

> Melody is fundamentally none other than the original, true and simple harmony itself, in which all intervals follow one *after* another, in *order*, and in *succession*. With music in parts, these selfsame intervals, and no others, sound one *with* another, *together*, and *simultaneously*.
>
> This central proposition puts an end to dispute on the matter. For everyone must concede that the prime elements from which part-writing is generated are [first] the very scale-degrees themselves, and second the innate natural learning [*Natur-Lehre*]

16 I am grateful to Keith Falconer for first suggesting this interpretation of Mattheson's *Misgeburt* to me.

17 It is tempting, but idle, to speculate that when using the geometer's term 'generation' later in his life, Rameau was aware of the natural historians' use of the term, over which fierce controversy raged. (Diderot's *Encyclopédie*, vol. VII (1757), under 'Génération', devoted three inches to geometry and thirty columns to natural history (physiology), with no reference to music at any point.) The notion that the source pitch had an interior moulding force which could shape entire pieces is an appealing one.

18 *Kern*, Foreword, p.b *verso*, §§6–7; 'in parts' for *vollstimmig* and 'part-writing' for *Vollstimmigkeit* are too contrapuntal in implication. This Foreword is not repeated in *Capellmeister*.

that any qualified musician must possess. The saying remains irrefutable: *The simple goes before the complex, hence is its origin and root.*

Here, *Natur-Lehre* is a play on words between natural (i.e. acoustical) theory and the innate wisdom of *human* nature. In 1735, Mattheson had listed seven 'erroneous, insupportable and mutually contradictory principles' that he had found in Rameau's *Treatise*.[19]

Rameau, then, was a controversial figure in his own century; and the dispute, far from petering out after 1800, continued unabated – if anything, sharpened – during the nineteenth century. The essentials of his theory were preserved by Momigny in 1803–05 and by Reicha in 1816–18; and some vestiges of it were retained by Vogler. The fundamental bass was revived in a limited form by Sechter in 1853, who directly influenced both Anton Bruckner's teaching methods and also the harmonic theory of Karl Mayrberger in 1878. Influenced by more recent acoustical work of Helmholtz and others, Arthur von Oettingen's *System of Harmony in Dual Development* (1866) built a new theory of chord structure, progression and modulation, based on the overtone series together with its inverse, the undertone series (itself proposed by Rameau in 1737), and Riemann was influenced by this, though developing a theory of harmonic function that derived in part from Hauptmann. Though Heinrich Schenker rejected Rameau's theory as neglecting voice-leading in its obsession with vertical sonority, he accepted the acoustical origin of the major triad – the 'chord of nature' – and projected the latter through time to form the *Ursatz* (for which the accepted translation, 'fundamental structure', is doubly anachronistic: 'primal counterpoint' might be more faithful, 'contrapuntal archetype' more immediate) as the basis of all musical form.[20]

In 1802, the Paris Conservatory adopted as its official harmony textbook a compact treatise that swept away the complexities of Rameau's theory and proclaimed with utmost simplicity: 'There exists in harmony but one solitary chord, which contains all the others', namely the ninth-chord, G–B–D–F–($\flat$)A. Independently opposing Rameau in 1817, Gottfried Weber cited the out-of-tuneness of many of the overtones of a fundamental, and the fact that the constituent notes of any one chord have mutually conflicting sets of overtones, robustly declaring:[21]

> Take all of this into account and you will easily become convinced that the resonance of the overtones of a string, far from being intrinsic to the essential nature and beauty of the sound, is an impurity, the harmful effect of which is averted only by the inaudibility of these resonating sounds.

19 Johann Mattheson, *Kleine General-Bass-Schule* (Hamburg: Kissner, 1735), Dedication, also p. 221, where he speaks of the augmented unison, augmented third, and the diminished sixth 'and other monstrosities [*Misgeburten*] that have been brought into the world [by Rameau, in whose works] one finds a generous 1,000 hundredweight of unrelieved tedium and obscure minutiae, 500 stone of wearisome caprice and eccentric absurdity, some 3lbs of genuine knowledge, not counting hearsay, 20zs of sound judgment, and scarcely a peck of good taste'.
20 Heinrich Schenker, 'Rameau oder Beethoven? Erstarrung oder geistiges Leben in der Musik?', *Das Meisterwerk in der Musik: ein Jahrbuch*, vol. III (1930), pp. 9–24. A complete English translation of *Das Meisterwerk* (1925–30) is forthcoming in the series Cambridge Studies in Music Theory and Analysis.
21 Gottfried Weber, *Versuch einer geordneten Theorie der Tonsezkunst*, vol. I (Mainz: Schott, 1817), §IV, Anmerkung.

The parading of arithmetical and algebraic formulas was in his view sheerest pedantry; the entire mathematical treatment of musical composition was an illusion.[22] This view was echoed in 1837 by the first volume of Marx's *Manual of Musical Composition in Theory and Practice*, a landmark in the history of music theory and pedagogy. Marx purged the whole apparatus of acoustics, believing that the calculated perception of relationships between overtones had nothing to do with the mental and spiritual activity of music creation and perception.[23]

Fétis, while conceding in 1840 that parallels might be found between harmonic practice and acoustical phenomena, denied that the latter were the origin of the former:[24]

> But, someone will ask, what is the origin of these scales; what is it that controls the order of their tones [i.e. provides the laws of tonality], if it is not acoustical phenomena, and the laws of calculus? I reply that their origin is purely metaphysical: we conceive this order, and the melodic and harmonic phenomena that ensue from it, as a consequence of our mental make-up and of our education. For us it exists as a fact in its own right, independent of all cause extraneous to us. [. . .] Mark my words: these acoustical phenomena, so badly analysed at first, do not possess the significance that they have so rashly been accorded.

Fétis derived this approach from the philosophy of Kant and also of Schelling. Sounds come from external sources, and the composer's organization of them takes place as mental process. The human cognitive system delivers impressions of sounds to the conscious mind; but it is the mind, prompted by the will, that correlates and organizes those impressions.[25] In place of the organizing principle of the fundamental bass, Fétis provided the innovatory and enduring paradigm of tonality, an indubitably human, mental creation.

For Moritz Hauptmann, in 1853, the false intonation of many overtones in the harmonic spectrum constituted an obstacle even more insurmountable than it had been for Weber. Whereas (if we take the fundamental to be C) the notes of the dominant chord, G, B and D (overtones 3, 9 and 15), were true in pitch, the F and A (11 and 13) of the subdominant chord were completely unusable. For Hauptmann, dominant and subdominant were mirror-images of one another a fifth above and below the tonic respectively, their symmetry central to his theory; hence the absence of one side of this symmetry in the natural tone-system was unacceptable, and he rejected acoustics as a basis in its entirety:[26]

> While these basic things remain undetermined, we surely cannot expect [to infer] from the data of such acoustical ratios alone a theoretical foundation for harmony in the wider sense – a foundation for the laws governing chord-to-chord connection, [let alone] for chord progression.

22   ibid, §X, Anmerkung.

23   A. B. Marx, *Die Lehre von der musikalischen Komposition, praktisch-theoretisch* (Leipzig: B&H, 1837), pp. 41–2. Marx disputed the evidence of acoustics in *Allgemeine Musiklehre* (Leipzig: B&H, 1839, 10/1884), pp. 49–51, and *Die alte Musiklehre im Streit mit unserer Zeit* (Leipzig: B&H, 1841), pp. 49, 77–84.

24   François-Joseph Fétis, *Esquisse de l'histoire de l'harmonie considérée comme art et comme science systématique* (Paris: 1840), pp. 169–70; restated in *Traité complet de la théorie et de la pratique de l'harmonie . . .* (Paris: Schlesinger, 1844, 3/1875), pp. 249–50.

25   This is summarized from Rosalie Schellhous, 'Fétis's "Tonality" as a Metaphysical Principle: Hypothesis for a New Science', *Music Theory Spectrum*, 13 (1991), pp. 225–30.

26   Moritz Hauptmann, *Die Natur der Harmonik und Metrik* (Leipzig: B&H, 1853, 2/1873), p. 4.

Instead, Hauptmann adduced the philosophical *triad* of Hegelian dialectics: thesis–antithesis–synthesis, or unity–duality–conjunction. His claim for this is as great as that of Rameau for the resonating body. It was the true organizing principle of all music. Thus the major triad was *generated by* root–fifth–third upwards, and the minor triad by root–fifth–third downwards as totalities; scale and chord progression were generated by subdominant–dominant–tonic chords; movement from key to key was generated by the combination of subdominant–dominant–tonic functions and root–fifth–third; metre was generated by duple–triple–quadruple beat-subdivision; and so forth.

These expressions of anti-Rameau sentiment all more or less point in one direction: to the *human mind* as the organizing principle of musical harmony, rather than to the acoustical phenomena in nature.

§6 Music as organism

Picking up again from the biological models of §4, the distinction between organic and inorganic matter had been articulated by de Buffon (1707–88), in his *Natural History* of 1749, the former being distinguished from the latter by its capacity to grow and to reproduce itself.[27] Bonnet in 1762 first put forward the idea of the 'germ' that constituted not the preformation but the *preorganization* of the mature structure, that carried 'the original imprint of the species'.[28] The unravelling of the mechanisms of reproduction continued in France; but from this point on it was with the work of German philosophers of the late eighteenth and early nineteenth centuries that the nascent science of biology now developed. These proponents of 'Nature Philosophy', which is closely associated with the beginnings of the Romantic movement, felt that the universe could not be explained by Newtonian mechanical principles alone. What had been a physiological search for prime cause now became a philosophical search for an understanding of living wholes as imbued with Spirit, or Will. These thinkers, including Fichte and Schelling, had a significant influence both on biology and on the arts.

Goethe's *Metamorphosis of Plants* (1790, published 1802) was an early example of a view of nature whereby the innumerable life-forms were to be understood as metamorphoses of a very small number of ideal-types or archetypes, each archetype standing for a particular group of plants or animals. All metamorphosis was controlled by the holistic relations between the parts of an organism and the totality. Goethe's ideas powerfully influenced Adolf Bernhard Marx as in the 1830s he schematized his theory of formal archetypes and the infinite multiplicity of variant and hybrid outward forms. It later lay at the heart of Heinrich Schenker's mature theory.

Organisms, then, were not self-sufficient mechanisms, explainable in purely physico-chemical terms, nor were they natural entities governed by some unmea-

---

27   G. L. Comte de Buffon, *Histoire naturelle*, vol. II *Des animaux* (Paris: Sonnini-Dupont, 1749), chap. 2, p. 2.
28   Quoted in Elizabeth B. Gasking, *Investigations into Generation 1651–1828* (Baltimore: Johns Hopkins Press, 1967), pp. 121–2.

surable external life-force; they were something between the two: functioning wholes that *regulate and control their own growth processes*. The notion of organism as a model for musical structure had found early expression in an author who was well-versed in the writings of Schlegel, Goethe, Schiller and other contemporary thinkers: E. T. A. Hoffmann (who was, incidentally, fascinated by the acoustical origins of music) wrote in his analysis of Beethoven's Fifth Symphony (see vol. II, Analysis 9), dating from 1810:

> Just as our aesthetic overseers have often complained of a total lack of real unity and inner coherence in Shakespeare, when only profounder contemplation shows the splendid tree, buds and leaves, blossom and fruit as springing from the same seed, so only the most penetrating study of the inner structure of Beethoven's music can reveal its high level of rational awareness, which is inseparable from true genius and nourished by continuing study of the art.

The Fifth Symphony's four-movement structure, Hoffmann repeatedly stresses, is whole and unitary. Features of the second movement thus 'express the character of the whole work and make this Andante a part of it'. Hoffmann was familiar with Schelling's *System of Transcendental Idealism* (1800), in which the philosopher had likened works of art to organisms. In both, the parts serve the whole, and the whole is purposive. In organisms, however, the organizing intelligence lies hidden or unconscious, and is manifest only in the product itself; whereas in the work of art, the organizing activity is conscious, while the work of art itself remains unconscious; art thus brings together self and nature, inward and outward reality, consciousness and unconsciousness. Hoffmann saw the orchestral and chamber works of Beethoven as the true embodiment of this view of art.

However, if the model of organism was successfully to supersede previous eighteenth-century models, it had to do two things: provide an aesthetic theory that replaced the Baroque principle of 'unity in diversity' and create the tools with which to describe musical structures in new ways.

As to the first of these, the principle of 'unity in diversity' is to be found as early as the fifth century, in St Augustine. By this principle, a whole was composite and heterogeneous, an aggregate of parts; those parts coexisted, they were related to one another by concinnity. This view of unity prevailed during the Middle Ages and Renaissance, and was strongly promulgated in the seventeenth and eighteenth centuries. Its classic articulation for music was given by Francis Hutcheson in 1725 ('The figures which excite in us the ideas of beauty seem to be those in which there is uniformity amidst variety'[29]). That this view survived into the nineteenth century is evidenced by some of the writers in the present volume: its tenets are to be found enunciated by Momigny in 1803–05 (e.g. in the 'Drumroll' Symphony, vol. II, Analysis 8: 'always faithful to variety without ever detracting from unity'[30]), by Reicha in his melody treatise of 1814 (section 'Observations on the Unity and Diversity of a Melody, and in general of a Piece of Music'[31]) and by Dehn (e.g. in

29   Francis Hutcheson, *An Inquiry into the Original of our Ideas of Beauty and Virtue . . .* (London: J. Darby, 1725, 4/1738), Treatise I, section 2, in le Huray/Day, p. 24.
30   See also Momigny, *Cours complet*, vol. II, pp. 645–6, 675.
31   Antoine Reicha, *Traité de mélodie* (Paris, 1814, 2/1832), pp. 54–6: 'Observations sur l'unité et la variété de la mélodie, et en général d'un morceau de musique'.

the D minor Fugue, *Well-tempered Clavier*, Book I: see Analysis 5 below: 'he has brought to the fugue a remarkable degree of variety within unity').

Already in the 1770s, Sulzer's definition of 'unity' in art (1771–4) shows a hint of a change in this view. Although it strikes the mechanistic analogy of a clock, it stresses that the parts of a whole possess a 'union' that gives the whole its 'essence'. This essence is the basis of the object's 'unity'; in turn, its unity is the basis of its perfection and beauty. In a particularly striking statement, he says that when the beholder contemplates an object, an impression is formed of that object's essence, and this essence becomes an 'ideal' against which the reality is compared. Correspondence of ideal with reality produces pleasure, non-correspondence displeasure. Heinrich Christoph Koch's adaptation of this definition to musical purposes in 1787 seems less progressive than Sulzer's original. While never suggesting that the sum of the parts of a work of art is greater than the whole, it does acknowledge that the whole itself is imbued with purpose. In order to attain the purpose of a work of art, a piece of music must possess three main qualities: it must be an expression of a specific affect, through its subsidiary ideas it must have diversity and:[32]

> Not only the main ideas of a piece but also the subsidiary ideas that are brought into conjunction with them must be so constituted that together they form a beautiful whole in which each part [i.e. phrase-unit] not only corresponds to the purpose of the whole but also in no way contradicts its connections with the other parts. No parts must be present which deflect us from the central subject-matter, or from the affect that it arouses and sustains. All principal parts must have one and the same goal, and the subsidiary ideas . . . must have the quality of showing that off in constantly changing aspects. This demands unity, being the third main quality of any piece that is to attain the purpose of art.

Vogler, with his limitation on modulatory distance, perhaps approaches this view, somewhere between Baroque aesthetic principles and nineteenth-century holistic thinking (see Analysis 7 below, from 1806). Czerny, in his own *School of Practical Composition* (c.1840?) represents it more forcibly: parsimony of material combined with richness of development and intelligibility of connection makes for unity (see the closing remarks of Analysis 11 below, from c.1832–4).

The organicist view of music is expressed with full clarity in Peter Lichtenthal's definition of 'unity' from 1826. Speaking of 'the rule that one strives for unity of idea in a composition', he says:[33]

> Amongst the works of the great masters may be found innumerable pieces that are built upon a single motif. What marvellous unity there is in the structure of these compositions! Everything relates to the subject: nothing extraneous or inappropriate is there. Not a single link could be detached from the chain without destroying the whole. Only the man of genius, only the learned composer can accomplish such a task, one that is as admirable as it is difficult.

32 H. C. Koch, *Versuch einer Anleitung zur Composition*, vol. II (Leipzig: Böhme, 1787), pp. 128, 131, 132–3. These three qualities are re-articulated in Koch's *Musikalisches Lexikon* (Frankfurt: Hermann, 1802), 'Ausdruck', 'Ausführung', 'Mannigfaltigkeit' and 'Einheit'. For Sulzer, see *Allgemeine Theorie der schönen Künste* (Leipzig: Weidmann, 1771–4), 'Einheit'.

33 Peter Lichtenthal, *Dizionario e bibliografia della musica* (Milan: A. Fontana, 1826), 'Unità', in le Huray/Day, pp. 374–5.

This conception was developed by Marx in a statement dating from 1859, beginning:[34]

> Each musical creation evolves, just as do organisms in nature, from a germ [*Keim*], which however, like vesicles or cells in plant and animal life-forms, must itself be a formation, a union of two or more elements (notes, chords, rhythmic units), an organism, if it is to be capable of propagating organisms. Such a germ is called a 'motif'. Every composition rests upon one or more motifs.

The mind, he says, 'does not just conceive the motif, but engages with it, moulds it, although at first without definite goal'. Only as the 'inexhaustible process of formation' continues does the process become purposive, so that ultimately 'the composition moves to mould and combine larger structural units into a whole'. This statement, which encapsulates the method taught by Marx in his composition manual, typifies the organic view of compositional process. Thereafter, the analogy with organism becomes a commonplace in writing about music in the later nineteenth century.

The second requirement for the establishment of the model of organism concerned the availability of tools for the adequate description of musical structures in such terms.

§7 Musical organism and the tools of description

The technical means of characterizing and detailing musical structures in organic terms in fact already existed in potential form among the writings of Friedrich Wilhelm Marpurg (1718–95), Joseph Riepel (1709–82) and other music theorists. Marpurg's approach to thematic fragmentation, as given in his *Treatise on Fugue* (1753–4), also exemplified there in his analysis of the *Kyrie Eleison* from J. S. Bach's Mass in G, and Riepel's discussion of repetition, extension and interpolation in musical phrases in his *First Principles of Musical Composition* (1755, 1765) offered the theorist a basis for conceiving musical structure in self-generating terms.[35] Marpurg showed how fragments could be broken off from a theme already stated, and then used to initiate new sections. In this way, a single theme could serve as the sole source of an entire work, engendering all of its material, primary and subsidiary. It may not be entirely fanciful, since the treatise was reprinted in 1806, 1843 and 1858, to imagine this method being likened in the nineteenth century to the taking of cuttings from an existing plant to create new ones; and, when considered together with Marpurg's detailed treatment of thematic repetition, sequence, imitation, augmentation and diminution, rhythmic displacement, abbreviation and

---

34 Adolf Bernhard Marx, *Ludwig van Beethoven: Leben und Schaffen* (Berlin: Janke, 1859), vol. I, p. 86; the passage spans pp. 86–98.

35 F. W. Marpurg, *Abhandlung von der Fuge* (Berlin: A. Haude and J. C. Spener, 1753–4): the Bach analysis, a brief sample of which is given below (Introduction to Part I), appears on pp. 136–41 of vol. II, and is available entire in translation in Alfred Mann, *The Study of Fugue* (New Brunswick, NJ: Rutgers University Press, 1958; reprint edn Westport, CT: Greenwood Press, 1981), pp. 204–12; unfortunately, the theoretical material on this, vol. I, pp. 115–20, and vol. II, pp. 142–4, is omitted by Mann. J. Riepel, *Anfangsgründe zur musikalischen Setzkunst*, vols. II *Grundregeln zur Tonkunst insgemein* (Frankfurt: n.p., 1755), pp. 36–66, and IV *Erlaeuterungen der Betrueglichen Tonordnung* (Augsburg: Lotter, 1765), pp. 81–2.

extension, and with the many analyses of these processes that he furnishes, the treatise might well have seemed like a thesaurus of organic development – a use undreamed of by its author.

Joseph Riepel's taxonomy of final and intermediate cadences (1755) offered a syntax of melody that far outstripped that of Mattheson's (discussed above) and a theory of melodic construction that was unrivalled in its flexibility. Later (1765) he demonstrated how a performer could take a number of motifs (*Figuren*) and use them in rotation, subjecting each to a range of developmental processes – variation, extension, compression, modulation – in improvising a cadenza. Koch, who in 1787 eloquently articulated the purpose of analysis in his time as the need 'to resolve the structure [of a composition (*Melodie*)] into its constituent parts, and to seek to derive from the types of linkage that exist among those parts, and at the same time the observable surface features, the laws and maxims whereby those parts combine to form a whole', spoke of Riepel's work as 'the first rays of light to be cast on these subjects [the lengths of phrases, and their types of ending] – subjects that in those days were from a theoretical point of view still entirely shrouded in darkness'. Riepel himself, Koch declared, 'was the first (and still is the only theorist known to me up to this time) to deal thoroughly with these subjects'.[36] It was Koch (and to a lesser extent also Kirnberger) who took Riepel's work and expanded it into a full-blown theory of musical construction in what he significantly called 'The Mechanical Rules of Melody'.[37]

Riepel's and Koch's conception of melodic construction fed directly or indirectly into those of Momigny and Reicha, the latter's *Treatise on Melody* (1814) paradoxically combining a relatively mechanistic constructional view with a pioneering essay 'On the Manner of Developing a Motif', the ideas of which emerged as a small treatise on the subject in 1826 (the change between Analyses 8 and 9 below is striking).[38] Continuation of this line of constructional theory can be traced in the work of Rudolf Westphal (1880), Mathis Lussy (1883, 1903) and Hugo Riemann (1884). However, with the first volume of his *Manual of Musical Composition* in 1837 Adolf Bernhard Marx took melodic theory in a profoundly different direction. Marx set out to teach composition by taking the student through the selfsame steps that the trained composer takes when creating a work: first conceiving of a motif (typically two, three or four crotchets in length), and then modifying and enlarging it into the form of phrase-segments and passage-work, and expanding it organically to form whole phrases and periods. Only at that point does he for the first time inject harmony, leading to the creation of harmonic motifs that can combine with melodic motifs to produce a motivically

36 H. C. Koch, *Versuch einer Anleitung zur Composition* (Leipzig: Böhme), vol. II (1787), pp. 6, 11.

37 ibid, vols. II, pp. 342–464, and III (1793), pp. 1–430; Eng. trans. Nancy Kovaleff Baker, as *Introductory Essay on Composition* (New Haven: Yale University Press, 1983). Koch's analysis of the aria 'Ein Gebeth um neue Stärke' from Carl Heinrich Graun's *Der Tod Jesu* (1755) appears in the *Versuch*, vol. II, pp. 59–64, and is discussed in the present author's 'The "Compositional Process" in Music Theory 1713–1850', *Music Analysis*, 3 (1984), 29–36, against the background of Koch's and Sulzer's views on the origin of music.

38 Antoine Reicha, *Traité de mélodie* (Paris, 1814, 2/1832), pp. 61–5 'Sur la manière de développer un motif'; *Traité de haute composition*, vol. II (Paris: Farrenc, 1826), pp. 235–359: 'L'art de tirer parti de ses idées, ou de les développer'.

saturated texture. Next he introduces a second voice, antecedent and consequent phrase-pairs, and finally the construction of small binary and ternary pieces. From there, the student is led up the ladder of increasingly complex forms, using the tools of organic development as he goes.

Thirteen years later, Johann Christian Lobe adopted an even more radical approach. Although starting in more orthodox fashion with elementary harmony, he began, after ten pages, to teach the student how to 'sketch' – just as Beethoven had done in his sketchbooks, inventing ideas, creating a stock of motivic material, and storing variant versions of these (see Analysis 12). As the sketching process became more adventurous, so Lobe supplied additional harmonic vocabulary. Unlike Marx, Lobe worked from the very beginning with existing music (by Haydn, Mozart, Beethoven, Mendelssohn and Schumann), using only the minimum of pedagogically contrived material.

With these two innovative works, the theory of composition had been changed from one of a phrase-structural framework driven by the Baroque theory of affect according to rhetorical strategies, to one of a potentially infinitely expanding structure triggered by an initial motivic inspiration and perpetuated by the laws of organic musical procreation, ultimately to be controlled and governed by one of a small number of underlying formal archetypes, the interaction between dynamic process and static archetype resulting in a metamorphosis of the archetype concerned. At the same time, the works by Marx and Lobe consummated the change that was already taking place in the work of Koch whereby vocal music, particularly expressive aria, was removed from the centre stage of music theory, to be replaced for the next 100 years or more by abstract instrumental music, especially those forms of it involving sonata form – symphony, quintet, quartet, trio and solo sonata. The prizing of formal musical relations over associative ideas that this entailed gained great aesthetic authority from Eduard Hanslick's famous *On the Musically Beautiful*, first published in 1854.

Precisely contemporaneously, however, an expanding motivic process *entered* the world of opera. In 1851, Wagner outlined a theory of motivic technique, a technique that he was to deploy powerfully in *Rhinegold* (1851–4), but of which some semblance had already been seen in *Lohengrin* (1848). 'Leitmotif', later to be codified by Hans von Wolzogen, though on the face of it a symbol-system, is at least obliquely related to Marx's notion of motif: the motif stock must be small, and must stretch unbroken across the work's entire fabric, imbuing it with unity; moreover, each motif must develop progressively, usually doing so in several directions at once, resulting in families, or clusters, of related leitmotif-forms.

Schoenberg and Schenker, while having such very different intellectual outlooks, had in common their conviction that music was living organism. Schenker, an early convert to the idea, ultimately developed a theory in which every true musical structure was considered an expansion from one of a number of two-voice contrapuntal archetypes (the *Ursatz* referred to earlier), 'blossoming' in successive layers of elaboration and temporal extension. He formulated a verbal language and graphic apparatus of great sophistication for explicating it. For Schoenberg, on the other hand, pieces of music were conceived as tiny motifs and motif-forms coherently connected as sentences, periods, sections and whole forms. With the theoretical developments of these two men among others such as Fritz Cassirer and Walter Engelsmann, and with Schoenberg's powerfully suggestive concepts of 'developing variation' and 'basic shape' (*Grundgestalt*), the organic model, aesthetic, and technical array of tools that can be seen to have arisen in the late eighteenth and early nineteenth centuries were transmitted to the twentieth century.

PART I

Analysis of fugue

Introduction

Nothing more vividly illustrates the tightly coupled system in which analysis and compositional theory coexisted in the eighteenth century than the German term *Zergliederung*. Its story is a fascinating one, and though we have touched on it already in the General Introduction, it is worth telling briefly here. The verb *zergliedern* means, literally, to dismember – as a German dictionary of 1691 put it: 'to cut off the limbs, to divide limb from limb, to truncate, to mutilate, to chop to pieces'; hence, by extension, the noun *Zergliederung* signified 'anatomy'.[1]

In 1730, the literary theorist Johann Christoph Gottsched (1700–66) listed *Zergliederung* as one of the figures of rhetoric, synonymous with the Latin *Distributio*, which he defined as: 'When [an author] dismembers something multifarious into its parts, in order to give his reader a full appreciation of the matter in hand'[2] – that is to say, when after making a complex statement he breaks that statement into its component parts, and elaborates each one in turn. In 1740, Johann Adolph Scheibe (1708–76), in his influential journal modelled on Gottsched's work, provided the following musical application of the device:[3]

> Zergliederung (Distributio). This arises when [a composer] articulates a main subject of a piece in such a way that he dwells upon each of its parts in turn individually; when, for example, he proceeds to *dismember* a fairly long fugue subject by first articulating one phrase or bar separately, and then doing the same for its remaining phrases, and consequently treating each of the main subject's parts as a phrase in its own right, and, by articulating each differently, setting them apart from one another. This [rhetorical] figure contributes very greatly to the skilled elaboration of a fugue.

Scheibe then cited its use in concerto and aria, but his initial choice of fugue was scarcely arbitrary: in Mattheson's *Essence of the Science of Melody*, published only three years earlier in 1737, fugue itself is cited as a rhetorical device, a 'figure of expansion', the citation reading 'Fugue, wherein are met Mimesis [sequence], Expolitio [embellishment], and *Distributio* . . .'.[4]

---

1 K. Stieler, *Der teutschen Sprache Stammbau und Fortwachs, oder teutscher Sprachsatz* . . . , vol. I (Nuremberg: Hoffmann, 1691; reprint edn 1968), 'Glidern/Entglidern/Zerglidern', col.670.
2 J. C. Gottsched, *Versuch einer critischen Dichtkunst* . . . (Leipzig: Breitkopf, 1730, 3/1742), 'Zergliederung (Distributio)', pp. 330–32; *Ausführliche Redekunst* . . . (Leipzig: Breitkopf, 5/1759), 'Distributio', p. 320.
3 J. A. Scheibe, *Der Critische Musicus*, vol. II (Hamburg: Wiering, 1740), No. 76 (9 February), p. 392. In these quotations, emphasis is mine.
4 *Kern melodischer Wissenschaft* (Hamburg: Herold, 1737; reprint edn Hildesheim: Olms, 1976), p. 143, repeated in *Der vollkommene Capellmeister* (Hamburg: Herold, 1739; reprint edn Kassel: Bärenreiter, 1954), p. 244. Fifty years later, J. N. Forkel listed *Zergliederung* as a rhetorical figure, though not associated with fugue: *Allgemeine Geschichte der Musik*, vol. I (Leipzig: Schwickert, 1788), pp. 51–2.

At the same time, *Zergliederung* is equated with the Greek loan-word *Analysis*. J. H. Zedler's *Universal Lexicon of the Arts and Sciences*, of 1729–54, not only defined it as 'anatomy', but also gave its applications as the philosophical 'analysis of concepts' and the linguistic 'analysis of propositions' into subject and predicate. Conversely, he used *zergliedern* in his definition of 'Analytical Method':[5]

> When one subdivides and *dismembers* a given issue or question into its parts or particulars, and then treats each of these in its own right, and compares them with one another, examines their causes and bases, in such a way that one arrives step by step at the origin and first basis . . .

Zergliederung, then, looked forward and backward. It was an agent that served both the production of a work and its reduction to prime causes. So, too, in music. Marpurg, in his *Treatise on Fugue* (1753–4), used it for the partitioning of a subject or countersubject into segments and their dispersal in what in modern terms would be called episodes, through imitation and transposition.[6] On the other hand, at the end of this great work, he took a triple fugue by J. S. Bach, the *Kyrie Eleison* from the Mass in G, BWV236, and subjected it to a detailed structural analysis, beginning: 'Finally, we should like to *dismember* the vocal fugue that is to be found in Plates XLVI–L'. The plates in question supply the entire fugue in five-part open score, its staves annotated at crucial points with letters (*a–z, aa–zz, A–H*) providing points of reference to the lengthy prose discussion, of which the following is but a tiny sample:[7]

> As, at (*dd*), the bass now takes up the first subject [inverted], the tenor at (*ee*) and (*gg*) gives out the opening [notes] of the third subject twice in quick succession, while the soprano at (*ff*) likewise embarks on the second subject [inverted], but with a continuation [*Melodie*] that derives from the first subject, and therefore continues by *dismemberment* of a part of that same [first] subject, as too does the alto immediately before that, after its introduction of the second subject truncated at (*cc*); and with this ends section II of the fugue.

Two senses of the term here come into conjunction: *Zergliederung* as the process being undertaken – that of analysing an entire fugue; and *Zergliederung* as a process being observed – that of partitioning fugal materials. The work of the analyst spirals round to become the work of the composer.

Matheson, in a passage already discussed and quoted in the General Introduction above, had used the term for the analysis of a minuet melody into its constituent parts (claiming to be the first ever to have done it).[8] This was (to enlist Zedler's definition) an 'analysis of propositions', for Matheson marked off the

---

5 J. H. Zedler, *Grosses vollständiges Universal-Lexicon aller Wissenschafften und Künste*, vol. LXI (Leipzig and Halle: Zedler, 1749), 'Zergliederung', 'Zergliederung der Begriffe', 'Zergliederung eines Satzes', cols.1643–5; vol. II (1732), 'Analysis' ('primarily, a dissection, a *dismemberment*, of a thing, body or discourse'), cols. 36–7, 'Analytische Methode', pp. 38–9.

6 F. W. Marpurg, *Abhandlung von der Fuge* (Berlin: A.Haude and J.C.Spener, 1753–4; reprint edn Hildesheim: Olms, 1970), vol. I, pp. 115–20; vol. II, pp. 142–4.

7 *Abhandlung*, vol. II, pp. 136–41. The index clearly distinguishes the two operations by having two separate entries, 'Zergliederung eines Fugensatzes . . .' and 'Zergliederung oder Analysis von Fugen'. The excerpt is p. 139,

8 *Kern*, pp. 109–11; reproduced in *Capellmeister*, pp. 224–5.

melodic sections by commas, colon, semicolon, period and paragraph-sign, performing a syntactic analysis in terms of natural language. The analogy between this *analysis* of a simple sixteen-bar melody and the *partitioning* of a fugue subject is striking, albeit the latter is purely compositional in intent whereas the former is (at least outwardly) formal. Composition and analysis, in melodic and fugal materials, were inextricably intertwined: as the composer of a fugue worked his materials, he was performing an implicit analysis of his subject.

Vogler used *Zergliederung* many times for analyses of his own pieces and those of others (Analysis 7). It was Sechter's term for his analysis of the fugal Finale of the 'Jupiter' Symphony (Analysis 4). It appeared in nineteenth-century music lexicons, and here a significant change came over it: segmented 'phrases' (*Sätze*) became 'motifs' (*Motive*), the fragmentation process came to be reinterpreted in organic terms – snap off a bud from the old stock, and a new life-form will grow from it. In a historic stroke of the editorial pen, Siegfried Dehn organicized Marpurg's definition of the word in 1858, when he wrote of extracting segments from a fugue subject for use as 'motifs from the Theme itself' (see Introduction to Analysis 5). Marx used it (though rarely) in his description of Beethoven's development sections, and here the motifs of the exposition, imbued with a sense of the Romantic titanic struggle, 'must be sent into battle, must overcome'.[9] Schumann used it to denote systematic analysis, sometimes employing diagrammatic means. With him, the word acquired a hint of disapproval, and nowhere is this more brilliantly and ironically displayed than in his aborted formal analysis of the first movement of Berlioz's *Symphonie fantastique*, with its play on words recalling Berlioz's earlier days as a medical student at the dissecting table (vol. II, Analysis 10). The word remains in the German language to this day, as a term for 'analysis' of music.

This, then, is the story of *Zergliederung*, a term intimately but never exclusively associated with fugue. It was not alone in having its centre of gravity outside of fugue, for very few of the terms that we now associate with fugue – fugue, that is, as crystallized in the works of Bach and Handel – are exclusive to it or originated with it: *fuga* and *contrapunctus*, for example, both date back to the Middle Ages, and *imitatio* to the late fifteenth century, whereas the concept of a fugue as we know it nowadays emerged only in the late seventeenth century. 'Fugue', 'counterpoint' and 'canon', as terms and as concepts in theoretical writing, remained intertwined even until the late eighteenth century. Only in the pages of the principal landmarks of eighteenth-century fugal theory do these concepts become separated out and given specific meaning, and only there, too, do such formal concepts as 'exposition', 'codetta' and 'episode' begin to find some measure of codification – those landmarks being Book II of Fux's *Gradus ad Parnassum* of 1725, Marpurg's *Treatise on Fugue* of 1753–4, volume II of Padre Martini's *Examples*,

---

9 G. Schilling, *Universal-Lexicon der Tonkunst*, vol. VI (Stuttgart: Köhler, 1838), pp. 962–3, 'Zergliederung'; H. Mendel, *Musikalisches Conversations-Lexikon*, new edn comp. A. Reissmann, vol. XI (Leipzig: List & Francke, n.d.), p. 474; A. B. Marx, *Ludwig van Beethoven: Leben und Schaffen* (Berlin: Janke, 1859), vol. I, p. 180, though as already stated in the General Introduction, Marx scarcely ever put a name to his own analytical activity.

or Fundamental Practical Manual of Counterpoint, of 1775, and chapters 23–31 of Albrechtsberger's *Basic Composition Method*, of 1790.[10]

Although in the nineteenth century, fugue declined as an artistic genre, it retained its place in compositional theory. In France, its alliance with counterpoint and canon as a free-standing discipline of study, a rigorous training in its own right, taught by specialist professors, is witnessed by a succession of independent treatises, notably Langlé's *Treatise on Fugue* (1805), Fétis's *Treatise on Counterpoint and Fugue* (1824), Reicha's *Treatise on Advanced Musical Composition* (1824–6), Cherubini's *Course in Counterpoint and Fugue* (1835) and ultimately Gédalge's *Treatise on Fugue* (1904), which concentrates exclusively on fugue, presenting the ahistorical construct of the 'scholastic fugue'.[11] In Germany, Marpurg's *Treatise*, reissued in 1806 and again in 1843 and 1858, thrust J. S. Bach's fugues forward as models embodying normative procedures. Although specialist treatises did appear – Dehn's *Theory of Counterpoint, Canon and Fugue* (1859) and Bussler's *Counterpoint and Fugue in Free (Modern) Tonal Composition* (1878) being two such[12] – fugue came to take its place in a comprehensive music curriculum, for which a new type of publication emerged mid-century: the multi-volume, all-embracing textbook of composition. Marx's *Manual of Musical Composition in Theory and Practice* (1837–47), Lobe's *Manual of Musical Composition* (1850–67) and Riemann's *Comprehensive Theory of Composition* (1902–13) are the classic works.[13]

The French treatises follow the analytical practice that we have seen was established by Marpurg in 1754 but employed intensively for the first time by Padre Martini in his *Examples* of 1775. Martini's 'examples' are in fact analytical models for the student: fugues by 'the masters' (Perti, Caresana and others) laid out complete, in full score, annotated with numbers at important structural points and accompanied with a detailed prose discussion of structure and technique in

10 J. J. Fux, *Gradus ad Parnassum* (Vienna: Ghelen, 1725; Ger. trans. L. Mizler, 1742), Book II, Exercitii IV, Exercitii V, Lectiones 1–7, pp. 140–239 of Latin edn; F. W. Marpurg, *Abhandlung von der Fuge* (Berlin: A. Haude & J. C. Spener, 1753–4); Padre G. Martini, *Esemplare o sia saggio fondamentale pratico di contrappunto* (Bologna: Volpe, 1774–5), vol. II *Regole per comporre la fuga – Saggio fondamentale pratico di contrappunto fugato*; J. G. Albrechtsberger, *Gründliche Anweisung zur Composition mit deutlichen und ausführlichen Exempeln, zum Selbstunterrichte, erläutert . . .* (Leipzig: Breitkopf, 1790), chaps. 23–31. Extended excerpts from the fugal sections of these four works constitute the bulk of Alfred Mann, *The Study of Fugue* (New Brunswick, NJ: Rutgers University Press, 1958; reprint edn Westport, CT: Greenwood Press, 1981).

11 H. F. M. Langlé, *Traité de la fugue* (Paris: Langlé, [1805]); F.-J. Fétis, *Traité du contrepoint et de la fugue . . . depuis deux jusqu'à huit parties réelles* (Paris: Ozu, [1824], 2/[1846]); A. Reicha, *Traité de haute composition musicale* (Paris: Zetter, [1824–6]), which however concludes with a chapter on melodic development (see Analysis 9, below); L. Cherubini, *Cours de contre-point et de fugue* (Paris: Schlesinger, [1835]); A. Gédalge, *Traité de la fugue* (Paris: Enoch, [1904]). Others include G. Kastner, *Théorie abregée de contrepoint et de la fugue* (Paris: Chabal, 1839); A. Elwart, *Le Contre-point et la fugue appliqués à la composition idéale* (Paris: Lemoine, 1840); F. Bazin, *Cours de contre-point théorique et pratique* (Paris: Lemoine, [after 1871]); T. Dubois, *Traité de contrepoint et de fugue* (Paris: Heugel, 1901).

12 S. Dehn, *Lehre vom Contrapunkt, dem Canon und der Fuge* (Berlin: Schneider, 1859, 2/1883); L. Bussler, *Contrapunct und Fuge im freien (modernen) Tonsatz* (Berlin: Habel, 1878).

13 A. B. Marx, *Die Lehre von der musikalischen Komposition praktisch-theoretisch . . .* , 4 vols. (Leipzig: B&H, 1837–47]; J. C. Lobe, *Lehrbuch der musikalischen Komposition*, 4 vols. (Leipzig: B&H, 1850–67); H. Riemann, *Grosse Kompositionslehre*, 3 vols. (Berlin and Stuttgart: Spemann, 1902–13). Of these works, the first two went through many editions.

the lower margin of the page. Volume II of this work is virtually entirely taken up with what are in fact, though not in name, fugal analyses. Although the nineteenth-century French treatises followed this precedent, they gave merely scores with structural labels of some detail, but without accompanying text (called 'examples of fugue with running analysis') – fugues, moreover, that had been written for pedagogical purposes.[14] The result is not unlike the edition of the *Well-tempered Clavier* published by Samuel Wesley and C. F. Horn in England in 1810–13, the engraving of which includes 'Annotations, explanatory of the several ingenious and surprizing Contrivances in the Treatment of the Subject throughout all the Fugues'. Wesley and Horn had devised a neat and compact set of symbols to accommodate any number of subjects, denoting for each whether in normal form, inverted, in diminution or augmentation; compound symbols indicated combinations of these conditions.[15]

Marx and Lobe, unlike the French theorists of fugue, drew liberally from the fugal repertory the musical examples in their treatises; but whereas Marx indulged in no analysis beyond a few bars at a time, Lobe enlisted full-length analysis as a primary teaching tool. He examined many fugues by Bach, notably Contrapuncti I–III and VIII from the *Art of Fugue* and several fugues from the *Well-tempered Clavier*, the *Kyrie* from the Mozart Requiem, the Finale of the 'Jupiter' Symphony – written in full knowledge of Sechter's analysis (Analysis 4) – a quadruple fugue and a double-choir fugue by Cherubini from the latter's *Course* and briefly a fugue from Liszt's 'Dante' Symphony, not to mention innumerable canons. Each of these he scrutinizes from several vantage points, exploiting the mixed media of annotated score, sketch, analytic reduction, single-stave graph, diagram and prose discussion in virtuosic fashion – just as he can be seen doing with quartet movements by Beethoven (Analysis 12 below, the introduction to which describes Lobe's startling pedagogical use of Contrapunctus I).

Two of the six analyses given below have direct links to Marpurg's *Treatise on Fugue*. Sechter's analysis of the 'Jupiter' Symphony (Analysis 4) belongs to the third edition of that work (1843), of which Sechter was the editor, and forms an appendix. Dehn's analysis of the D minor fugue from Book I of the *Well-tempered Clavier* (Analysis 5) is a by-product of the fourth edition, mentioned a moment ago (1858). Written by Dehn while seeing that edition through, it was published from his posthumous papers. None of the other four has any connection with the treatises or textbooks cited above. Two come from other composition manuals: Momigny's analysis of an F♯ minor fugue by Handel (Analysis 1) comes from his idiosyncratic *Complete Course in Harmony and Counterpoint* (1803–05), already

---

14　Reicha (1824–6) offered more than 100 pages of such analyses, all of fugues by either himself or named pupils. Cherubini appended analyses of nine fugues: one by his teacher, Sarti, is perhaps the only exception to the above remark.

15　*S. Wesley and C. F. Horn's New and Correct Edition of the Preludes and Fugues of John Sebastian Bach* (London: Birchall, 1810–13). A forerunner of this edition was apparently an edition of four fugues by Bach, with analytical elucidations, dating from 1803, by Joseph Diettenhofer. I am grateful to Robert Pascall for drawing this to my attention, and sharing with me his unpublished materials on the work.

noted above in the General Introduction for its empirical spirit and richness of analytical materials; Reicha's analysis of an unidentified fugue (Analysis 2) is from a purely harmonic treatise, his *Course in Musical Composition* (?1816–18). Riemann's analysis of the B♭ minor Prelude and Fugue from Book II of the *Well-tempered Clavier* (Analysis 6) can be associated with a popular introductory manual of form: it comes from a set of three companion volumes to Riemann's *Catechism of the Theory of Composition*, which comprise an analysis of the entire *Well-tempered Clavier* and also the *Art of Fugue*. Finally, Hauptmann's analysis of this latter work (Analysis 3) came about quite differently, as the critical commentary to an edition of the *Art of Fugue*.

The six analyses reveal debts to a number of prior traditions. The oldest of these is a coherent lineage that stretches back to a five-voice fugue with continuo, *Laboravi clamans*, printed in Rameau's *Treatise on Harmony* of 1722, presented on seven staves with fundamental bass, as discussed in the General Introduction above.[16] Some fifty years later Kirnberger and Schulz published not dissimilar analyses: Kirnberger, an analysis of a fugue of his own in *The Art of Strict Musical Composition* (1771) (to which Kollmann published revisions in 1806), while Schulz published analyses of two items from Bach's *Well-tempered Clavier*: the Fugue in B minor from Book I (chosen for its reputed insolubility), and (incompletely) the Prelude in A minor from Book II, in *The True Principles for the Practice of Harmony* (1773).[17] Then, some thirty years later Momigny took over this layered-score analytical display for the first movement of Mozart's String Quartet in D minor, K421/417b, adapting it to his own theoretical precepts of phrase structure and cadence, incorporating his own technique of affective analysis, yet still including a fundamental bass, though of highly unorthodox type.[18] It is this tradition to which the analysis given here by Reicha (Analysis 2) belongs: a harmonic analysis laid out on multiple staves, looking much like an orchestral score, but in fact comprising a series of horizontal layers displaying successive analytical reinterpretations of the piece presented at the top, and incorporating a fundamental bass.

Most influential upon the analyses included here is the tradition that stems from Marpurg and Martini, which has already been quoted and discussed above. Its presence is felt in the analyses by Momigny, Sechter and Dehn. Closest to that tradition, at first sight, are the initial three-quarters of Momigny's analysis of the

16   J.-P. Rameau, *Traité d'harmonie* (Paris: Ballard, 1722), pp. 341–55; Eng. trans. P. Gossett (New York: Dover, 1971), pp. 357–66.

17   J. P. Kirnberger, *Die Kunst des reinen Satzes in der Musik . . .* , vol. I (Berlin: Voss, 1771), pp. 248–50; Eng. trans. D. W. Beach and J. Thym (New Haven: Yale University Press, 1982), pp. 266–75; A. F. C. Kollmann, *A New Theory of Musical Harmony . . .* (London: Bulmer, 1806), p. 48, Plate XX, where see similar analysis of part of the Fantasia of Bach's *Chromatic Fantasia and Fugue*, p. 84, Plates XXXIV–XXXVI; J. A. P. Schulz (published over Kirnberger's name), *Die wahren Grundsätze zum Gebrauch der Harmonie . . .* (Berlin and Königsberg: Decker and Hartung, 1773; reprint edn Hildesheim: Olms, 1970); Eng. trans. D. W. Beach and J. Thym, *JMT*, 23 (1979), 163–225.

18   J.-J. de Momigny, *Cours complet d'harmonie et de composition . . .* (Paris: Momigny, 1803–05), vols. I, pp. 307–39, 362–82; II, pp. 387–403; III, pp. 109–36 (= Plate 30A–B). For sample facsimiles, with discussion, of the analyses by Schulz and Momigny, see I. Bent with W. Drabkin, *Analysis* (London: Macmillan, 1987), pp. 10–11, 20–22.

Handel F♯ minor fugue (Analysis 1), which comprises an uninterrupted verbal text keyed to a separate, annotated score (though on two staves only), diverging graphically only in its use of Arabic and Roman numerals to provide not a single but a double system of annotation, and in its labelling of each set of middle entries. Momigny's text, however, differs significantly: first, it conducts a segmentation of the subject and countersubject at the outset, rather than retroactively later in the discussion, and thus sets out the possibilities more clearly; second, it transforms the tone of the discussion by speaking of the fugue in dynamic terms – of 'vibrancy', 'intensification', 'momentum' and 'respite'. The spirit of Marpurg is probably most fully preserved in Sechter's Mozart analysis, designed as it was to fit into Marpurg's own *Treatise*. The interpolated musical examples, however, give it a superficially different appearance, and the use of 'violins and flute' or 'bassoon', where Marpurg might have had 'soprano' or 'tenor', and the consequent substitution of instrumentation for texture and spacing, also give a changed air to the commentary. (It is astonishing how little difference the presence of sonata form makes!) Dehn's analysis of the D minor fugue from Book I of the *Well-tempered Clavier*, while still close to Marpurg, has, like Momigny's, a segmentation of the subject at the outset, and uses, as does Sechter's, interpolated music examples. There is one important difference, however: it talks in consciously tonal terms, speaking frequently of tonic and dominant functions and modulation, and identifying key-areas.

Hauptmann's analysis of the *Art of Fugue* (Analysis 3) and the final quarter of Momigny's Handel analysis (Analysis 1) have one thing in common: a concern with *content* in abstract instrumental music. Yet the content that the two analysts seek is very different. Hauptmann seems to wrestle with the Hegelian notion that satisfaction as achieved by absolute music through technical devices alone is 'empty, without significance', and that only when something of 'spiritual import' is expressed through tone can instrumental music attain its position as true art.[19] Hauptmann seems to say that the latent content of Bach's principal subject, its contrapuntal potentiality as progressively and logically unfolded fugue-by-fugue, 'animates' the work. (Hauptmann's notion of content is discussed further in the Introduction to Part I of vol. II of the present work.) Momigny, on the other hand, in objectifying content through dramatic analogy, draws on the practice of certain French 'parodists', as he calls them, who used to translate music into verse, a practice that goes back to musico-literary experiments conducted by a group of north German poets in the mid-eighteenth century.[20]

19   Georg Wilhelm Friedrich Hegel, *Vorlesung über die Ästhetik* (1818–20), quoted from *Musical Aesthetics: A Historical Reader*, ed. E. A. Lippman, vol. II *The Nineteenth Century* (New York: Pendragon, 1988), pp. 99–100 (from the translation by F. P. B. Osmaston); see also le Huray/Day, p. 343.
20   See the latter part of vol. II, Analysis 8 for another dramatic analogy. Momigny's use of Dido's monologue at the departure of Aeneas as his analogue to the first movement of Mozart's Quartet in D minor is close in spirit to Heinrich Wilhelm von Gerstenberg's experimental adaptation of C. P. E. Bach's keyboard Fantasy in C minor to Hamlet's monologue 'To be, or not to be', and alternatively to Socrates' monologue as he takes hemlock. See Eugene Helm, 'The "Hamlet" Fantasy and the Literary Element in C. P. E. Bach's Music', *The Musical Quarterly*, 58 (1972), 277–96. Momigny identifes one of the 'parodistes' as André-Joseph Grétry, blind nephew of the composer, and offers rules on how to execute such a parody (*Cours*, vol. I, pp. 372, 376, 379–82).

Finally, the tradition of phrase-structure theory that comes from Riepel, through Kirnberger and Koch to Momigny and Reicha, the graphic devices of which seem to have influenced Dehn's musical examples, is the clear forerunner of the phrasing material in Riemann's analysis of the B♭ minor Prelude and Fugue from Book II of the *Well-tempered Clavier* (Analysis 6). At the same time, this analysis has other elements – motivic analysis and figurative description – that derive from mid-century sources and notably from the elucidatory tradition discussed in volume II, Part I.

Jérôme-Joseph de Momigny (1762–1842)
Cours complet d'harmonie et de composition (1805)

As we have already seen in the General Introduction above, Momigny averred that 'musical masterpieces' were primary source materials for the music theorist. Nowhere in his *Complete Course in Harmony and Composition* of 1803–05 does this assertion manifest itself more keenly than in the chapter on fugue,[1] for Momigny can hardly wait to get on with the analysis. What precedes it – a bare statement that strict counterpoint is single, double, triple or quadruple; a brief definition of single counterpoint; derivation and definition of 'fugue' as 'a succession of imitations, regular and periodic, on one or several themes or subjects, single fugue being based on only one theme, double fugue on two subjects, triple on three' – takes less than one page, before the reader is whisked into a seventeen-page analysis of the C major fugue from Book I of J. S. Bach's *Well-tempered Clavier*. Starting from known instances and arriving at generalizations, Momigny's method would appear to be classically inductive. In practice, it is a mixture of demonstration and prescription. Thus, for example, in treating the entry of the answer, he first takes Bach's subject and sets out seven possible entry points and pitches, laying them out in parallel on eight staves (his Plate 39 H), then draws attention to Bach's choice of entry point, finally invoking the precept 'in the first exposition of the subject, the answer should not be allowed to enter until a large portion of the subject has been sounded, so that the subject may be assimilated' (p. 519). This is the method, too, in the present analysis. Thus in §258, prescribed rule and justification for the answering of fifth by tonic follow observation.

Examination of the Handel fugue in F♯ minor leads directly on from that of the Bach, comprising the second half of the chapter, which is then rounded off with passing reference to fugue by inversion and some closing remarks. Thus, of the chapter's twenty-seven pages, twenty-five are more or less continuous analysis. These are supported by thirteen pages of plates, including the complete musical text of each fugue (for the Handel fugue, see the Appendix below), annotated along the lines of Marpurg's *Treatise on Fugue* of 1753–4 with letters *a–z*, *aa–* and so forth, Roman and Arabic numerals and verbal indications (Sechter used this same device: see Analysis 4 below).

For Momigny, the principal structural marker in fugue is the exposition. He coins a word for it: *Révolution*, which he prefers to the established *Répercussion*. He defines exposition as 'the circle or space which [the subject] traverses before

---

1 Chap. 39 (vol. II, pp. 517–43) is entitled 'De la composition asservie <à un ou à plusieurs Desseins>, ou <du> Contre-point obligé: de la Fugue <et de ce qui y a rapport>' (words in the Table of Contents (vol. II, p. 710) but not at the head of the chapter are given in angle-brackets).

being repeated in the same voice', and furthers the implicit analogy thus: 'the four voices are in something like the same relation to the subject that the zodiac is to the sun; that is, the subject appears successively in the four voices, just as the sun appears to visit each of the celestial signs before seeming to return to its starting-point' (p. 520). He does not consistently point out episodes – the fact that he has several words for them (*digression, Andamento, Promenade*) suggests that there is in his mind no single concept clearly separated from that of exposition. He offers interesting remarks on part-crossing, thematic fragmentation, contrasted rates of movement and rhythmic impetus. Finally – and perhaps surprisingly for so 'scientific' a genre as fugue – he devises a short scene, writes a script and underlays it to the fugue, thereby providing a *raison d'être* for the contrasts in affective content of the various *portions* of the two subjects that he has earlier segmented, and for the fluctuations in rhythmic activity.

Belgian by birth, Momigny worked for a time as teacher and organist in Lyon before establishing a music publishing and printing house in Paris in 1800, by which means he published not only his own theoretical and didactic works and many compositions, but also an extensive list of music by other composers. He wrote the *Complete Course* over a period of at least two years, issuing it in the meantime by instalments. Essentially in accord with Rameau that the laws of harmony derived from the harmonic spectrum of a sonorous body, and that harmony precedes melody, he laid emphasis on his own theoretical innovations, seeking to distance himself from his illustrious predecessor.[2] After issuing the *Complete Course* three times (1803–05, 1806, 1808), he published a summary of his theory, *Succint Exposé of the Only Musical System*, in 1808 and one further treatise, *The Only True Theory of Music*, in 1821. Momigny formally submitted the *Complete Course* to the Institut National. At the end of his life, deeply embittered, he had still failed to win the official approval for which he had so long petitioned.

---

2   Ian Bent, 'Momigny's "Type de la Musique" and a Treatise in the Making', in *Music Theory and the Exploration of the Past*, ed. C. Hatch and D. Bernstein (Chicago: Chicago University Press, 1993).

'Double Fugue [Handel: Fugue from Harpsichord Suite No. 6 in F♯ Minor³]'

Complete Course in Harmony and Composition

> Source:
> 'De la Fugue à deux Sujets', *Cours complet d'harmonie et de composition, d'après une théorie nouvelle et générale de la musique*, vol. II (Paris: Momigny, 1805), pp. 535–43; vol. III (Paris: Momigny, 1803–05), pp. 198–204 (Plate 39 I).

Double fugue

First exposition⁴

254. The soprano gives out subject 1 for the first time (at 1) [in the score: bb. 1–8], the tenor subject 2 [bb. 2–4]. The bass restates subject 1 (2) [bb. 6–10], and the soprano restates subject 2 (II) [bb. 8–10]. [See Appendix, pp. 333–5 below.] *NB* Arabic numerals indicate successive statements of subject 1, Roman numerals those of subject 2.

255. Subject 2 is nothing other than an answer [*Réponse*] to subject 1, but one not involving its imitation. It is, so to speak, a dissenting voice raised against theme 1.⁵

256. Four distinct segments [*portions*] are to be observed in theme 1 [see Example 1]: C♯, B A, G♯ F[♯], E♯ F♯, D C♯⁶ comprises the first of these segments, and was probably the only one that Handel had invented prior to the first segment of subject 2.

Example 1

Subject 1

---

3 *Hallische Händel-Ausgabe*, Ser.IV: *Instrumentalmusik*, vol. I, *Klavierwerke I*, ed. R.Steglich (Kassel and Basel: Bärenreiter, 1955), pp. 56–8. This fugue appears also in the opening Symphony of Chandos Anthem No. 2, *In the Lord put I my Trust*, and in the second movement of the Concerto Grosso Op. 3, No. 5, both in D minor. See *Händel-Handbuch*, ed. B. Baselt, vol. III *Thematisch-systematisches Verzeichnis: Instrumentalmusik, Pasticci und Fragmente* (Kassel and Basel: Bärenreiter, 1986), pp. 222–4. It dates from *c.*1717–20; order of precedence of the three versions is unclear.

4 'Exposition': *Révolution*. 'I term *Révolution du Sujet* the circle or interval that [the subject] traverses without repeating itself in any one voice,' to which the footnote is appended: 'It is what some call *Répercussion*, a word singularly ill-adapted to the thing at issue here' (p. 520); see also '*Répercussion*' (p. 695).

5 'Subject' and 'theme' are interchangeable in this analysis.

6 Momigny punctuates his musical examples with commas according to the upbeat-downbeat patterns of the *motifs* that are the basis of his theoretical system.

The second segment of subject 1, C♯ D, F♯ B, E C♯, A, A B, D G♯, C♯ A, F♯, can only have {536} been conceived in conjunction with the first segment of subject 2, namely A, G♯, F♯, E♯ F♯.

The third segment of subject 1, C♯, F♯ B, A♯ B, is of secondary importance [*accessoire*], as also is the fourth segment, F♯, G♯ A, G♯ A, B G♯, F♯ E, D♯ E, C♯ C♯, D♯ B♯, G♯. Indeed, this fourth segment does not really belong to subject 1: it is an extension [*ajoute*] which fills the gap that would otherwise exist in the soprano between the end of subject 1 and the answer to theme 2.

257. It is possible to treat the two subjects separately throughout the first two or three expositions, and not to treat them in conjunction until the fourth or fifth exposition.

258. Why does the bass (2) [in b. 6] not begin as follows: G♯, F♯ E, D♯ C♯, B♯ C♯, A G♯, which would answer exactly C♯, B A, G♯ F♯, E♯ F♯, D C♯?

Because the rule is that the fifth must be answered only by the tonic. This is why F♯, and not G♯, has to answer C♯.

Can that rule never be overridden?

It is perfectly possible to do so, since only practice stands against it. However, unless one were to give good reason for the infringement one would risk being taken for an ignoramus.

What is the basis of this practice? The fact that the [diatonic] scale comprises two unequal halves when the dominant is taken as the dividing point, there being in ascent five notes from C to G but only four from G to C, such that C D E F G must be answered with G G A B C, or G G A B C with C D E F G. {537}

259. Worthy of note in this first exposition is a brief canon at the fourth comprising five notes between bass and tenor at letter *b* and number 3 [b. 12]. The bass states G♯, F♯ E[♯], D♯ C♯, the tenor C♯, B A, G♯ F♯. This is an imitation *alla stretta* of subject 1.

Second exposition

260. In this, the second exposition, subject 1 appears only in the soprano (4) [bb. 18–22], and subject 2 only in the tenor (IV) [bb. 19–21].

From letter *d* up to the fifth statement of subject 1 (5) [i.e. from b. 23 to b. 28] there is nothing but free counterpoint, save for brief points of imitation at letters *e* and *f* [bb. 26, 27]. This constitutes an episode [*digression*][7] that allows the two subjects a brief respite.

Third exposition

261. Once again the soprano gives out subject 1 first (5) [bb. 29–30]. It states the first segment of subject 1, and then proceeds directly to subject 2 (V) [bb. 30–32],

---

7   Other terms for 'episode' in Momigny's vocabulary are *Andamento* and *Promenade* (p. 680): 'a sort of extension located within an exposition, after a subject and its answers, to allow the theme a brief respite, and separate one exposition from the next. In short, it is a moment of relaxation [*hors-d'œuvre*].'

stating only the first segment of that before reverting to the second segment of subject 1 (*h*).

[Two] voices have been interchanged at this point. It is not in fact the tenor that ought to continue subject 1 at *g* [b. 30], but rather the soprano, the voice which began it; for it is the tenor that ought properly to carry the statement of theme 2, G♯, F♯, E, D♯ E (V), though an octave lower.

Handel chose instead to locate subject 2 in the soprano, {538} or at any rate [to place it] an octave higher, so as to make a stronger effect. It is possible to do this in a fugue for organ or harpsichord without giving rise to complications.

Would this not, then, work equally well with a fugue written for three separate parts? No, because it is not possible to retrieve the voices from an octave displacement [*diapason*] without endangering the coherence of the part-writing.

262. Moreover, there are several passages in this fugue that presuppose the existence of four voices – for example, at number 5.

This would not be feasible in a three-part fugue for anything other than a polyphonic [*collectif*] instrument such as piano or organ, whereas on such instruments as these this kind of amplification of texture [*remplissage*][8] can occasionally be permitted, more orthodox though it would be to avoid it.

Fourth exposition

263. The opening of subject 1 is given out twice in quick succession by the bass (6, 7) [bb. 35–7, 37–9], the first time in A major, the second in B minor.[9] It is as well to exploit such immediate repetitions from time to time, for they bring a certain vibrancy to the style. They are especially effective when the restatement is one step higher [as here], the rise in pitch bringing an intensification which conveys a sense of gathering momentum in the voice [*personnage*][10] making the repetition.

The quavers that occurred in the bass during the third exposition, themselves a free variant [*imitation libre*][11] of the second segment of subject 1 inverted, bring a momentum to the present exposition which is {539} most effective. It is important

8   The function of *remplissage* is best seen in the following explanation of the four 'roles' of fugal part-writing:

> The primary role is played at any given moment by the voice assigned to state the first segment of the subject . . . ; the secondary role . . . by the voice assigned to state the second segment of the subject; the third role . . . by that which presents some segment or other of the theme, or a variant of a segment . . . while the other two voices play the role of the two leading characters [*personnages*]; the fourth role is played by the voice that does nothing but add to the harmony, and consists of *pur remplissage*, because it is not slave to any of the thematic material nor variant . . . The great masters, however, . . . avoid *simple remplissage* and harness it . . . to some segment of the theme, in inversion or not. (p. 522)

   It is thus roughly equivalent to the contemporary German term *Gegenharmonie*, but with an element of *Zergliederung*.

9   Plate 39 I signals the beginning of the fourth exposition as the middle of b. 37, but this text implies the middle of b. 35.

10 *personnage*: see note 8.

11 In keeping with eighteenth-century writers, Momigny includes repetition and sequential restatement *in the same voice* within the definition of *imitation*. In addition, he defines several degrees of 'imperfect imitation', the most imperfect of which approximates more closely in modern terminology to 'variant' or 'variation' (pp. 262–7).

always to be on one's guard against tedium. So long as the parts do not degene-
rate into chaos, a little agitation never does any harm – unless, that is, it is out of
keeping with what has to be expressed.

See how carefully Handel has contrived the bass so that, while soprano and
tenor move relatively slowly, it supplies renewed impetus at *l*, *m* and *n*, against
entries VI, VII and VIII of subject 2 [bb. 39, 41, 43].

264. At *o*, *p*, *q*, *r*, *s*, *t*, *u*, *v* and *x* [bb. 45–53], he seems to toy playfully with the
second segment of subject 1, as it is tossed continually from voice to voice. Then
after a truncated entry [*petite Attaque*] which recalls the rhythm of notes 2–3 of
subject 1 [bb. 55–6],[12] he at last reintroduces this subject in close stretto in a three-
part canon at the octave which continues unabated from letter *y* right through
to *z* [bb. 57–63].

This canon is a real jewel, and would be ample evidence alone of Handel's
technical skill [*science*], were that not plain to see in every bar of the fugue.

Fifth exposition

265. The moment this three-part canon ends, the fifth exposition is launched [b. 63]
with a two-part canon, subject 1 making its eighth and ninth appearances (8 and 9).

The two-part canon continues as far as letter *aa* [b. 66], at which point the
truncated entry reappears; hot on the heels of this comes the tenth statement of
subject 1, making its appearance in the bass [b. 67].

{540}

Sixth exposition

266. The soprano presents the eleventh statement of subject 1 (11); and this same
voice bears also the ninth and tenth statements of theme 2 [bb. 69–74].

Worthy of note is the variant of the second segment of subject [1], which enters
simultaneously in tenor and bass at letters *bb* and *cc* [b. 71], further stimulating
interest.

The *tasto solo*, the pedal-point or sustained bass note that now ensues is no less
remarkable. How skilful is the gradual rise and fall now of the soprano line! What
a rich tableau of life Handel has unfolded before us!

Conclusion

267. It is essential that the two themes of a double fugue be clearly distinguishable
from one another; if one of them has a lot of rhythmic activity the other should
have very little. These two themes may be introduced virtually simultaneously,
as is the case here, or at some distance from one another, be it large or small. It is
however obligatory that they appear together at the end, in several of the fugue's
expositions, or at least in the final ones. It follows that they must be constructed
one against the other in counterpoint, if not in totality then in part, unless some

---

12 '*Attaque* [in fugue] is a short subject of two or three notes, whether or not drawn from the
    theme' (p. 680).

stroke of fortune should happen to produce what is normally the job of technical skill to contrive.

Although it is generally agreed that the highest realms and most subtle devices of contrapuntal technique [*science*] should be reserved until the end, it is {541} even more important that careful attention be given to increasing its effects gradually. In music, as in the art of oratory, to fail to move one's listeners is to miss the whole point. But even before moving them must come pleasing them and engaging their interest; and to achieve this, the subject must be well chosen.

As to the subject of Handel's fugue, the first segment – which is particularly identified with the theme – is noble in character, whereas the segment that works in counterpoint with theme 2 requires a higher level of rhythmic activity.

Here is how one might set about interpreting the expressive content of this subject.

268. A father, respectable but at the same time severe, commands his daughter, who has fallen into an infatuation, to sacrifice her love. Unable to banish from her mind and heart the object of her affections, the latter says to her father: 'Father dear, I beg you, soften your heart' (C♯, B A, G♯ F♯, E♯ F♯, D C♯) [bb. 1–2]. The father, unbending, replies: 'No, obey you must' (A, G♯, F♯, E♯ F[♯]) [bb. 2–4]. While the father delivers his uncompromising rebuttal, the daughter turns and says to her mother: 'Oh plead for me, dear mother' [(C♯ D, F♯ B, E C♯, A) [bb. 2–3, 3–4].

Example 2

(a) Fa - ther dear, I beg you, soft'n your heart   (b) No,___ o - bey___ you must

(c) Oh plead for me, dear mo - ther

The delineation of the characters is reflected not only in the interaction of the voices, but also in the higher register at which the daughter's entreaties ring out at 4 and 5 [bb. 18–19, 29–30], and in the increasing frequency {542} with which the subjects occur between 5 and *x*.

Following *g* and *h*, the fretful movement of the bass [bb. 32, 33–4] portrays vividly the father's wrath, which, far from abating, grows steadily more furious. This ire bursts forth for a second time at *u*, *v* and *x* [bb. 51–3]. At this point, the exchanges become so vehement and so rapid that the words of *father*, *mother* and *daughter* seem to be heard in brief snatches.

Soon everybody is so agitated that they pay no heed to each other, pursuing their own protestations while ignoring all rejoinders. The canon that begins at y [b. 57] in all three parts conveys this perfectly.

Enraged, the father thunders: 'I insist, don't waste your breath, obey me, I insist' (D, C♯ B, A G♯, F[♯] E♯, D♯ C♯, B A, G♯ F♯) [bb. 62–4].

The two-part canon [bb. 63–6] is a portrayal of mother and daughter lamenting their inability to soften the heart of the wrathful father.

At letter *dd*, in despair the daughter breaks off her passionate entreaties abruptly, and declares in ringing tones [bb. 74–81] that, tear out her heart though he might, he would not succeed in banishing the image of her loved-one. She forgets herself, mixing protestations of undying love for the object of her desires with reckless reproaches to her father, full of bitterness at his heartlessness.

The latter, shocked by her audacity, stands stupefied – as the sustained bass note portrays. The mother, ever loving, tries to coax her daughter back to the filial duty and respect required of her towards her father.

{543} This, or something like it, is the range of feeling that we believe Handel might have experienced, or the image that he might have had in mind, as he composed this fugue.

Antoine Reicha (1770–1836)
'Observation sur la méthode d'analyser avec fruit un morceau sous le rapport de l'harmonie'
Cours de composition musicale (?1816–18)

An analysis admittedly *of a* fugue, yet not *concerning* fugue (in the sense of thematic logistics, strategy, contrapuntal artifice), this is the most conservative of the three analyses by Reicha presented in this volume. As discussed in the Introduction to Part I, it is the end of a line that extends backwards through Vogler (1806), Momigny (1803–05), Kirnberger and Schulz (1771; 1773) ultimately to the *Treatise on Harmony* (1722) of Rameau: a slender lineage not at all intrinsically concerned with fugue, despite four of its instances being analyses of fugues.

In Reicha's case, the titles bring this out. The item itself is headed *Fugue analysée sous le rapport de l'harmonie* – i.e. what follows relates not so much to fugal as to harmonic process. The table of contents puts a wider perspective on it: *Observation sur la méthode d'analyser avec fruit* – he is concerned primarily with (fruitful) methodology rather than with the work in its own right – *un morceau sous le rapport de l'harmonie* – the choice of a fugue is actually irrelevant. We also learn that the method is designed for 'pupils' in composition, and is effective on 'the works of celebrated composers'. In short, we have an essay on method in harmonic analysis, for self-instructional purposes, for which a fugue (by a celebrated composer?) happens to have been selected as the object of a prototype.

The brief text of this essay recommends a three-stage process. The first two stages require manuscript paper and pen for the preparation of (1) a two-stave harmonic reduction, and (2) a stave of fundamentals; the third is an exercise in comparison and deduction, the long-term result being a mental thesaurus of harmonic features.

In the event, the prototype does not exactly correspond: instead of two written stages, there are five. If stages 2, 3 and 4 are really a trifurcation of the prescribed second stage, then stage 5 is surplus to specification. What Reicha calls his 'model' is laid out on nine staves, the upper brace supplying the finished composition, the next brace the reduction to 'essential notes', the next three single staves three aspects of the *basse fondamentale* and the lowest brace a figured-bass reading of the piece. Of the three staves of *basse fondamentale*, the first (i.e. stage 2, stave 5) transmits the root of each chord (with presence of ninth or seventh, diminished fifth or altered fifth or third noted in figures). Fugue presents special difficulties at this stage, integral to its strategy being that the bass line rest for long stretches, and that the texture often reduce to a single line or two, in all of which situations a series of roots has to be inferred. This information is then carried down to stave 6 (stage 3), reinterpreted according to a chord-labelling system that Reicha has formulated earlier in the volume. The labels used here are:

1 = major triad	2 = minor triad
3 = diminished triad	4 = augmented triad
5 = dominant seventh chord	6 = minor triad with minor seventh
7 = half-diminished seventh chord	8 = major triad with major seventh
9 = dominant major ninth chord	10 = dominant minor ninth chord.

It is at this point that Reicha diverges most markedly from Kirnberger/Schulz. The latter simplify the figuring so that only perfect triads and seventh chords remain, in accordance with Rameau's stipulations.[1]

Stave 7 (stage 4) has the significant function of making the fundamental bass conform to the paths laid down for it by Rameau: paths that, in Reicha's words, constitute the *enchaînement des accords*. Reicha has set out rules for fundamental bass progression earlier in the volume (pp. 21–5). Summarily: (1) best are those root progressions that move by descending third, fourth or fifth (or their inverses); (2) progressions by step are unacceptable *except* for three cases: I–II, IV–V, V–VI; (3) an ascending third (or its inverse) is acceptable only if followed by a descending fifth. We can now understand why Reicha speaks in his analysis of 'exceptions' such as that in the second half of b. 2, E–F♯ (I–II). For each such exception he interpolates a note a third below the first (here C♯), following the practice frequently demonstrated in the examples of Rameau's *Treatise*.[2]

It is important to realize that these stages work purely successively: each one processes only the data presented to it by the previous stage. Ironically, if only the answer had not been reduced differently from the subject (cf. bb. 1 and 2), many of the stepwise progressions would never have arisen in the first place. For example, in bb. 31–4, the necessity to avoid the first such progression in each bar would have been obviated, leaving a fundamental bass of c♯–g♯–c♯–(A♯)–d♯–(G♯)–e, and so on.

Antoine-Joseph Reicha, although born and educated in Prague, and employed first in Bonn and Hamburg, belongs to the long line of 'French' theorists who were also composers of stature – including Rameau, Berlioz, d'Indy and in modern times Messiaen, Schaeffer and Boulez. Reicha finally settled in Paris only in 1808 and set himself up as a teacher of composition. He envisaged a course in musical composition for which the student should count on not less than 'eight years of assiduous work'. Such a course would involve the study of melody, of harmony, and of double, triple and quadruple counterpoint and fugue, all of which constitute a 'necessary preliminary to the study of composition', which begins only after all of this. Reicha's first three major treatises provide the teaching material for precisely that preliminary work: manuals on melody (*Treatise on Melody*, 1814: see Analysis 8 below), harmony (*Course in Musical Composition*, ?1816–18: see the present analysis) and the higher levels of counterpoint and fugue (*Treatise on Advanced Musical Composition*, 1824–6: see Analysis 9 below).

1   Rameau, *Traité*, trans. P. Gossett, p. 357: 'The fundamental bass has been added to the other parts simply to prove that there are only perfect chords or seventh chords throughout the piece . . .'.
2   ibid, 234: 'We remarked in the preceding book that, whenever it is permissible to have the fundamental bass ascend a tone or semitone, the progression of a third or fourth is always implied.'

'Fruitful Method of Analysing a Piece of Music with Respect to Harmony'[3]

Course in Musical Composition

Source:
'Observation sur la méthode d'analyser avec fruit un morceau sous le rapport de l'harmonie', *Cours de composition musicale ou Traité complet et raisonné d'harmonie pratique* (Paris: Gambaro, ?1816–18), pp. 131, 263–9.

Here is the method that we suggest to pupils who wish to analyse fruitfully the works [*productions*] of celebrated composers:

(1)   first, all the inessential notes of the piece under analysis are eliminated, and the essential notes alone are entered separately [on two staves];

(2)   then the fundamentals of the chords are entered on a separate staff;

(3)   the piece in its original form is compared with that giving just the essential notes; then the succession of fundamentals is examined so as to see how the chord successions form progressions [*s'enchaînent*].

This exercise, if carried out repeatedly, presents the pupil with a whole host of noteworthy cases with regard to chord progressions [*l'enchaînement des accords*], modulations, different procedures for employing inessential notes, and also distribution of parts. These cases will, in time, engrave themselves on his memory. A model of this [method of] analysis [is given below].

---

3   The title is taken from the table of contents (p. 1).

Harmonic Analysis of a Fugue[4]

FUGUE

No.1 For the fortepiano:

No.2 The same fugue reduced to its more essential elements, and with all inessential notes eliminated except for the notes of the pedal:

No.3 Principal notes of the chords expressed as fundamental bass:

No.4 The figures on this staff indicate the species of chord according to its position in our classification system: '2' = chord no. 2, '5' = chord no. 5 of the system, and so on:

No.5 This staff shows how the hiatuses could have been avoided in constructing the succession of perfect chords and in resolving the dissonant chords.
The semiquavers imply notes of larger value, since the chord-progressions would occur too rapidly at these points:

The rests indicate that the harmony of the fugue proceeds without exceptions in the chord successions.

No.6 The lower staff on No.6 shows a figured bass of the fugue still further reduced. The upper staff supplies the realization of these same figures. No.6 should be used as a model for study by anyone who wishes to practise figuring and realizing complicated harmonies:

4   The table of contents: 'This piece serves as an example of the method already indicated of fruitfully analysing musical works [*productions musicales*].'

Pedal

As can be seen from this staff, it is almost never necessary to add more than a single chord in order to avoid an exception in the chord successions.

Moritz Hauptmann (1792–1868)

Erläuterungen zu Johann Sebastian Bach's 'Kunst der Fuge' (1841)

Hauptmann's 'Elucidations' of Bach's *Art of Fugue* are a rare, if not unique, phenomenon for their time. As analysis they are technical hook, line and sinker, and yet they do not emanate from the realm of compositional instruction. They differ in this sense from the analyses in this volume by Reicha, Sechter, Czerny and Lobe. The only items which at first sight bear comparison with them are the *Analysen dreier Fugen* of Dehn and the *Zergliederungen* of Vogler (Analyses 5 and 7), which are analyses of whole pieces, contained in discrete, specifically analytical publications. However, both of the latter are aimed, at least in part, at the pupil in composition, despite their not forming part of a manual. Hauptmann's *Elucidations*, on the other hand, arise from a purely abstract engagement with contrapuntal process, and were brought about by wholly unusual circumstances.

In 1837 a new collected edition of the keyboard works of J. S. Bach was launched by C. F. Peters of Leipzig. It was the second such enterprise that Peters had begun: the first they embarked upon in 1817, itself preceded by a similar enterprise from Hoffmeister of Vienna, begun in 1801.[1] The primary editor of the 'new edition, carefully revised, corrected, annotated with metronome marks and fingerings, by a committee of artists' was Carl Czerny, who edited the first five volumes and had a hand in at least one other. Also involved, though his involvement was less expressly stated, was Moritz Hauptmann. For example, he 'revised and collated' the two- and three-part Inventions on the basis of the Spohr manuscripts for volume VII, edited by Friedrich Griepenkerl.

More particularly, for volume III, *The Art of Fugue*, issued in 1839, he contributed something very familiar in present-day collected editions but most unfamiliar in the early nineteenth century: a supplementary volume.[2] It is this, comprising fourteen quarto pages, that is reproduced below. In providing cross-references by page number, and in co-ordinating the wording of the headings, he made its association with the edition plain to see. Only ten years later, Hauptmann was to be involved in another – historically even more significant – collected edition: that of the Bach Gesellschaft (of which he was a founding member and its president), editing three volumes of its *Works*.[3]

1 See Max Schneider, 'Verzeichnis der bis zum Jahre 1851 gedruckten (und der geschrieben im Handel gewesenen) Werke von Johann Sebastian Bach', *Bach-Jahrbuch 1906*, pp. 84–113.
2 A footnote to the edition stated 'The very valuable Elucidations to *The Art of Fugue* written by Chamber Musician M. Hauptmann are obtainable from the same publisher [i.e. C. F. Peters] price 12 gr.'. They were reviewed by G. W. Fink in *AmZ*, 43 (15 September 1841), cols. 737–9.
3 *Johann Sebastian Bach's Werke*, vols. I (Leipzig: B&H, 1851: ten church cantatas), II (ten church cantatas), VIII (four masses). It is no more than a curiosity that while the *Erläuterungen* were published by C. F. Peters, according to the colophon of this work (p. 15) and to Fink's review (see note 2 above) they were produced at the printing works (*Offizin*) of Breitkopf und Härtel.

Hauptmann addressed his 'Elucidations' not to the theoretically-trained musician but to the 'wider musical circle' of those who used Czerny's edition. What he offered them, accordingly, was in his own words *einige Nachweisungen* – 'a little information', or perhaps 'a few words of clarification'. However, this diffident phrase cloaks something much more substantial: a close description of the technical processes at work in each of the items making up *The Art of Fugue*, together with excursions into the theory of double (i.e. invertible) counterpoint – notably that into inversion with respect to mode (following Fugue IV), that on double counterpoint at the octave, twelfth and tenth (following Fugue XI and continuing through Fugues IX–X), and that on the writing of mirror fugue (in Fugue XII). The description that accompanies each item is not a blow-by-blow account of the fugue in real time but rather a description of the contrapuntal mechanism that impels it. It is, so to speak, a synchronic analysis. Its purpose is to lay bare the *Inhalt* of each piece – and its *Inhalt* is that essentialized mechanism that projects the piece in time.

Nowhere is this special notion of 'content' more apparent than in a remark associated with Fugue X. Hauptmann there explains that in double counterpoint at the tenth, cantus firmus and countersubject can be used to generate good *three*-part counterpoint: first, the two positions of the countersubject can for once be used not merely as alternatives but *simultaneously* (i.e. in parallel thirds or tenths) against the cantus firmus; or secondly, with the countersubject lying below the cantus firmus, the latter can be doubled in thirds below itself. Furthermore, Hauptmann tells us, these two conditions can apply *concurrently*, to produce *four*-part counterpoint. Bach does not avail himself of this possibility; nevertheless Hauptmann sets it out in a music example along with the three-part forms, 'so as to display the full *content* of the contrapuntal procedure at work here' – indeed, he sets it out in two separate forms. Thus for Fugue X, the 'content' projects beyond the *actual* piece to a *potential* piece of which Hauptmann wishes the reader to be aware. This in turn demonstrates Bach's parsimony in the use of his contrapuntal resources, underlying the aesthetic point that a piece exists within a larger field of possibilities – a universe of potential pieces – of which it is the representative. Put in other terms, Hauptmann draws attention to Bach's discarded paradigms, and makes us aware of his margin of security.

All of this brings a delightful irony to Hauptmann's use of the term *Erläuterung(en)*. This term tended to be used during the nineteenth century in two very different contexts: for text-critical commentary on a piece, and for essays in drawing out the inner poetic essence of a work – for the latter, see Part I of volume II of the present work. Hauptmann's work inhabits a shadow-land between these two contexts: it is editorial commentary, at the same time it penetrates essence – albeit contrapuntal essence. Hauptmann even alludes in his opening sentence to 'musical-poetic essence and value' as the antithesis of his present undertaking. And yet what his elucidations uncover are precisely *content* – the word so often used by those who search for inner poetic essence. In the final section of his discourse, Hauptmann distinguishes the synchronic ('disjunct elements') from the diachronic ('the living work'), and goes on to speak of *content* in the sense of emotion and feeling. He makes the point that while, at the level of detail, form is alien to feeling and acts as a restraining element upon it, in the larger perspective, 'form is conditioned by the collective content of all that is utterable in musical terms in a given age'.

Hauptmann displays in his own style of writing a vagueness of syntax that is surprising in so theoretical a work and makes for difficulty in translation. Confusion arises out of a 'play' of synonyms (*Führer*, *Subject* and *Thema*, for example), and out of a tendency for individual terms to shift meaning unannounced (*Contrapunct*, for instance, shunts between 'countersubject', 'double counterpoint' and 'contrapuntal procedure', all of which are legitimate usages, indeed all of which are in a sense one and the same thing, but which need distinguishing for the English-speaking reader; *Lage* is another case, signifying variously 'register', 'position' and 'permutation').

Since Hauptmann is popularly thought of as a 'Hegelian' music theorist, the question will inevitably arise as to whether that philosophical cast is exhibited in the present essay, as it is in his later, and more familiar writings. The notion of the triad thesis–antithesis–synthesis surfaces during the excursion into double counterpoint (in Fugue XI). Counterpoint at the octave possesses, he says, 'absolute oneness', lacking variety, that at the twelfth 'absolute disjunction', lacking unity. From this he concludes that the three species of double counterpoint belong conceptually together: that at the octave as 'unity' (*Einheit*), that at the twelfth as 'duality' (*Trennung*), that at the tenth as 'conjunction' (*Verbindung*). The three form a harmonic triad (tonic–fifth–third) 'of a higher order'. Note that Hauptmann reorders the fugues XI–IX–X so as to introduce them in the order of double counterpoint at the octave, twelfth and tenth respectively. While the Hegelian triad in no way dominates the 'elucidations' as a whole, it does surface from time to time.

Born in Dresden, Hauptmann studied violin and piano, becoming a violinist at the court chapel in Dresden, later in Leipzig. He studied composition with Theodor Weinlig (who taught Wagner briefly) and Spohr. In 1842, the year after publication of his *Elucidations* (which went through a second edition in 1861), he succeeded Weinlig in Bach's former position as Kantor of the Thomasschule at Leipzig and in 1843 became a teacher of music theory at the newly founded Leipzig Conservatory. One of the nineteenth century's foremost theorists, and a protagonist of harmonic dualism, his principal theoretical writings are *The Nature of Harmony and Metre* (1853) and *The Theory of Harmony* (1868). His pupils included Josef Joachim, Hans von Bülow and the theorists Carl Friedrich Weitzmann and Salomon Jadassohn.

Elucidations of Johann Sebastian Bach's 'Art of Fugue'

Source:
Moritz Hauptmann: *Erläuterungen zu Joh. Sebastian Bachs KUNST DER FUGE ... Beilage zum III. Bande der in obiger Verlags-Handlung erschienenen neuen Ausgabe von J. S. Bachs Werken* (Leipzig: C. F. Peters, 1841), pp. 3–14.

Were one to examine the twenty items that make up this work solely from the point of view of their musical-poetic essence and value, the hand of the sublime master would still be instantly recognizable behind it. However, the work has a purpose that goes beyond the merely aesthetic: it is that of instruction. It teaches the higher realms of counterpoint: not in abstract rules and prescriptions, but by the setting out of fully-fledged, model compositions, each one taking as its essential subject-matter [*wesentlicher Inhalt*] a specific aspect of this art. Except for the final item, each is elaborated over one and the same underlying theme. Most of the resultant counterpoints [*Sätze*] begin with this theme, which is so constructed as to work in combination [*Combination*] with itself in many different ways; others start with a countersubject [*Contrapunct*] to this theme, treated first in its own right before later being drawn into conjunction [*Verbindung*] with the theme itself.

While the musician with training in music theory will not need explained to him the technical intricacies of these compositions, there are plenty of people in the wider musical circle for whom the present edition is intended who will not find a little information unwelcome. What follows presupposes, however, a broad acquaintance with contrapuntal technique in general [*Contrapunct überhaupt*] and with the structure and essential nature of fugue and canon, and concentrates exclusively upon what is extraordinary and characteristic in the compositions at hand. To those who have no need of such explications, its external ordering of items may serve as a *catalogue raisonnée*, providing a simpler conspectus of the work as a whole.[4]

The work includes thirteen fugues, based on the principal theme in various guises; two of these are for three voices, the remainder[5] for four. In addition, there are four two-part canons and two fugues for two keyboards.

---

4   Previous catalogues of Bach's works were those by C. P. E. Bach and J. F. Agricola in Mizler's *Musikalische Bibliothek*, vol. IV (1754), pp. 158–76, reprinted separately as *Der Nekrolog auf Johann Sebastian Bach*, facs. ed. C. Trautmann (Leipzig and Hannover, 1965); the relevant parts of the *Verzeichnis des musikalischen Nachlasses des verstorbenen Capellmeisters Carl Philipp Emanuel Bach* (Hamburg: Schniebes, 1790); and that in J. N. Forkel's *Ueber Johann Sebastian Bachs Leben, Kunst und Kunstwerke* (Leipzig: Hoffmeister and Kühnel, 1802), pp. 49–62. All of these were without thematic incipits. The first published thematic catalogue (as apart from Franz Hauser's unpublished catalogue of the 1830s) was A. Dörffel's *Thematisches Verzeichniss der Instrumentalwerke Joh. Seb. Bach* (Leipzig and Berlin: Peters, 1867), based on the Bach-Gesellschaft collected edition.

5   *brüigen* should read *übrigen*.

Fuga I, *a 4 voci* (p. 2)[6]

Example 1

In simple counterpoint.

Fuga II, *a 4 voci* (p. 4)

Example 2

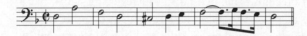

As the previous fugue, but with different order of voices.

Fuga III, *a 4 voci* (p. 6)

Example 3

The theme in contrary motion. In simple counterpoint.

Fuga IV, *a 4 voci* (p. 8)

Example 4

As the previous fugue, but with different order of voices.

Rich and elegant though the harmonic fabric of each is, these four fugues together constitute so far no more than the exposition [*Exposition*] of the theme. All the combinations available under double counterpoint, literal restatements of counterpoints at different registers, and stretti [*Engführungen*], are so far deliberately avoided, so reserving them for the later fugues, where they will receive special and systematic treatment. The way in which the theme is presented in

6   The page numbers are those of the edition for which this analysis served as editorial commentary: *L'ART DE LA FUGUE* | *Kunst der Fuge* | *par* | [portrait] | *Jean Sebastien Bach.* | *Edition nouvelle, soigneusement revue, corrigée, et doigtée,* | *ainsi que pourvue de notifications sur l'exécution* | *et sur les mesures des temps (d'après le Métronome de Maelzel)* | *et accompagnée d'une préface* | *par* | *UN COMITÉ D'ARTISTES.* | [. . .] | *LEIPZIG,* | *au Bureau de Musique de C. F. Peters.* | *Oeuvre complets Liv. III* ||. Vols. I–II of the *Oeuvre complets,* or *Ouevres complettes,* were the two volumes of *The Well-tempered Clavier,* edited by Carl Czerny.

Fugues III and IV calls for a word on *contrary motion* in general, and its bearing upon the manner of answering [*Beantwortung*] of a fugue subject [*Fugenthema*]. As is well known, the terms 'contrary motion' [*Gegenbewegung*] and 'inversion' [*Umkehrung*], when applied to melodic forms, signify transformations of a melodic line in which the rising intervals become falling ones of the same size, the falling ones rising ones. In the major scale, the semitone – which is the crucial factor here – occurs above the third and seventh; and exact inversion is obtained when ascent from the tonic is reciprocated by descent from the third:

Example 5

If the notes of a melodic line from the one scale are set against corresponding notes drawn from the other scale, then an essential relationship is observable between the newly derived melodic line and the original line – an inner rather than an outer reciprocation, and a mutual answering is perceived. This is detectable especially in the semitones, E–F, B♮–C being answered[7] by {4} C–B♮, F–E, and in the intervals which are associated with them:

Example 6

In the minor key, contrary motion is to be sought on a different degree of the scale. The greatest compatibility between the semitones is achieved where the tonic of the ascending scale is answered by the fifth of the descending scale. It is in this form that Sebastian Bach consistently uses it:

Example 7

Contrary motion as demonstrated for the major key has deeper implications for tonal scheme [*Modulation*], in that every chromatic alteration in the one direction generates a reciprocating alteration in the other direction, for B♭ in the inversion corresponds to F♯ in the original, E♭ to C♯; the modulation [*Ausweichung*] to F corresponds to the modulation to G, and so forth.

---

7 *sich beantworteden* should read *sich beantwortenden*.

Example 8

For contrary motion in the minor key, this relationship is lacking. Against that, it should be said that just as the former [i.e. major] is better suited to strictly canonic movements, so the latter is better adapted for use in fugue, because it answers the tonic with the fifth. It is for this reason that movements in the minor key lend themselves more readily to fugal treatment than do movements in the major key. This is because in the latter case inversion at the fifth can easily yield unmelodic results, while at the same time lacking inner reciprocation, whereas inversion at the third is ill-suited to the nature of fugue. In general, however, with this way of answering a theme, the element of reciprocation lies in the contrary motion itself. The answer [*Gefährte*] is not contained within the inversion of the answer, as is otherwise true in the laws of fugue, but in the inversion of the subject [*Führer*] itself. This should become apparent in the following fugues; the preceding two fugues treat the inverted theme as the given subject. Direct motion and contrary motion have not hitherto been used side-by-side in one and the same item: so far they have been isolated from each other as between the first pair and second pair of fugues.

Fuga V, *a 4 voci* (p. 12)

Example 9

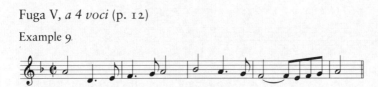

The answer [is] in direct motion, the subject in contrary motion. With this fugue begins the counterpointing of the theme against itself: the *stretti*. The very first entry of the answer is itself a stretto, entering as it does before the close of the theme. For ease of inspection, the later occurrences are set out in the accompanying schema in decreasing distance of stretto; and for the same reason they are all given in the tonic key. In this and all other musical quotations, only those combinations are included which present the theme entire in the form of either subject or answer. Even transposition or inversion of voices at the octave, which is possible and indeed occurs in most of them, has been excluded from the two-voice combinations, in the interests of concise presentation.

Example 10

{5} Fuga VI, *a 4 voci. In stile francese.* (p. 14)

Example 11

The epithet *in stile francese*[8] relates not to the type of counterpoint in which this fugue is written as a whole, but solely to tiny figures that occur in demisemiquavers – the 'graces' [*Grazie*] of the French keyboard music of the time, by Couperin and his contemporaries. The theme is here answered in diminution and

---

8   The epithet is present in the first edition (1751?) as 'Contrapunctus 6. a 4 in Stylo Francese', but not in the composer's autograph (*c.*1745–50).

contrary motion, in fact this manner of answering is maintained throughout the entire course of the fugue with the exception of a few passages in which the answer proceeds in notes of double value, so anticipating the fugue that follows. The combinations encountered here are set out in the accompanying example in the same order as in the previous example.

Example 12

Fuga VII, *a 4 voci* (p. 18)

Example 13

In contrast to the previous fugue, here we have a study in the answering of the theme in contrary motion by augmentation. The theme itself also occurs in double values in each of the four voices, interspersed with entries in original note values in a variety of forms. The combinations in these last two fugues are most ingeniously devised, and woven with such skill into a full harmonic texture as befits a work whose purpose is to display the art [of counterpoint]: profoundly complex though Sebastian Bach's other compositions often are in other respects, they employ this particular type of thematic treatment only very rarely. Rhythmic diversity within metrical unity – the use of tied notes and syncopations – is an essential condition of double counterpoint, indeed, it is the very soul of it; whereas metrical diversity, disparity between the time signatures for the subjects [*Subjecte*] being combined together, will never make for a truly musical effect in contrapuntal composition. The conjunction of such metrically diverse voices will always be something foreign, it will not yield a detectable unity, and the inherent contradiction can easily give rise to comic effect. Just as the previous fugue brought into play certain raw material belonging to the {6} present fugue, so there are several passages in the latter in which combinations from the former are taken up again. Here we need only note what does not occur in the previous fugue. The introduction of the theme in notes of double value, the deployment of which occupies the bulk of the fugue, results even here, unlike the beginning, in most of the answers [*Antworten*] being in diminution.

Example 14

The earlier two-part combinations which now recur acquire a new meaning in that both voices enter into a relationship with a third, given one. In No. 2 the outer voices are taken from the beginning of Fugue V, schema 1a; in No. 3 both pairs of entries of the upper two voices come from this same source.

Fuga VIII, *a 3 voci* (p. 21)

Example 15

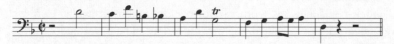

The subject [*Thema*] with which this three-part fugue begins, as also a second one which joins it later (b. 39), are countersubjects to the principal theme in a some-what varied guise (see b. 171). They have moreover the special property that all three combine together at any octave transposition to form a perfectly satisfactory three-part counterpoint – a property that distinguishes them fundamentally from the preceding combinations, all of which required extra voices to fill out the harmony to an acceptable level. Three voices generate six possible permutations [*Lagen*]. To save space, it will suffice to quote just one of these permutations in full, and to indicate the remainder by their beginnings alone:

Example 16

{7} Of these permutations, Nos 3 and 6 are not used. The others are to be found between b. 147 and the end of the fugue, which has proceeded up to now by turns with the two counter-themes [*Gegenthemen*] and the principal theme, the latter as yet not in conjunction with the former.

Fuga XI, *a 4 voci* (p. 34)

Example 17

Fugue XI needs to be taken out of order and considered now, in advance of Nos IX and X. It presents the two subjects of the preceding fugue set in contrary motion, and in other respects too belongs at this point. A new ingredient, and a very important one for the character of the fugue, interposes itself via the fourth voice, not that this new figure deserves to be named as a fourth subject, for it is never placed in full-scale conjunction with the principal theme. It contributes colour rather than form, primarily adhering to the first subject from the previous fugue [i.e. Fugue VIII], counterpointing it in its direct- and contrary-motion forms, and raising the level of chromaticism in this fugue to the highest point:

Example 18

Only Nos 1, 2 and 3 of the six possible permutations of the three subjects are exploited in this fugue, the third subject being used neither complete nor strictly in contrary motion. The missing harmony notes are supplied by the fourth voice:

Example 19

Under the contrapuntal inversions that have so far taken place in Fugues V, VI and VII with one and the same theme, and even more so those in Fugues VIII and XI with several subjects, the harmony produced by the counterpointing voices themselves has remained unchanged, since these same pitches come into fresh combinations with each other with respect to their vertical ordering only. In the following two fugues this is no longer the case. The transposed countersubject falls into an essentially different relationship with the given voice. The intervals that result from the inversion belong to different chords, or form different intervals of the same chord. In addition to double counterpoint at the *octave* [*Contrapunct der Octave*], in which Fugues VIII and XI are studies, there are two other categories [*Gattungen*] which lend themselves to artistic exploitation: double counterpoint at the *fifth*, or *twelfth*, and double counterpoint at the *third*, or *tenth*. It is not just that in both cases the original consonances [*Grundconsonanzen*] of the one position [*Lage*]⁹ yield equally consonant intervals at the other position – that is a *sine qua non* without which the [system] would be technically unworkable. There is much more to it than that: an inner relationship and affinity is at work here, whereby it emerges that these three categories of double counterpoint belong together conceptually and constitute a unified system. For any one of these [categories], we need only think of the two positions available to it as a single, self-contained relationship, and we have precisely what gives each of the categories its essential character. To {8} consider just one of these positions in isolation is to lose all sense of the special significance of such counterpoints [*Sätze*], the very *Doppelgänger* spirit that animates them; and in view of the technical constraints associated with their use, what remains would in most cases seem not worth all the effort. It clearly takes a special mode of listening to fathom the musical individuality of such products; but who can deny that every product of art has its own special mode of understanding?

Whereas double counterpoint at the octave merely replicates itself melodically and harmonically at its two available positions, double counterpoint at the twelfth yields precisely the reverse of this situation [*Gegenbild*]. In the former there is the lack of diversity, the absolute oneness of parallel octaves, in the latter the lack of unity, the absolute disjunction of the parallel fifths which would result if the two positions were to be sounded simultaneously – a degree of unification forbidden in contrapuntal practice. In both categories, only one position or the other may be used at a time. With double counterpoint at the tenth the negative attributes of the other two no longer apply. Its two positions embody essentially different things, so may be sounded together.

In this sense, these three categories of double counterpoint can be viewed as a harmonic 'triad' [*Trias*] of a higher order. Thus, to double counterpoint at the octave, corresponding in significance to the tonic, can be attributed the character of unity [*Einheit*]; to that at the twelfth, corresponding to the fifth, the character of duality [*Trennung*]; and to that at the tenth, corresponding to the third, the

9 The passage is somewhat confusing. By *Lage* at this point, Hauptmann is referring not to the alternatives of simple or compound inversional interval – third *or* tenth, fifth *or* twelfth – but to the two possible positions of countersubject in relation to given voice – either below or above. By *Gattung*, Hauptmann is referring to any of the three categories of invertible counterpoint [*Contrapunct*]: at the octave, at the third or tenth, at the fifth or twelfth.

character of conjunction [*Verbindung*]. The extent to which the first of these three categories is employed outside fugue as well as within is well known. However, only the last of the categories, double counterpoint at the tenth, is in everyday use. For where two voices proceed in parallel thirds against a third voice, providing that that third voice is not a pedal-point, the basic conditions of this method are met, albeit not with the strictness necessary for a counterpoint designed to be inverted. Double counterpoint at the twelfth is rarely found in more recent music, and is even rarer in earlier music. Examples of counterpoint [*Sätze*] in which one voice remains constant while another stating the same melody alternates a third below and a third above it can be included among these, as for instance in the first fugue of Mozart's Requiem.[10]

Fuga IX, *a 4 voci* (p. 26)

Example 20

In double counterpoint at the twelfth. The fugue begins with the counter-theme on its own. Once this has passed through all four voices, the principal theme then enters (p. 27, top), accompanied by the counter-theme alternately at the two positions that are stipulated for this type of counterpoint. For the counter-theme is so constructed that it can enter at the octave below the principal theme or at the fifth above it. The raw material of this fugue therefore comprises essentially the following counterpoint:

Example 21

10 'Kyrie eleison'/'Christe eleison', bb. 48– of the first movement, e.g. Bass/Alto, bb. 48–50 and Soprano/Tenor, bb. 51–53.

This is not the place in which to set out the specific rules for this type of counter-point, or that of the following fugue. They are to be found exhaustively stated in that comprehensive work of music theory, André's *Compositionslehre*, published by Breitkopf und Härtel.[11] The fact that double counterpoint at the twelfth permits parallel thirds against the cantus firmus but excludes the sixth as a consonance gives a character to its resultant counterpoints, even to their separate positions, that is quite unlike those of double counterpoint at the tenth.[12]

Fuga X, *a 4 voci* (p. 30)

Example 22

In double counterpoint at the tenth. This fugue, too, begins with the exposition [*Durchführung*] of the counter-theme on its own. Conjunction with the principal theme does not begin until b. 44; but in the meantime the latter has again received independent exposition starting at b. 23. The countersubject, together with its transposition to the tenth, are as follows:

{9}

Example 23

As remarked earlier, it is a feature of this category of double counterpoint that the two positions, a third or tenth apart, can be used simultaneously, and that these make good three-part counterpoint when placed in conjunction with the cantus firmus, which is in this case the principal theme. What is more, it is inherent in the construction [*Construction*] of this particular [category of counterpoint] that at its first position the cantus firmus may be doubled at the third below. Furthermore, so long as freely approached and quitted sixths are avoided, this [category of counterpoint] allows a doubling in parallel thirds such that a doubling of the cantus firmus at the third below will still prove to be consonant with the counter-subject in both of its positions. The present countersubject is designed to meet this condition, yet Sebastian Bach has avoided its four-part application entirely in

11   The reference may perhaps be to Johann Anton André (1775–1842), *Lehrbuch der Tonsetzkunst*, vols. I–II (Offenbach: André, 1832–42). I have been unable to consult it.
12   The meaning of this sentence is not entirely clear.

this fugue, and has taken advantage even of its three-part application only in the closing six bars. For this combination, based as it is on the conditions set out above, should not be confused with the remaining three-part combinations. A four-part counterpoint of this type could also be achieved if one were to avoid in double counterpoint at the twelfth anything that is incompatible with double counterpoint at the tenth, namely parallel motion in thirds with the cantus firmus – just as here in double counterpoint at the tenth the sixth, which is an inadmissible interval in double counterpoint at the twelfth, has had to be avoided. For ultimately it arises out of a fusion of these two categories – or all three – of double counterpoint, whereby everything that is contrary to the nature of any one of them has to be excluded. An entire composition in this manner would be a very cramped affair. It would convey the sense of an object born of numbing compulsion rather than of a free aesthetic spirit. We cannot even entertain such a thought: we can talk only of the nature and validity of such combinations in specific applications, occurring frequently in all types of music as they do, and making the best of effects in their proper place. So as to display the full potential [*Inhalt*] of the contrapuntal procedure at work here, the four-part combination has been included below. In this, as in all previous fugues except for No. VII, we should not lose sight of the fact that in the three-part combinations a fourth part is always available to supply the root or fill out the harmony.

Example 24

{10} With this item ends a succession of fugues that hang together systematically in their content and order of events, and can be summarized as follows:

A. Simple counterpoint
   a. subject in direct motion
      1. exposition: A–S–T–B   Fugue I
      2. exposition: B–T–A–S   Fugue II
   b. subject in contrary motion
      1. exposition: A–S–T–B   Fugue III
      2. exposition: S–A–T–B   Fugue IV

B. Double counterpoint
   a. subject, in direct and contrary motion, combined with itself
      1. in notes of normal value   Fugue V
      2. in diminution   Fugue VI
      3. in augmentation   Fugue VII
   b. subject combined with others
      1. in double counterpoint at the octave   Fugue VIII (XI)
      2. in double counterpoint at the fifth (twelfth)   Fugue IX
      3. in double counterpoint at the third (tenth)   Fugue X

In the double counterpoint of Fugues V and VI, there occur isolated contrapuntal passages in two and three parts that permit inversion in contrary motion. In schemas V: 1, 2, 3, and VI: 1, 2 they are given in both forms. Likewise, Fugue XI includes at least two voices of Fugue VIII set in strict contrary motion. The two items that now follow deal exclusively with this type of inversion. Again, however, they are essentially distinct from one another.

Fuga XII, *a 4 voci* (p. 40)

Example 25

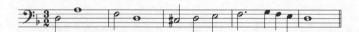

In inversion and contrary motion in all four voices, such that voice 4 becomes voice 1, voice 3 becomes voice 2, voice 2 becomes voice 3, and voice 1 becomes voice 4. In this way, the intervallic relationships between the voices in the two versions [i.e. the original and the inversion] remain constant, but the harmony is totally changed. The chords, so to speak, appear turned on their heads. This is a type of contrapuntal procedure for which prescriptions are not easy to lay down but are even harder to put into practice. In essence, they depend on an extremely restricted use of dissonances in the underlying harmony, since under inversion and contrary motion they would appear improperly prepared and resolved. Where in normal counterpoint the fourth above the lowest pitch has to be avoided, here the fourth below the highest pitch must also be avoided, since under inversion [*Versetzung*] the latter becomes the former. In other words, the upper voice must, apart from in passing harmonies, always supply the third or fifth of the basic chord [*Grundaccord*]. It may not be so very difficult for the musician skilled in harmony to devise a handful of phrases that will work equally well in either version under such conditions. On the other hand, a piece as complex and extended as the present one will always stand out as one of the most remarkable products of the harmonic control of counterpoint; for with all the restrictions that hold it in check, this item betrays scarcely a hint of constraint. There is a strong sense of progression within individual lines, and at the same time a mighty flow from voice to voice. The piece is austere and disciplined in character; its absence of suspensions [*gebundene Dissonanzen*] gives it a rather distinctively grandiose coldness, which seems to withdraw beyond the realm of human sentiment.

The second version, designated *inversa*, was placed *first* in earlier issues of the present edition, as also in other earlier editions, and the version *here* placed first was itself considered to be the inversion. This is based on a misunderstanding, as can be seen not only from the theme itself in direct motion, but also from the more persuasive fact that it requires inversion [*Versetzung*] for the answer to acquire the form that it has in the following fugue, whereas the previous fugue gives it correctly in direct motion.[13]

Fuga XIII, *a 3 voci* (p. 44)

Example 26

The same as for the previous fugue, except that under inversion [*Versetzung*] voice 1 becomes voice 2, voice 2 becomes voice 3, and voice 3 becomes voice 1. The reduced number of voices might seem to make the counterpoint less difficult to write; but, because of the various positions [*Stellung*] which the voices may now occupy in relation to one another, it now becomes necessary to conform to the rules for double counterpoint at the octave – avoidance of parallel fourths – since this rearrangement produces conflicting intervals.

{11} Fuga XIV, *a 4 voci* (p. 150)

Example 27

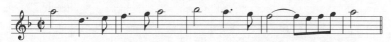

This item is a repetition of Fugue X with the omission of the latter's opening twenty-two bars. To account for this strange state of affairs, we can only assume that Sebastian Bach first noted it down in the form that it is in here, and then later added the opening which appears in No. X. In so doing, he evidently wished

13   This clause gives rise to some confusion, since Hauptmann discusses the three preceding fugues out of order. He seems to be referring to the sequence of pitches in the answer of Fugue XI, which proceeds a'–(e")–d"–c"–(b♭')–a'–g♯'–a'–b♭'–c"–d"–c"–b♭'–a', thus corresponding in tonal terms to the answer of what he considers to be the uninverted form of Fugue XII. The meaning of the previous clause is, on the other hand, less clear.

to do in the present fugue, which inverts at the tenth, what he did with its earlier counterpart, which inverts at the twelfth: namely, to introduce the second subject [*Thema*] on its own before presenting it in conjunction with the principal theme. This is even more necessary since the first encounter of the two [subjects] is less well prepared, and a counter-theme would not be so instantly recognizable at this point. This incomplete 'double' was at any rate not designated by the composer for inclusion within the work – the publication of which did not occur until after Sebastian Bach's death. On the evidence of the numerous small variants between this and Fugue X, the version of the latter clearly represents Bach's later intentions.

Just as the items so far cited furnish in themselves as rich a set of specimens and as valuable a body of instruction in three- and four-part counterpoint as one could find outside the realm of fugal theory, such as only Sebastian Bach himself could provide, so the following four canons offer a set of models every bit as perfect for the ingenious treatment of two-part counterpoint.

I. (II.) Canone all' Ottava (p. 58)

Example 28

To start with one of the simpler ones, let us take first the canon designated no. II. It is at the octave, in direct motion, and in original note values. This type of two-part contrapuntal writing stands in contrast to the fugal studies that precede it. Seen purely and simply as a constant flow of musical ideas it is not among the more taxing, though it is never easy to produce something musically really satisfying with only two voices. Serious difficulties do not arise until the initiating voice is obliged to take up the theme anew (which in this canon occurs at bb. 25, 41 and 77). At these points, the initiating voice must supply a countersubject invertible at the octave which will also work against what follows:

Example 29

Here, for example, in bb. 73–80, voice a in the first four bars is set against the predetermined material of voice b, yet must in the next four bars, at d, also do service as the lower voice to c. It is not a case of a different countersubject to the same cantus firmus, but rather of the same countersubject to a different cantus firmus.

II. (I.) Canon per augmentationem in motu contrario (p. 54)

Example 30

The working out of this canon, which must answer itself in augmentation and contrary motion, may appear to involve conditions more stringent than those of the previous canon. In practice, however, it poses fewer problems, since the initiating voice has no predetermined entries to take account of, and can instead evolve freely over the augmented and inverted ensuing voice until the latter in b. 52 has reached the point corresponding to b. 24 in the upper part. At this moment, the lower part takes up the opening, and the upper part its canonic imitation; hence what has been the countersubject thus far is now {12} transposed to the octave. It continues until four bars from the end, when the bass introduces a cadential passage, where at the opening and midpoint of the canon the ensuing voice had had rests.

It will be apparent that a canon of this type cannot continue indefinitely in strict imitation, because the ensuing voice with its doubled note values can only, no matter how long it persists, cover half the ground of the initiating voice. For this reason, the process of imitation must be halted at the midpoint of the canon and the rate of motion reversed, and what was the initiating voice must now become the ensuing one. The second half of the first section – that which was not imitated in longer note values – still now fails to appear in augmentation: it is impossible for it to do so. Nevertheless, the canon is so constructed that the content of the two parts as a whole is the same: for voice 2 from the midpoint on inherits what voice 1 has been presenting since the outset, and voice 1 from then on correspondingly inherits the augmented half [of voice 2].

Canone III, alla Decima (p. 62)

Example 31

By the superscription *alla Decima* should be understood not so much that the second voice in this canon follows the first voice a tenth higher – although this is in fact so from the beginning as far as b. 39. It signifies rather that the canon is set in double counterpoint at the tenth. Bb. 9–12, which are the inversion at the tenth

[*Decimen-Umkehrung*] of bb. 5–8, are only a spontaneous use of this opening. The actual full-scale inversion of the contrapuntal materials that appear between bb. 5 and 39 begins in earnest at b. 44 and continues to the end with the exception of the last four bars, which supply a cadence in free style. This is at the same time an example of the other type of inversion, the opposite of that used in Fugue X. There, the lower voice was inverted at the tenth above, here it is the upper voice which is inverted at the tenth below. Nor is this randomly done, for it is the initiating voice in this case that adopts the role of cantus firmus and therefore must maintain its pitch. Even though the ensuing voice begins with the theme, its role is that of countersubject and it is therefore liable to transposition.

Example 32

Canonic treatment ceases to be possible at bb. 36–43 of the lower voice because the upper voice at this point [bb. 40–47] is obliged to introduce the theme in readiness for its inversion [at b. 44]. The first four of these non-canonic bars do eventually undergo inversion, near the end, at bb. 75–8.

Canone IV, alla Duodecima (p. 66)

Example 33

In its form, and in the succession of its entries, the canon is similar to the previous one, save for the fact that it incorporates a repeat, and that it inverts at the twelfth. Inversion begins at b. 42. However, as the theme was obliged to enter eight bars earlier [b. 33] in the upper voice, [canonic] imitation came to an end at this point. The passage concerned [bb. 25–33] appears under inversion as bb. 58–66. Bar 67 sees a change which is worth noting: it is not part of the canon, and brings about an exchange of inversion. Bar 66, which corresponds to b. 33, is a transposition of the upper voice to the twelfth below; b. 68, parallel to b. 34, is a transposition of the lower voice to the twelfth above. This exchange became necessary if the canon was to repeat. If the disposition of registers had simply continued, the lower voice would have arrived at the repetition on the fifth below instead of the tonic. The coda derives from bb. 40–41, which are appended [after b. 75].

Fuga I, per due Pianoforti (p. 68)

Example 34

{13} Fuga II, per due Pianoforti (p. 71)

Example 35

Exemplifying a freer style of melodic-harmonic inversion, there follow now two four-part fugues for two keyboards, the second fugue presenting one or more parts of the first throughout in contrary motion. Bar for bar, then, in its essentials the one is a mirror image of the other, and each achieves its individuality through its free-composed parts. The fugues are for four voices, but are so devised that each instrument is apportioned a virtually self-sufficient keyboard part.

Fuga XV, a tre soggetti (p. 74)

Example 36

The work closes with a four-part fugue on three subjects [*Themen*], which alas remained unfinished. Of the three subjects, only the first two appear in conjunction with one another, the third being developed entirely on its own, after which the fugue breaks off without a final cadence.[14] (The most satisfactory solution is to

14   The Peters edition ends at the second beat of b. 233, with the words 'See Preface'. The Preface states:

the final fugue (p. 74), which involves three subjects of which the third states the letters of his name, B–A–C–H, survives incomplete. Moreover, Bach, from all accounts, had the extraordinary idea, alas never realized, of ending his mighty work with a fugue involving four subjects, subsequently inverted in all four voices, supplying the crowning masterpiece and forming the keystone of the *Art of Fugue*.

This Preface, unsigned, leans heavily on Forkel's commentary (pp. 52–4). In fact, although the first edition (1751?) breaks off at the first beat of b. 233, the autograph manuscript continues for a further six and a half bars, to the end of b. 239, the upper voices finishing before the lower. It is precisely where the edition breaks off that the three subjects are for the first (and only) time

close on the first chord of the last bar, preparing the way with a ritardando in the penultimate bar.) The second subject does not permit inversion at the octave against the first on account of its suspended ninths [e.g. bb. 151, 152, 160, 162]. In compensation, it offers entry points for the first subject at different places, and even a stretto of that subject [bb. 180, 182, 183]. The job of collating these and the other strettos for the first theme and drawing up a schema of them seemed unnecessary in the present context. This fugue, despite its incomplete state, is a priceless bonus, both because it is Bach's last work, and because of its content [*Gehalt*]. Yet it cannot ever be more than a bonus, for the work has already been concluded by the previous item. Every movement up to now has had the set purpose of demonstrating a particular variety of double counterpoint, or a specific aspect of fugal technique, against one theme which remains constant. This final fugue departs from such a plan not only in abandoning the theme but also in not contributing anything essential to the work as a whole. For even the combination of the three subjects, with which the fugue would undoubtedly have ended,[15] would have been in essence only a further example of what had already been realized in Fugues VIII and X.

The above commentary deals for the most part only with disjunct elements from the items that go to make up this work, or touches on the general issues of their purpose or subject-matter [*Inhalt*]. There was little scope for discussing what animates this music, or what epitomizes it. The living work cannot be isolated in abstract moments, it is not to be found in the particular or the general as such, but rather in the conjunction, the coexistence [*Verbindung*], the concurrence, the oneness [*Zugleich- und Einssein*] of these linear elements that are set against one another – and it is this that is, here as elsewhere, so difficult to put into words. Technical problems, and mechanics of solutions – these can be expressed. What it is, on the other hand, that enables a work of art to communicate with us as a living source deep within; or what it is that empowers the often recalcitrant raw materials, under such irksome constraints as these, to take shape in the master's hand as free and profoundly inspired forms, and that reveals its creator to us, the object equally of our admiration and our astonishment; – all of this can be understood and appreciated only through kindred feeling.

That which is the product of such heights of artistic mastery need no longer suffer the accusation of cold technical dexterity, any more than the poet of classical odes, or the Italian or Spaniard with his sestinas, need suffer blame for the self-imposed limitations of form. For within this form these artists range free and untramelled; through these very restrictions they raise its content high above the

---

combined, in the order 2–1–3. Arguments have since been advanced that the three subjects combine satisfactorily with the main theme, that this is the four-subject work that Bach intended, and that the fugue may once have been complete: see C. Wolff, 'The Last Fugue: Unfinished?', *Current Musicology*, 19 (1975), 71–7, and the edition by P. Williams (London: Eulenburg, 1986), pp. vi–xi, xxxvi–xxxvii. For a further discussion, and a reconstruction, of this fugue, see the *Urtext* edition by Davitt Moroney, *Joh. Seb. Bach: Die Kunst der Fuge* (Munich: Henle, [1989]), pp. 120–21, 62–9.

15   See note 14.

realm of congenial feeling. Ultimately, every constraint by whose agency unformed poetic materials are refined for artistic purposes is one that is alien to the direct feeling associated with this content. Quantity and metre in poetry of the classical tongue, rhyme and accent in verse of the modern era, measure in music, regularity of {14} periodic structure, uniformity in the flux of emotional states – these are the self-serving demands of artistic form, made without regard for content in its individuality and variability. Much that obtains in music, not only fugue, canon, double counterpoint and all of these specialist techniques, but much else besides, would be dispensable if direct expression of feeling were the highest, or even the sole function of art. However, nobody in his right mind would want to see created a music devoid of measure, least of all anybody who is musically sane. – Even after the most poignant recitative, we sense we have not entered the realms of true art until we can feel the metrical basis of the aria underway. This is true no matter how close that recitative may have come to it through regular rhythmic and harmonic patterns. Large expanses of recitative quickly become tedious, and they do so the sooner, the more dramatic the subject-matter, because we still lack a vehicle, an independent form, a framework, something that cushions for us the disturbing effect, the raw impact of the emotional state.

After all, emotional involvement at the aesthetic level strives to be free, not oppressed. Whereas on the small scale, form subdues content, overall it is content that determines form. In the case of music, form is conditioned by the collective content of all that is utterable in musical terms in a given age. Hence it is every bit as much determined as it is itself determinant; and only in so far as these two forces subsist side by side can it prove perfectly suited to expression in the poetic and artistic sense. Fugal form, as a mode of expression determined by the nature of content, belongs to an earlier age. With Sebastian Bach, indubitably the greatest and most deeply feeling composer of fugues, the era of fugue seems to have reached its close, or at least to draw towards its end. Soon after him, this genre is invaded by a certain conventional quality, a purely formalistic character, which replaces its earlier driving force, now cleft from the roots that once nourished it. In our more recent times, it remains hard to bring the special qualities of the genre into consonance with the very different *raison d'être* of modern music: for the music of our time is more harmonic; the fugal style – indeed early music as a whole – is more melodic in quality. The polyphony of the latter is essentially a process of combining melodies, whereas that of our own time is essentially the formation of chord successions marked off by lyric caesura.

Thus the modern composer, if he is to think in fugal terms, must disavow something that is inborn and inbred within him – he must proceed from this negative, or else be like a poet writing in a foreign language. If a few of our contemporary composers have succeeded in producing something of real quality in fugal style, then the very paucity of their numbers is evidence in itself that it is not intrinsically an art of our own time but rather the result of immersing oneself in a practice from a bygone age. Thus did *Platen* immerse himself in the verse forms of the classical era and bring them to life in his own language, achieving a richer and more poetic mode of expression than when writing in a less formal style.[16] If only the respected composer *A. A. Klengel*, whom we venture to liken to the poet just cited, would produce the contrapuntal work that was promised so long ago – a work that from its principal content we might entitle *The Art of Canon*, and that far surpasses mere technical accomplishment – and keep us no longer in suspense, then our own age could enjoy its fruits, and he could assure himself of lasting recognition by future generations.[17]

16 August, Graf von Platen(-Hallermünde) (1796–1835), German poet and dramatist who, though initially schooled in Romanticism, strove for classical purity of rhyme and versification, and austerity of style. His poetry rekindled the Persian ghasel, the Renaissance sonnet and the Pindaric ode (*Ghaseln* (1821), *Sonnetten aus Venedig* (1825), etc.), the epic poem (*Die Abbassiden* (1834)) and historical drama (*Die Liga von Cambrai* (1833)). He also directed his sharp wit against the fate-tragedies of Immermann and others in his Aristophanes-style comedies, *Die verhängnisvolle Gabel* (1826) and *Der romantische Ödipus* (1829).

17 August Alexander Klengel (1783–1852), who edited J. S. Bach's *Well-tempered Clavier* and as a pianist performed Bach's fugues as early as 1814. Klengel's principal work was *Canons et fugues dans tous les tons majeurs et mineurs pour le piano . . . en deux parties*, each book containing 24 *Canons et 24 Fugues*. Hauptmann himself, an old friend of Klengel, saw this work through the press posthumously in 1854, stating: 'For years before the composer's death the manuscript lay ready for the engraver. Virtually every musician of any significance in recent decades knew and valued this work, and longed to see it published' (vol. I, p. iv). Its layout on the page and style of heading are modelled on the Peters edition of *Art of Fugue* (though Canon I/1 is set out in full score parallel with keyboard score). In the second edition of the *Erläuterungen* (1861) Hauptmann stated (p. 14): 'Since the appearance of the first edition of these *Elucidations*, the work was published in Leipzig by Breitkopf und Härtel in the year 1854, under the title: *Canons et Fugues dans tous les tons majeurs et mineurs pour le Piano, composés par August Alexandre Klengel*. The author did not live to see this edition: he died in 1852.'

Simon Sechter (1788–1867)
'Zergliederung des Finale aus Mozarts 4ter Sinfonie in C'

F. W. Marpurg: *Abhandlung von der Fuge, nach den Grundsätzen und Beispielen der besten in- und ausländischen Meister entworfen*, ed. S. Sechter (1843)

His analysis of the Finale of Mozart's 'Jupiter' Symphony is the only example of extended analytical treatment ever published by Simon Sechter. That it nowhere reflects the principal tenets of his very celebrated theory – root-progression by third and fifth, interpolated roots, root-substitutes, hybrid chords and so forth – should come as no surprise for two reasons. First, as in the case of the analysis by Hauptmann (Analysis 3 above), it was published a full decade before his principal treatise, *The Fundamentals of Musical Composition* (1853–4), in which those tenets were expounded. It is to the work of Sechter's later adherents that we must look for analyses that implement his theoretical ideas, one particularly powerful example of which is published below: Mayrberger's analysis of the harmonic language of Wagner's *Tristan and Isolde* (Analysis 13). Secondly, and even more to the point, it was designed as an appendix to the third edition of a treatise on counterpoint, canon and fugue written ninety years earlier: Marpurg's *Treatise on Fugue* of 1753–4.

Sechter was the editor of the third edition of Marpurg's *Treatise* (the second, and minimally changed, edition of which had been issued in 1806). Sechter preserved Marpurg's original text and sequence of ideas largely intact. He occasionally glossed an outmoded term, or substituted a more current term for it; he interpolated additional material, meticulously demarcated by smaller type and parentheses, and finally he incorporated the music examples, which had in previous editions been presented collectively, into the main body of the text (a policy which the volume's next editor, Dehn, incidentally, reversed in 1858). However, his main contribution was the 'Appendix' reproduced below (also reversed, i.e. suppressed by Dehn in 1858).

Context conditioned the nature of the analysis. We should not look to it for a free-standing account of sonata form, or for a study of harmonic process. Sechter's Preface (vol. I, p. 3) speaks of his 'analysis of Mozart's *instrumental fugue* from the Symphony in C' (my italics), and from this we might think the movement destined to be viewed through contrapuntal, canonic and fugal spectacles.

Sechter offered his Mozart analysis 'as a model for an instrumental fugue in free style'. Marpurg's definition of a *freye Fuge* (1753, p. 20) is of a fugue in which 'whenever the subject is abandoned, a well-chosen, short episode, having an affinity with the nature of the subject itself, or with that of the [countersubject], homogeneous with it if not always actually derived from it, is developed by means of imitation and transposition', and instances Handel's fugues as examples. The 'Jupiter' finale hardly matches that description, as Sechter must have realized. Nearer to the mark is Marx's definition, given only seven years before Sechter's analysis. Marx defined *freie Fuge* first negatively as fugue not possessing all the accoutrements of *strenge Fuge* (strictly maintained subject and answer, and regular countersubject, developments of these providing material for episodes; at least some stretti; canonic treatment of motifs in episodes), and then positively as a fugue 'whose course is interrupted by unrelated, interjacent sections, the result being an alternation of fugal and non-fugal styles'.[1]

Sechter in fact knew exactly what he was dealing with. Despite his spurious 'orthodox rondo theme' early on (a deliberate red herring?[2]), and his coy reference to Mozart's stopping a rather good canon in mid-flight 'in order that the movement satisfy the requirements of *the other form*' (my italics – does this betray a flash of annoyance: is fugue cast in the role of jealous husband here as canon is found to be flirting with symphony?), it is clear that Sechter not only recognized the presence of sonata form, but also viewed it in binary rather than ternary terms. His pinpointing remark, 'After the repetition of section II is complete . . .', for the onset of the coda at b. 356, following the repeat-sign at the end of the (in modern terms) recapitulation, reveals this. If we marry this to his reference to the close of section I and the opening of section II (b. 158: beginning of the development), and that to the 'return of the main subject' (b. 225: retransition and recapitulation), to bars then being 'destined to follow faithfully the course of section I', and to the return of the second subject, 'which in section I was in G major, and must now appear, obeying the dictates of form, in C major' (b. 272), it is plain that he discerns the gross features of sonata form in this movement, referring to it on two occasions as 'symphonic form'.

Sechter mediates successfully between the two very different formal worlds. He strives in his analysis, one might say, to emulate Mozart's own 'effortless fusion of free composition with strict'. He manipulates two technical vocabulary-sets side by side, treating them as if they were terminological 'screens', the reader being allowed to look through now one, now the other, and occasionally through the two superimposed. In the one he handles such terms as *Sinfonieform*, *Hauptsatz*, *Mittelsatz*, *Nebensache*, *Theil*, *Abtheilung* and *Zurückkehren*, in the other such terms as *Fuge*, *Canon*, *Führer*, *Gefährte*, *Contrathema*, *Contrapunct*, *Hauptstimme*, *Gegenharmonie*, *Verbindung* and *Nachahmung*. His principal difficulties must have lain in that group of terms that forms the intersection of these two sets. Of these, he is careful to reserve *Antwort* for an implied consequent-to-antecedent

---

1   in Gustav Schilling, *Encyclopädie der gesammten musikalischen Wissenschaften, oder Universal-Lexicon der Tonkunst* (Stuttgart: Köhler, 1835–42; reprint edn Hildesheim: Olms, 1974), vol. III (1836), pp. 84–5.

2   Sechter may, however, be using 'rondo' as a generic term or character-substitute for 'finale'. Finales were sometimes referred to as rondos almost as a matter of course. I am grateful to Elaine Sisman for drawing my attention to this usage.

relationship, and *Wiederholung* for phrase-restatement and recapitulation, both in the sonata orbit; whereas he keeps *Durchführung* for contrapuntal development. *Thema* is kept essentially for the five fugue subjects; but since these are identified also with the materials of the sonata form (bringing to mind Marpurg's requirement of affinity, homogeneity, if not derivation for an episode), the term carries a certain *double-entendre*.

Sechter adopted Marpurg's medium of presenting the entire score, marked with letters and other annotations, as the backbone of his music examples. Incorporating examples into the text caused him to split the score into sections (most of these have been omitted from the translation below and replaced by references to bar numbers) and at the same time gave him the opportunity to interpolate additional, explanatory examples. These are of considerable interest (and all have been retained here), some of them representing the contrapuntal processes at work, some demonstrating possibilities that Mozart might have exploited, and one simplifying the part-writing and providing a harmonic reduction (Example 7).

Of considerable interest is Sechter's handling of orchestration. He refers to it constantly, devoting time to problems of instrumental doubling, and pointing out many of the subtleties in Mozart's scoring, such as the reinforcement of the dominant note by horns, trumpets and timpani in bb. 223–4 at the crucial moment in the retransition. It is only a slight exaggeration to say that Sechter treats the orchestra as integral to the formal structure.

Born in Bohemia, Simon Sechter went to Vienna for further musical study. He schooled himself in the writings of Marpurg, Kirnberger and Albrechtsberger. Between 1810 and 1825 he taught music at the Blind Institute there, after which he was appointed principal court organist. He became professor of thoroughbass and counterpoint at the Vienna Conservatory in 1851 and served in that capacity until his retirement. Long before that, he had adopted the mantle of Albrechtsberger and established himself as Austria's principal music theorist. Schubert sought instruction from him, and took one lesson in 1828 just before his death. He was a major influence on Bruckner, who studied with him between 1857 and 1861, and indeed influenced directly or indirectly the course of Viennese music in the late nineteenth and early twentieth centuries. A prolific composer, it is said that he never let a day go by without writing a fugue.

'Analysis of the Finale of Mozart's Symphony No.[41] in C [K551 ("Jupiter")]'[3]

S.Sechter, ed.: F.W.Marpurg: *Treatise on Fugue*

Source:
'Zergliederung des Finale aus Mozarts 4ter Sinfonie in C', *Abhandlung von der Fuge, nach den Grundsätzen und Beispielen der besten in- und ausländischen Meister entworfen, von Friedrich Wilhelm Marpurg, neu bearbeitet, mit erläuternden Anmerkungen und Beispielen vermehrt von S. Sechter . . .* (Vienna: Anton Diabelli, [1843]), vol. II, pp. 161–93 'Anhang von S. Sechter'.

Although the original author [Marpurg, in 1753–4] was able to instance exemplary models in his own day, we are in a position now to cite, from among the many outstanding works of more recent times, the Finale[4] from Mozart's Fourth Symphony in C [= No. 41, K551 ('Jupiter')], as a model for an instrumental fugue in free style. This is a work which in terms of skill and taste can enter the lists alongside any composition in the world. Its greatest perfection is its effortless fusion of free composition with strict, this being an art of which Mozart had full command. It therefore behoves every music lover to become acquainted with the way in which Mozart's thought processes [*Ideengang*] evolved. Without doubt, his first conception [*Idee*] was to fashion an artistic product the elaborateness of whose deployment should not be foreseeable at its outset. The five themes that combine contrapuntally in the final section must unquestionably have been worked together in counterpoint right from the start. Only after that did he begin to develop each theme in its own right, unfolding the various delightful features of each one individually, as we shall see when we come to look at each more closely.

His first theme (a favourite theme of his) is as follows:

Example 1

[bb.1–4]

He wished, however, to introduce it first in the guise of an orthodox rondo theme, and tacked four freely-composed bars on to it. The violins, violas[, cellos] and basses begin as can be seen in [bb. 1–8].[5]

The master's hand is clearly detectable even in these four appended bars, however, for the [cellos and] basses, together with the violas that reinforce them, promptly imitate the last two bars of the theme (i.e. bb. 3–4) in bb. 5–6. After this

3   Title in the table of contents to vol. II reads *Anhang von S. Sechter. Zergliederung des Finale aus Mozarts 4ter Sinfonie.*
4   '. . . *folgendes Finale* . . .': the presentation of the entire movement in score during Sechter's analysis has been suppressed in this translation, hence also 'following' at this point.
5   Bb. 1–8 quoted at this point in full score.

imperfect cadence [*Halbcadenz*], the natural expectation is of a restatement of the theme followed by a perfect cadence [*ganze Cadenz*]; and this is just what occurs, although it is accompanied by full orchestra, and given different harmonic treatment, already involving notes tied over the barline.[6] I[7] must point out that, contrary to Marpurg's rule,[8] Mozart makes great use of the doubling of voices in octaves, a practice that is no more incorrect than to play the organ using sixteen-, eight-, four- and two-foot registers simultaneously. Thus in the first four bars of the passage that follows [bb. 9–12], the violas, timpani, trumpets and horns reinforce the [cellos and] basses in octaves, as do the bassoons and flute the oboes, and the second violins the firsts. So that no more need be said on this hereafter, let me also remind the reader that because the double bass sounds an octave lower than it would if played on the keyboard, it should not surprise us if the bassoon when playing inner parts appears to go below the basses, an impression which will be corrected the moment the latter are thought of, as is proper, an octave lower.[9] The fact that the style of composition [*Satz*] in the Finale as a whole is freer and more daring than in earlier times needs no further justification of any sort; after all, [the music of] Bach abounds in bold turns of phrase, as my readers will already have had occasion to notice. Now, to resume our account.[10]

{162} The violins take up the first theme in octaves [in b. 9], and the [cellos and] basses, doubled by violas, take up the four semiquavers from b. 6 of the previous unit [*Abtheilung*] and reiterate them at different pitch levels against the first theme. The timpani, trumpets and horns simply sound the main notes [*Grundtöne*] [of the basses' line].[11] Against these, the flute, oboes and bassoons provide a

---

6   *mit einer andern Harmonie, die schon Bindungen enthält.* The use of *Bindungen* for 'notes tied over the barline' carries clear overtones of the fifth species of strict counterpoint. Tellingly, this same passage (bb. 9–12: flute, oboes, bassoons) is referred to in the next paragraph in quite different terms, from the point of view of phrase structure, as *einen syncopirten Satz*, and its extended form in bb. 233–42 differently yet again as *Rückungen* (lit., 'displacements'?) and *rückende Figur*.

7   The sentence begins 'Before I reproduce more from Mozart's orchestral score . . .'.

8   In chap. 7 of vol. II (1754), 'Vocal Fugue and Canon', Marpurg subdivides vocal fugue into that with, and that without obbligato instrumental parts. For the latter, he offers a scheme for doubling the four vocal lines at the unison with strings and, optionally, oboes. (Sechter, in 1843, amplifies this scheme by inclusion of clarinets, bassoons and trombones.) Marpurg then proceeds:

> The appetite for change exhibited by the younger generation does not allow it to leave well alone where this scheme is concerned. A different disposition of parts has been introduced whereby the first violins double the altos at the octave above, the seconds the sopranos in unison, and the violas the tenors, sometimes in unison, sometimes at the octave above. The oboes play in unison with the violins all the time. In practice, however, this disposition can give rise to irregular progressions, since it cannot ensure that two voices will proceed always in consistent registers against each other. For example, when two fourths occur in succession between the inner voices, and in the instrumental doublings these fourths become two fifths, [it is hard] not to hear the doubling of the dissonances, etc. Hence such a scheme will not satisfy thoroughly all good composers, if the intention of adopting it is greatly to heighten the impression which the harmony makes.

> To which Sechter adds 'In no case in which parallel fifths arise from such doubling can they be tolerated.' (1754: vol. II, p. 128; [1843]: vol. II, pp. 141–2).

9   Sechter presumably refers to the semiquavers D–C in the cellos and basses in b. 11. Sechter returns to this topic in relation to bb. 256 and 258, where the offset is momentarily greater than a written octave.

10   Bb. 9–19[2] quoted at this point in full score.

11   *Grundtöne*: it is unclear whether Sechter is speaking in reductionist terms, referring to the essential note of each five-note group, or in functional terms, referring to tonic and dominant as the primary pitches of the diatonic.

syncopated counterpoint that is to figure frequently in what follows. It is in the last seven bars of this unit [bb. 13–19 of bb. 9–19] that the perfect cadence, itself repeated, occurs in answer to the preceding imperfect cadence. Now follows the second theme, in unison between violins, oboes and violas, and reinforced at the lower octave by [cellos,] basses and bassoons, as follows:

Example 2

[bb.19–22]

That this is capable of working in counterpoint against the first theme, albeit the contrapuntal combination is not put to use until much later, is shown by the following juxtaposition of the two:

Example 3

Now follows the first development [*Durchführung*] of this same theme, with its accompanying instruments [bb. 19–28], and a coda appended to it in free style [bb. 28–35] that once again ends with an imperfect cadence.[12]

{164} As is easily discerned, this development contains at its outset the following three-part canon:[13]

Example 4

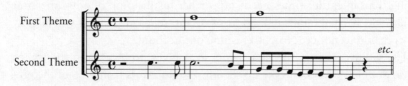

[bb.19–28]

This is accompanied by the following ostinato [*Grundgesang*], the second statement of which is treated with figuration by [cellos,] basses and violas.

Example 5

[bb.19–22]

12   Bb. 193–354 quoted at this point in full score as Ex. *a* = {163}.
13   This sentence begins with a lower-case letter, as if running on from the previous sentence by way of the music example.

The coda following this canon leads, as in the style of a festive symphony,[14] to an imperfect cadence. This introduces the development of the first theme, which then proceeds in the style of an orthodox fugue. Mozart continues [as can be seen in bb. 36–56].[15]

{165} The modification that the last bar of the theme has undergone [b. 39] gives rise to a pleasing effect, because the figure that replaces the last note of the theme is imitated among the various voices, in the supporting harmonies [*Gegenharmonie*].[16] The double basses, as the fifth voice to enter, have just reached the last note of the theme when the first violins introduce the theme again [b. 53], in unison with the oboes, doubled by second violins at the octave below and by flute at the octave above. The [cellos and] basses give out the counter-theme [*Contrathema*], which is accompanied, mostly in thirds, by the bassoons and violas. At the same moment, the trumpets and horns [*Waldhörner*] enter with a figure derived from the opening notes of the second theme. At the end [b. 56²],[17] the violins embark on the third theme, straight away canonically imitated in the next bar by the [cellos and] basses at the seventh below, as follows:

Example 6

[bb.56–62]

If some of my readers find the harmony between these two voices not pure enough for their liking, they may care to think of this canonic imitation in the following way:

Example 7

or:

14 *nach Art einer feierlichen Sinfonie*: Sechter may have had in mind a specific genre, or perhaps just the typical tonic–dominant alternation at bb. 28–30, 32–5, scored with trumpets and timpani.
15 Bb. 36–56 quoted at this point in full score as Ex. *b*.
16 *Gegenharmonie*: Marpurg, 1753–4: 'that material which is set against the fugue subject in the remaining voices' (vol. I, p. 18). Marpurg devotes the whole of vol. I, chap. 5 (pp. 147–50) to *Gegenharmonie*, making the distinction as to its operation in vocal and instrumental fugues as against keyboard fugues.
17 'marked *NB*'.

The following example shows how this third theme relates to the two preceding ones:

Example 8

or:

To see how Mozart envisaged the harmony as a whole in this passage, my readers should consult bb. 57–64^2 in the full score.[18]

{166} The figure in the first violins [b. 62^2][19] is worth noting because it will occur later in free inversion [*Gegenbewegung*]. Next comes a second canon: canon at the octave, on the second theme, on conflicting halves of the bar[20] (if the *Allabreve* unit is equated with the bar) in close imitation, thus:

Example 9

[bb.64–7]

18   This sentence reads in the original: 'So that my readers may see how Mozart envisaged the harmony as a whole in this passage, I shall lay out all the voices, picking up where we previously left off:' followed by bb. 57–64^2 quoted in full score as Ex. *c*.

19   'marked *NB*'.

20   *im widrigen Takttheile*: Marpurg, 1753–4: '. . . when the first voice begins on a weak part or unit of the bar [*Takttheile oder Gliede*], and the other answers on a strong part or unit of the bar, then this is known as "imitation on conflicting or mixed halves of the bar", *imitatio per arsin & thesin* or *in contrario tempore*' (vol. I, p. 6). Marpurg defines 'fugue on mixed halves of the bar [*im vermischten Takttheile*]' as the fourth class of fugue (vol. I, p. 22), and devotes a paragraph to the class (p. 25), in which he states that it belongs 'to the art of canonic writing'. Of Allabreve, Marpurg states: 'In rapid 4/4–beat or Allabreve time, the strong beat [*gute Takttheil*] falls on the first half of the bar, i.e. the first minim, and consequently on the downbeat or *Thesin*; the weak beat [*schlimme Takttheil*] on the second half of the bar, is the second minim, consequently on the upbeat or *Arsin*' (vol. I, p. 9). In this context, *Takttheil* relates directly to the medieval concept of *tactus*, with which the first element of the German term is cognate. See also Analysis 10 below, §466^{2}4.

The violins and flute take the lead [*Führer*], and the violas, [cellos,] basses, bassoons and oboes give the answer [*Gefährte*].[21] The horns pick up the initial three notes of the same theme, giving rise at least to the impression that the canon is to be three-part, although strictly speaking it is never in more than two parts. The free extension of the last portion of the theme [bb. 70–73] serves as a preparation for what is to come.[22]

What follows now [bb. 74–7] is the fourth theme, which Mozart introduces *piano* as the second subject [*Mittelsatz*]. Hot on its heels comes the fifth theme [oboes, bb. 76–7], which has already been heard in free inversion [b. 62].[23] Immediately after that follows the third theme in thirds [bassoon, bb. 77–8], the voice accompanying at the third [first bassoon] at the same time forming an extension of the fifth theme. Scarcely has the third theme begun when the second theme enters again. However, everything fits together so effortlessly that the listener is aware merely of an intermingling of these themes rather than a contrapuntal combination as such. Here they are:

{167}

Example 10

The following example [Example 11] shows how the fourth and fifth themes combine with the first, second and third.

But even though he had this combination ready-made in his mind, Mozart chooses not to reveal it for some time, introducing instead an apparently simple and unpretentious-looking accompaniment designed [bb. 74–86^1] so that the themes may first be grasped individually, while at the same time casting light on the structure [*Bau*] of the piece as a whole.[24]

21 Marpurg, 1753–4:

The *Führer*, otherwise known as *Hauptsatz*, *Vorsatz*, *Thema* (Gr. *Phonagogus*; Lat: *dux*, *thema*, *subiectum*; Ital: *guida*; Fr: *sujet*): the name for the phrase [*Satz*] which forms the basis of and begins the fugue. [. . .] The *Gefährte*, otherwise know as *Nachsatz* (Lat: *comes*, *vox consequens*; Ital: *risposta* or *conseguenza*; Fr: *réponse*): the name for the near-repetition of the *Führer* in another voice and transposed to higher or lower pitches. (vol. I, pp. 17–18)

22 The original has 'This is how it looks in the orchestral score:' followed by bb. 64–73 quoted in full score as Ex. *d*.
23 'at the last *NB*'.
24 The original has 'Here is what it looks like in the orchestral score:' followed by bb. 74–86^1 quoted in full score as Ex. *e*.

Example 11

{168} Notice that the accompaniment [in bb. 74–80¹], although remaining simple throughout, is radically altered during the repetition [bb. 80²–86¹], so that the listener may for ever be hearing something new in it.

Now, over a sustained bass note on the dominant of the scale of G [bb. 86–93], the third theme is developed in canonic imitation between flute and first bassoon at the seventh below. Against this, the violins weave a flowing quaver figure that is new and yet conforms well with the character of the movement [Stück] as a whole, the seconds doubling the firsts at the octave below, while the violas sustain the dominant note along with the [cellos and] basses.[25]

Mozart now develops the first three notes of the fourth theme canonically between first violins and [cellos and] basses, doing so at the fifth below [bb. 94³–99²]. The first oboe plays in parallel sixths below the first violins, which are supported in unison by the flute, and the second oboe plays along with the first bassoon in parallel thirds above the [cellos and] basses, who are reinforced at the unison by the second bassoon. Against this, the second violins and violas develop the running figure of this fourth theme in free fashion, imitating each other in alternation at different pitch levels. The horns, trumpets and timpani join in only intermittently, sounding harmony notes.[26]

{169} At [b. 98³],[27] the first violins now take up the fourth theme in earnest and begin to explore its possibilities thoroughly. Half a bar later, the seconds enter with the same theme at the octave below; a further half [bar] later the [cellos and] basses enter likewise at the twelfth below, though actually shifted to an octave below that; and finally yet another half bar later the violas take up the same theme an octave above the [cellos and] basses. Not only do all voices carry this through, but when the first violins start the whole process all over again a third lower [b. 102³], they all follow suit in the same canonic scheme. Only after the third recurrence [b. 106³] does Mozart call a halt to it, although it would have been

25   The original has 'as can be seen here:' followed by bb. 86–94² quoted in full score as Ex. *f*.
26   The original has 'as can be seen here:' followed by bb. 94³–99² quoted in full score as Ex. *g*.
27   'the *NB*'.

possible to continue the canon through all the keys [*Canon durch die Töne*], in order that the movement satisfy the requirements of the other form.

Here is the canon, shown through its principal voice:

Example 12

§8.   §9.   §12.

He now takes up the running figure from this theme [b. 110] and deploys it in free imitation between the [cellos and] basses, reinforced by violas and bassoons, and the first violins, reinforced by the seconds and by the flute, until the harmony is steered [*sich hinlenkt*] towards the tonic chord of G major [bb. 112–15]. Here too, as is generally the case, the horns, trumpets and timpani merely fill out the texture.[28]

{171} At this point, Mozart once again takes up a figure that made an appearance right at the beginning of the movement as a subsidiary idea in bb. 5–6 and bb. 13–14, and now develops it through transposition leading to a cadence in G [bb. 115–23]. This figure, originally presented in the first violins, is now seized by the [cellos,] basses and bassoons, reinforced by violas at the octave above, in a drive towards a cadence in G via several modulatory shifts [*Mudulationen [sic]*: bb. 115–135²].[29]

{172} At this point, [cellos,] basses and violas enter with the second theme, stating it three times in succession, each time a third higher than the last [bb. 135³–144²]. On each occasion, the violins enter with the beginning of the theme in the next bar one step higher, and then extend it in a free form that nevertheless has a strong affinity to the theme itself. Half a bar before the violins' entry each time, the oboes and flute give out the first three notes of the theme, after which, like the bassoons, they provide a free counterpoint [*Contrapunct*] to the other lines. Soon after this comes a rousing cadence [bb. 144³–151²], then finally, over a pedal-point on the tonic of G major, this same second theme makes a further appearance [bb. 151³–157²], initially on first oboe then on first bassoon, accompanied sparingly and simply by strings. With this, section I comes to a close.[30]

{174} Section II opens with the first theme again in sixths in the two violins, thus:

Example 13

28   The original has 'This is what the orchestral score looks like at this point:' followed by bb. 98²–114 quoted in full score as Ex. *h* = {170}.
29   The original has 'as can be seen here:' followed by bb. 115–135² quoted in full score as Ex. *i*. *Modulation* in Marpurg (1753–4) refers to the pendulum-like alternation between tonic and dominant of subject and answer in a fugue (e.g. vol. II, p. 38).
30   The original has 'as can be seen here:' followed by bb. 135³–157 quoted in full score as Ex. *k* = {173}.

Meanwhile, [cellos,] basses and horns prolong the dominant note of C minor [bb. 158–61], at the end of which the first oboe and first bassoon promptly seize upon the second theme. By means of a linking bar [*Zwischentakt*: b. 165] in unison, the modulatory shift [*Modulation*] is effected from the dominant note of the scale of C minor to that of A minor. Immediately, the first theme enters once again, while the horns[, cellos] and basses prolong the dominant note of A minor, at the end of which the flute and first bassoon seize upon the second theme in inversion.[31]

Now the second theme adapts itself, by a slight modification towards its end, to form a modulating canon [*Canon durch die Töne*] between the [cellos and] basses and the first violins, as can be seen here from the principal voice:

Example 14

The first violins enter, as marked, at the fifteenth (*Decima Quinta*) above [i.e. b. 173^1], and respond to each transposition of the canon with this same interval [bb. 176^3, 180^1, 183^3]. The violas, which enter half a bar later, present the theme each time in a curtailed form and then continue with a free extension [*Zusatz*]. The second violins, which enter a further half bar later, present it in even more curtailed form. The flute, bassoons and oboes reinforce the entry of the violas and then continue with a free extension. The horns, trumpets and timpani simply reinforce each entry of the [cellos and] basses and then have rests.[32]

{176} At [b. 186^3],[33] the [cellos and] basses first, immediately followed by the first violins, take up the second theme in inversion with canonic imitation at the twelfth above. The violas reinforce the entry of the first violins [at the tenth below], and then fall into unisons with the [cellos and] basses. The second violins, entering a further half bar later, soon resort to free imitation. The first oboe at [b. 189^3][34] enters with the first theme, though the opening is compressed and the end speeded up, accompanied boldly by the second oboe and first bassoon *piano*. The first violins at [b. 191^3][35] enter again *forte* with the second theme in contrary motion, [cellos and] basses imitating this canonically half a bar later at the fifth below, this time however in direct motion [bb. 191^3–194].

31   The original has 'Up to this point, the orchestral score is as follows:' followed by bb. 158–172^2 quoted in full score as Ex. *l*.
32   The original has 'as can be seen in the orchestral score as follows:' followed by bb. 172^3–191 quoted in full score as Ex. *m* = {175}.
33   'the *NB*'. There is an *NB* also in the first violins at b. 187^1.
34   'the *'. An * also appears in the bassoon part at b. 190^3 in Ex. *m*.
35   'the **'.

Example 15

[bb.191–4]

As the last bass note sounds, the first theme enters once again, as previously but a fifth higher and consequently on flute accompanied by the two oboes, in similar fashion to the last time. With the final note of this [b. 196³] the [cellos and] basses enter once again *forte* with the second theme in inversion, immediately followed by the first violins, also in inversion. These two voices, and the two free inner parts also, proceed as at [bb. 186³–187¹],[36] now in G minor instead of F major. Flute and oboes now present the first theme in D minor [bb. 199³–201], corresponding to the previous G minor. With the final note of this [b. 201³], the first violins enter again with the second theme in contrary motion, the [cellos and] basses once again imitating it canonically half a bar later at the fifth below but in direct motion. These two voices, and the two freer inner parts also, proceed as on the previous occasion [bb. 191–4], now in D minor instead of C minor.[37]

{177} At [b. 204³],[38] the flute takes up the first theme for the third time, now in A minor, accompanied by the two oboes and the first bassoon. While a modulatory shift is being effected towards E minor, more precisely towards an imperfect cadence [bb. 209–10], the two violins embark on the second theme in inversion. Immediately after that, it appears again, over a prolonged dominant in the [cellos and] basses, this time in the first violins and in direct motion, accompanied by a harmonic progression which brings back the imperfect cadence in E minor for a second time [bb. 212–13]. It appears for a third time [bb. 215–16] after the [cellos,] basses, bassoons and violas have stated the second theme, and for a fourth time [bb. 218–19] as the theme is taken up by all the strings in contrary motion.[39]

{178} At [b. 219³],[40] there begins a chromatic enharmonic passage, and this, contrary[41] to all expectations, leads back into the scale of the home key, C major. The first three notes of the second theme are initially introduced by the first bassoon, then by the second, then by the horns, and finally by the first violins, with the last of these playing it right through to the end, which in turn marks the arrival of the return [*Wiederholung*] of the main subject [*Hauptsatz*: b. 225]. It should not pass unremarked that the dominant note of the home key is reinforced by horns, trumpets and timpani so as to draw attention to the return [*Zurückkehren*].

36 'the previous *NB*'.
37 The original has 'This is what it looks like in the orchestral score:' followed by bb. 192–204 quoted in full score as Ex. *n*.
38 'the *NB*'. The *NB* appears in the flute, oboe and cello/bass parts simultaneously.
39 The original has 'as can be seen here:' followed by bb. 205–19 quoted in full score as Ex. *o*.
40 'the *NB*'.
41 *wieder*: recte *wider*.

Whether Mozart failed to spot the consecutive fifths at [b. 222–3],[42] or introduced them deliberately, I cannot say; but I would point out that they could easily have been avoided if only a 6/4–chord on the dominant had been introduced instead of a 7/5/4–chord.[43]

It is easy to detect that, starting at [b. 225 in the first violins],[44] the first eight bars of the movement are restated, and that this is the point at which the first theme makes its entrance. On the other hand, it may not be quite so obvious at first sight that at [b. 227 in the cellos and basses][45] the four notes of the first theme are canonically imitated not in approximate form but actually in retrograde. If the four notes:

Example 16

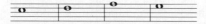

are read backwards in the bass clef, then the result is precisely what appears at [b. 227].[46] Moreover, by sounding this in parallel thirds above, the first bassoon answers the semitones and whole tones of the first violins in exact retrograde. The octave doubling surely needs no justification.

Just as the bars to come seem destined to follow faithfully the course of section I, the supporting harmonies to the first theme, and the theme itself, are developed in a rich manner by means of {179} transposition [bb. 233–52]. The first violins state the first theme three times, each repetition lying a whole tone higher. On the first two occasions the second violins double them at the octave below; on the third occasion, however, they break off and imitate the theme canonically at the fifth below; whereupon the first violins abandon their upward transpositions and state the theme twice more, each time a whole tone lower, each time imitated by the second violins. The flute, oboes and bassoons develop their syncopations [*Rückungen*] throughout [bb. 233–42, cf. bb. 9–12], and the [cellos,] basses and violas develop the figure from the corresponding point in section I. At first they play this figure together; later, [in b. 243,] the [cellos and] basses turn just to playing the last two notes of the first theme several times over, each time in thirds below [the first and second violins alternately], while the violas interpolate their earlier figure from time to time. The syncopated figure [*rückende Figur*] of the woodwind instruments just mentioned changes at this point: instead of falling, it now rises chromatically. The horns, trumpets and timpani merely fill out the texture.[47]

{180} At this point [b. 253] the third theme returns in the [cellos and] basses, with the first violins in canon against it at the sixth above. A word is necessary here about the fact that the second bassoon, as an inner part merely filling out the

42   'the *NB* in the following example [=Ex. *p*]', the *NB* being placed beneath the bassoon. The fifths referred to occur between second bassoon and cellos/basses.
43   The original has 'This is how it appears in the orchestral score:' followed by bb. 220–32 quoted in full score as Ex. *p*.
44   'the *'.
45   'the **'.
46   'the **'.
47   The original has 'as will be seen from the orchestral score below:' followed by bb. 233–52 quoted in full score as Ex. *q*.

texture, several times goes too low in relation to the bass line, even when the latter is thought of as sounding an octave lower. Added to this is the fact that it (the second bassoon) not only proceeds in consecutive compound octaves with the flute – if that were not startling enough – but also interacts with the horns and trumpets to produce an effect even uglier than that of straightforward consecutive octaves, namely [bb. 253–60]:

Example 17

[bb.253–60]

This lapse on the composer's part should however not be taken as encouragement to commit errors.

This piece of counterpoint [*Satz*], together with the next two bars, which form an imperfect cadence, should be viewed in the orchestral score [bb. 253–62].[48] {181} The way the horns, trumpets and timpani in the first and last two bars of this passage recall the second theme should not go unremarked.

The second theme now reasserts itself forcefully [bb. 262³–265³] as a canon at the octave below between first violins and [cellos and] basses, the former doubled at the lower octave by the seconds and the upper octave by the flute, while the

---

48 The original has 'Here is what this piece of counterpoint, together with the next two bars, which form an imperfect cadence, looks like in the orchestral score:' followed by bb. 253–262² quoted in full score as Ex. *r*.

[cellos and] basses are reinforced [in unison] by the bassoons, at the upper octave by the violas, and at the double octave above by the oboes. Because the horns and trumpets enter half a bar later with the first three notes of the same theme, followed by the identical three notes on timpani a moment later, the effect is almost that of a four-part canon, albeit not running its full course. This canon is repeated once [bb. 265^3–268^3], this being made possible only by the fact that it has the properties of a circular canon. After this, a brief coda [*Anhang*] is introduced [bb. 268^2–271], based on a figure from the last portion of the canon, leading to a rest in all parts [*Abschnitt*].[49] This heralds the return of the second subject, which in section I was in G major and must now appear, obeying the dictates of form, in C major.[50]

{182} As symphonic form [*die Form der Sinfonie*] demands, the second subject, which in section I was in the key of the dominant, now makes its appearance in the tonic key. My readers may care now to compare the following passages: bb. 272–284^1 with that of bb. 74–86^1, bb. 284–292^2 with bb. 86–94^2, bb. 292^3–296^2 with bb. 94^3–98^2, bb. 296^3–312 with bb. 98^3–114, bb. 313–334^2 with bb. 115–135^2 and bb. 334^3–356^2 with bb. 135^3–157^2.[51] On grounds of orchestration alone, the small-scale modifications that are revealed by so doing will be of interest to my readers. The passages comprising bb. 272–356,[52] in the course of which no new material of significance is introduced, all now follow in unbroken succession.[53]

{188} After the repetition of section II is complete [b. 356], the first violins and [cellos and] basses reintroduce the second theme simultaneously, the latter in direct motion and the former in inversion, though with a small modification after the first three notes, thus [bb. 356–9]:

Example 18

[bb. 356–9]

Second violins and violas reinforce this entry freely in parallel motion. Horns, trumpets and timpani also enter at this point, and then reiterate the first three notes of the theme. Because the flute, oboes and bassoons sound the opening of the theme half a bar later [than the initial entry], this gives the illusion of three thematic entries in quick succession.[54]

49 *Abschnitt*: contemporary use of this term conveys not only a phrase unit but also a rest punctuating such a unit. Koch (1802), e.g. defines it thus: 'With this term are often designated the points of rest [*Ruhepunkte*] that demarcate a melody, when the extent of its sections [*Theile*] is left unspecified. The specific extent of melodic sections and units [*Glieder*] are designated by the terms *Periode*, *Absatz* and *Einschnitt* (q.v.).'

50 The original has 'This passage appears as follows in the orchestral score:' followed by bb. 263^3–271 quoted in full score as Ex. *s*.

51 'that of *t* with that of *e*, *u* with *f*, *v* with *g*, *w* with *h*, *x* with *i*, and *z* with *k*'.

52 '*t* to *z*'.

53 At this point bb. 272–356^2 (2nd-time bar) are quoted in full score on pp. 183–7, the letters *t*, *u*, *v*, *w*, *x* and *z* marking off the sections corresponding to earlier full-score examples.

54 The original has 'This is how it looks in the orchestral score:' followed by bb. 356^3 (2nd-time bar)–359 quoted in full score as Ex. *aa*.

Following this, the two violins introduce the first theme (*piano*) in free inversion in thirds, and promptly restate it one step lower [bb. 360–67]. Violas and cellos together imitate it in thirds, the flute reinforcing the violas at the octave above.[55]

{189} Now the first violins take up this same theme at [b. 368][56] in direct motion, whereas the first oboe and first bassoon take up the syncopated counterpoint which first appeared right at the very beginning, this time slightly extended. The second violins, violas, [cellos and] basses merely fill out the texture at this point.[57] Scarcely have the first violins completed this statement of the first theme when the violas at [b. 371][58] seize powerfully upon the fourth theme. With the cellos, bassoons and horns promptly launching into the first theme in energetic fashion, the onset of the fugue proper is signalled at this point. At [b. 375][59] the second violins take up the fourth theme, followed by the violas, oboes and flute with the first theme and simultaneously the cellos with the third theme. At [b. 379][60] the first violins take up the fourth theme, followed by second violins, oboes and flute with the first theme and simultaneously the violas with the third theme, whereupon the cellos embark on the fifth theme, which is extended by shadowing the [viola's] third theme in thirds above. At [b. 383][61] the double basses take up the fourth theme, followed by first violins, oboes and flute with the first theme, and again simultaneously the second violins with the third theme, whereupon the cellos launch into the second theme, the violas finally adding the fifth theme plus its extension. At [b. 387][62] the cellos and first bassoon take up the fourth theme, followed by the double basses and second bassoon with the first theme, and the horns, trumpets and timpani entering simultaneously to fill out the texture. Thereupon the first violins and flute promptly plunge into the third theme, while the violas and second oboe immediately take up the second theme. Finally the second violins and first oboe add the fifth theme plus its extension. At [b. 391][63] the violas, which have by now stated all five themes, one after another, as can be seen below:

Example 19

[bb.371–91]

restate the fourth theme, doubled by second oboe, followed immediately by the cellos, who by now have also stated all five themes one after another, as can be

55 The original has 'as follows:' followed by bb. 360–67 quoted in full score as Ex. *bb*.
56 '*cc*'.
57 It is surprising that Sechter does not claim the cellos and basses in bb. 370–71 (hence by association bb. 368–9) as playing the last two notes of the first theme at the third below the first violins, by analogy with bb. 243–52.
58 '*dd*'.   59 '*ee*'.   60 '*ff*'.
61 '*gg*'.   62 '*hh*'.   63 '*ii*'.

seen from the orchestral score, with the first theme again, doubled by first bassoon. Thereupon, the double basses seize upon the third theme, doubled by the second bassoon, while the second violins immediately take up the second theme, doubled by the first oboe. Finally the first violins, doubled by flute, add the fifth theme plus its extension. At [b. 395][64] the second violins, which have meanwhile also stated all five themes, one after another, moreover in the same order as the violas, take up the fourth theme yet again, doubled by first oboe. The violas promptly launch into the first theme, in unison with the second oboe, whereupon the cellos and first bassoon appear with the third theme, followed by the first violins and flute with the second theme. Finally the double basses, doubling the second bassoon, add the fifth theme. At [b. 398],[65] where the violas have reached only the penultimate note of the first theme, this same note can be seen as carrying double duty for the first note of the fourth theme, and the following note, which completes the first theme, does duty for the second note of the fourth theme, which then continues to its con-clusion. The first violins, which have now stated all five themes one after another in the same order as the violas, now immediately take up the first theme once again, whereupon the second violins take up the third theme, followed by the double basses and second bassoon with the second theme. Finally the cellos and the first bassoon add the fifth theme; but this time, instead of being extended in thirds above the third theme, as previously, they merge into the double bass and second bassoon line. With this, now that the basses have stated in the same order as the second violins all five themes one after another, as have each of the four other principal voices,[66] Mozart evidently wished to close the fugue proper and resume composition in free style, which is the mainstay of symphonic form [*Sinfonieform*].

At [b. 402][67] there now recurs exactly what initially appeared in bb. 13–29. However, instead of leading to an imperfect cadence, as occurred there [b. 35], it leads now, at [b. 419][68] to a full close, whereupon the tonic chord is prolonged thunderously for a further five bars.[69]

{193} Mozart has given us here, as in so many of his works, proof positive that counterpoint, fugue and canon, far from being the sole preserve of solemn music, can also be used with excellent effect in light-hearted compositions. That he succeeded in this purpose can be deduced easily from the fact that at virtually every performance, this movement, despite its quite considerable duration, has had to be repeated because even those who were not connoisseurs were greatly excited by it. Anyone who takes the trouble to study them attentively will quickly find that in many of his greatest works he adopted a similar plan.

---

64   '*kk*'.   65   '*ll*'.
66   While implying that, with the separation of cellos from double basses, there are five principal voices [*Hauptstimmen*], Sechter does not actually state that the cellos present the five themes in the same order as the second violins (bb. 387–402), which they do except for the elision of the fifth and second themes such that the distinctive opening of the second theme is not sounded. Sechter's attention to detail is notable in the way in which he separates out two successions of entries by their different pitch levels. After equating the succession of entries of the second violins with that of the violas on order alone, he thereafter carefully equates that of the first violins with that of the violas, that of the double basses with that of the second violins.
67   '*mm*'.   68   '*nn*'.
69   At this point (pp. 190–92) bb. 368–423 (the end) are quoted in full score, with letters *cc* to *nn* marking off the points discussed in the preceding text.

Siegfried Wilhelm Dehn (1799–1858)
'Dreistimmige Fuge aus dem "Wohltemperirten Clavier" von J. S. Bach'

Analysen dreier Fugen aus Joh. Seb. Bach's 'wohltemperirtem Clavier' (1858)

Siegfried Dehn was the next and last editor of Marpurg's *Treatise on Fugue*, succeeding Sechter by taking charge of the fourth edition, dated 1858. Expunging Sechter's analysis of Mozart's 'Jupiter' Finale (Analysis 4), eliminating his explanatory interpolations and reversing his inclusion of music examples in the text, Dehn's was a restoration of Marpurg's work.[1] Yet it was in a small way also a modernization. Take, for example, his definition of *zergliedern* – italics here mark changes from Marpurg's original: 'To segment a *theme* is to partition it into distinct *smaller sections*, so as to use one of them *as a melodic motif* in imitation between the different voices, either on its own, or along with other *motifs from the theme* itself . . .'[2] The supporting music examples remain the same, but the change from *Glieder* to *kleinere Theile* and the introduction of *Motiv* twice here (like the use of *Figur* in the analysis) tinge the passage with the language of organic mid-nineteenth-century theory, as discussed earlier in the General Introduction. Even *Thema* (a fugal usage going back to Zarlino) takes on a faint Romantic aura in context.

The analysis given below does not come from, or relate directly to, his edition of the *Treatise*. Dehn's intention had allegedly been to analyse a substantial number of fugues from the *Well-tempered Clavier*, along with fugues by other great composers. However, he died before completing this project. Analyses of only three fugues by Bach and one by Bononcini were found among his papers, and these were brought together by Bernhard Scholz in a modest publication of about fifty pages entitled *Analyses of Three Fugues*.

For Dehn, analysis involved two distinct processes: segmentation, and structural critique. Work began with placing a fugue in open score (four such scores appear at the end of the volume), and then with functional annotation of the parts (some trace of this can been seen with fugues 2 and 3). Textual commentary then proceeded by identification of the basic motivic material of subject, countersubject and other initial counterpoints, and by close study of the distribution of this

1 In the interests of low price and wide dissemination, Dehn chose to use the surviving original plates. He resisted pressure to add examples from 'Joseph and Michael Haydn, Mozart, Cherubini and other masters', preserved the 1753 dedication and foreword, and drew in places on Marpurg's own French translation (Berlin: Haude and Spener, 1756): *Abhandlung von der Fuge nach den Grundsätzen der besten deutschen und ausländischen Meister entworfen von Friedrich Wilhelm Marpurg*, rev. and ed. S. W. Dehn (Leipzig: C. F. Peters, 1858), vol. I, pp. xiv (note), xv.
2 ibid, I, 67.

material throughout the fugue. Built into this was observation of the major structural components – exposition, episodes, middle-entry series, stretti.

It is one aspect of this last which perhaps gives individuality to the analysis of the D minor fugue. Dehn was greatly concerned with uncovering how, while achieving maximum unity, Bach contrived the avoidance of monotony. As the analysis proceeds, Dehn builds us a map of parallel passages – between bb. 13–14 and 21–22, for example. These parallelisms are often covert, and involve passages of markedly different length – bb. 1–6 and 27–9, for example. The result is an elaborate internal cross-referencing of the fugue. Dehn ignores the one truly obvious parallelism – that between bb. 17–21 and 39–43 – perhaps precisely because this was a formal concluding repetition rather than an inner relationship.

His portrayal of the D minor subject here contrasts incisively with that of the Eb major subject from Book II No. 7, given later in *Analyses*. The former unfolds the identity of the minor mode by gradually disclosing its distinguishing scale degrees (. . . f' . . . c#' . . . bb' . . .); the latter asserts the major mode by thrusting its distinguishing notes (eb–bb . . . g–c') upon the listener. Dehn delimits the subject as lasting to the initial quaver e' of b. 4, tacitly sanctioning the overlap of the answer by a full measure. Modern analysts would probably terminate it at a crotchet's value (or a quaver's value, or even at the attack-point) of the initial a' of b. 3, leaving the following measure as a non-obligatory codetta.

There are anomalies in the segmentation of the D minor subject: according to the text, figures 4 and 5 both begin on a tied note, for example, and the first semiquaver of b. 2 has a place in neither figure 1 nor figure 2. On the other hand, Example 1 half includes this note in figure 1. Indeed, the inflexibilities of moveable type (which have been reproduced as faithfully as possible here) give rise to several ambiguities in the figure-bracketing of Examples 1 and 4 – does the initial quaver rest belong to figure 1 or not? – do theme and countersubject really intersect at the e' of b. 4? Notably, in terms of the text, four of the five figures are multiples of a single note value; only figure 2 includes different values. The overlaying of figures 2 and 3 represents an interesting conceptual leap; also interesting is the fact that both are upbeat–downbeat patterns. (These remarks should not mask the existence of some innovative structural music examples later in the volume.) Dehn was apparently unaware of Bach's authority for a slur on the three semiquavers of figure 2, a staccato on the first crotchet and a trill on the second. He thus attributes the notes of the upper voice in b. 5 to figure 2, whereas Tovey insisted, on grounds of the absence of these signs, that they 'do not allude to the subject'.[3] Note how he treats the Eb major chord in b. 9 as a 'passing modulation', showing no conception of the flattened second degree as a chromatic identity within a key.[4] Comparison with Vogler's treatment of the same phenomenon some fifty years earlier is striking. He observes (Analysis 7 below) with extraordinary

3   *J. S. Bach: Forty-eight Preludes and Fugues*, ed. D. F. Tovey (London: Associated Board, 1924), vol. I, p. 57; Tovey speaks only of 'the final crotchets of bar 5'.
4   The term 'Neapolitan sixth' appears in Riemann's *Handbuch der Harmonie* (Leipzig: B&H, 4/1906), and perhaps goes back to his earlier *Skizze einer neuen Methode der Harmonielehre* (1880). I do not know who used the term first.

acuity that an extended E♭ major passage, seven bars in duration, is not heard as a discrete key area precisely because the listener is familiar with the first-inversion flattened second degree as a localized phenomenon.

Born in Altona, Dehn studied law in Leipzig, 1819–22, before becoming a pupil of Bernhard Klein in Berlin, from which time he increasingly involved himself in musical scholarship. In 1842 he was appointed curator of the music division of the Königliche Bibliothek zu Berlin (later called the Preussische Staatsbibliothek, since 1954 the Deutsche Staatsbibliothek in East Berlin, now in unified Germany). That this division, founded in 1824, is one of the world's greatest collections of music manuscripts and books is appreciably due to Dehn's acquisition and cataloguing of materials. He edited works of Lassus, de Rore and other sixteenth- and seventeenth-century composers, and he took over from Griepenkerl in 1849 the Peters *Oeuvres complets* of J. S. Bach, editing volumes XV–XXIII, including the Brandenburg Concertos. In addition to the *Analyses of Three Fugues*, he produced two works of music theory: *Theoretical-Practical Manual of Harmony* (1840) and *Theory of Counterpoint, Canon and Fugue* (1859).[5]

5   *Theoretisch-praktische Harmonielehre* (Leipzig: Thome, 1840, 2/1860); *Lehre vom Contrapunkt, dem Canon und der Fuge* (Berlin: Schneider, 1859, 2/1883).

'Three-part Fugue [Bk I No. 6 in D minor] from J. S. Bach's *Well-tempered Clavier*'

Analyses of Three Fugues from J. S. Bach's 'Well-tempered Clavier'

Source:
'Dreistimmige Fuge aus dem "Wohltemperirten Clavier" von J. S. Bach', *Analysen dreier Fugen aus Joh. Seb. Bach's 'wohltemperirtem Clavier' und einer Vocal-Doppelfuge A. M. Bononcini's* (Leipzig: C. F. Peters, 1858), pp. 1–7.

The subject begins at the second quaver, on the tonic of the home key, occupies three bars, and brings into play one by one the *cordae principales* or distinguishing pitches of the minor key, that is, the minor third, the leading-note and the minor sixth (cf. *Theory of Harmony*, 79[6]). Any difficulty that might have arisen in answering the subject is obviated by the late arrival of the fifth of the key, appearing as it does for the first time in b. 3. Consequently, every note is answered at the fifth – or rather at the fourth below, which amounts to the same thing. From the subsequent course of the fugue it is apparent that, in order to provide the figures necessary for development, the composer segments [*zergliedert*] the subject in the following way. The first segment [*Glied*] of the subject comprises the quaver figure of b. 1; figure 2 comprises the whole of b. 2 save only for the first semiquaver; figure 3 consists of the two crotchets of b. 2 and the first crotchet value of b. 3; figure 4 comprises the eight semiquavers of b. 3. Lastly, to these four figures is added [figure 5,] the semiquaver figure of the countersubject in b. 4. The material for development is thus as follows:

Example 1

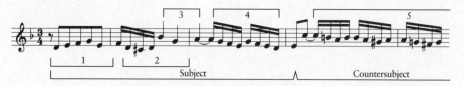

The answer appears in the middle voice well before the end of the subject, as early as b. 3. Since the subject is in the minor, the answer must appear in the minor too. Hence it introduces the same *cordae principales* or distinguishing pitches of the minor as did the subject, this time at the fourth below, thus in A minor. To pave the way for the entry of the subject in the third voice, due to recur as in the first voice in the tonic key, a brief but fully-fledged modulation to the key of the dominant, made explicit by means of the major third and major sixth, C♯ and F♯, is now effected in b. 5. Noteworthy during this modulation is the

6   See note 5.

juxtaposition of various figures derived from the subject: the second bar of the subject occurs in the upper voice against the third bar of the subject in the middle voice. In this instance, the modulation to the key of the dominant is brought about not, as is usually the case, by a codetta [*Zwischensatz*] interpolated immediately after the conclusion of the answer, but merely by the adjustment of certain notes in the latter part of the answer itself. That is, instead of the last eight semiquavers of the subject being answered at the perfect fifth they are subjected to chromatic alteration by a sharp, e.g.:

Example 2

and it is through this that the dominant harmony with congruent major third – here C♯ – arises and thereby forms the chord of the leading-note [*Leitaccord*] of D minor. At the completion of the answer, the subject now makes its entry in the third voice reverting to the tonic key, though of course an octave lower than the upper voice in b. 1. The answer in b. 3 enters before the completion {2} of the subject, whereas the subject in the third voice – the lowest voice – does not enter until the answer is finished. It is as a result of this that, in an apparently quite unaffected way, the three voices enter not equidistantly but after differing time-intervals, the second voice following on from the first after only two bars, the third voice following on from the second after three bars. By means of these varying entry points, the rhythmic monotony that prevails in so many fugues, in which the voices follow each other in precise succession every two or every three bars, is avoided. With the entry of the third voice the fugal texture ought now to be three-part; in fact it remains two-part in b. 6 because as the third voice enters the middle voice has rests. Just as previously in b. 3 two figures of the subject appeared juxtaposed, so this juxtaposition occurs also in b. 6; and although the selfsame figures occur here as there, they occur in not quite the same voices and on totally different degrees of the scale. Not until b. 7 does the fugal texture become three-part once more, as the middle voice enters again after its rests with a figure from the countersubject which comes from b. 4, in accordance with a time-honoured rule that no voice shall re-enter after a protracted rest except with either the subject itself or a principal figure from the subject or countersubject. Just as b. 6 was noted as a repetition of b. 3 with modifications, so too b. 7 is a repetition of b. 4; however, the monotony that would inevitably set in with a direct repetition of bars so recently sounded is avoided by being modified also through transposition, and what is more also by the introduction of a third voice, which fills out the texture.

Before the end of the subject is reached another entry occurs, this time not a strict answer, in the upper voice of b. 8, on the second degree of the tonic key. By comparison with b. 8, b. 3 is inverted, for the upper voice of b. 3 occurs as the lowest voice of b. 8 whilst the lower voice of the former now becomes the upper voice. Since, however, the two voices are not set in counterpoint at the same interval, but rather the upper voice is an octave below and against that the lower voice a fifth higher, so the deployment of invertible counterpoint at the fifth or twelfth stands out clearly, as the following example demonstrates.

Example 3

In addition to the invertible counterpoint just cited, a further ingenuity in the treatment of the subject is worth mentioning at this point. The entry of the subject in the upper voice, in b. 8, provides the means of connecting the next section of the fugue tightly to the exposition [*Exposition*]. Throughout the exposition, nothing other than the tonic and dominant keys have arisen: nothing remote or alien. Now, to avoid any danger of monotony, a passing modulation is effected which touches fleetingly on E♭ major. This key does not come about by transposition of the subject up one step but rather in an entirely natural and unforced way through a tiny melodic modification of the subject. Whenever a subject is modified, it must always be plainly recognizable – so runs a time-honoured rule the reasons for which need no further enlargement. In the passage under discussion, the melodic modification brings to the subject a new upward momentum [*Aufschwung*]: instead of the semitone step (E–F) that can be seen in the subject in the upper voice between bb. 1 and 2, and then in the bass between bb. 6 and 7, and in the answer in the middle voice {3} [B–C] between bb. 3 and 4, what is now interpolated in the upper voice between bb. 8 and 9 is a leap of a fourth [F–B♭].

Episode [*Zwischensatz*] 1 of the fugue begins in b. 9. Each of the three voices presents a figure from either the subject or the countersubject out of b. 4, this time not successively but simultaneously. Consequently nothing the slightest bit alien is introduced into the fugue in the course of this first episode. In the upper voice, b. 9 sees the continuation of the subject as it entered melodically modified in b. 8 on the second degree of the tonic key, but not the completion of the subject; instead, figure 3 is repeated (the last two crotchets of b. 2 and the first crotchet value of b. 3 in the segmentation of the subject given earlier). Against this figure there enters, from b. 10 onwards in the middle voice, a rhythmic imitation of figure 2 of the subject (the whole of b. 2 except for the first semiquaver); and before that, in the third voice in b. 9, there enters figure 5 (from the countersubject in b. 4). An extension of this episode with its various figures begins with the middle voice in b. 12 using figure [1] (the first bar of the subject) – the figure which ushered in this episode in b. 8, made no further appearance and now brings the episode to a close, at the same time providing a link to the series of middle entries [*Repercussion*] that follows.[7] This entry of figure 1 is in inversion, and against it appears,

7   *Repercussion*: often translates as 'exposition'; however, it here refers to successions of entries that
    do not encompass all three voices and therefore do not qualify for that term.

in b. 12, the second bar of the subject in normal form in the lowest voice, followed by the third bar in b. 13. In this way, the entire subject is heard again at the end of the episode, presented in its various parts by the different voices. Even before the third [i.e. lowest] voice has completed the last two bars of the subject, the *first series of middle entries* cuts in in b. 13 in the dominant major key. The subject appears in full only in one voice – the upper voice; in the middle voice no more than the first two bars are given, while in the bass only figure 1 is stated. Although it was the upper voice that opened the entire fugue, just as it does now the series of middle entries, there is one essential difference to be noted, namely that in b. 1 the upper voice entered on the tonic of the home key and proceeded via the minor third, whereas here it enters on the dominant and proceeds via the major third. Equally well, there is an unmistakeable similarity between the first answer, in b. 3, and the answer in b. 14, and yet here too there is an essential difference. In the former, imitation, at the fourth below, starts with the second quaver of b. 3, whereas in the latter, the imitation, also at the fourth below, enters with the second quaver of the *second* bar (i.e. b. 14), and moreover it is in inversion. By this, unity and variety are achieved. This series of middle entries, with the selfsame stretto, occurs once again later in the fugue [bb. 21–3], though further modified, this time in invertible counterpoint at the octave, from which still greater variety is achieved in the presentation of the counterpoint.

While the upper two voices execute the ingenious stretto[8] in bb. 13–15, the bass fills out the texture with something that states, or at least recalls, figure 1 of the subject. Close on the heels of this series of middle entries comes the upper voice, initiating episode 2 with figure 4 (the semiquaver figure from b. 3 of the subject), which the middle voice has failed to present in bb. 14–15 in giving out only the first two bars of the subject. This figure flows directly into figure 5 (from the countersubject in b. 4), and against it the *second series of middle entries* makes its appearance in the bass of b. 17; the middle voice meanwhile rests, thus reducing the fugal texture to two voices. The bass, which {4} up to now has presented the subject only on the tonic (b. 6), now states it on the dominant of the home key, at first with the minor third but followed immediately by the major third. This in turn brings about a modification to the middle voice, which when it originally presented the subject as answer in b. 3 stated it likewise on the dominant but preserved the minor third throughout. This small modification is not the only change to the subject [in the lowest voice], for the third bar is dispensed with entirely, such that the first bar of the countersubject (the upper voice of b. 4 of the fugue), modified in its interval structure though not in its rhythm, connects up directly with the second bar [of the subject]. In this series of middle entries, imitation occurs at the octave, and moreover in the middle voice, which, having rested for a whole bar's worth, enters with the subject and once again establishes a stretto. While no closer, this stretto works rather differently from its immediate predecessor in bb. 13–14, where imitation took place at the fourth below and in

---

8 *künstliche Engführung*: this could imply 'false stretto', i.e. a stretto whose statements are incomplete; however, the later description of bb. 27–30 as *künstlicher wie alle bisherigen Repercussionen* invalidates this reasoning, since the stretto in those bars is not 'more false' than preceding stretti.

inversion. Other respects in which these two series of middle entries differ are that the former, bb. 13–14, was executed by the upper and middle voices, whereas the latter is executed by the lower and middle voices; and finally that in the latter no voice presents the subject in its entirety, whereas in the former the upper voice did so. The third of the dominant has been heard vacillating between major and minor in bb. 17–19, giving the tonality a somewhat indeterminate quality. Now in b. 20, which forms a brief episode, the voices coalesce as they drive towards a cadence on the dominant at the beginning of b. 21, but they fail to dispel the indeterminacy as they leave behind a bare A. At this point the middle voice falls silent, only to remain so appreciably longer than hitherto, and the texture reverts to two-part counterpoint in an inversion of the stretto in the two upper voices[9] from bb. 13–15, in invertible counterpoint at the octave, as the following juxtaposition reveals. What is more, b. 21 taken on its own is an inversion, of the same type, of the *outermost* voices of b. 13.

Example 4

The upper voice of b. 13, the subject beginning on the second quaver of the bar, appears now in b. 21 as the lower voice. The imitation of the subject in b. 14, formerly located *beneath* the first voice, now lies above it in b. 22. The fact that several notes of the subject are modified in b. 23 (namely A and C in b. 15 become G and B♭ in b. 23) is not a matter for concern, because when counterpoint is inverted not only can accidentals be added but also individual notes can be modified under the exigencies of good part-writing. It is directly after this stretto, during the course of the *third series of middle entries* which presents the dominant key with *major* third at its clearest, that the composer allows the minor character of the tonic key to reassert itself, as he introduces the subject in the lowest voice

9 Dehn conducts his discussion here at first as two abstract voices, before acknowledging that one of these voices in bb. 13–15 is in reality a conflation of the lower (up to b. 14, note 1) and middle voices, as is indicated by the clef change in b. 14 of the music example, and as is implicit in the sentence that follows.

on the second quaver of b. 23 with the minor third in the key of D while interpolating the leading-note, or the major seventh of the same key, C♯, and then
cadences by way of the same note at the end of b. 24 in the tonic key.

Three-part fugal texture resumes in b. 25, and episode [4], which follows,
involves all three voices. In the upper voice of bb. 25–6 appears figure [5] (from
the countersubject in b. 4) now for the first time in inversion. The middle voice,
which has been silent since b. 21 and is thus obliged to enter with the subject or a
principal figure, {5} now makes its reappearance with the opening of the subject,
moreover on the tonic of the home key and in inversion. The interval at which this
tonic subject entry is now imitated in b. 26 is the *fifth below* – the first time that
this interval has been used for this purpose, all previous imitations having been
without exception at the fifth above (or fourth below) or, as in bb. 17–18, at the
octave. The *fourth series of middle entries* begins in b. 27: the *third* series, bb. 21ff,
having been in two parts, this is once again in three parts. It is the *first stretto in
three parts* and moreover is more ingenious than all of the series of middle entries
so far. The first to enter, the upper voice, introduces the subject on the second
quaver of b. 27 on the dominant of the home key, presenting its first two bars in
inversion, against which in the bass the third bar of the subject serves as countersubject. The second to enter, the middle voice, having rested for one bar's worth,
responds early on the tonic of the home key, against the second bar of the previous
entry, and likewise presents the first two bars of the subject in bb. 28–9, this time
not in inversion but in normal form. Finally, before the statement in the second
voice is complete the third voice enters, once again on the dominant of the home
key like the first voice, once again in inversion. If the entries of the three voices in
bb. 27, 28 and 29 are compared with those in bb. 1, 3 and 6, where all three
voices likewise stated the subject, what emerges is that the composer made one
change to the succession of entries on the tonic and dominant of the home key. At
the opening of the fugue, the succession of scale-degrees on which the voices entered
was: tonic, dominant, then back to tonic; tonic was thus heard twice, and dominant
only once. By contrast, in bb. 27, 28 and 29 the dominant begins, then comes
tonic and this is followed by dominant once again; thus in this case dominant is
heard twice, and tonic only once.

Even before the third voice to enter has completed the first two bars of the subject, figure [5] (from the countersubject in b. 4) appears to launch the episode which
now follows in b. 30. This figure continues as far as b. 33; unlike its recent appearance in inversion and ascent in bb. 25–6, however, it is now in its original form
and descent, as it was initially in bb. 9–11. As in bb. 10–11, the middle voice of
bb. 31–2 presents a rhythmic imitation of figure 2 of the subject (comprising the
whole second bar of the subject save for the first semiquaver). Despite this similarity of material between the episodes of bb. 9–11 and bb. 30–32, the composer
has once again distinguished these two episodes, [this time] by varying the deployment of the voices. In bb. 9–11, figure 5 (from the countersubject of b. 4) appears
in the lower voice, whereas in bb. 30, 31 and 32 it appears in the upper voice.
Then there is figure 2, or a rhythmic imitation of the same, which appears in the
middle voice in bb. 10–11; now, though still in the middle voice, it has one

component (the two crotchets) inverted. Yet another distinction is the presence of figure 3 (the two crotchets of b. 2 and the first crotchet value of b. 3 taken together) in the upper voice of bb. 9–11, and its absence from bb. 30–32, where instead the bass fills out the three-part contrapuntal texture with a purely free part. Finally, as regards tonality, the earlier episode is remarkable for the fleeting appearance of a remote key (E♭ major), this never being established by a fully-fledged modulation involving a cadence.[10] In the present episode also there is a modulation, but it differs crucially from its counterpart in that (1) it comes about by way of a perfect cadence,[11] and (2) [it leads to] a related key (G minor). Specifically in b. 30 the {6} harmony

Example 5

occurs: fundamentally [the] chord of the leading-note in G minor by means of which the transition [*Uebergang*] to the tonic chord [*Grunddreiklang*] of this key is effected and carried through (cf. *Theory of Harmony*: Arbitrary and Specified Modulations, pp. 230ff, also the tabular synopsis of the key relationships, p. 235, where G minor is shown as closely related to D minor[12]). At the end of this episode, different bars of the subject appear simultaneously in different voices, just as was the case earlier in b. 6. Up to this point, whenever stating again something that has been heard before, the composer has been at pains to ensure a difference in presentation, and precisely in so doing, he has brought to the fugue a remarkable degree of variety within unity. Thus in b. 6 he juxtaposes the first bar of the subject with the third, whereas in b. 33 he juxtaposes the first with the second, to be followed immediately by the third in b. 34, the result being that fragments comprising the entire subject are assembled within the space of two bars. A comparable assemblage has already taken place in bb. 12–13, but that was markedly different from the present case. In that, the second bar of the subject appeared *beneath* the first, whereas now the first appears beneath the second; in that, the first bar was inverted, now it is in its original form.

Bar 34 sees the beginning of the *fifth series of middle entries*, its initial note being the tonic of the home key. The subject, only the first two bars of which appear here in the bass, the voice which opens the series of entries, is in neither the major nor the minor of the tonic key, for the major third (F♯) rules out minor, and yet the minor sixth (B♭) rules out major. In the light of the fully-fledged modulation to G minor just noted in b. 30, which patently did not come about fortuitously, it is on the dominant of that key that the subject now makes its appearance. Should there be any argument that the E in the first bar of the subject is not in the domain of G minor, G minor requiring E♭, it can be argued in return that the minor scale is often modified under melodic conditions by taking the major

10   *nicht durch eine* Cadenz *vollständig gemachte Ausweichung festgestellte fremde Tonart*: it is not clear whether Dehn intends *vollständig* to be attributed to *Cadenz*, thus implying a 'perfect cadence', as later in the sentence.

11   *mittelst einer vollständigen Cadenz*: see note 10. Below, however, this is described as a *vollständige Ausweichung*.

12   [Dehn:] In the older schools, a basis for the relationship of keys was seen to lie in speculative theory.

sixth in ascent, so as to avoid the leap, or more properly the augmented tone, from the minor sixth to the leading-note (in this case E♭ to F♯), an interval which would severely change the character of the subject (cf. *Theory of Harmony*, p. 67ff, Remarks on the Minor Key). The juxtaposition of individual whole bars of the subject in different voices, of which we have had occasion to speak briefly already, becomes increasingly interesting from b. 34 onwards, and so shall be dealt with once again now, at the close of this analysis, looking back over the fugue as whole.

With the entry of the subject in the bass, the third bar [of the subject] in the upper voice is set simultaneously against the first bar, as it was in b. 6, but this time with the tonality altered and with an additional voice to fill out the texture. Against the second bar in the bass (b. 35) is set the first bar, now in both of the other voices, and moreover in the original form in the upper voice and in inversion in the middle voice. This means that no single voice in bb. 34–5 presents the subject in full; rather, the bass presents only the first two bars while at the same time the upper voice gives out the third bar, so that once again the entire subject is sounded by different voices almost concurrently. After this brief fifth series of middle entries follows episode [6], occupying bb. 36–8, and featuring figures 1 and 4 of the subject superimposed. This episode is in three parts, yet comprises only two principal voices and one subordinate one to fill out the texture, in that the middle voice presents figure 1 in inversion against figure 4, while being for the most part {7} accompanied by the bass in thirds below. As to harmony, several remote keys can be heard, transitory and lightly touched upon, in the course of this episode, after which in b. 38 the dominant harmony of the tonic key reasserts itself. Then, while the semiquaver figure [5] (deriving from the countersubject in b. 4) chimes in at b. 39 in the upper voice to maintain the existing flow of semiquavers, the first bar of the subject, now for the first time on the tonic of the home key, makes its entrance against this. The bass, once again presenting only the first two bars of the subject, is promptly imitated at the octave by the middle voice, which likewise states only the first two bars of the subject. Against this, the bass in b. 41 once more brings back figure 5, to which the upper voice has just alluded in b. 40.

Bar 42 sees the onset of the *coda* of the fugue. In the course of this, in b. 43 the tonic note is sustained by the bass doubled in the uppermost voice, while figure 1 of the subject recurs yet again, in its original form and simultaneously in inversion, both statements accompanied by parallel thirds, after which the fugue ends on the tonic major triad of the home key. It was not uncommon in Bach's day to increase the number of voices in clavier and organ fugues[13] as the fugue drew to a close; doing so serves to reinforce the volume of sound[14] at the conclusion of a piece. Equally well, there is nothing unusual in a minor fugue having a major ending; the effect is more pleasing to the ear than a minor ending. To some extent, the way is paved for the major ending in this case by the alternation of tonic major and minor third that has taken place in b. 39.

---

13   *in Clavier- und Orgelfugen*: lit. 'in keyboard and organ fugues'. The present, admittedly infelicitous, rendering of *Clavier* was preferred to 'piano' out of respect for Dehn's knowledge of early music and to 'harpsichord and clavichord' as over-specific.

14   *die Tonmasse . . . verstärken.*

Hugo Riemann (1849–1919)
'[J. S. Bach:] II.22. Präludium und Fuge B-moll'

Katechismus der Fugen-Komposition (Analyse von J. S. Bachs 'Wohltemperiertem Klavier' und 'Kunst der Fuge') (1890)

It may seem bizarre that Hugo Riemann's analyses of J. S. Bach's *Well-tempered Clavier* and *Art of Fugue* should have appeared in a series alongside handbooks on chess, indoor gardening, decorum and good manners, proper behaviour in children and taste in the art of toiletry. Such was Max Hesse Verlag's *Illustrated Catechisms*; however, it was at first solidly based in music, and Riemann himself contributed most of the initial twenty-one volumes.

These volumes alone – he produced them between 1888 and 1902 – reveal Riemann as the culmination of eighteenth- and nineteenth-century music theory, for in these little handbooks he covers musical rudiments and also technical subjects such as acoustics, musical instruments, thoroughbass, harmony, modulation, composition (i.e. form and construction), fugue and vocal composition, with two volumes on music history, as well as practical manuals on organ playing, piano playing, musical dictation and orchestration.

But there are signs even within this series of another side to Riemann, for he produced manuals also on phrase structure and on music perception. One of his few joint ventures, Riemann published the *Catechism of Phrasing* with Dr Carl Fuchs in 1890. Subtitled 'Practical introduction to phrasing: exposition of the criteria governing the establishment of phrasing-signs, together with complete thematic, harmonic and rhythmic analyses of classical and romantic pieces of music [by Bach, Clementi, Mendelssohn, Schubert and Chopin]', it was the outcome of an on-going series of editions that he had published in the 1880s of the major baroque, classical and romantic repertory – editions which had 'many critics', and to which Schenker was presumably referring in his polemical essay 'Away with the phrase-slur' (1925).[1] In these, he sought to locate for the performer the 'boundaries of phrases', laying bare the inner dynamics of phrase units with an increasingly complex system of symbols. His *Catechism of Musical Aesthetics (How do we Listen to Music?)* of 1888 deals not so much with aesthetics as with the new field of music perception. Out of his concern for tangible musical processes, he sees the listening experience as a flux, as a constant ebb and flow of energy, of 'life-force' (*Lebenskraft*).

---

1 With C. Fuchs, *Katechismus der Phrasierung (Praktische Anleitung zum Phrasieren)* (Leipzig: Hesse, 1890, 2/1900 as *Vademecum der Phrasierung*, 8/1912 as *Handbuch der Phrasierung*); *Wie hören wir Musik?: drei Vorträge* (Leipzig: Hesse, 1888; 1890 as *Katechismus der Musik-Ästhetik (Wie hören wir Musik?)*). Heinrich Schenker, 'Weg mit dem Phrasierungsbogen', *Das Meisterwerk in der Musik*, vol. I (1925), pp. 41–60.

To see Riemann's work exclusively through Hesse's *Illustrated Catechisms*, rich though his contributions are, would be to view only the more popular face of his work. In his dissertation 'On Musical Listening' (1873), later published as *Musical Logic*, in his *Musical Syntax: Outline of a Theory of Harmonic Phrase Construction* (1877), in *The Nature of Harmony* (1882) and perhaps above all in *Musical Dynamic and Agogic: a Treatise on Musical Phrasing* (1884), he laid the theoretical groundwork for a view of musical processes.[2] These were powered by atomistic units of energy, *Motive*, networked together hierarchically against a normative background in complex and subtle interactions, and manifested in a harmony comprising three functions (a tonic, and two dominants, a fifth to either side of the tonic) and resting on a harmonic dualism whereby minor was seen as the inverse of major. In these, we see Riemann the twentieth-century theory-builder, the constructor of a unitary theory to account for all pitch- and time-related phenomena within a tonal structure, and of an analytical system to report these phenomena. We see him alongside Schoenberg and Schenker – as one of the three primary theory-builders of the century, and one who has influenced musical thinking profoundly to this day. Nor should we overlook the other sides of this man's output: Riemann the lexicographer, the music historian, the notationer, the editor, the historian of music theory.

The advertisement for the *Catechism of Fugal Composition* (as placed on the endpapers of volumes of the *Illustrated Catechisms*) describes it thus: 'A manual of fugal theory in the form of full-length analyses. All of the fugues and preludes are exhaustively analysed according to their thematic and modulatory structure. A major contribution to the theory of form and of phrase structure.' Riemann never wrote a purely instructional manual on fugue. Nor does his *Catechism of Fugal Composition* offer even an introduction on fugal technique or construction. When he wrote it, it was an extension of his *Catechism of the Theory of Composition (Theory of Musical Form)*, published the previous year, 1889, the first volume of which devoted twenty-six pages to 'Fugue and Fugato'.[3]

In this latter he presented fugue as a form like any other, having only the special quality of 'making possible the constructing of longer pieces of compelling logic using only a single theme' (p. 186). Thus he offered formal schemata and discussed the production of answer from subject, treating all other matters only sketchily, and illustrating copiously from Bach's *Well-tempered Clavier* and *Art of Fugue*. Hence his *Catechism of Fugal Composition* emerged as a by-product of this, offering thorough-going analyses of precisely these two works, and enlarging on these selfsame concerns.

However, the work rests on other prior publications too, most specifically on his *Manual of Simple, Double and Imitative Counterpoint* of 1888, itself resting

---

2 'Über das musikalische Hören' (PhD dissertation, University of Göttingen; Leipzig: Andrä, 1874); *Musikalische Logik* (Leipzig: Andrä, 1874); *Musikalische Syntaxis: Grundriss einer harmonischen Satzbildungslehre* (Leipzig: B&H, 1877); 'Die Natur der Harmonik', *Sammlung musikalischer Vorträge*, 1/lx (1882), pp. 157–90; *Musikalische Dynamik und Agogik: Lehrbuch der musikalischen Phrasierung* (Hamburg: Rahter, 1884).

3 *Katechismus der Kompositionslehre (Musikalische Formenlehre)* (Leipzig: Hesse, 1889, 3/1905 as *Grundriss der Kompositionslehre (Musikalische Formenlehre)*, 5/1916 as *Handbuch der Kompositionslehre*).

on his *New School of Melodic Composition* of 1883, subtitled 'a manual of counterpoint based on a new method'.[4] It derives more generally from the theory of harmony that he had been developing throughout the 1880s.

In the 1888 edition of his *Catechism of Musical Aesthetics*, Riemann spoke of 'my editions, known as "phrase-structure editions", of the sonatas of Mozart and Beethoven, and the sonatinas of Clementi and Hässler, not to mention of keyboard works by Bach and Schubert' (p. 45), which in later editions became '. . . of the sonatas of Mozart, Beethoven and Haydn, and sonatinas by Clementi, Kuhlau and others, not to mention keyboard works by Bach, Schumann, Schubert, Chopin etc' (6/1923, p. 47). Riemann had indeed produced just such editions of the *Well-tempered Clavier* and of the *Art of Fugue*.[5]

The status of Riemann's analysis of Bach's *Well-tempered Clavier* is not unlike that of Hauptmann's *Elucidations* of Bach's *Art of Fugue*. Both are commentaries of editions already published. In both, elements of the edition break through into the commentary. Yet there are substantial differences between these two commentaries.

A typical analysis by Riemann comprises three principal components: graphic elements, discussion of the compositional materials and description of the formal structure. The first of these includes harmonic tabulations and charts, and for some of the preludes full-scale melodic-structural graphs deploying the whole panoply of symbols for phrase structure and chords (see Example 1). Even the many short music examples are in fact extracts from the phrase-structure edition and are thus as much graph as excerpt.

The second of these components involves, for a prelude, the identification of a principal motif and attendant counterpoint; and, for a fugue, a close examination of the structure of subject, answer and countersubjects. In a prelude, the third component addresses periodic structure and quality of symmetry, while, in a fugue, it marks out the succession of expositions and episodes, normative eight-bar structure prevailing within expositions, with period (*Satz*) dividing into antecedent and consequent (*Vordersatz* and *Nachsatz*), the latter often being *frei* – that is, not based on subject or answer. Riemann states his view of fugal structure as follows (Foreword to the first edition):

> What these fugal analyses bring home most strikingly is the perfect correspondence of Bach's fugal structure with the norms of all other musical conformation [*Formgebung*]. The tripartite nature, schematically A–B–A (primary section in the tonic, modulatory transitional section, closing section in the tonic) is everywhere plainly in evidence [. . .] The free episodes do not function as linking units interpolated between main sections of the fugue, but belong within those main sections themselves, complementing the entries of the theme, acting as a foil to them, or surpassing and crowning them.

4 *Lehrbuch des einfachen, doppelten und imitierenden Kontrapunkts* (Leipzig: B&H, 1888, 3/1915); *Neue Schule der Melodik: Entwurf einer Lehre des Contrapunkts nach einer gänzlich neuen Methode* (Hamburg: Richter, 1883).

5 *Joh. Seb. Bach's Wohltemperirtes Clavier mit Phrasierungs- und Fingersatzbezeichung herausgegeben* (London: Augener, [n.d.]) and *Die Kunst der Fuge [The Art of Fugue] von Johann Sebastian Bach: Phrasierungsausgabe* (London: Augener, [n.d.]); endpaper advertisements give also *Joh. Seb. Bach's Inventionen für Piano. Mit genauer Bezeichnung der Phrasierung und neuem Fingersatz* (London: Augener, [n.d.]).

Example 1

However, most analyses begin with at least a brief characterizing description. Thus the C major Prelude of Book I is 'of truly Olympian peace and serenity [. . .] forming the portal to Bach's exalted work'. Occasionally these remarks become more fulsome, and are often said to be in agreement or disagreement with Spitta (to whom he dedicated the volume) or 'Debrois van Bruck'[6]. Riemann explains that 'since the preludes stand in so close a spiritual relationship to the fugues, I felt bound to make some reference to their aesthetic content [*ästhetischer Gehalt*]'. At least by hindsight, Riemann intended a theoretical basis for such descriptions, for a quarter of a century later he stated: 'How the character of keys influences thematic invention in those keys is something I sought to establish in my analyses of the *Well-tempered Clavier*.'[7] Nowhere is this purpose declared in the Preface;

6   I have been unable to identify Debrois van Bruck.

7   'Ideen zu einer "Lehre von den Tonvorstellungen" ', *Jahrbuch der Musikbibliothek Peters für 1914/15*, 21/22 (1916), p. 23. His article 'Charakter der Tonarten' in his *Musik-Lexikon* expounds the basis of his theory, in which mode interacts with position on the sharp–flat spectrum: 'The major keys with sharps have as a result an exaggerated brilliance, just as the minor keys with flats are exaggeratedly dark; distinctive mixtures of the two effects are [produced by] the chiaroscuro of major keys with flats, and the subdued luminosity of minor keys with sharps' (1/1882, p. 156).

but frequently in the first volume mood is correlated with key-character. Thus of Book I No. 3: 'That keys influenced [Bach's] feeling and invention in specific ways is strikingly demonstrated by the C♯ major prelude: this ardent midsummer mood, this "flashing, flittering and glistening" was born out of the spirit of the C♯ major key; the veiled, soft D♭ major would have set him off in quite a different direction.' Of Book I No. 22 he says: 'The deep darkness of the key of B♭ minor inspired the old master with ideas of holy earnestness, and imbued his tones with a sacred aura such as they rarely exhibit.'[8]

The analysis of the B♭ minor Prelude and Fugue from Book II is broadly representative of these features. The discussion of the stock of raw materials is of particular interest since Riemann treats the fugue as a model of voluntary self-limitation, alluding to, and even reconstructing, possibilities that Bach rejected in order not to let the work be 'sacrificed on the altar of contrapuntal artifice'. As in the analysis by Sechter (Analysis 4 above), the term *Thema* shows its Janus-like nature, serving in the prelude as a balanced melodic construct (though asymmetricalized by elision of its notional first bar, in Riemann's interpretation) and in the fugue as the neutral sum total of subject and answer (for which Riemann uses *Dux* and *Comes*), where it often takes subject and answer to encompass an eight-bar period (bb. 11–20, for example, where subject = bb. 11–14, answer = bb. 17–20, with a codetta in bb. 15–16 interpolating two bars between the half-period statements: *ten* bars in all, though normatively eight).

Riemann offers a hermeneutic reading of the fugue which may surprise us: subject suffused with anger, first countersubject milder yet with dark growlings, then sinking into resignation, and second countersubject wracked with sobs. This reading scarcely survives further than the discussion of raw contrapuntal materials, surfacing only fleetingly once the account of fugal structure has started, and so robbing the interpretation of any dramatic force. Structure is presented as a narrative, the prelude in a relaxed travelogue, the fugue with prose quickly lapsing into telegraphese. Riemann controls the fugue by contrapuntal procedure: normal–stretto–total inversion–stretto in inversion–stretto normal against inversion. While distinguishing subject entries from codettas and episodes, he simultaneously divides each main section into periods, analysing their internal functions.

The analysis of the B♭ minor Prelude and Fugue lacks only the tabular and fully-graphed elements that we find in many of the other preludes and fugues. Example 1 shows Riemann's graph of the Prelude in E♭ minor from Book I; this will serve as a brief introduction to his vocabulary of symbols. This example, though relatively compact, nonetheless presents the main features of his graphing technique: reduction to a single line stripped of embellishment; division into large-scale sections; subdivision of all material into normative eight-bar 'periods' shown by bold parenthesized numbers beneath the staff such that the numbering never exceeds '(8)'; recycling of functions '(3)' and '(4)' in bb. 21–2 and of an entire half-period ([(6a)]–(8a)) at b. 27–9, and substitution of a strong bar for a weak bar at bb. 36–7 with '(8=5)'; idiosyncratic use of slurs to represent phrase structure, with a slur

8   Vol. I, p. 16 (also especially p. 65, E major and p. 82, F minor), p. 147.

characteristically open to the left in b. 26 designating a 'cadential restatement', crossed slurs in bb. 28–9 representing the telescoping of two phrases and the square bracket in bb. 32–4 denoting a 'triplet' of bars.

Example 1 also illustrates Riemann's chord-symbol system, a letter being in each case the 'prime' of the chord, Arabic numerals intervals counted upwards (as in conventional figured bass), Roman numerals intervals counted downwards, superscript zero and plus representing minor and major triads respectively. Hence the chord symbol in b. 1 shows a minor triad whose 'prime' is B♭, with its 'fifth' (i.e. E♭) in the bass represented by the subscript V, yielding (since minor triads are inverse constructs) an E♭ minor chord in root position, the E♭ forming a pedal note beneath bb. 1–4. Harmonic function is shown by T, S and D for tonic, subdominant and dominant. In b. 10, an E♭ minor triad undergoes substitution of minor subdominant function for minor tonic as the music moves from E♭ minor to B♭ minor.

Riemann's normative eight-bar numbering has in this translation been distinguished from raw bar numbers by enclosure in parentheses (as they appear in Riemann's editions, hence music examples). However, there is one difficulty, which we shall encounter later in Momigny's analysis of Haydn's Symphony No. 103 (vol. II, Analysis 8). Riemann's basic rhythmic cell, the motif, like Momigny's from which it is in a sense derived, runs always from weak beat to strong. In consequence, his normative bars, which are compounds of such motifs, always straddle the barline (despite the fact that the principal thematic material of both prelude and fugue begins on the strong beat). When editorially supplying bar numbers in explanation of Riemann's normative numbers, it has often been necessary to show the beat-number within the bar as a superscript number, as employed also in Analyses 4, 7 and 9.

'Prelude and Fugue in B♭ minor, Bk II No. 22'

Catechism of Fugal Composition (Analysis of J. S. Bach's 'Well-tempered Clavier' and 'Art of Fugue')

Source:
'II. 22. Präludium und Fuge B-moll', *Katechismus der Fugen-Komposition (Analyse von J. S. Bachs 'Wohltemperiertem Klavier' und 'Kunst der Fuge')*, vol. II, Max Hesses illustrierte Katechismen, vol. XIX (Leipzig: Max Hesse, 1890), pp. 183–97.

[Prelude]

Before us lie two of the mightiest pieces from Book II. In both, the art of counterpoint appears with unusual richness, but it is never for one moment overdone. In the prelude, opportunities for more cunning stratagems present themselves at every turn, but Bach has resisted them. Consider just the initial motif (a turn, and a step of a second approached from the fourth): innumerable possibilities seem to call our attention in the four bars:

Example 2

{184} We find none of these possibilities taken up in the finished piece. It is for us to concentrate on what Bach has selected from the wealth of possibilities – that is, the theme and its fugal-style treatment. Not that the theme comprises the paltry scraps shown above: on the contrary, it is a full-phrased melodic unit [*ganzer Satz*]:

Example 3[9]

This unit, with slight modifications at the final cadence, commands the entire prelude, in all its eighty-three bars. Fugue-like, it is promptly restated at the dominant (plunging straight in [with b. (2) [=b. 8]], b. 1 being elided[10]), with a two-bar enhancement of the close:

Example 4

In the minims of this extension we can easily discern an echo of the principal countersubject [*Hauptkontrapunkt*] to the first half of the theme [LH, bb. 1–3]. Very much {185} along the lines of a fugue, an eight-bar episode [*Zwischenspiel*] [bb. 16–23] now ensues (without elision), its character stamped by the graceful ebb and flow of the crotchets:

Example 5

The counterpoint in quavers that asserts itself against this can be traced back to the principal countersubject to the second half of the theme [LH, b. 4], which made its first appearance specifically as a link between first and second statement of the theme (in the alto) [b. 7]:

9   Though this example seems to contain seven bars, Riemann counts it *structurally* as an eight-bar unit, numbering the final bar '(8)'. For him the first sounding bar is structurally bar 2 (the notional first bar being elided). Moreover, even his second bar starts after its notional upbeat beginning; hence all of the first bar and part of the second are non-activated, yielding in all twenty-five beats where thirty-two normatively exist.

10   *mit Überspringung des 1. Taktes*: unlike later situations (e.g. b. 31), in which b. (2) is super-imposed direct upon b. (8), b. (8) is here stated in its own right, after which b. (2) enters. Riemann calls this (the same happens in b. 62) an 'elision' (*Überspringung, Elision*) because an even-numbered bar replaces an odd-numbered bar rather than another even-numbered one.

Example 6

When the first episode is finished, the motif is combined with its own inversion to form the next linking passage:

Example 7

Now the bass takes up the narrative (with the subject [*Dux*]) [bb. 25–31], whilst the soprano with the second half of the theme makes contrapuntal play against the first half. The theme relinquishes its leading-note in b. (5) [b. 28] in the process of modulating towards D♭ major. The close of the theme this time appears as follows:

Example 8

(8)

{186} At b. (8) [b. 31] (with (8=2))[11] the soprano introduces the theme in the relative key, D♭ major. In the counterpointing voices, it should be noted that this time the quaver motif makes its appearance against the first half of the theme (displaced by half a bar).[12] The close appears in a different guise yet again, modulating to A♭ major:

Example 9

NB.   (8)

With this, the quaver motif now sallies forth as a theme in its own right, catching the ear as it is imitated several times [in the bass], and with b. (8) calling b. (5) to mind. A♭ major returns with b. (8a) [b. 40?], and this is confirmed in the following two bars, whereupon the bass introduces the theme in F minor (as answer [*Comes*]) (8=2) [b. 42]. The quaver motif waxes ever stronger against it, alternating between direct and contrary motion. The second half of the theme appears not in the bass

11   Once again, the structural 'eighth bar' is only the seventh surface bar of the unit beginning at b. 25. The sign '(8=2)' signifies not only that the unit which follows likewise begins at its second structural bar but also that b. 8 of the present unit and b. 2 of the next are coexistent.
12   i.e. displaced from the first to the third beat of the bar.

but in the alto [bb. 44–7] and shifted one step lower (e♭ e♭ | e♭ d♮ instead of f f | f e♮); it modulates via E♭ minor to G♭ major [b. 48].

Out of the midst of the cadence, the alto takes up the theme in the same key, only for it to be snatched away by the soprano [in b. 50], which gives it in complete form through to its end except for the quaver motif being stated twice in conclusion [bb. 53–4]. The soprano then plunges [b. 55] (8=2) directly into the theme in E♭ minor (the subdominant), and here for the first time the theme is played out exactly as it was at its original statement [in bb. 1–7]. Once again the alto takes it up (with b. (1) elided[13]), restoring it to B♭ minor. This time it is complete, though the last few notes are varied, fashioning a half close on F^7 [b. 68]. A two-bar codetta, however, then transmutes this into a full close [bb. 68^2–70^1]. At this point, a new consequent [*Nachsatz*][14] materializes [bb. 70–74], but its arrival together with the bass on F by b. (7) [b. 73] frustrates the natural progression towards a close in b. (8), producing a 6/4–chord. What follows is a phrase divided into three segments, each comprising a 'triplet' [*Taktriole*] of three bars, the first one while the {187} pedal F is still sounding [bb. 74–6],[15] and this brings the piece to a broad and effective close.

[Fugue]

The prevailing spirit of the *fugue*[16] (in four parts) is imperious and commanding. [The theme] rises with elemental power from the tonic, first to the fourth above, then, retreating, surges mightily, reaching up to the sixth before breaking off abruptly at the fifth:

Example 10

It now turns gently aside, dropping to the third, and we find ourselves already in the countersubject, which is altogether milder in character:

---

13 See note 10 above.
14 This is the sole use of 'consequent' in the analysis of the prelude – i.e. to refer to the functional second half of a period (*Satz*) which begins in b. 62. The term is frequently used in the analysis of the fugue – see the footnoted discussion.
15 *dreigliedriger Satz . . . drei Takttriolen*: Riemann alludes here to the *Triolenbildung* – a large-scale triplet formation, one of the standard devices in his theory of phrase structure for disturbing normative symmetry: 'When a triplet function arises at a higher-than-normal level of note value, replacing two segments by three, this is called the *Takttriole*. It consists of the placing of three bars' distance between two strong beats [. . .] In the *Triole*, two weak beats [i.e. bars] occur in succession . . .', *Vademecum* [=*Handbuch*], pp. 86–7; also *Katechismus der Kompositionslehre*, pp. 82–3, and other sources. See also note 19.
16 *Fuge*: spaced type.

Example 11

Even so, it accompanies the theme, so to speak, with dark growlings, while the theme itself blazes forth in anger. The {188} cadence motif of this, the primary countersubject, sinks step by step as if in resignation during the episode which heralds the third entry:

Example 12

During the third statement of the theme [bb. 11^1–14^1], the first voice [i.e. soprano] puts forward elements of a second countersubject:[17]

Example 13

It seems to be gathering strength once more, but only to break off as if sobbing in violent, spasmodic outbursts. Although this second countersubject never recurs as a whole, the syncopation of the second and third crotchets followed by quaver figure surface again and again in the course of the fugue, as too do the sobbing crotchets.

{189} The fugue falls naturally into five clearly discernible sections [*Abschnitte*]:

> I. *Exposition of the theme in original form* in the customary manner as subject and answer, accompanied by the countersubjects given above [bb. 1–26]. *Period* [*Satz*] 1 [bb. 1–10^3]: subject in the alto, answer in the soprano, followed by a codetta [*Anhang*] three bars in length (6a–8a) [bb. 8^2–11^1] leading back to the tonic. *Period* 2 [bb. 11^1–20^1] (beginning at (8=1)): subject in the bass, followed by a three-bar codetta (4a, 3b–4b [bb. 14^3–17^1]); consequent [*Nachsatz*][18] (4b=5) [bb. 17^1–20^1] with answer in

17   *des dritten Gegensatz*: presumably 'third' is a typesetting error, since two sentences later the countersubject is referred to as *dieser zweite*. However, it remained uncorrected in the third edition of 1916.
18   In analyses of other fugues in the *Wohltemperirtes Klavier* (e.g. Book I No. 6) Riemann speaks also of 'antecedent' [*Vordersatz*]. Normatively, a 'period' [*Satz*] comprises eight bars, of which the first four are antecedent and the last four consequent, though these may be compressed or expanded by any of the usual devices, or extended by interpolation of a 'codetta' [*Anhang*].

the tenor. An eight-bar episode [bb. 20²–27¹] ensues, leading back to the tonic.

  II. *Stretto of the theme in original form* (without countersubject) [bb. 27¹–41³], first between tenor and alto (the bass rests) at the seventh above and at one minim's distance:

Example 14

(2)   (4)

(4a)

{190} and then, after a 'triplet' of 2/2 bars¹⁹ (forming one 3/1 bar) which shifts the cadence towards D♭ major (4b), between soprano and bass in D♭ major (starting at (4b=5) [bb. 33¹]) at the same interval and distance, but with the two voices transposed.

Example 15

(8ᵛᵃ bassa)

This, too, is followed by a one-bar codetta [bb. 36²–37¹], which transforms a half close into a full close (8a). A four-bar episode [*Zwischenhalbsatz*]²⁰ [bb. 37¹–42¹] now provides a most ingenious preparation for section III, deploying a one-bar descending chromatic motif [in the alto]. The resemblance of this motif to the [first] countersubject is obvious: the stabbing, isolated notes in one of the accompanying voices [soprano] and the anapests (♪♪ ♩ | ♩) in the other [bass] are already also familiar to us [from the second countersubject]:

19 *Triole von . . . Takten*: in Riemann's phrase-structure system, *Taktriole* is one of the devices for breaking rigid normative symmetry by introducing elements of three-bar structure (*Dreitaktigkeiten*), thereby interpolating a second weak unit (strong–weak–weak) into the construction. The present case is self-compensating in that each unit is 2/2, the whole functioning as a *hemiola*. See *Vademecum* [=*Handbuch*], pp. 86–7; also *Grundriss* [=*Handbuch*], vol. I, pp. 99–100. See also note 15.

20 *Zwischenhalbsatz*: a *Halbsatz* is a notionally four-bar phrase (i.e. half a *Satz*), built up of four *Taktmotive* in some pattern such as la a b al or la b a bl, the current one being la a a al: see *Grundriss* [=*Handbuch*], vol. I, pp. 20–30. In fact, through expansion this comprises five bars and one beat.

Example 16

etc.

It continues thus for four further bars (G♭ major, C♭ major, A♭ major, D♭ major). With the fifth bar, a cadential restatement (B♭ minor: (4a) becoming (1)), section III begins.

{191} *III. Exposition in inversion of the theme, countersubject and subsidiary countersubjects* [bb. 42¹–66³]: a veritable *inversione della fuga*! Bach has opted for that form of inversion which preserves the tonic triad unimpaired, interchanging root with fifth while leaving the third fixed. As is well known (see my *Counterpoint*, p. 168²¹), this causes dominant and subdominant²² to exchange their roles in the process; on the other hand, the diminished seventh chord with two possible interpretations (A♮ C E♭ G♭ = F⁹> or B♭^{IX}< ²³) remain unchanged. Thanks to this, the subject when under inversion still traverses the tonic triad, whereas the answer traverses the subdominant instead of the dominant triad. I quote only the inversions of the theme and countersubject in the example below, but would stress that all other contrapuntal materials are for the most part inverted too, as should in fact be obvious. The section begins with all four voices; this works well because the preceding episode has laid the groundwork for the inversion. *Period 1* [42¹–51³]: (beginning with (4a=1)): inversion of the subject in the tenor, inversion of the countersubject in the alto, and after a one-bar cadential restatement [*Schlussbestätigung*]²⁴ (at (4a=5)) [b. 45²–46¹], inversion of the answer in the alto and inversion of the countersubject in the tenor (while the soprano is silent) [bb. 46¹–49¹], with three one-bar cadential restatements [bb. 49²–50¹, 50²–51¹, 51²–52¹] (displacing the cadence successively to

21   *Lehrbuch des . . . Kontrapunkts*: on p. 168 begins §26 'Canon in Contrary Motion', which states the principle of distinguishing such canonic imitations in terms of those scale-degrees that remain constant and those that are exchanged under inversion. His first category (60, schema 280) is 'canon by inversion with retention of the third of the tonic [. . .] i.e. the tonic chord reappears also in the answer as such and the diminished seventh chord remains constant; on the other hand, dominant and subdominant exchange their roles [exx. 281–2]'.

22   *die Dominanten*, i.e. 'the dominants': the notion of 'overdominant' and 'underdominant' (*Oberdominant* and *Unterdominant*; Riemann later changed these terms to *Dominant* and *Subdominant*), in a mirror-like dual system, is fundamental to Riemann's thought.

23   i.e. F dominant minor ninth chord, or inverted minor ninth chord from B♭ (reading downwards, B♭, G♭, E♭, C, A♮) with the B♭ itself omitted.

24   *Schlussbestätigung*: in Riemann's phrase-structure system, the repetition of the final element of a symmetrical phrase, i.e. repetition of the strong bar of a cadence, thereby forming a three-element unit (weak–strong–strong) and 'confirming' the cadence. One of the principal devices for 'disturbing symmetry' [*die Störungen des symmetrischen Aufbaues*], it is the opposite of *Taktriole* (strong–weak–weak: see bb. 31–3 above and note). See *Vademecum* [=*Handbuch*], pp. 79–82; also *Grundriss* [=*Handbuch*], vol. I, pp. 94–9, and other sources. What is 'confirmed' is not the tonality of the cadence, but its structure; indeed, the restatement may effect a 'shifting of the cadence' [*Schlussverschiebung*] to another harmony or key, as happens in bb. 49–52 and elsewhere.

E♭ minor, B♭ minor, then D♭ major). *Period 2* [bb. 52^1–58^1] (beginning at
(8c=1)): inversion of the theme in the soprano, inversion of the countersubject in the alto, the theme beginning on D♭ (subject in G♭ major) but
entering over a D♭ major chord with a feint towards B♭ minor (the tonic key);
the consequent [bb. 55^2–58^1], with b. (5) elided, without statement of the
subject, modulates to the subdominant of the subdominant (A♭ minor): G♭+
D♭^{7} I(6) G♭$^{1<}$ [=E♭^{7}] ᵒE♭ A♭^{VII} [=F♭^{6}] G♭^{7} I(7) C♭+ F♭^{6} [=A♭^{VII}] E♭^{7} I(8) ᵒE♭.^{25}
Period 3 [bb. 58^1–67^1] (beginning at (8=1)): inversion of the theme (subject)
in the bass, inversion of the countersubject in the tenor, but transferring to
the soprano in b. (2), remaining in {192} A♭ minor throughout, the first
cadential restatement reasserting that key (4a) [bb. 61^2–62^1], whereas the
second [bb. 62^2–63^1] (4b) brings about a shift to D♭ major (E♭$^{III<}$ = A♭^{7}).^{26}
The consequent [bb. 63^2–67^1], without statement of subject, finds its way
back home to B♭ minor (8) via E♭ minor (6) by way of the chords D♭^{7} ..1<
(=B♭$^{9>}$) ᵒB♭ ..^{VII} F^7 ᵒF.^{27} The inversion of the theme and countersubject
appear as follows:

Example 17

Gone now is the towering ascendancy that characterized the earlier part
of the fugue, but in its place the wrath seems to deepen.

IV. Stretto of the theme in inversion [bb. 67^1–79^3]: this is constructed like
that of the theme in its original form; that is, at the seventh *below* (or ninth
above), and at a minim's distance. Nor is the countersubject used here, though
it reappears, as if in compensation, in the foreshortened consequent – reappears, moreover, in its original (i.e. ascending) form. *Period 1* [bb. 67^1–73^1]:
inversion of the subject in the tenor, inversion of the theme at the ninth
above (starting on G♭) in the soprano:

Example 18

25 i.e. (b. 55^2–) chords of G♭ major, D♭ dominant seventh, G♭ major with raised root [= E♭ dominant
    seventh], A♭ minor, B♭ half-diminished seventh [= F♭ with added major sixth], G♭ dominant seventh,
    C♭ major, F♭ with added major sixth [= B♭ half-diminished seventh], E♭ dominant seventh, A♭ minor.
26 i.e. chord of A♭ minor with raised third = A♭ dominant seventh.
27 i.e. (bb. 63^2–) chords of D♭ dominant seventh, D♭ dominant seventh with raised root (=B♭ domi-
    nant minor ninth), E♭ minor, C half-diminished seventh, F dominant seventh, B♭ minor.

{193} Consequent [bb. 70²–73¹] (with b. (5) elided), no statement of subject, but chromatic countersubject in bb. (7–8). *Period 2* [bb. 73¹–80¹] (beginning with (8=1)): inversion of the subject in F minor (starting on C) in the alto, inversion of the theme (starting on D♭) in the bass [bb. 73¹–76²]. Codetta [bb. 76²–77¹]: one-bar restatement of the F minor cadence, after which comes a new foreshortened consequent [bb. 77¹–80¹] (with b. (5) elided), with no statement of the subject, and modulating to A♭ major (relative major of the subdominant) (°C |(6) F^VII (=E♭⁷) A♭⁺ D♭⁶ |(8) E♭⁷).²⁸ The half-close here leads us into:

V. *Stretto of the theme in original form against its own inversion* [bb. 80¹–101]: *period 1* [bb. 80¹–89¹]: introduces (at (8=1)) the inverted subject [in the soprano] in A♭ (though over E♭⁷ harmony to support the starting note, E♭) and the theme in its original form [in the tenor] starting on G (its design would therefore permit combination in stretto with the subject in original form in A♭ major). Hints of the countersubject are to be found in bb. (3)–(4) [bb. 81¹–83¹] (in the former, the stabbing, isolated crotchets [bb. 81²–82¹], in the latter the chromatic principal countersubject [bb. 82¹–83¹]). The combination is as follows:

Example 19

The cadence in A♭ has a one-bar restatement [bb. 83²–84¹], but {194} frustrated by a mixolydian inflection in the bass (G♭). The consequent [bb. 84²–89¹] is a free episode which makes three feints at b. (6) [bb. 85², 86³, 88¹], using a motif that cuts across the bar (making three bars of 4/2):

Example 20

and then comes metrically into line again as it flows back to the tonic key. *Period 2* [bb. 89¹–101] (starting at (8=1)): the subject returns in the bass in original form, against which the inversion appears in the alto starting on G♭ (such that it would fit with the inversion starting on F):

---

28   i.e. (bb. 78¹–) chords of C minor, G half-diminished seventh [= E♭ dominant seventh], A♭ major, D♭ with added major sixth, E♭ dominant seventh.

29   Riemann gives them reversed: *mit Terzen- bzw. Sextenverdopplung.*

Example 21

(2)   (4)

{195} The consequent [bb. 92²–95³] contains no statement of the subject, occupies a full four bars, and serves formally to establish the tonic key. The bass, however, at the last moment effects a deceptive cadence (G♭ instead of B♭), thereby necessitating a second consequent [bb. 96¹–101]. This introduces (at (8=5) [b. 96¹]) the final combination, a stretto of the subject (soprano) with inversion of the theme (tenor), each doubled by the remaining voices at the sixth and third respectively:[29]

Example 22

(6)   (8a)

Nobody could ever say of this fugue that it is sacrificed on the altar of contrapuntal artifice. Even the final combination is free, a direct outcome of the nature of the theme. A more doctrinaire logical next step after this last combination might have been for Bach to launch a stretto of the theme simultaneously with a stretto {196} of the inversion – and this would have been perfectly possible, indeed available in a number of different permutations of the voices:

Example 23

etc.

[See previous page for n.29]

He would have achieved no more by this than what a straightforward doubling in thirds would have yielded, which is what this combination comes down to in the end. Similarly, a number of three-part stretti could with ease have been effected:

Example 24

{197} etc. etc. For Bach to have renounced all such combinations as derive from these types of relationships and contented himself with just what he felt met the needs of the work's structure demonstrates once again the capacity of the true master to impose upon himself prudent limitations.

PART II

Technical analysis of form and style

Introduction

At the heart of fugue lies a primary mechanism: the rapid reiteration of a theme at discrete pitch levels among different voices. In the analyses presented in Part I, this mechanism was given several names: 'repercussion' (Lat. *repercussio*; Fr. *répercussion*; Ger. *Wiederschlag*), 'revolution' (Fr. *révolution*), 'exposition' (Ger. *Exposition*), and literally 'carrying through' (Ger. *Durchführung*). These four names embody two alternative views of the function of this mechanism.

'Repercussion' and 'revolution' both suggest *periodic visitation* to each voice-part by a single entity (the theme, in its two guises: subject and answer) – many images come to mind: the hour hand passing the numerals on a clock face, the year's seasonal rotation, the stations of the cross, or, in Momigny's delightful simile, the sun entering each of the signs of the zodiac in turn.[1] These two terms imply circuition or spiral rotation, or some kind of ritual revisiting. They thus suggest a closed time system. By contrast, 'exposition' and 'carrying through' both suggest *propulsion* of a theme on a journey, during which it is cast in various lights by its changing environment, or undergoes a series of experiences. Now such images come to mind – almost inevitably male-oriented, even phallic – as the hero undertaking exploits, the traveller on adventures, the youth undergoing initiation tests and the journey along the path of human life. These images imply linear motion; they suggest an open time system.

The German word *durchführen* had from the early eighteenth century (Heinichen, Scheibe, J. S. Bach) also signified the keeping in play of a theme (not necessarily the only theme) throughout the entire course of a composition.[2] At some point around 1800, possibly under the influence of Haydn's sonata structures, these two senses of *durchführen* – as monothematic fugal process, and as thematic retention – converged. The result was a monothematic, non-fugal compositional process. Old and new, fugal and non-fugal definitions are juxtaposed in Koch's *Musical Lexicon* of 1802:[3]

> *Durchführung*. By this term, most commonly used in fugue, is understood the respective imitation of the subject [*Hauptsatz*] of the fugue in all of the extant voices. *See* 'Fugue'. In pieces not composed in the stricter form of fugue, it is understood to

1 J.-J. de Momigny, *Cours complet*, vol. II (1805), p. 520. See also Marpurg's definition, 'Wiederschlag (Lat. repercussio): the name given to the order in which the subject and answer are stated in turn by the various voices' (*Abhandlung von der Fuge*, vol. I (1753), p. 18).
2 This discussion of development-related terms is derived largely from Siegfried Schmalzriedt, 'Durchführen, Durchführung' (1979), *HwMT*. See also ibid, 'Expositio' (1979), and Peter Cahn, 'Repercussio' (1981).
3 H. C. Koch, *Musikalisches Lexikon* (Frankfurt: Hermann, 1802; reprint edn Hildesheim: Olms, 1964), col. 506, 'Durchführung'.

denote adherence to the main idea [*Hauptgedanke*], and its constant reworking [*Bearbeitung*], in different guises or modifications.

In this definition (which was adopted *verbatim* by three other music dictionaries in the 1820s and 1830s), the mutation from formalized 'subject' to less-structured 'idea' is striking, as too is the change of implication that *durchführen* undergoes from restatement to constant transformation. From about this time, the verb took on some of the meaning of *entwickeln*, 'to unfold', and came into the orbit of the French *développer* and its English cognate 'to develop'.

The new language employed by Koch is to be found in many articles in the Leipzig *Allgemeine musikalische Zeitung*, not least in E. T. A. Hoffmann's analysis of Beethoven's Fifth Symphony (1810) (vol. II, Analysis 9). 'Idea' (*Gedanke*) and in particular 'main idea' (*Hauptgedanke*) frequently appear there, always to designate the four-note opening motif of the symphony in its original form or in some transformation. *Durchführen* and *entwickeln* come into close proximity in discussion of the finale (my italics):

> This theme [bb. 90–] is now *developed* for thirty-four bars, in abbreviated and stretto configurations, and during this *development* the character already apparent in its original guise *unfolds* fully . . .

Although there is still a remnant of fugal thinking in this passage, what happens to the theme is precisely the varying of guises or modifications (*Wendungen oder Modifikationen*) of which Koch spoke.

The French musical term *développement* extends some way back before 1800. Bernard Lacépède (1756–1825), in his *The Poetics of Music* of 1785, likened sonata form to the three overarching phases of a drama: presentation–complication–resolution. He portrayed the middle phase of a musical structure as 'developments, a type of intrigue'.[4] In 1805, Momigny described the first part of section II of sonata form as follows:[5]

> It is there above all that the genius must depend on technical skill [*science*]. It is there that must be developed all the richness that harmony possesses, all the profundity that counterpoint holds, and lastly all that is unexpected and ravishing in the magical art of modulation [*transitions*].

In 1814, Reicha used the term in a semi-formal sense:[6]

> Section II of this form [the large binary form, i.e. sonata form] can never be shorter than section I; but it can be longer by a third, even half; for section I is no more than the *exposition*, whilst section II is the *development* of that [. . .] In general, section II is made up of, and develops, the ideas of section I, especially in instrumental music . . .

Reicha defined 'to develop' as: 'to make something really big out of an idea, a phrase, a motif, or a theme'. He recounted and illustrated five methods of developing

---

4   Bernard Lacépède, *La poétique de la musique* (Paris, 1785, 2/1787), vol. II, p. 234.
5   J.-J. de Momigny, *Cours complet*, vol. II (1805), p. 387, embarking on section II of Mozart's String Quartet in D minor, K421/417b. Momigny used the phrase *exposition du sujet* in his analysis of Haydn's 'Drumroll' Symphony (vol. II, Analysis 8), but to designate his account of the pictorial subject-matter of the symphony rather than any formal feature.
6   A. Reicha, *Traité de mélodie* (Paris: Farrenc, 1814, 2/1832), pp. 41, 42 (my italics).

a motif, referring to these as 'Haydn's great secret'.[7] These methods are demonstrated in the analysis that he made in 1826 of an Andante for wind quintet (Analysis 9), a very early example of motivic analytical technique the 'modern' spirit of which contrasts strikingly with the non-developmental style of his analysis of Mozart's 'Non so più' made in 1814 (Analysis 8), akin as that is not only to the first half of Momigny's analysis of Haydn's 'Drumroll' Symphony from 1805 (vol. II, Analysis 8), but also to Koch's melodic analyses (1787, 1793). Twelve years later, in 1826, Reicha provided a structural diagram of sonata form, labelling section I 'exposition of the ideas' and the first part of section II as 'principal development, modulating continuously'. This diagram and its surrounding discussion of form is preceded by a miniature treatise on motivic development.[8]

In this way, terms denoting propulsive thematic unfolding and open time system eventually came to serve as labels – '*the* development section', '*die* Durchführung' – for a middle phase that contrasted structurally and temporally with the first and last phases, these latter made up of rounded units in closed time systems. This new conception led to the increasingly popular view of sonata form as ternary, the whole transformation graphically encapsulated in Marx's diagram (HS = main subject, SS = second subject, G = continuation, SZ = closing subject, or coda):[9]

Theil 1.	Theil 2.	Theil 3.
HS. SS. G. SZ.	——	HS. SS. G. SZ.

To put it in the jargon of the 1990s, the legitimizing of the developmental process within sonata form led to the reifying of a polarity between middle and outer sections that had not existed (if it ever had) since Haydn. It was perhaps out of awareness of this very reification that Lobe, when describing sonata form in the string quartet (Analysis 12), so studiously avoided the term *durchführen*, preferring near-synonyms such as *Ausführung* and *Verarbeitung*, and frequently deploying the powerful *umwandeln*, 'to transform'.

From the middle of the nineteenth century onwards, there appeared a growing stream of manuals devoted to matters of form, many of them employing analysis. What had been one of the many functions of the comprehensive multi-volume textbook of composition – as was the case with Marx's *Manual of Musical Composition* (vols. II and III: 1838, 1845), and with Czerny's *School of Practical Composition* (*c.*1848: Parts I–III) – now became the preserve of the independent textbook of form, the principal examples being Richter's *The Fundamentals of Musical Forms and Their Analysis* (1851), Widmann's *Theory of Form in Instrumental Music* (1862), Skuherský's *Concerning Musical Form* (1873), Bussler's *The Theory of Musical Form in Thirty-Three Exercises* (1878), Cornell's *The Theory and Practice of Musical Form* (1883), Jadassohn's *Forms in Musical Works Analysed* (1885), Riemann's *Theory of Musical Form* (1889), Prout's *Musical Form* (1893) and *Applied Forms* (1895) and Goetschius's *Complete Musical Analysis* (1889), *Models of the Principal Musical Forms* (1894), *The*

---

7 ibid, 61–5.
8 *Traité de haute composition musicale*, vol. II (Paris: Zetter, 1826), pp. 300, 234–95.
9 Marx, *Die Lehre von der musikalischen Komposition*, vol. III (Leipzig: B&H, 1845, 2/1848), p. 221.

Homophonic Forms of Musical Composition (1898) and other books. These culminated in Leichtentritt's paradigmatic *Theory of Musical Forms* (1911).[10]

It would be wrong to give the impression that music theory in the nineteenth century was obsessed solely with questions of form and process. It had at least as strong a concern with the nature of harmony. At first, its task was to come to terms with the harmonic language of the Viennese Classical composers – a language very different from that of the Italian, French and German Baroque on which much eighteenth-century harmonic theory was predicated: a language that no longer dealt in vertical sound-slices, each slice expressible in terms of intervals measured upwards from the bass, but rather a language dealing in harmonic functions that could last for long time spans, functions governed and determined by a syntax in which not only pitch structures but also rhythm and metre, phraseology, and even form, partook. Thereafter, its task was to take account of the rapid expansion of harmonic language that occurred throughout the century. As Gottfried Weber said in 1817: by comparison with the other arts, in which theory had kept pace with practice, 'in the case of our art, the lead that practical composition, which has risen to such glorious heights during the last few decades, has over compositional theory, which is still in so rudimentary a state, is out of all proportion'.[11]

Weber himself made a very significant contribution to harmonic theory at the beginning of the century. Denying any acoustical basis for tonal harmony, and rejecting harmonic generation (as we saw in the General Introduction, above), in his eminently practical *Attempt at a Systematic Theory of Musical Composition* (1817–21) he enumerated seven 'fundamental harmonies' that formed the basis of all of the 'almost infinite variety of chords' that occur at the surface of music. To these seven could be referred all musically viable simultaneities of notes. Surface simultaneities differed from their fundamental harmonies – which were thought of as situated not within a fundamental bass, but simply on the ordered notes of the diatonic scale of each key, the 'scale-degrees' – by respacing of existing notes, by chromatic alteration of those notes, and by addition and omission. Moreover, surface simultaneities could often be referred equally well not just to one, but to two or even more fundamental harmonies in different keys, giving rise to the all-important and near-ubiquitous phenomenon of 'ambiguity', a phenomenon that furnished a theoretical basis for the psychological experiences of expectation, satisfaction and disappointment.

Weber chose to represent these fundamental harmonies by a symbol-system of great simplicity and power. For this purpose, he had appropriated an innovative though rudimentary device from Abbé Vogler that can be seen in the last line of the table in Analysis 7. The line above that presents not a 'fundamental bass' (which would have implied procedural rules and generation), but rather a succession simply of 'Roots' (*Hauptklänge*). Beneath each root – back in the bottom line – is a Roman numeral identifying the scale-degree on which the root is situated,

---

10   For details of these and other works cited only by title and date, see the Bibliographical Essay at the end of this volume.

11   Gottfried Weber, *Versuch einer geordneten Theorie der Tonsezkunst*, vol. 1 (Mainz: B. Schott, 1817), Vorwort.

this itself inferring the key to which that root belongs. Taking over the device of the Roman numeral, Weber turned it into a composite symbol, packing more information into it by the use of modifiers in order to signal whether a triad was major, minor or diminished, whether it had a seventh, and if so what type of seventh. He applied these modifiers also directly to the letters denoting roots. Examples of cases relating to numerals and letters can be seen in Analysis 10. This system was capable of representing all seven fundamental harmonies, and of showing them in any context, by root or by scale-degree.

At the same time, the sheer efficiency of the system, the very independence of the symbols, threw emphasis onto what historians of theory have come to call 'chord-quality' – that is, the individual character of a chord rather than the place that it occupies in a progression. The influence of this shift can be seen in many subsequent manuals, perhaps above all in the *Textbook of Harmony* (1853) of Ernst Friedrich Richter, in which Weber's symbols were adopted and the augmented triad was admitted as a fundamental chord. This widely circulated manual went through at least thirty-six editions, and was translated into French, Italian, Spanish, Danish, Dutch, Russian and several times into English, influencing music pedagogy for the best part of a century. The result of this shift of emphasis, and of developments in French harmonic theory by Catel, Choron, Fétis and others, was a greater preparedness to probe the workings of chromatic harmony as practised by Schumann, Chopin, Mendelssohn and their contemporaries. Other such manuals were the monographs on the augmented triad and diminished seventh chord (1853, 1854) by Carl Friedrich Weitzmann, advocate of the music of Liszt and Wagner, and author of a treatise entitled *The New Harmonic Theory in Conflict with the Old* (1861), and Salomon Jadassohn's *Textbook of Harmony* (1883) and *Melody and Harmony in the Music of Richard Wagner* (1899). Both theorists perpetuated Weber's symbol-system.

The harmonic style of Wagner constituted the challenge *par excellence* to theorists, a challenge taken up not only by Weitzmann and Jadassohn, but also by a succession of theorists belonging to a tradition very different from that of Gottfried Weber. The first of these were the Viennese theorists Cyrill Kistler, adherent of Moritz Hauptmann's dialectical theory of harmony, and Karl Mayrberger, who brought a mixture of theoretical tenets from Hauptmann and Sechter to bear on *Tristan and Isolde* (Analysis 13). After these, and influenced by them, were Cyrill Hynais and Josef Schalk, both former students of Bruckner. Significant advances after the turn of the century were made by Rudolf Louis and Ludwig Thuille, their joint *Theory of Harmony* (1907) dealing extensively with the harmonic styles of Brahms, Wagner and Richard Strauss, this whole line of enquiry culminating in Ernst Kurth's massive study, *Romantic Harmony and its Crisis in Wagner's 'Tristan'* (1920).

Georg Joseph Vogler (1749–1814)
'[Prelude] Nro. 8'

Zwei und dreisig Präludien . . . nebst einer Zergliederung (1806)

Midway through this extraordinarily interesting analysis, Vogler presents a 'segmentation into periods'. Though it uses terms familiar from the vocabulary of Heinrich Christoph Koch (*Versuch*, 1787, 1793), and though these two writers have not only terms but also concepts in common, the linkages between the terminological and conceptual planes do not conform.[1]

The differences, however, go deeper. Koch thinks hierarchically: his 'incises' *nest within* the phrase, his phrases (*Sätze*) *within* the period. Vogler thinks along a single time line: his 'phrases' (*Rhythmen*) are simply *shorter than* periods, coexisting but not partitioning them (analogous to Lobe's use of *Satz* alongside *Periode* (Analysis 12)); any markedly shorter unit finds him unprepared, leaving him to resort to metaphor ('aphorism') or neutral measurement ('bar'). Moreover, for Koch the 'period' is an enclosed sense-unit, interiorly clustered, and in turn clustering within overarching sections. Vogler's notion of structure is quite different from this. Like a series of relays in an electrical circuit, his 'units' (*Sätze*) extend contiguously from the beginning, to an end that is not initially determinable. The first of these units has the status of 'model, theme and initial groundplan'; the remainder are 'ensuing units'.

The entire segmentation is located within something essentially different: an analysis of *harmonic logic*. This is why it peters out after b. 73 (the restatement of b. 29), at which point the tonic key has finally been re-established; this is why it never exhibits any concern with intrinsically phrase-structural matters (it turns a blind eye to a nine-bar formation, bb. 21–9, describing it as 'metrical and regularly constructed'). Harmonic logic – the real issue here – is analysed in two stages: first the detailed operation of harmonies – beat to beat and bar to bar, as disclosed by the table of roots and figurings; secondly the teleology of these harmonies, that is, the goal-centred succession of tonal centres. For the latter, the segmentation into periods and phrases provides a structural scaffold, carrying the reader through the furthest tonal extremity of E♭ and arriving at the most *frappant* moment: the implied thirteenth-chords in bb. 73 and 74.

---

1 For subdivision of the 'period', Vogler (perhaps under French influence) uses *Rhythmus* (the term Koch uses for 'periodicity') whereas Koch uses at the upper level *Satz* (a term that Vogler uses here either for 'material' or 'subject', or neutrally 'unit') and at the lower level *Einschnitt* (the term Vogler uses for 'caesura', for which Koch has *Cäsur*). Vogler uses *der Period* at the notional four-bar level, whereas Koch uses *die Periode* (they disagree even on gender) at the notional eight-bar level. The central constructional unit, in both cases notionally four bars in length, is for Vogler the *Period* and for Koch the *Satz*.

The table just referred to is a fascinating hybrid. In one sense, it belongs to the lineage of multi-stave fundamental-bass gràphings described above in the Introduction to Part I, which stretches from Rameau (1722), through Kirnberger (1771) and Schulz (1773) to Momigny (1805) and Reicha (?1816–18), in that the musical original represented at the top is reprocessed in the lower layers of the table. Not that this is a true fundamental-bass analysis: it has no concern with bass progression, merely with roots; and the resultant data are scale-degrees. The table uses not staff but figured-bass notation (which lends it the superficial appearance of a keyboard tablature), and yet negates the very principle of figured-bass thought by interpreting the vertical sonorities in terms of roots and then rewriting the figurings as chords of those roots. It is perhaps best described, then, as the interpretation of (a) an initial figured-bass stratum (b) in fundamental-bass terms, which then returns to the realm of figured-bass thought by (c) rewriting the figures, and then (d) converting the roots into scale-degrees, these latter in turn implying (e) a succession of tonal centres that forms an invisible final analytical layer.

Vogler's overall agenda (see the General Introduction, above, on analytical agendas) comprises three items: (1) rhetoric, (2) harmonic logic, (3) aesthetics. To conceptualize a piece of music as a 'rhetorical discourse' (*Gang der Rede*) would seem to be to identify its author with the Baroque analytical disposition. Traces of the latter indeed appear: the *Epiphonema* which concludes a discourse in a spectacular way; the *Anlage* (also *Entwurf*) or 'groundplan' from which a finished composition is elaborated; the *suspensio*, or 'digression' strategically placed just before the conclusion. On the other hand, his perception of musical structure is as a discourse that constantly augments itself from within (*oratio crescit eundo*);[2] he holds a surprisingly modern view, conceiving structure as 'tension' (*Spannung*) progressively built up and then released, this leading inexorably to conclusion. To be sure, Vogler's paradigm for musical structure was that quintessentially Baroque form, the fugue, and its ideal type the Handelian vocal fugue; but fugue, while open in form, was nonetheless punctuated by structural norms and expectations.

However, Prelude No. 8 (reproduced in full in the Appendix) is only a quasi-fugue in which orthodox expositions and episodes have been dispensed with (indeed, it is precisely because the prelude lacks either clear fugal structure or truly independent part-writing that Vogler's analysis of it has been included in Part II of the present volume rather than Part I). Invoking the established term *fuga d'imitazione*, Vogler claims that the prelude achieves the ends of fugue while jettisoning most of the means. 'Free or imitating fugues' (*fugae liberae sive imitantes*) were defined in 1650 in Athanasius Kircher's *Musurgia universalis* as fugues 'that do not adhere so closely to the rigorous laws as do strict fugues and canons [. . .] but wander at will hither and thither, [entries] answering each other now at the beginning, now at the middle, now at the end . . .'[3] Padre Martini, in his *Examples*

2 *System für den Fugenbau als Einleitung zur harmonischen Gesang-Verbindungs-Lehre* (Offenbach: André, c.1817), 72.
3 *Musurgia universalis sive ars magna consoni et dissoni . . .* (Rome: Corbelletti, 1650), Book V, p. 393.

of 1775, provided a separate discussion of *fuga d'imitazione*: inferior in rank to strict fugue but more pleasing and grateful to the ear, it was freer in that the answer must correspond only in some, not in all, respects to the subject, and in that there was no prescribed distance or interval at which the one must answer the other.[4] It is the remainder of Martini's statement, however, that explains those final words of Kircher, and at the same time casts light on Vogler's own prelude:

> If the *subject* be made up of several segments [*parti*], it will be possible in the course of the fugue to reintroduce one or another of these segments, with mutual answering of one or another, such that a contest will result among the segments, and in this manner pleasure and delight will be restored.

The subject of Vogler's prelude (like that of the example that Martini gives) is subdivisible into segments in just such a way. It is also implicitly in three voices (Vogler does not even explain this away, as well he might have done, as a simultaneous double fugue, the lower voice moving mostly in thirds). The result is a subject well supplied with motivic materials for development, which Vogler fragments, uses in imitation and builds up to a remarkable climax.

Because Vogler's view of structure, then, is of an open-ended, forward-streaming musical phraseology, rather than either the exposition–episode alternation of late Baroque and Classical fugue, or the striated phrase hierarchy typical of Viennese Classical forms, Vogler wrote in terms extraordinarily well adapted to interpreting the new structures of the early nineteenth century. The *Thema* of fugue (in the eighteenth century, an amalgam of subject and answer) is here liberated to become the 'theme' of a progressively unfolding melodic structure. The relays are activated in five distinct ways – repetition, transposition, proliferation, elaboration and development – that uncannily adumbrate the processes of Beethovenian thematic evolution, guaranteeing internal genesis (*ex visceribus causae*) for all that arises.

Elsewhere, Vogler defined aesthetics as 'the science of disposing [or analysing] feelings' (*die Zergliederungs-Wissenschaft der Empfindungen*).[5] 'Feelings' here implies not emotions, but rather fluid states of mind. If this third item on his agenda seems to lack character, it is because aesthetics is a series of controls upon the operations of items 1 and 2: it ensures that everything is done without mannerism or extraneous agency, that discourse and logic are effected in the most convincing manner.[6] Ultimately, it is the watchdog of teleology. It falls to aesthetics to perform an act of what we might in modern jargon call damage limitation, for the piece undeniably breaks the 'one single law for modulation' by moving further than one flat or sharp away from the home key. Vogler, with a technical wizardry which is at the same time an astonishing insight, accounts for the extended E♭ major passage bb. 57–64 as a mere dwelling-upon a single chord that is perfectly accepted within D minor: the E♭ triad in first inversion. At one stroke he identifies without name the Neapolitan sixth chord, tonicization and prolongation!

4 Giovanni Battista Martini, *Esemplare o sia saggio fondamentale pratico di contrapunto* (Bologna: Volpe, 1774–5; reprint edn Ridgewood: Gregg, 1965), vol. II, pp. xxxii–xxxiii.
5 *System*, 23. *Zergliederung* can be seen in either its active or its reflective capacities here. See General Introduction, above.
6 'If an aesthetician wishes to let his feeling [*Empfindung*] speak, then it is conviction [*Ueberzeugung*] that should be the order of the day' (ibid, 74).

While employed as chaplain to the Mannheim court in the early 1770s, Georg Joseph Vogler was sent to Italy for musical studies and there worked with Padre Martini and Francesco Antonio Vallotti, the latter making a great impact on him. In 1775 he founded his Mannheim School of Music, setting out the musical theories on which the School was based in a succession of publications: *The Science of Music and the Art of Composition* (1776 – 'more useful for teaching arithmetic than for teaching composition', Mozart wrote in 1777), *The Kuhrpfalz School of Music* (1778) and the monthly periodical *Reflections of the Mannheim School of Music* (1778–81), the last of which contained pioneering analyses of his own works and those of contemporaries such as the Mannheim composer Peter Winter, as well as 'improvements' of works by J. S. Bach and others, including Pergolesi's *Stabat mater*.[7]

Vogler subsequently spent a decade in the service of the King of Sweden, followed by years of travel as a keyboard recitalist and advocate of reform in organ tuning and design during which he published many theoretical works. Most notable among these was his *Handbook of Harmonic Theory and of Thoroughbass* (1802), in which he brought to fruition his theory of 'reduction' (*Redukzion*), whereby the entire surface fabric of a composition could be restated in terms of root-position triads, each represented as a Roman numeral, and also his theory of modulation by pivot-chords, involving tonal 'ambiguity' (*Mehrdeutigkeit*). Both of these aspects of his theory had a significant influence upon Gottfried Weber (Analysis 10), hence upon the course of German nineteenth-century harmonic theory. From this period also came the *Thirty-two Preludes for Organ or Piano* and their analyses (1806), from which the analysis below is taken. These 1806 analyses, as their subtitle indicates, serve as a practical appendix to the 1802 *Handbook*. Vogler spent the final years of his life as director of music at the ducal court in Darmstadt, also publishing his *Analytical Edition of the Setting of the Penitential Psalms* (1807) and *System for Fugal Construction* (?1811).[8]

7   *Tonwissenschaft und Tonsetzkunst* (Mannheim: Kurfürstliche Hofbuchdruckerei, 1776; reprint edn Hildesheim: Olms, 1970); *Kuhrpfälzische Tonschule* (Mannheim: Schwan & Götz, 1778); *Betrachtungen der Mannheimer Tonschule*, vols. I–III (Mannheim, 1778–81; reprint edn Hildesheim: Olms, 1974); Emily Anderson, ed., *Letters of Mozart and his Family* (London: Macmillan, 1938, 2/1966), vol. I, pp. 369–70 (13 November 1777). For excellent accounts of Vogler's life and work, see Margaret H. Grave in *NGDM*, and Floyd K. and Margaret H. Grave, *In Praise of Harmony: The Teachings of Abbé Georg Joseph Vogler* (Lincoln: University of Nebraska Press, 1987).
8   *Handbuch zur Harmonielehre und für den Generalbass, nach den Grundsätze der Mannheimer Tonschule . . .* (Prague: Barth, 1802); *Zergliederung der musikalischen Bearbeitung der Busspsalmen* (Munich, 1807).

[Vogler: Prelude] No. 8 [in D minor]

Thirty-two Preludes for Organ or Piano, together with an Aesthetic, Rhetorical and Harmonic Analysis . . .

Source:
'Nro. 8', *Zwei und dreisig Präludien für die Orgel und für das Fortepiano: nebst einer Zergliederung in ästhetischer, rhetorischer und harmonischer Rücksicht, mit praktischem Bezug auf das Handbuch der Tonlehre von Abt Vogler* (Munich: Falter, 1806), 18–29.

This piece of music, in strictly contrapuntal style, moreover fugal in treatment, calls for consideration in three separate respects: (1) as a rhetorical *fuga d'imitazione*, (2) as a meticulously constructed harmonic series of modulations, (3) as a not infelicitous assortment of aesthetic delights.[9]

(1) It is perfectly possible to link together units in strict counterpoint without producing a fugue in the orthodox sense. Precisely by avoiding the tedium of routine [fugal] entries, entries that oftentimes become tiresome even before the stretto is concluded,[10] a greater concentration is achieved, and a greater freshness maintained, because there is less of the conventional about it. In this way, means and ends[11] are kept separate; ends are achieved without resort to hackneyed means. When contrapuntal imitations, alternating allusions to one and the same subject [*Satz*], proliferate, develop and elaborate[12] the theme in a constant and logical stream, a fugue results, a strict fugue, and yet not a fugue by conventional

---

9   *ästhetische Unterhaltungen*: under influence from French *entretenir*, *soutenir* and *diversion* in the late eighteenth century, *unterhalten* came to mean not only 'support' but also 'maintain', hence by extension to 'pass the time pleasurably' (including 'converse'), and 'entertain' In *System für den Fugenbau*, Vogler defines his three 'aspects' as 'rhetoric'='the art of discourse [*Redekunst*]', 'logic'='the art of conclusion [*Schlusskunst*]' and 'aesthetics'='the theory of feelings [*Empfindungs-Theorie*]' (p. 70). He amplifies the last: 'aesthetics, which concerns delight as well as persuasion [*Ueberzeugung*] and feeling [*Gefühl*]'. Of these, 'delight' recurs later under (3), and 'persuasion' under (3)(c) and after 3(g).

10   *noch eh die Spannung befriedigt wird*: Vogler appears to associate *Spannung* ('tension') with the rhetorical device *suspensio*, a skilfully timed digression which delays the conclusion only to make it ultimately the more powerful. In the master's fugue of *System* (p. 74), the *suspensio* takes the form of a stretto on a fragment of the subject at the half-bar in all four voices, of which he remarks 'a general tension spreads over [the passage]'.

11   [Vogler:] I still well remember the time when double counterpoint was considered the ultimate end of musical composition, and was associated with formal models that had sanctioned slavish con-formity and sedulously fostered blind orthodoxy. [I have taken sing. *hatte* for plural *hatten*, here.]

12   *fort-, durch- und ausführen*. For Vogler in 1779 (*Betrachtungen*, vol. II, pp. 366–7), the generic term *componere*, signifying 'to place together', was subdivisible into four distinct subprocesses: *wiederholen* ('to repeat'), *versezen* ('to transpose'), *fortführen* ('to proliferate') and *ausführen* ('to elaborate'). He distinguished three of them succinctly: 'To transpose is to present the same at different pitches, to elaborate is to present the same in different guises [*Gestalten*], to proliferate is to present different [material] in the same guise. This should be sufficient to illuminate the present-day symphony.' *Fortführen* is thus associative free invention: 'to devise ideas that, having a close affinity and kinship to what precedes them, promote manifold unity. This [new] material has never appeared before, thus is not a repetition.' Later, c.1817, Vogler added a fifth sub-process, *durchführen* ('to develop'):

formal models [*Formen*]. A masterpiece of this inimitable[13] type we call an 'imitation', or *fuga d'imitazione*. Under this modest mantle, I do not deny, has often been cloaked the work of bungling incompetents. Whether this [Prelude] No. 8 {19} is worthy of emulation[14] I cannot say. I merely make the claim for this new verity that something that is not strict in appearance or name as regards formal models and routine conventions may yet be counted more purposeful, more inspired in effect as regards its treatment of mechanical procedures.

I shall begin by unravelling all the interrelationships between the ensuing units and the model [*Vortrag*], the theme and the initial groundplan [*Entwürffe*].

The first period comprises four bars, and is played in three parts by the left hand. The second period, which begins at b. 5, does not answer it, but bears a relationship to it, its two upper voices forming a double counterpoint at the tenth [*in der Dez*], its two lower accompanying voices likewise supplying double counterpoint at the tenth.

Relationships to b. 1 exist as follows:

bb. 5, 9, 11, 13, 17, 24, 30, 32, 34, 36, 38, 40, 42, 43, 44, 45, 46, 47, 50, 61, 68, 72, 80, 81, 82, 83, 84: hence twenty-eight mutually analogous bars in all.

Relationships to bb. 1^3–2^2 exist at bb. 2^3–3^2, and also at:[15]

bb. 5^3–6^2, 6^3–7^2, 13^3–14^2, 14^3–15^2, 15^3–16^2, 17^3–18^2, 18^3–19^2, 19^3–20^2, 20^3–21^2, 21^3–22^2, 22^3–23^2, 25^3–26^2, 26^3–27^2, 27^3–28^2, 30^3–31^2, 32^3–33^2, 34^3–35^2, 36^3–37^2, 38^3–39^2, 40^3–41^2, 44^3–45^2, 46^3–47^2, 50^3–51^2, 51^3–52^2, 52^3–53^2, 53^3–54^2, 54^3–55^2, 55^3–56^2, 56^3–57^2, 57^3–58^2, 58^3–59^2, 59^3–60^2, 61^3–62^2, 62^3–63^2, 63^3–64^2, 64^3–65^2, 65^3–66^2, 66^3–67^2, 68^3–69^2, 69^3–70^2, 70^3–71^2, 71^3–72^2, 72^3–73^2, 73^3–74^2, 74^3–75^2, 75^3–76^2, 80^3–81^2, 81^3–82^2, 82^3–83^2, 83^3–84^2: hence fifty-two mutually analogous bars in all.

Relationships to bb. 1–2 exist as follows:[16]

bb. 5–6, 13–14, 17–18, 30–31, 32–3, 34–5, 36–7, 38–9, 40–41, 61–2, 72–3, 80–81, 82–3: hence twenty-eight mutually analogous bars in all.

Relationships to bb. 1–3 exist as follows:

bb. 5–6–7, 13–14–15, 17–18–19, 61–62–63: hence fifteen mutually analogous bars in all.

{20} Relationships to the melodic line of b. 4 exist in the alto part at bb. 10 and 12.

The four-part harmony that first occurred in bb. 13–28, partly in C major, partly in A minor, occurs again in bb. 58–71, partly in E♭ major, partly in D minor. It is

By 'proliferate' I understand [. . .] a homogeneous succession of the main thematic ideas, all of which are derived [*entlehnt*] from the opening unit [*Sazze*], but more appropriately continued rather than recast or elaborated [. . .] By 'develop' I understand the bald juxtaposition of the principal ideas [*Hauptideen*], in a context that would appear totally unsuited to such a combination [. . .] Variety [hence 'elaboration'] consists in maintaining the original outline, but subjecting it to combination with new elements, forms and keys, reharmonizations, modulations, etc. (*System*, 66–7)

13   *unnachahmliches*: Vogler perhaps intended a play on words.
14   *nachahmungswürdig*, lit. 'worthy of imitation'.
15   Within the list, Vogler refers by single bar number. Each case has been editorially rendered specific, e.g. his '6' amplified to '5^3–6^2' and so forth (without square brackets).
16   In the following two lists, bars are listed individually in the original, without the editorially supplied en-rules: '5. 6. 13. 14.' etc, and '5. 6. 7. 13. 14. 15.' etc.

not E♭ major to D minor that corresponds with C major to A minor, but E♭ major to C minor; because of this, a deceptive, artful, unobtrusively modulating key-progression [*Tonfolge*] from E♭ to D has to be manoeuvred.[17] Compare:

> b. 63[3–64²] with b. 19[3–20²]
>
> b. 64[3–65²] with b. 20[3–21²].

Relationships to the movement of the lower voices in b. 8 exist as follows: (1) the bass of bb. 24, 68, 76, 78, 82, 84, 85; (2) the middle voice of bb. 25, 69, 76, 78; (3) the upper melodic line of the whole bar[18] in bb. 22, 23, 27, 28, 31, 33, 35, 37, 39, 41, 65, 66, 67, 70, 71, 72, 81, 83, 85: hence once again twenty[19] mutually analogous bars.

In order to crown this strict set of relationships, involving an elaborately worked theme that makes its presence felt at more than 150 points, with a conclusion that derives convincingly *ex visceribus causae*, what was needed was a further bifurcation of melodic relationships over the same harmonies. Thus it is that in the concluding section at b. 72[–3] the soprano recalls b. 28[–9] while the bass reinvokes bb. 1–2; in bb. 81 and 83 the soprano recalls b. 28 while the bass recaptures b. 1, and in bb. 82 and 84 the soprano recalls b. 1 while the bass recaptures b. 28.

(2) Beneath the figured lowest voice, or bass, I have set out the roots, identifying them by Roman numerals, thus rendering the key-progression readily interpretable without elucidatory commentary. Now, thanks to this, I need only carry out a segmentation into periods [*periodologische Eintheilung*]. This in itself will provide a link [backwards] from the present issue {21} to that of rhetorical foundations, and prepare the way for aesthetic considerations.

The first two periods, each of four bars, furnish the model [*Vortrag*]. The two-bar phrase [*Rhythmus*] beginning at b. 9 modulates [*lenkt ein*] into F major. The two-bar phrase at b. 11 modulates into A minor.

C major is the prevailing key throughout bb. 13–203; A minor prevails throughout bb. 21–9 and at the same time brings section I to a close with this metrical and regularly constructed development.[20] This observation should give the lie to the old delusion that the more confusing a fugue is, the more learned one should imagine it to be.[21]

17   *eine betrügerische, täuschende, unvermerkt abweichende Tonfolge vom Es ins D einlenken*: the implication of *unvermerkt abweichend* is that a remote modulation (from a three-flat to a one-flat key signature, as against the neutral-to-neutral modulation in bb. 13–28) should not be perceived as remote but rather as a neighbouring modulation (*Uebergang*). The presence of two words signifying modulation here, *abweichend* and *einlenken*, suggests the two-level process involved: E♭–D minor is a modulation *upon* the modulation C–A minor.

18   [Vogler:] I say 'of the whole bar' here since previously where an analogy or relationship has existed between one bar and another, the bar unit has started with the third crotchet and extended through to the second crotchet of the following.

19   '20' refers only to (3): the total number of bars in the network comprising b. 8 and (1), (2) and (3) is 28. Moreover, Vogler overlooks bb. 21 and 26 in the upper line, hence 30 *in toto*.

20   *in dieser metrischen, genau zugeschnittenen Arbeit*: Vogler here disguises his awareness (later revealed in another context: see notes 30 and 34) of the irregularity of bb. 21–9: a *nine*-bar unit. One way of viewing this is that b. 24 has been expanded to two bars, bb. 24–5.

21   Cf. 'People used to believe that the more confusing a fugue, the more learned it was, because by "counterpoint" they understood something contrary, something very ingenious but alien to the ear and to nature' (*System*, 23).

The contrapuntal tug-of-war that rages between the player's two hands in bb. 30–42, casting each hand in the role of an antiphonal three-voice chorus, comprises a very simple key-progression. After the initial pair of two-bar phrases in C major, two further phrases revert with the same material at b. 34 to A minor, and then two more at b. 38 in F major.

Between b. 42 and b. 48 we have, so to speak, aphorisms where before we had full sentences – fewer words, but more telling ones, trenchant and meaningful, such that each bar speaks distinctively, contributing to the contrapuntal fabric an imitative entry as well as a modulation [Ausweichung] in its own right.

Bb. 29 and 49 both end in A minor, the former with a cadence [Schlussfall][22] from V to I, the latter from I to V.

At b. 49 a modulation, deriving from existing material, is set in motion, which starts in A minor and reaches E♭ minor[23] by b. 57, then picking up in E♭ major at b. 57³ the selfsame material [Satz] that had appeared in C major at b. 13³.[24]

Of far-flung modulations and enharmonic shifts there is no trace here. All the more striking to ear and eye are the dissonances [Uebelklänge] between bass and pedal-point: for example, {22} the thirteenth in bb. 73 and 74, especially when we look at the figuring for the bass line that derives from this, and which looks entirely consonant.[25] The B♭ bears the figures 5 and 3: only the preparation and resolution betray the fact that B♭ cannot be the root. In my Summa of Harmony, which stems from my monthly journal for the year 1780,[26] and has appeared in a new edition the place of publication of which I do not know, but most excellently of all in the copper-engraved Table I of my Handbook of Harmony,[27] can be found in a clear and graded presentation all the possible types of figuring.

Here follows the detailed table for [Prelude] No. 8.

	1	2	3	4	5	6	7
						6 5 –	9 8
						4 3 –	7 6#
	5 6		6 5 7	4	5	5 – –	5♮
	3♮	7 6	4 – 3#	5 5 3♮	3♮ 7♭	3♮ – –	3♮
Bass-line	D –	C# – D	A –	D A D	D C#	D –	E – C#
		9 8	13 12 7	11 – 10		13 12 –	11 10
		3# –	11 – 10#	9 – 8		11 10 –	9 8#
Roots	D B♭	A – D	A –	D – –		D	C# –
	I VI	V – I	V	I	VII#	I	VII#

22 'Schlussfall or Tonschluss, see Cadenz.': Koch: Musikalisches Lexikon (1802).

23 Presumably Vogler means that E♭ minor is implied in bb. 57–8 by the g♭ in b. 56, though in fact E♭ materializes only as major, in b. 58. Later, Vogler claims that the farthest-flung key of the piece from D minor is E♭ major.

24 'at b. 58 . . . at b. 13'.

25 harmonisch: [Vogler:] It appears purely consonant because the fifth of the root D is absent. Compare the situation in bb. 73 and 74 with that in b. 75, where the major seventh, i.e. the fifth of the root D, arises there against the B♭.

26 Original reads '1776': the work is dated '15 June 1780': 'Summe der Harmonik', Betrachtungen, vol. III (1780–81), pp. 1–117 (text), vol. IV (1781–2) Gegenstände der Betrachtungen, [pp. 318–32] (plates).

27 [Vogler:] That I had published in Prague for my public lectures on the science of music, aesthetics and acoustics in the acoustic Orchestrions-Saal of the Karl Ferdinand University.

Bars 8–15

	8	9	10	11	12	13	14	15
	4 – 8	5 6	4 3		4 3#	5	4 3	4 3♮ –
	9 – 6	3♮ –	5 –	5 6	5♮ –	5♮ 6	5 – 6#	5 – –
Bass-line	D E F	D –	C –	F –	E –	C B	C – A	G – –
	11 – 10	5	11 10		11 10#	7	11 10 5♮	11 10♮7
	9 – 8					3♮		–
Roots	D – –	B♭	C –		D E –	G	C – F#	G – –
	I	VI IV	V	I IV	V	I V	I IV#	V

Bars 16–22

	16	17	18	19	20	21	22
	5 4			7	5 3♮	4 3	4 3
	6 – 3♮	5	4 3	4 3♮ –	6 6♮		6♮
	4 –	5 6	5 – 6#	5 – –	4 6 4#	6 – 7♮	5 –
Bass-line	G –	C B	C – A	G – –	G E D	C – G#	A – D
	9 8 3♮	7	11 10 5♮	11 10♮ 7	9 8 7♮	13 12	5♮
		3♮					
Roots	C – G	G	C – F#	G – –	C G#	A –	B
	I V	I V	I IV#	V	I VII#	I VII#	I II

Bars 23–29

	23	24	25	26	27	28	29
	5♮ 4 7	6	6♭ 3♮				
	6 5♮	5 4 6♭	6♮	4 3	4 3	5♮ 4 7	
	4 – 3#	2	4#	6 – 7♮	5 – 6♮	6 – 3#	3♮
Bass-line	E – –	F E♭ D	D –	C – G#	A – D	E – –	A
	7		5 7	13 12	11 10 5♮	7	
	9♮ 8 3#	7♭	3♮			9♮ 8 3#	
Roots	A – E	F – B♭	B♭ G#	A –	A – B	A – E	I
	I V	VI V I	VII#	I	VII#	II	I V

Bars 30–43

	30 / 32	31 / 33	34 / 36	35 / 37	38 / 40	39 / 41	42	43
	5 6	7 6 5	5 6	7♮ 6 5	5 6	7 6 5	5 6	4 3 7♭
Bass-line	C –	B – –	A –	G# – –	F –	E – –	F D	C – F#
		7		7				
	3♮	7 3♮ –	7♮ 3# –	5 3♮	7 5 7♭	5	11 10	
Roots	A	B G –	F	G# E –	F D	E C –	B♭	C
	I VI	VII V	I VI	VII# V	I VI	VII V	I IV	V VII#

	44	45	46	47	48	49	50		51	
					7			3	–	6	7
	5	6	7		4	3♯	6	5♮	6	5♮	5	6	–	4♮	5♮
	3♭	4	3♯	3♮	3♮	6	5♮	–	4	3♯	4	3♯		4♭	4♮	2♯	3♯
Bass-line	G	E♭	D	–	G♯	A	F	E	–	–	E	–	E	F	–	F	–	E
												–		7♮
		3♭	11	10♯		3♮	11	10♯	3♮		3♮		7	7	3♮
Roots		C	D	–		D	E	–	A	A		F	B♭	B	G♯
	I	IV	V	VII♯	I	IV	V		I	V	I	V	I	IV	II	VII♯	V

	52		53		54		55		56		57		58		59	
	7	3	3		7	3	3		7	3♭	3♭		7♭	6	3♭	4	3
	5♭	6♯	6	7	5♭	6♮	6♭	7♭	5♭	6♮	6♭	7♭	6	–			7♭
	3♮	4	4	3♯	3♮	4	4	3♮	3♭	4	4	3♮	4♭	–	6♮	5	–
Bass-line	E	–	E♭	D	D	–	D♭	C	C	–	C♭	B♭	B♭	–	C	B♭	–	–
			7				7				7♭					
		3♯	5♭			3♮	5♭				5♭				11	10
		3♮				3♭			7♭	3♭	11♭	10	5♭		7♭
Roots	A	A		G	G		F	F	E♭	A	B♭	–	–
	II	V	II	V	II	V	II	V	II	V	II	V	I	IV♯	V
											VII	I	V

	60		61		62		63		64		65		66	
	5	4♭		5♭				6	7	6♭	3♭				
	6	–	5	5♭	5♭	4♭	3	3♭	4♭	3	4	6♮	4	3	4	3
	4♭	–	3	6	5	–	6♮	5	–	2	6♭	–	4♯	6	–	7♭	5	–	6♮
Bass-line	B♭	–	–	E♭	D	E♭	–	C	B♭	–	A♭	G	–	–	F	–	C♯	D	–	G
										9	8♭	7♭			
	9	8	5	7♭	11♭	10	5♭	11♭	10	7♭	3♮	13	12	11	10	5♭
Roots	E♭	–	B♭	B♭	E♭	–	A	B♭	–	–	E♭	–	C♯	D	–	D	–	E
	I	V	I	V	I	IV♯	V	I	VII♯	I	VII♯	I	II
			VII	I	V

	67		68		69		70		71		72		73	
													74	
	5	4	7	6			3♭					5	4	6		6
	6	–	5	4	6♭	6♮	4	3	4	3	6	–	4	5	6	4
	4	–	3♯	5	2	6♭	4♯	6	–	7♭	5	–	6	4	–	2♯	3	4	2♯
Bass-line	A	–	–	B♭	A♭	G	G	–	F	C♯	D	–	G	A	–	B♭	B♭	A	B♭
						7♭								
	9	8	7♭	3♮	13	12	11	10	5♭	9	8	7♭	13	12	7♭
Roots	D	–	B♭	E♭	E♭	C♯	D	–	–	D	E	D	–	C♯	D	–	C♯
	I	V	VI	V	I	VII♯	I	VII♯	I	II	I	VII♯	I	VII♯

	75	76	77	78	79	80
		6 3b		6 3b		
	5 6	4 5 6		4 5 6		
	3 4 5	2# 3# 4#	6	2# 3# 4#	6 6#	6 6
Bass-line	Bb A Bb	Bb A G	F#	Eb D C	B Bb	F D
		7b 5 7b		5		
	13 12 5	3#	3X	7♮ 3# 7b	3♮ 3b	3♮ 5
Roots	D – Bb	C# A C#	D	F# D F#	G G#	D Bb
	I VI	VII# V VII#	V	VII# V VII#	V IV#	I VI

	81	82	83	84	85	86	87	88
	9 8 3	4	9 8 3	4 3b	3	7		
	5 6 6	2# 6 7	5 6 6	2# 6 6	6#	5		
	3# 4 4	7 4	3# 4 4	7 4 4#	6 4 3♮	3♮	3#	3♮
Bass-line	A – Bb	Bb A G	A – Bb	Bb A G	F E D	G#	A	D
	9	9 5	9 5	9 5	7			
	3# 5 7	3# 3♮	3# 3♮	3# 3♮ 7b	3♮ 3# 3♮			
Roots	A D E	A D	A D E	A D C#	D A D			
	V I II	V I IV	V I II	V I VII#	I V I	VII#	V	I

{25} B. 4^2 seems to call for A as its root, but the e is no more than an appoggiatura, the A in any case the fifth of the root D. There is a fortunate turn of events for b. 8^2, where the passing notes in the lower voices form consonances with the dissonances of the upper voices. To generalize, from this passage can be seen the merit of my system, which did not invent or devise the eleventh and thirteenth in a spirit of harmonic progress, but rather rediscovered them (for as early as 1549 *Luigi Prenestini*[28] under *Marcellus II* in Rome made use of these dissonances).

{26} (3) With respect to aesthetic delight, it is necessary to enquire (a) whether the upper melodic line is simple, (b) whether the harmony flows smoothly, (c) whether the key-progression is consistent, (d) whether the ordering of periods is correct, (e) whether the deployment of phrases corresponds to it, (f) whether the rhetorical discourse conveys meaning, [and] (g) whether the conclusion is energetic – if the inner content [*innere Gehalt*] meets these requirements, then there need be no doubt that the groundplan [*Anlage*] has been aesthetically designed and aesthetically elaborated.

(a) All music must sing. A soprano would be able to perform the *upper* melodic line of No. 8. Even though:

28   i.e. Palestrina. [Vogler:]

> Joseph FUX, Emperor Charles VI's Kapellmeister in Vienna, as he was writing Part II of his *Gradus ad Parnassum* in Socratic style in 1720–30, allotted to the enquiring Pupil his own first name, *Joseph*, {26} and to the Master, whose job it was to answer these questions on the basis of his musical compositions from the sixteenth century, the first name of this *Prenestini* (that extraordinary genius, born in the town [*Staat*] of *Preneste*, near Rome), namely *Ludwig* [*Aloysius*]. *Fux* sought to abstract from the consummate *chef-d'œuvres* of this Prenestini's church music rules for musical composition, as if he were a Horace, a Quintilian and a Boileau from the masterworks of the ancient orators and poets. However, *Prenestini's practical* compositions contain the correctly prepared, sounded and resolved eleventh and thirteenth; of these, Fux's *theoretical* prescriptions are wholly oblivious!

the c''' in b. 53, taken on its own,

the b♭'' in b. 55[, and]

the a♭'' in b. 57

may appear difficult to pitch, each is in fact easy to locate because the latter note of the leap is already audible in the harmonies.

(b) *All* voices must sing. This organ piece could be performed by four singers as a quartet.

Because the bass asserts its own character, indeed all four vocal lines, even the middle voices whose range is much more restricted, have their own distinctive and shapely melodic line, we can anticipate that this harmony, if nothing untoward occurs, will be consistently aesthetic in effect throughout all its modulations to other keys remote and local.

{27} (c) Since all the key centres employed here are related to the principal tonic D and are no more than a single step away from it in key signature (for the keys at the opposite ends of the spectrum appear remote from one another only as a result of admixture and juxtaposition),[29] and since even E♭ major, which is two steps away, and which is familiar in the following context:

	6	5♮	.	3♮
6♭	4	3×		
G	A	–		D

exercises its sovereign rights only by lingering for a while [*beim Verweilen*], reliant upon the principal tonic and clinging to it as a neighbour, one has only to go through the table set out [above] to be persuaded of its consistency – a consistency that will be found in other respects as well.

(d) The periods have already been analysed [*zergliedert*] under the heading of harmonic progression, their caesuras [*Einschnitte*] noted and their ordering discussed. In addition, there was the fact that:

(e) the phrases [*Rhythmen*] were found to be well rounded and to fall into pairs, except where the *stretto* creates an effect of increasing constriction, concentration and foreshortening, as a result of which:

(f) the rhetorical discourse and the conclusion follow logically.

(g) There are composers who, in seeking a sense of direction for all that they write, resort to rapid tempi and the proliferation of hosts of short note values – and miss the target completely.

In this piece there is not a single quaver, there is no tremolando in the strings, no thunder-clap on timpani – none of the conventional remedies to which so many composers turn. The melodic line retains its simplicity throughout, the

---

29   There is only one single law for modulation, but it is a general one: that there should be no going beyond a step that is one ♯ or one ♭ removed from the key signature [. . .] Every piece of music [. . .] is named by reference to a certain key. In order to preserve its unity, it must not modulate to a key more than one step away [. . . .] From this is it clear that in any one key there are only six that can appear as principal or primary keys: e.g. in C: C major, A minor; F major, D minor; G major, E minor. (*Tonwissenschaft und Tonsezkunst*, 70–72)

   Stufe here implicitly denotes a 'step' on the circle of fifths, rather than a scale-degree.

harmony yields shapely lines in all voices and flows forward uninterruptedly; the key-progression, colouring the periods and phrases as it does, enlivens the rhetorical discourse through its orderly succession and moves unswervingly towards its constant goal, its logical conclusion, which is never lost from sight. Only compare the model in bb. 1–8 with the subsequent twenty bars {28} in which the theme undergoes proliferation. Note, further, how in the passage bb. 30–42 the *same material* [*idem*] persistently recurs, and in ever-changing guise begets *diversity* [*varium*], and how the theme is developed. Whereas the periods from b. 1 to b. 30 have been mostly[30] four bars in length, they contract at this point to two bars' length, and then in bb. 42–58 to *one* bar's length: during these last sixteen bars, first b. 1 [bb. 42–9] then b. 2 [bb. 50–58] is forcefully elaborated. Bb. 58–72 appear at first sight to be a straight repetition of the material heard earlier in bb. 13–29. It has in fact a much more conclusive effect, because E♭ (1) is now the remotest key, and (2) is more remote from D minor than C was from A [minor]. Ultimately, however, the *Epiphonema*[31] in bb. 72 and 81 consists in the introduction of the theme in the bass, the appearance of the thirteenth above the root in b. 73 and of the ninth in b. 82, and finally the presentation of two themes in counterpoint against one another in one and the same bar,[32] thereby making a convincing and crowning effect.

Not content at having prepared a double reward for the player and reader, as promised, by way of this edition,[33] and wanting by way of this analysis to render him a competent judge [of music], I feel bound to point out that two bars could be excised to the significant improvement of the rhetorical discourse, namely if the player will cut from b. 67^2 to b. 69^3.[34] In an earlier draft, b. 79 comprised only a crotchet and two rests, and I had interpolated two bars that contained the material of bb. 78–9 a tone higher:

after | E♭ D C | B♮ | F E D | C♯.

However, the transposition weakened the effect of the conclusion, so I discarded it. {29} The above two bars (bb. 68–9) I decided to leave in so as to afford the reader the satisfaction of rendering it aesthetically truer by his own hand.

30   Having disregarded it earlier (see notes 20 and 34), Vogler here betrays his awareness that bb. 21–9 comprise either 4 + 5 or 5 + 4.

31   *Epiphonema*: '*Rhet*. An exclamatory sentence or striking reflection, which sums up or concludes a discourse . . .' (*OED*). See also *System*, 58: 'a compressed *Resumé*, a conclusive *Epiphonema*, closes the fugue'.

32   [Vogler:] In bb. 81 and 83, b. 1 appears in the bass, b. 2 in the soprano; in bb. 82 and 84, b. 2 appears in the bass, b. 1 in the soprano.

33   In producing reworkings of his *112 petits préludes pour l'orgue ou fortepiano* (Munich, 1776), Vogler stated:

> to the owners of the earlier edition [who might purchase it] I hoped to offer a small compensation [in the differences between the two editions], but to those true amateurs and connoisseurs of music who desire to penetrate to the essence of its individuality, [I hoped] to proffer a double reward by way of the aesthetic, rhetorical and harmonic enquiries of the following analysis. (p. I)

34   [Vogler:] Were I to perform this piece, I should cut from b. 65 to b. 71. [This remarkable and surprising remark relates to the recurrence of the very passage referred to earlier in notes 20 and 30. In the present context, however, the periodic construction is no longer irregular, since bb. 50–73 make up (4 + 4) (4 + 4) (4 + 4): whereas b. 14 fell on a structural upbeat, its counterpart, b. 58, falls on a structural downbeat, reversing out the stress patterns of the two-bar phrases. If, however, one considers bb. 61–71 as an enclosed unit (4 + 5 + 4) – or (4 + 4 + 5) – then the text recommendation renders that (4 + 3 + 4), whereas the footnote renders it (4 + 4), the latter evidently being what Vogler had in mind.]

Since this analysis on its own has turned out to be longer than I had expected for all thirty-two, I hope that it will be of real value with regard not only to the strict contrapuntal style [*gebundener Styl*] (a type of counterpoint that is not pedantic), but also to the science of harmony [*Harmoniekenntnis*] (a rational thoroughbass) and lastly also to aesthetic treatment, rhetorical design and so forth.

The pedal requires no special directions, since it follows the lowest bass notes.

Antoine Reicha (1770–1836)
'Aria de Mozart ["Non so più"] des *Nozze di Figaro*'
Traité de mélodie (1814)

Reicha's *Treatise on Melody* offers the first really cogent study of melody – perhaps the only one to be produced in the nineteenth century. It is at one and the same time an essay on the nature of melody and a pedagogical manual (sixty-five pages of hypothesis and analysis followed by sixteen pages of instruction). For Reicha (unlike Momigny), music rested on two equal pillars: melody and harmony. His purpose in the *Traité* was to counter the erstwhile neglect of the former by ensuring both a vocabulary and a syntax for it. This he did by first establishing a terminology for the structural units of melody; second, positing the rules by which those units function; third, carrying out analyses of a wide selection of melodies from Handel to Cimarosa, in the process of which the rules become qualified and extended.

Reicha's vocabulary appears to derive in part by transference from German into French (*Periode* = *période*, *Glied* = *membre*, *Theil* = *partie*, *Rhythmus* = *rhytme*, etc, as used by Koch, Kirnberger and others), as does his use of punctuation signs (used by Mattheson, Riepel, Kirnberger) to mark phrase boundaries. His smallest structural unit is the *dessein* (occasionally also *petit dessein*); *desseins* combine to form the *membre*, *membres* to form the *période*, *périodes* to form the *partie*, *parties* to form the *morceau*, the formal structure of which is synonymously termed *cadre*, *coupe* or *dimension*. He has an additional term for *membre*, namely *rhytme* (or *rythme*). Significantly, these are not alternatives: *membre* and *rhytme* coexist. Whereas *membre* refers to a given unit as content, *rhytme* refers to it as number. Effectively, it is at this level of structure that a melody is brought into balance and symmetry: *rhytme* is a controlling force that equalizes the *membres* that follow one another. It acts as a kind of temporal grid into which the material invented at the level of the *dessein* must fit. The grid operates only at this one level, requiring that *membres* with few exceptions combine in pairs of equal length and parallel construction. The second of such a pair (labelled 'the same' in Reicha's graphic analyses) can have the status of a *compagnon* if much of its material is identical with that of the first – if, in other words, the two form an antecedent–consequent relationship.

A certain kinship between Reicha and Vogler is pointed up by the opening remarks of this analysis. Both writers consider periodicity and symmetry of phrase structure crucial in musical utterance, both assert the superiority of this over special orchestral effects (which they regard as currently fashionable), both counsel against extremes of modulation. Their differences are equally clear: for Vogler these qualities guarantee effectiveness of discourse, whereas for Reicha they ensure power of feeling expressed; and Vogler speaks in terms of harmony, Reicha of independent melody.

Reicha's theory includes a doctrine of phrase morphology. Two footnotes to the present analysis reveal his interpretation of a seven-bar unit as having eight bars of which the final bar has been suppressed (Reicha's *supposition* is not to be confused with Rameau's use of the term), and of a five-bar unit as having six bars of which the third and fourth have been expressed as half bars with fermatas. He graphs out one instance in the analysis with overlapping brackets (at 'spegiar, un desio'). Reicha's doctrine is remarkably libertarian: in the analysis below he accepts a three-bar *membre* in its own right, provided only that it is one of a pair of such three-bar units; he accepts that three *membres* should function in parallel instead of two, as happens towards the end of this analysis. He also on occasion tolerates *membres* of five, ten and twelve bars.

Other terms needing explanation here are *complément*, a filling-in figure usually forming a bridge from one phrase to the next without extending the first phrase, and the various forms of *cadence*. A *½-cad:* is a cadence that marks the end of a *membre* (in modern terms an imperfect, plagal or lightly-stressed perfect cadence); a *cad:perf:* a cadence that marks the end of a period (a perfect cadence on the tonic, with the melody coming to rest on the tonic note at a strong beat); a *cad:inter:* a cadence in which the melody 'falls to some other note than the tonic, or leaps suddenly from the tonic to another note' (undifferentiated by harmony, it is not the modern interrupted or evaded cadence – see the cadence before the Adagio).

Reicha was the first analyst (he used *analyser* and *décomposer* for the analyst's work) to take advantage of musical engraving to employ thorough-going graphic means. Like Riemann (whose publisher, however, used moveable type), and later Schenker (whose fold-out plates at their best were exquisite), the graph becomes the focus of the presentation, and the verbal text is demoted to commentary. This commentary usually contains a list of the *membres* expressed as a succession of numbers. This he calls the *patron* of the piece.

'Aria ["Non so più"] from Mozart's *The Marriage of Figaro*'
Treatise on Melody

Source:
'*Traité de mélodie: abstraction faite de ses rapports avec l'harmonie . . . le tout appuyé sur les meilleurs modèles mélodiques* (Paris: pubd privately, 1814, 2/1832), vol. I, p. 43; vol. II *Soixante-dix-sept planches graves, contenant les éxamples auquels renvoie le texte du Traité de mélodie* (Paris: pubd privately, 1814), pl. E4, pp. 23–5.

This is an example of an *aria agitato* in large binary form. The rhythm of this aria, delightfully regular, is as follows: Part I: 4;–4;–3;–3.–6;–4;–6:–6. Part II: 4;–4;–3;–3.–4;–4;–6;–8.–4;–4;–4;–8:–4;–6. The half cadence has been indicated here by the semicolon (;), the perfect cadence by the full point (.) and the interrupted cadence by the colon (:).

This aria is from all points of view a perfect model. It demonstrates in the most convincing manner (1) that melody is capable of expressing the most animated feelings of our hearts just as well as the sweetest; (2) that regularity of rhythm, without which there can be no true melody, can and should have a place in the one as in the other; (3) that this way of expressing the agitations of our hearts is infinitely better than all the orchestral fracas with which composers nowadays try to portray similar situations and in which the vocal part is for all intents and purposes redundant; (4) it shows, moreover, that music can and should delight us, even when expressing powerful emotions; it shows lastly (5) that there is no reason to go running after bizarre modulations in order to achieve this goal, and that it can be attained by the simplest and most natural means. Exemplary also is the manner in which this aria is accompanied: the orchestra expresses the agitation of the singer covering the voice, without diverting our attention from its melody; in short, it does no more than second it, and second it perfectly (see the full score).

Example 1[1]

fon - ti   a l'ecco a l'aria ai ven - ti   che il suon de vani ac - cen - ti___

por- ta- no via con se,___   por - ta - no via con   se.   par- lo d'a-mor ve -

glian - do   par - la d'a-mor so - gnan-do   a l'ac - qua a l'om - bra

ai monti ai   fio - ri   a l'er - be   ai fon - ti   a l'e - co a l'a - ria ai

ven - ti che il suon-de vani ac - cen - ti ___ por - ta - no via con   se___

(*) In order to convince oneself that this *rythme* (in a tempo as fast as this) is really eight bars long, not seven, one needs to imagine it written in the following way:

This demonstrates that one needs to count two bars in place of one, with regard to *rythme*, at the end of Mozart's phrase, e.g.:

(*) This *rythme* comprises six, not five, bars, because of the fermatas in b. 13, which one should count here as two bars, e.g.:

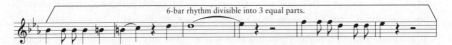

In the following period by Grétry it is necessary to count the final bar (which has a fermata) as two bars. The *rythme* demands this, as anyone can feel:

Since the last note of *rythme 1* here (the d") has the value of five crotchets, the last note of *rythme 2* has to have the same value, without which the second would be lop-sided and could not serve as the *compagnon* to the first.

Antoine Reicha (1770–1836)

Traité de haute composition musicale, vol. II (1826)

Reicha's *Course in Musical Composition* (see Analysis 2 above), which not only presented its own classification of intervals and rules of progression and modulation, but also dealt with harmonic writing for choir, instrumental groupings and full orchestra, had unseated Charles-Simon Catel's influential *Treatise on Harmony* (1802) as the official harmony textbook of the Paris Conservatoire, Reicha being appointed professor of counterpoint there in 1817 after the death of Méhul.[1] Fétis (Analysis 16b), who later attacked this work violently in his *Universal Biography*, was appointed professor of counterpoint and fugue at the Conservatoire in 1821, while Cherubini became its Director in 1822 (Marmontel later recalled the side-long glances that were constantly exchanged in the 1830s 'between Italy, Bohemia and the Low Countries'[2]).

It was against this background of rivalry that Reicha wrote his two mighty volumes encompassing 600 folio pages, the *Treatise on Advanced Musical Composition* (1824–6), which exploded upon the scene, splitting the Conservatoire from top to bottom for its total disregard of species counterpoint. Baini devoted ten pages of his great study of Palestrina in 1828 (Analysis 14 below) to refuting Reicha's historical statements. Fétis lashed the work in his *Universal Biography*. Cherubini published his own *Course in Counterpoint and Fugue* (1835), reinstating the method established by Fux's *Gradus ad Parnassum* in 1725 of teaching species counterpoint, though with reference to only major and minor modes, as an implicit refutation of Reicha's treatise. As a result, while Cherubini discarded the church modes but retained species counterpoint, Reicha discarded the species but retained the modes for their practical compositional value.[3]

However, having led the 'advanced' student through part-writing in traditional and modern styles, double, triple and quadruple counterpoint, imitation and canon, and fugue in all its aspects, Reicha embarked upon a still more radical enterprise in the sixth and final book of the *Traité*, flaccidly entitled 'The Art of Making the Most of One's Ideas, or of Developing Them' (vol. II, pp. 234–359). *Idée* in that context is a very general term for a musical element ('roughly speaking between two and twenty-four bars in length') that embodies feelings and is memorable.

---

1   Eitner's *Quellenlexikon*: 'Prof. der Komposition' and '1818'.
2   Antoine François Marmontel (1816–98) taught *solfège* at the Conservatoire 1837–87; see M. Emmanuel, *Antonin Reicha* (Paris: Henri Laurens, 1937), 48–50.
3   To submit oneself nowadays to [strict] composition in all its severity is entirely to disregard the progress that the art of music has made in the past century; armed with compass and ruler, one has to calculate rather than to feel [. . .] He who is trained only in this style is incapable of writing a pleasing tune, a striking dramatic scene, even less a piece of instrumental music that has verve, taste and warmth. (*Traité de haute*, vol. I, p. 6)

Ideas arise through the creative faculty and are usually 'rough diamonds that need to be polished later'. Reicha's views on genius and inspiration were not far in advance of those of Sulzer's *General Theory of the Fine Arts* (1771–4); but whereas for the latter, inspiration[4] was a state of heightened awareness produced by undivided concentration and resulting in effortlessness of invention, for Reicha a more dynamic condition prevailed: 'an electric current circulates in the veins, and the imagination is as if it were set on fire [. . .] it would be dangerous to remain in this state for a long time' (vol. II, p. 235). Like Czerny after him, and Lobe, too (Analyses 11, 12), Reicha offered advice on how to manage this 'primitive' state and how to capture the often crude ideas to which it gives rise. We ought to guard against construing these various remarks as full-bloodedly Romantic in outlook: it was Haydn and Mozart that he had in mind more than Beethoven, and it was to the *Marriage of Figaro* overture that he turned, analysing and repeatedly rewriting parts of it in illustration. Reicha recognized the irrational element in artistic creation, appreciated its power and yet believed that the rational mind must master its forces.

The principal tools of the composer were exposition and development of ideas; only through these tools, which called for the full range of the composer's skills, could an extended form be properly sustained. After demonstrating these tools, Reicha went on to supply a manual of those musical forms that lent themselves best to development. Systematically classified and described, the main forms are also elegantly graphed in engraved diagrams. In an exquisitely ambiguous moment that positions him midway between Koch and A. B. Marx (vol. II, Analysis 12), he named sonata form as binary yet graphed it as tripartite.[5]

The analysis given below is itself a halfway house. It is close to Vogler's rhetorical treatment (Analysis 7) in providing a semiotic analysis, although in purely thematic, non-harmonic terms. At the same time, it looks forward to the motivic analytical method exemplified in compositional terms by Marx and practised by many twentieth-century analysts. However, the term *motif* is used here not as it was in the mid-nineteenth century and after, but as almost the equivalent of *thème*, i.e. a balanced melodic structure made up of small elements called *desseins*. It has been translated here as 'principal theme'. The term *phrase* is used indeterminately as a subdivision of a *motif* but never formally equated with *dessein*, *membre* or *rythme*. It has been translated below as 'phrase', though it is closer to the modern 'motif'.

4 'Begeisterung', *Allgemeine Theorie der schönen Künste* (Leipzig: Weidmann, 1771–4, 2/1792–4; reprint edn Hildesheim: Olms, 1967–70), vol. I, pp. 349–56; Eng. trans. le Huray/Day, 130–33.
5 See B. P. V. Moyer, 'Concepts of Musical Form in the Nineteenth Century with Special Reference to A. B. Marx and Sonata Form' (PhD diss.: Stanford University, 1969), 46–58.

'Analysis of [Reicha?: Andante for Wind Quintet in G] with Respect to Thematic Development'[6]

Treatise on Advanced Musical Composition

Source:
'Sur le développement des idées musicales en général', *Traité de haute composition musicale*, vol. II (Paris: Farrenc, [1826]), pp. 240–95; passage taken from pp. 273 [analysis], 263–72 [music in score].

This Andante comprises 196 bars. However, its central core of ideas amounts to only fifty-six of these; the remainder (nearly three-quarters, that is) is taken up with development. It is, admittedly, remarkable that a piece can be prolonged to as much as 196 bars when its core of ideas is as little as fifty-six and still retain interest.

An analysis of the piece shows:

1. that the phrase [Example 1] attaching to the principal theme [*motif*] is repeated immediately so as to make the idea symmetrical [*quarrée*];

Example 1

2. that bb. 3_{17}–26^I answer (with a different arrangement of the parts) bb. 3_1–5_3, 7^I–11^I (suppressing b. 6);[7]

3. that bb. 3_{32}–35^I are repeated immediately [as bb. 3_{36}–39^I] with modified harmony;

4. that the repeated phrase [Example 2] is none other than a transposition with a slight alteration of Example 1;

Example 2

6   This title has been derived from the sentence preceding the music example containing the piece in score, on p. 263, which reads: 'In order to render this section [*article*] more useful, instructive, and complete, we will now analyse the two following pieces with respect to thematic development'. I have been unable to trace the piece, so have assumed it to be by Reicha himself; it is reproduced in the Appendix below.

7   Reicha equates bb. 17–28 with bb. 1–5, 7–10. Neither set of numbers is satisfactory. Leaving aside phrase compressions and expansions, one can say that 3_1–11^I = 3_{17}–26^I, or that 3_1–14 = 3_{17}–28, or that 3_1–16^I = 3_{17}–31^I. However, the latter two equations involve transposition from b. 26 to which Reicha does not refer. A special system of bar-reference has been adopted here since Reicha fails to indicate what is often critical: the beat of the bar on which a phrase begins or ends. Hence '3_{17}' signifies the third beat of the bar preceding b. 17 (i.e. b. 16); '26^I' signifies the first beat of b. 26.

5. that bb. $366-71^2$ contain the opening of the principal theme transposed, with a concluding turn of phrase which is different on account of the modulation; the same thing happens in the following six bars [bb. $372-77^1$];

6. that 77^2-85^1 are a transposition (with a different arrangement of the parts) of bb. 57^2-65^1;[8]

7. that the same thing happens (with a new transposition and a new arrangement of the parts) between b. 100^2 and b. 108^1;

8. that between b. ^{3109} and b. 120^1 the first six bars of the principal theme are heard twice in succession, though with a different arrangement of the parts on each occasion;

9. that Example 1 is reiterated several times in the following bars [bb. $^3121-124^1$] and closes by way of a sequence [*progression*: bb. 124^2-127^1];

10. that the imitation between the four voices (see bb. 128–32) is a transposition of that in bb. 52–6;

11. that the phrase [Example 3] is introduced three times in succession transposed and played in turn by flute, clarinet and bassoon (see bb. 133–45); this phrase was heard originally in E♭ in bb. 48–52;[9]

Example 3

12. that in bb. $146-153^1$ there is a linking passage [*conduit*][10] which leads from C to D major; and that bb. $^3149-153^2$ recall an idea first heard at the beginning (bb. $^312-16^2$);

13. that bb. $^3154-161^1$ are a transposition of the idea in bb. $^332-39^1$;[11]

14. that between bb. 164 and 172^1 the phrase [Example 4] that has been previously heard [in bb. 133–145] is now presented in dialogue (between horn and bassoon);

Example 4

---

8   Reicha: 57–64 = 77–84 = (in §7) 100–107.

9   Reicha: 48–51.

10 The term *conduit* is for Reicha well defined. It is generally associated, as here, with a pause: *Traité de mélodie*, vol. I, p. 27:

> CONDUIT, Pause on the last [bar] of the first *rythme* (that is, at the midpoint of the period) or on the last [bar] of the period itself, on which may be introduced several free decorative melodic passages which serve as a transition or link from one *membre* to the other [i.e. from antecedent to consequent] or from one period to another. Sometimes the composer writes out this bar, more often it is left to the taste and talent of the performer.

11 Reicha: 32–38 = 154–60.

15. that in the ten bars following this [bb. ^{2}173–182^1], a phrase which was heard near the beginning in bb. ^{2}27–31^1 is reiterated twice (the second time an octave higher in both melody and harmony);[12]

16. that the same happens with the idea [Example 5] [from bb. 3$32$–35^2] in bb. 3$183$–190^2; and that the four bars following that [bb. 3$191$–194] derive from the last seven notes of this same phrase [bb. 3$34$–35^1].

Example 5

12   Reicha: 27–37 (*sic*).

Gottfried Weber (1779–1839)
'Ueber eine besonders merkwürdige Stelle in einem
Mozart'schen Violinquartett aus C'

Versuch einer geordneten Theorie der Tonsetzkunst (3/1832)

For sheer vividness, for immediacy of descriptive power, there is perhaps nothing in this volume to rival Weber's account of the introduction to Mozart's 'Dissonance' Quartet. Take only two instances. In discussing the combined effect of various technical processes that he has so far described, Weber lights (in §466[18]) upon the first beat of b. 3, and the c#' in the second violin. Where another writer might have said of this neighbouring note [*Nebennote*] that it 'displaces its main note, d', by a crotchet-value . . .', Weber introduces an adjectival phrase in apposition, *als frech hervortretende Wechselnote*, the total effect of the passage, rendered slightly freely, being: '*this upstart changing note*, that *so rudely* displaces its own main note, d', by a full crotchet-value and *robs* it of the stressed beat . . .'.

Secondly, in examining the tonal coherence of bb. 1–5 (in §466[9]) he turns his attention to the third beat of b. 4, and the high b♭" in the violin I that follows a succession of B♮s in the lower instruments. What occurs at this point is for Weber not just a 'modulation' but an *Ab- und Ausweichung* – a 'deflection and modulation'. Moreover, it does not just 'occur', but *Epoche* [*macht*] – 'creates a sensation'; and not just on a 'weak beat' but a 'beat ill-equipped' for the job. The result is no mere 'change' but a *Reform*; it is a matter of 'taking the law into its own hands', of 'seeking to overthrow [*reformiren*] the G major triad'.

This is to *personify* a passing note, to *dramatize* a tonal process!

But let us return to the former case. The ear, already confounded by what has happened in b. 2, 'yearns for a G major chord simple and unadorned'.

> But that this c#' should forcibly displace the harmony note d', that it should mar its arrival, indeed subvert the entry of the long-desired G major chord, on the first beat of the bar, and distort the chord into [B♮ g c#' a"], [. . .] – the likes of this [the ear] never expected

The style is almost that of the old-fashioned serialized who-dun-it: 'in doubt, the ear looks and listens eagerly for what will happen next . . .', 'totally contrary to all expectations . . .', and so forth.

The central character in this impassioned description is *das Gehör* – the ear. Behind it stands *das Gehörsinn* – the faculty of hearing (mentioned only in Weber's introductory remarks). The tense is the present. Experience is constant and active: the ear perpetually listens, receives, reacts. What Weber offers us, though not in so many words, is a real-time experiential model, complete with feed-back. The ear seeks 'contentment' (*Befriedigung*), but finds instead 'disturbing effects' (*das Befremdliche*), whereupon it is forced to reconsider and reinterpret. Tonal samples are repeatedly rerun for us like some taped fragment of sound under laboratory analysis. In one paragraph (§466[19]), Weber – like Reicha in 1824–6 (see Introduction to Analysis 9) – adopts the strategy of rewriting the music: using musical notation, he makes a series of modifications to the musical text, letting us sample the differences in our mind's ear as he removes the dissonant complexities one by one – a kind of early commutative test.

Then, suddenly, the model is turned off. From the beginning of §466[22] to the end of §466[27], the central character is banished. With its departure, the present tense largely disappears. In their place are *der Tonsetzer* – the composer – and the past tense. The music becomes static, the discourse objective.

Significantly, this section is entitled 'The rhetorical import of the passage'. Here Weber examines the passage for evidence of those musical devices of rhetoric codified by Burmeister, Kircher, Mattheson and others, interpreting them in the more limited guise of what he calls 'contrapuntal-imitative' devices. He does indeed find imitation; and he diagnoses Mozart's 'governing idea' [*Idee*] as the consistent introduction of imitative entries at one crotchet's distance in a harmonic environment that is hostile to that process. It is noticeable that precisely in this section, which looks back (though only in principle, not in reality) to the theory of ancient Greece and Rome, Weber cloaks himself in more learned language by using latinate German word-forms. He abandons *Erklärung* for *Explication*, mixes *Imitation* and *imitirend* with *Nachahmung* and *nachahmend*, prefers *Phrase* to *Satz* (in the sense of 'passage', reserving *Satz* now for 'counterpoint'); he introduces *Melodie* and *grammatical* for the first time; he even flaunts *imitatio per thesin et arsin*, making a play of sparing the poor reader the burden of an explanation, only then to overpower him with the neologistic construction *apodictische Assurance*.[1]

Over the entire section hovers the word *Intention*, announced at the head of §466[23], and bade farewell to in the second paragraph of the 'Conclusion' (where it is signalled by spaced type). Throughout this section on rhetoric, Weber's purpose is to explore motivation, intentionality. As he embarks on it, we perceive two shifts in his mode of discourse. First, he now faces the composer frontally – indeed, he utters the name 'Mozart' for the first time in nineteen pages (since three pages before the analysis proper starts). As he does so, he asks the question *Why*? Why did Mozart do this? Why did he choose to avoid that? And secondly, while meeting Mozart, we also meet the instruments. With two exceptions, Weber had hitherto spoken of the material in abstract terms as 'the upper voice', 'voice 2', 'voice 3', 'the middle voices', 'the lower voices' and 'the bass'. In so doing, he had neutralized precisely the vivid sound that he had been conjuring up for us. Now, in an odd reversal, he speaks freely of 'violin I', 'violin II' and 'the viola' (though never of 'the cello').

In short, the first section of the analysis (§§466[1-21]) is *experiential*, whereas the second section (§§466[22-27]) is *intentional*. This distinction is neatly encapsulated in

---

1   To be sure, the words *grammatical* and *Phrase* appear in the heading of section 5 and in §466[21], but not in the *Caecilia* version, which, as demonstrated below, was the first to be published. It is in *Caecilia* that *apodictische Assurance* appears (see note 35).

a single sentence (of the German, that is: split into five here) of the second paragraph of the 'Conclusion' (§466²⁷), complete with matching tenses (my italics):

> Of what *does* the disturbing effect consist? Through what concatenation of circumstances *is* it effected? What *were* the intentions that *lay* behind it and *prompted* it? These things we *have learned* in the course of the foregoing analysis. All that technical theory *could have done*, it *has* here *done*.

There is an important clue here as to how this analysis took shape. In the *Caecilia* version, the clause 'What were the intentions that lay behind it and prompted it?' is *absent*, and for the good reason that the discussion of rhetoric and intention has not yet taken place. Careful comparison of the *Caecilia* and *Attempt* versions shows two major shifts of material. The less significant is the fact that while the *Attempt* version could resort to cross-references backwards to earlier paragraphs in volume III and forwards to volume IV, the *Caecilia* version was obliged to import large portions of these paragraphs in order to be free-standing (see relevant footnotes). Much more striking, however, is the fact that the *Caecilia* version appeared in *two instalments*, the first omitting the discussion of rhetoric altogether, continuing with most of the 'Conclusion', and ending with an air of finality then belied by the second instalment, the *Inhalt* of which describes it as '*continuation* and *conclusion* of the article *left incomplete* in the previous issue' (all italics mine).

There is clear evidence that the entire section '6. The rhetorical import of the passage' was an afterthought at first appended to an analysis complete in its own right and that Weber subsequently incorporated it into the body of the analysis, displacing its four last paragraphs, joining them to his final personal comment, and making a separate section, '7. Conclusion'. However, Weber failed to assimilate the material entirely, leaving one tell-tale clue: the fact that the schema given in §466¹ includes no reference to section 6.

Of the countless minor differences between the two texts, most of which Weber made in the interests of correctness or clearer expression, only the most significant have been recorded in footnotes here.

Gottfried Weber, a German theorist and composer working in Mannheim, Mainz and ultimately Darmstadt, wrote several treatises, of which the four-volume *Attempt at a Systematic Theory of Musical Composition* is his principal contribution to music theory. First published in 1817–21, it went through a second edition in 1824 and a third in 1832. His analysis of the opening bars of the introduction to Mozart's 'Dissonance' Quartet was presumably written in 1831 and 1832, for it constitutes a response to a heated debate between François-Joseph Fétis, writing in his *La revue musicale*, and the pseudonymous 'A. C. Leduc', writing in the Leipzig *Allgemeine musikalische Zeitung*,[2] which took place in the years 1829–31. Weber's analysis was itself published in his journal *Caecilia* in 1831–2, and also in the third edition of the *Attempt* (1832). It subsequently reached

---

2 For a full account of this debate, which was started by Carl Cramer in 1787 and vigorously joined by Giuseppe Sarti (writing somewhere between 1785 and 1802) and included a number of other writers, see Julie Anne Vertrees, 'Mozart's String Quartet K.465: the History of a Controversy', *Current Musicology*, 17 (1974), 96–114. Vertrees proposes Peter Lichtenthal as the identity of 'Leduc'.

a much wider readership through French and English translations of the third edition,[3] and itself prompted a challenge from Fétis.

Weber summarizes the views of Fétis (whose own rewritings of 'faulty' passages presumably prompted those by Weber referred to above) and 'Leduc', preceded by those of Giuseppe Sarti, in the introduction to his analysis (the summary is here omitted); and it is doubtless against Sarti and Fétis that his barbed references to 'critics' (§466[22]) and 'fools and jealous ones' (§466[28]) are directed, as well as the obvious scornful allusion to the '"two plus two is four" fashion' of formulating compositional theory.

Weber had discussed and quoted these bars of Mozart in several earlier paragraphs of the *Attempt*, in illustration of passing notes, cross-relations and parallel progressions. Accordingly, when he now reached these matters, he merely referred the reader to those paragraphs. In the *Caecilia* version of the analysis, on the other hand, Weber imported large portions of these paragraphs, and in so doing he made the analysis much more diffuse; even so, he failed to include some of the extant allusions to the Mozart passage. In the present translation, all references to the passage have been incorporated, together with just the most essential statements from the surrounding paragraphs, with explanatory footnotes. The resultant surgery, while less than perfect, was inevitable. On the other hand, Weber's network of cross-references to tangential discussions elsewhere in his four volumes, which would have served no purpose in this context, has been replaced by bracketed ellipses.

When stating the pitches of a chord, Weber adopts the orthographical device of surrounding the letter-names with square brackets, thus: [c f♯ d' a"]. Despite the normal reservation of square brackets in the present volume for editorially supplied matter, this device has been preserved. There should be no confusion: *all* such sets of letter-names are in Weber's original text, all other items in square brackets are editorial. Weber's use of typography (for which he is justly famed in the history of theory) has also been retained: Gothic letters signify roots, Roman letters keys; Roman numerals signify scale-degrees; and in all these cases, large capitals denote major triads, small capitals minor triads.

---

3   French trans. said to be by J. G. Kastner, *Essai d'un théorie systématique de la composition* (1837), place of publication and publisher unknown; Eng. trans. by J. Bishop in his edition (London: Cocks, 1851), pp. 733–54, of the Eng. trans. by J. F. Warner, *The Theory of Musical Composition* (London: Novello, [Preface: 1842]).

'A Particularly Remarkable Passage in a String Quartet in C by Mozart [K465 ("Dissonance")]'⁴

Attempt at a Systematic Theory of Musical Composition

Source:
'Ueber eine besonders merkwürdige Stelle in einem Mozart'schen Violinquartett aus C', *Versuch einer geordneten Theorie der Tonsetzkunst zum Selbstunterricht* (Mainz: Schott, 3/1830–32), vol. III, pp. 196–226; published also in *Caecilia: eine Zeitschrift für die musikalische Welt*, 14/53 (1831), 1–49; 14/54 (1832), 122–9.

§466bis

All that remains for me at the close of this volume is to discharge the duty that I gave myself at the end of §225 (vol. II, p. 186) of undertaking an analysis [*Analyse*] of the intricate web of passing notes [*Geflecht der Durchgänge*], and at the same time of the tonal scheme [*modulatorischer Gang*] and other unusual features of the introduction to the String Quartet in C [K465 'Dissonance'] by *Mozart*, with which fault has been found over the past few years in many periodicals.⁵

{197} The passage, as is well known, forms the opening of the *Introduction* [. . .] of *Mozart's* sublime String Quartet, No. 6 of a set of six that *Mozart* inscribed on the dedication page of the original printed edition (Vienna: Artaria & Co), as 'the fruit of a long and toilsome labour (*il frutto di una lunga e laboriosa fatica*), devoted to his best friend (*al suo migliore amico*) *Joseph Haydn*'.⁶

The opening eight or nine bars of this introduction had already created a sensation immediately after the quartet's first appearance, and caused offence to the ears of its listeners, who found it difficult to determine whether the harsh and jarring effects that they experienced were admissible or contrary to the rules.

[. . .]

---

4 [Weber:] These considerations are published also in Heft 53 of the periodical *Caecilia*, in the volume for 1831.

5 This first paragraph does not appear in the *Caecilia* version. For the promise, see vol. II, p. 186:

> It is our intention to make an analysis [*Zergliederung*], in the same manner that we have analysed [*zergliedert*] the above pieces, of *Mozart's* famous *Introduction* to his sublime *String Quartet in C major* – a passage whose interpretation has kept so many pens busy in Italy, German and France for many a year now. However, since for this passage it is essential to take into account so many notes foreign to chords, it will be best, for this reason and also in view of the considerable size of the present volume by comparison with the third, to reserve until the end of vol. III the analysis of this extraordinarily interesting passage.

> Note that the *Zergliederung* of the promise becomes an *Analyse* in the fulfilment. This promise is mentioned again, also with shift from *Zergliederung* to *Analyse*, in §466¹² below.

6 This first edition of the set of six quartets (K387, 421/417*b*, 428/421*b*, 458, 464 and 465) was published in 1785.

{200} If [. . .] I now venture my own personal consideration of this oft-discussed composition, using it, much as I did with several other pieces in §225, as a practical demonstration of how to analyse [*zur Uebung im Analysiren*] a given tonal scheme and so forth, I must entreat my readers at the outset *not* to expect any sort of *verdict on the so fiercely contested theoretical admissibility or contrariness to the rules* of the passage in question.

Anyone who is acquainted with my theory and knows its way of working will be aware that clear-cut directives and prohibitions, declarations as to whether this or that conjunction of pitches, sequence of notes, chord progression, etc., etc., is or is not admissible, is simply not my forte. I once casually described this tendency of my theory, which amounts in essence purely to *observations* upon that which sounds well or badly, smooth or harsh, and in no way deals in *a priori* and dogmatic theoretical *demonstrations* {201} *as to why* this or that must be such and such, or may not be so and so, in the Commentary to §95, in the following words:

> Since I have for once just been speaking of *greater or lesser strictness*, [let me say that] in general the reader will find the present theory neither freer nor stricter than any other, but rather just as strict, and at the same time just as free as any other. I shall draw attention to *every* harshness that other writers have passed over without so much as a caution, and again that others have forbidden unconditionally. To what extent, then, are more or less harsh or smooth conjunctions of notes *to be used* for this or that artistic purpose? Determining this is not a technical question; it is a matter of the appropriate feeling; in the last resort it is a question for aesthetics.

This much, at least, is clear: the task of music is by no means merely to present the faculty of hearing only with soft and sickly conjunctions of pitches, such as will ingratiate the ear as much as possible. Rather, it should include confronting the aural senses with conjunctions of pitches that up to a point sound harsh, jarring, pungent or disturbing; and indeed it does this not infrequently for purposes of contrast. *How far* it should go in this, *just how* harsh it should be, *how great* a demand it should make on the ear – these are matters in which, as with all things relative, the theorist can set no absolute limits. The composer must have the right to make significant use of harsh, jarring, coarse or shrill tonal effects [*Tongebilde*] to the extent that he aims to express something harsh, coarse, etc. Only that which is harsh and odious to the point of being absolutely *painful* to the ear should be absolutely forbidden. Whether this is the case for any given conjunction of pitches, whether the harsh and jarring effects combine to produce a sum total of harshness that is literally unbearable to the ear – ultimately there is no final arbiter of this other than the aural faculty and good taste of a musically trained ear.

{202} Music is, after all, not a science endowed with mathematical consistency and absoluteness; it is not a system that presents us with directives and prohibitions in the form of unconditional rules, by means of which any given conjunction or combination of pitches may be determined, in 'two plus two is four' fashion, as worthy or worthless, correct or incorrect, admissible or inadmissible. All presumptions to this effect, which imagine that compositional theory [*Tonsatzlehre*] is mathematically based and can thereby derive and lay down absolute precepts, can with the simplest of proofs be shown to be empty, derisory dreams, the falsehood of which is palpable with the very first example. [. . .]

[. . .]

Therefore nobody should expect from me a verdict as to whether and how far this or that feature of the Introduction in question *should be admitted or prohibited and categorically forbidden.*

What *I* have to offer, however, is the following.

Clearly the passage [*Satz*] in question does sound disturbing to the ear – very disturbing. The causes of this disturbing effect, operating at times singly and at times in consort, can be identified by the theorist [. . .].

A thorough-going *analysis* of the entire *harmonic and melodic fabric* [*Textur*] of the passage in question will enable us to detect all these causes, to isolate them and see them interacting with one another, and thus to specify *what* it is in these tonal constructs [*Anklängen*] that disturbs us so much, and what it is that strikes our faculty of hearing as so undeniably harsh.

The sole task that I have set myself here is to carry out just such an enquiry, to produce just such an analysis. Once I have done this, I am bound then to leave to the individual, to his faculty of hearing and good taste, to decide whether he finds the {203} level of harshnesses, of idiosyncrasy, of eccentricity resulting from the combined operation of these individual features that we have identified excessive or not excessive for presentation to the ear.

§466[1]

I believe that I can best carry out the promised analysis of the passage in question if first, in preparation, I:

1   examine it from the point of view of *its* underlying *chord progression* or *tonal scheme*; then

2   consider the *notes foreign to chords*, otherwise known as *passing notes*, that occur in the passage, and then

3   a few so-called *cross-relations* that are lurking there; as well as

4   some *parallel progressions between voices* that are worthy of note; but finally

5   examine the entire passage once again, bringing all the above points *into conjunction with one another.*

1 Tonal scheme

§466[2]

Right at the very beginning of the movement, and continuing into b. 2, the ear encounters a succession of interesting, aurally intriguing and highly agreeable *ambiguities* [*Mehrdeutigkeiten*] of key and of chord progression.

Right at the outset, the bass note c sounds in isolation. In view of the undeniable ambiguity of the opening, the ear is inclined initially to hear this solitary bass note as the tonic, whether of C major or of C minor.

{204}

Example 1

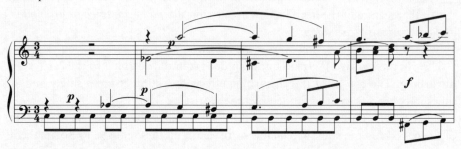

§466[3]

On the last crotchet-beat of b. 1, the note a♭ enters against this c. This leaves the ear with a new element of uncertainty: is this latter note to be heard as g♯ or a♭? [. . .]

It would be notated as g♯ if, for example, the passage were to continue along the following lines:

Example 2

If, however, it is heard as a♭, much ambiguity remains, in that the ear still has the choice of regarding the dyad [*Zusammenklang*] [c a♭] as belonging to the chord of . . . . A♭ thus as the chord on the sixth scale-degree in C minor . . . . c: VI or as the tonic chord of A♭ major. . . . . A♭: I; or as belonging instead to the minor triad . . . . f, thus as the chord on the fourth scale-degree in C minor . . . . c: IV; or perhaps as the tonic chord of F minor. f: I.

Example 3

{205} Initially, the ear must await more precise specification, in what follows, of the intended key – of which there is as yet no intimation. [. . .]

With the entry of the note e♭' at the beginning of the next bar, the dyad of the hitherto isolated notes [c and a♭] now takes the form of a complete A♭ triad. With this, the ear experiences the pleasant sense of relief which it always associates with the gradual resolution of harmonic ambiguities.

Example 4

But at this stage it is still no more than a friendly premonition of the required information, leaving the ear the choice of hearing the triad . . . . *A♭*

either as . . . . .c: VI

or as . . . . A♭: I.

Is it to be the former or the latter? As yet there is still no good foundation on which to base a decision. For all we know, the A♭ may yet turn out to be merely a passing note to G, and the chord come to rest on a C minor triad.

Example 5

Still in doubt as to the key, the ear now waits to hear what will come next.

§466⁴

In this state of continuing tonal uncertainty,[7] in which the ear longs to hear the arrival of confirmation that the key is either C minor or A♭ major, it now hears the A♭ move to G on the second crotchet-beat of b. 2. At precisely that moment, {206} startling us rather than fulfilling our expectations, the note a♮" appears in the upper voice, contradicting the expected key, so that the previous triad [c a♭ e♭'] now sounds as the chord [c g e♭' a"], which

Example 6

considered as a four-note chord with diminished fifth . . . . °a⁷

can be heard as the seventh scale-degree in B♭ major. . . . . B♭: °VII⁷

or – closer to the ear's previous assumption – as the second

scale-degree in G minor [. . .] . . . . g: °II⁷.

Instead of either of these assumptions (which in any case presuppose a modulation [*Ausweichung*] from one of the keys heard as prevailing hitherto, either into B♭ major or into G minor), the ear can hear the g as merely a passing note, not belonging to the chord at all. Its relationship in that case may perhaps prove to be something simpler on the next beat.

Still in doubt, the ear looks and listens eagerly for what will happen next.

Example 7

§466⁵

As it turns out, on the next crotchet-beat the g moves down to f♯, yielding the chord [c f♯ d' a"], which the ear has no difficulty in assimilating in the light of what has preceded it as the chord of the dominant of the dominant of C minor (in the third inversion), thus as . . . . 𝔇⁷.

7 *unentschiedene Stimmung*: the enforced circumlocution of this translation conceals the true meaning of *Stimmung*, Weber's term for the process whereby the ear 'perceives this or that chord as the tonic chord'. Warner translates it as 'attunement': see chap. 4, section 3, §§190–225. See also below, §466⁹, *sich umstimmen*, lit. 'to change attunement'.

This now confirms that the g of the chord {207} [c g e♭' a"] on the second crotchet-beat was in reality only a passing note to f♯, whose place it took for a fleeting moment. The chord progression of b. 2 has thus not in fact been:

$$\mathcal{A}♭ - {}^{\circ}a^7 - \mathcal{D}^7 - (!)$$

but more simply and more directly:

$$\mathcal{A}♭ - \mathcal{D}^7.$$

After this $\mathcal{D}^7$ chord, dominant of the dominant of C minor, the ear now expects a $\mathcal{G}$ major triad to follow.

Example 8

§466[6]

The chord that does appear in the next bar seems to fulfil the ear's expectations

completely as . . . . $\mathcal{G}$
(the c♯' in voice 2 of which functions as an unprepared [*schwer*] chromatic passing note (changing note) to the harmony note d' that follows it, as too does the a" function as a prepared changing note [. . .] to the g" that follows it. The f♯" that ensues immediately in the upper voice, the a' in voice 2 and the a and c' in voice 3 all interact as passing notes).

Thanks to the emergence of this $\mathcal{G}$ major chord, the ambiguity that has prevailed hitherto is now at last sufficiently eradicated for the ear to hear the chord as an established dominant chord, or fifth scale-degree, of C minor or C major [. . .].

{208}

§466[7]

Throughout the first two beats of the next bar, the ear continues to hear this same dominant chord, until on the final beat (the fifth quaver-beat) a b♭" enters in the upper voice contradicting this chord. This note, foreign to the scales of both C major and C minor [. . .], forces the ear to interpret the

Example 9

dyad [G b♭"] as some other chord, belonging to a different key; $\mathcal{G}$ $\mathcal{D}^7$? forces it, indeed, for reasons of coherence to take it initially as a $\mathcal{G}$ minor triad . . . . $\mathfrak{g}$
and as the tonic chord of G minor . . . . g: I.

The chord progression of this bar is thus:

		$\mathcal{G}$	–		$\mathcal{D}$	–		$\mathfrak{g}$
	G:	I	–		V	–	g:	I
or	C:	V	–	G:	V	–	g:	I

or otherwise, if the F♯ and a″ are considered purely as passing notes:

G: I   –   g: I;

or   C: V   –   g: I.

§466[8]

There are several things about this interpretation, albeit provisional, that need to be said.

For a start, a modulation of this sort (one, that is, that comes about through a dominant chord (say a Ⓖ major triad as dominant of C major or minor) being followed immediately (or virtually so) by the tonic chord of the minor key a perfect fifth higher (thus a Ⓖ minor chord as g:I)) is very uncommon, most unfamiliar to the ear. The ear is as a result disinclined to tolerate it in this manner.

{209}

§466[9]

Secondly, however, the way in which this modulation comes about is hardly propitious, in that the b♭″ enters almost casually, on the weak final beat of the bar [. . .], the ear having previously grown accustomed to the long-extended b♮. After having heard during the course of b. 3 and the first two beats of b. 4, first the quavers a–b♮ in voice 3, then similarly a′–b♮′ in voice 2, then again likewise a′–b♮′ in voice 3:

Example 10

and now into the bargain the rising progression from a″ in the upper voice, one can be excused for confidently expecting this last a″ to rise in analogous fashion to b♮″.

Example 11

Totally contrary to all expectations, however, it does nothing of the sort. Instead it deviates from the model of the other voices – wrongly, we cannot help feeling, and for what reason? – suddenly introducing in place of the previous b♮ a b♭:

Example 12

introducing immediately after voice 3's

a–b♮–c'   and then   a'–b♮'–c"

and likewise after voice 2's {210}

a'–b♮'–c"

out of the blue, in complete disregard for what has gone before,

not a♮"–b♮"–c'''   but instead   a"–b♭"–c'''.

This happens, moreover, on a beat (the weak final beat of the 3/4 bar) that is ill-equipped, because of its brevity and lack of inherent stress [. . .] for carrying so momentous a deflection and modulation [*Ab- und Ausweichung*] to the unsuspecting ear. So revolutionary a move [*eine solche Reform*] [the first voice] tries to foist upon the ear (which might have accepted it, had it been presented in a rather more imposing manner, or even just with fuller texture, such as:[8]

Example 13),

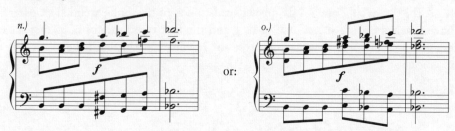

not only at a point of such weak stress but also in bare two-part texture, accompanied solely by the bass's G, without support from the other voices, who are resting, and whose b♮s are still ringing in our ears. On its own authority, and without any apparent motivation, it takes the law into its own hands and seeks to overthrow the 𝔊 major triad which has been in force as a result of the combined efforts of all four voices up to this point throughout the greater and more stressed part of the bar, transforming it now unilaterally into the triad of 𝔊 minor. In so doing, moreover, [the upper voice] is given less than satisfactory support by the bass, its sole accompaniment: the space separating the two notes, {211} G–b♭", unmediated as it is by middle voices, is so *extreme* as not to present them to the ear as a functional unity. [. . .]

Confronted by the emergence of so indecisive a change of harmony [*Harmoniewechsel*], the ear almost goes astray, and is left in some doubt as to whether to believe, whether to take seriously, what it has heard. Will the first violinist, with his remote, tenuous, etiolated b♭", now restore the hitherto ubiquitous b♮, all casual like, during the last beat of the bar [*im letzten Tactviertel*]? Or has he

---

8   Music example not in *Caecilia* version.

perhaps stopped the string at the wrong place, at b♭" instead of b♮"?[9] Or, it wonders equally well, is the b♭" really an a♯", and thus a chromatic passing note to a b♮" which will now follow, such as

Example 14

But this conjecture is clearly dashed when not b♮" but c''' ensues –

Example 15

and the ear is forced to abandon [. . .] this comfortable means of explaining the problem away (a♯" instead of b♭"), and to adjust itself [*sich umstimmen*] all too hastily in the weak final beat of the bar to G minor as a reality.

§466[10]

Scarcely has it had time to make this enforced adjustment when right at the {212} beginning of the next bar (b. 5) yet another unexpected chord progression awaits it, with the emergence of the dyad [B♭ d♭'''], brought about when the upper voice, in immediate response to the

a   b♮   c'   d'

and   a'   b♮'   c"   d"

in the lower voices, now suddenly, in flagrant contradiction, introduces

a"   b♭"   c'''   d♭'''

---

9   The *AmZ*, 1 (11 September 1799), col. 855, reports that Count Grassalkowich, on hearing Mozart's Haydn Quartets, at first accused the players of making mistakes, and then tore up the parts on the spot; see Vertrees, 'Mozart's String Quartet K.465', 97.

The ear, already taxed as to how to account for the appearance of the bb", and to understand how it came about, is now at an even greater loss as to how to make intelligible sense out of the dyad [Bb db'''].

The dyad, seen in the context of the next bar (b. 6), emerges as a genuine 𝕭b minor triad in intention – indeed as the tonic chord of Bb minor:

Example 16

It has therefore precipitated a modulation from G minor, which has barely had time to establish itself, into Bb minor (a key remote from C major, C minor, G major and G minor [. . .]); and precipitated it, furthermore, by way of a wholly unprepared chord of bb: I following directly on from the 𝕲 minor triad g: I; in short, two utterly remote keys stated one immediately after another.

{213}

§466¹¹

Maybe the ear could avoid making the assumption of yet another remote modulation by interpreting the db''' in violin I as a c♯''', hence as a chromatic passing note to a putative d♮''' to follow:

Example 17.

But this hypothesis is no more borne out than was the earlier one of a♯" for bb": for no d♮''' now ensues. Instead, the db''' marks the close of the phrase, while the bass with its reiterated Bbs introduces the selfsame figure [Formel] that occurred in b. 1 and what followed, except that it is in a key one step lower.

Example 18

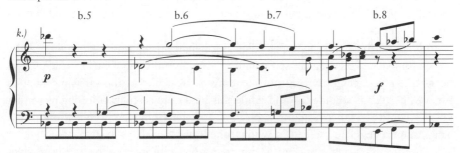

The whole of bb. 1–4 is now restated a whole tone lower, with the sole difference that in b. 9 violin I proceeds not to c♭''' but to c♮''' (the latter being a great deal less foreign to the ear than was the d♭''' of b. 5).

§466[12]

With this analysis of the passage under discussion, the understanding of which will present no further difficulties for the advanced {214} reader, I have fulfilled my promise (made at the end of §225)[10] to provide an *Analysis [Analyse] of the tonal scheme* of this passage. This analysis will become all the clearer during a consideration of the interaction [*Verflechtung*] of the piece's melodic lines or parts which now follows.[11]

2 Passing notes

§466[13]

The many passing notes that occur in the passage under discussion constitute a second respect in which this passage exhibits noteworthy, at times even surprising features.[12]

10   vol. II, p. 186. See note 5 above, relating to the first allusion to this promise, at the beginning of §466[bis]. As there, the term *Zergliederung* of the promise becomes *Analyse* here.

11   In place of this paragraph in the *Caecilia* version there appears the following:

> In closing the analysis of the *tonal scheme* of the passage concerned at this point, I hope therein to have been understood by those who are not yet familiar from my *Theory of Composition* with the fundamental issues underlying the question – How does the ear assimilate each of the conjunctions of pitches that confront it as belonging to this or that preceding or new, closely or remotely related key? In that volume (1st edn, vol. II, §§33–68; 2nd and 3rd edns, vol. II, §§190–225), I have for the first time ever ventured an attempt at this theory (which has so far been dealt with by only *one* music theorist [Vogler?]), and only wish I could, in the interests of a fuller understanding of the processes described above, reproduce it here in the context of this extraordinarily difficult passage, unusually developed, opaque and ambiguous as its tonal scheme is. I must, however, suppress this wish so as not to make the present article too long, and content myself with the hope of having been sufficiently clear and comprehensible even so.

12   What follows at this point in the original is simply a series of cross-references, thus:

> However, all that is noteworthy in this respect has already been discussed at length in §§360, 361, 362, 363, 408 of the present volume, to which I respectfully request the reader to refer at this point in order (see pp. 68, 71, 72, 73 and 136 of the present third edition).

<[. . .] Not infrequently, a neighbouring note immediately precedes a note of a chord, *while at the same moment in another voice* the note of that chord is itself sounded. [. . .]

In b. 3, a" appears in the upper voice as a neighbouring note to g", while at the same moment in voice 3 g is itself sounded. Again, in the same bar, in voice 3, one hears the a as a neighbouring note leading to b♮, while at the same moment in the bass B♮ itself is sounded; – and while this bass note is still continuing to sound, voice 2, and then voice 3 again, present a' as a neighbouring note leading to b♮'. The same process can be seen [a whole tone lower] in bb. 7–8.>[13]

<The simultaneous sounding of the main note with its neighouring note gives the least harsh effect when the former is the root of the chord [. . .]. The effect is less mild when a neighbouring note sounds simultaneously with *one of the other* notes [of the chord], for example the fifth, [. . .] and still more offensive to the ear when sounding simultaneously with the third [. . .].

This may be the reason why the passing notes already mentioned in bb. 4 and 8 [. . .] are so ungrateful to the ear.>.[14]

<[. . .] Sometimes the passing note is struck at exactly the same moment as other [notes] of harmonic status – sometimes not. [. . .]

Thus in b. 2 [. . .] a" in the upper voice is struck at exactly the same moment as g [in voice 3], this g evidently being a passing note to f♯, along with c in the bass. Again, in b. 3, where the two passing notes a" and c♯' sound simultaneously [. . .], the latter passing note, c♯', is struck at exactly the same moment as B♮ and g in the lower voices. The process repeats itself [a whole tone lower] in bb. 6 and 7.>[15]

<Such increased harshness is doubly perceptible when the *very harmony note* to which the passing note pertains is struck simultaneously with it, so that main note and passing note are not merely *heard together* but are actually *struck at one and the same moment*. [. . .]

The paragraphs thus cross-referred all occur in chapter VIII 'Passing notes': section II 'Different ways in which passing notes may occur', (F) 'Main note sounding simultaneously with its neighbouring note' (§§360, 361) and (G) 'Passing notes struck simultaneously' (§§362, 363), and section IV 'Ambiguity', (C) 'Mediating effect of ambiguity' (§§407, 408). The passages given in angle-brackets in translation are the relevant extracts from these cross-referred paragraphs, and are identified by individual footnote below.

In the *Caecilia* version, the following paragraph appears:

In order to present the most noteworthy features in this respect, I have quoted *verbatim* as conveniently as possible those paragraphs of my manual of composition in which the relevant principles (admittedly in a way which, while as self-explanatory as possible, deviates from the fragmentary treatment in this analysis up to now) are set forth, and in which I (as already mentioned in the introduction to the present article) have used by way of illustration the *Mozart* composition now under discussion (itself debated by others). I have reproduced what was relevant in the paragraphs concerned word for word (according to the second and especially the third editions).

Weber then incorporates passages from §§354, 355, 358, 360, 361, 362, 363, 407, 408, 490, 491, 492 (omitting the discussion of Mozart, but transferring the example to the next paragraph), 493, 494, 495 (excluding the last clause and example), 496, 499, 500.

13   The passage in angle-brackets is extracted from §360 (vol. III, pp. 68–9). In the original, it includes bb. 1–8 in short score (as Ex. 177 *i*), and concludes with a cross-reference to §466[bis], i.e. the main discussion of the Mozart passage.

14   The passage in angle-brackets is extracted from §361 (vol. III, pp. 70–71). The original cross-refers to Ex. 177 *i* of the previous passage, and concludes with a cross-reference to §466[bis].

15   The passage in angle-brackets is extracted from §362 (vol. III, pp. 71–2). The original cross-refers to Ex. 177 *i* of the penultimate passage, and concludes with a cross-reference to §466[bis].

This offers a further reason why in bb. 3 and 4 [. . .] the neighbouring notes to b♮ and b♮' clash so harshly with the B♮ in the bass, which is struck afresh against them each time. [. . .]>[16]

< [. . .] Many a combination of notes that might otherwise be expected to strike the ear as unpleasant in fact sounds far more agreeable than it might have done because when viewed as a set of pure harmony notes it would form a chord that does not sound harsh in its own right; that is, it constitutes a chord-semblance [*Scheinaccord*] [. . .] which, when viewed as a chord-reality [*wirklicher Accord*] does not belong to the class of harsh-sounding chords.

By contrast, [. . .] at the beginning of b. 3 the ear is unable to make out of the combination [B♮ g c♯' a"] even so much as a chord-semblance – yet another reason why this chord sounds (to put it mildly) not particularly appealing.>[17]

3 Cross-relations

§466[14]

The above heading indicates yet another respect in which the passage in question exhibits quite remarkable features.[18]

<When a voice moves by leap to a note that has been heard moments before in a chromatically different form, [that leap] usually sounds harsh and unpleasant. [. . .] Theorists have termed such part-writing 'cross-relation' [*Querstand*] or *relatio non harmonica*. [. . .]

Cross-relations are not infrequently audible even when the leap to the chromatically different note is filled with notes of transient value and importance. [. . .]

A cross-relation of this sort is formed in b. 4 by the b♭" [in the upper voice] with respect to the B♮ heard only moments before [in the bass and voices 2 and 3]:

g"   a"   b♭"   c'"   d♭'"

B♮   F♯   G   A   B♭ >[19]

< A case closely analogous to the cross-relations just discussed is that in which a voice, instead of moving by leap, enters *quite independently*, striking a note which has just before been heard in a chromatically different form. [. . .]

16 The passage in angle-brackets is extracted from §363 (vol. III, pp. 72–3). The original cross-refers to Ex. 177 *i* of the earlier passage, and concludes with a cross-reference to §466[bis].
17 The passage in angle-brackets is extracted from §§407–408 (vol. III, pp. 134–6). In the original, it includes bb. 1–4 in short score (as Ex. 177), and concludes with a cross-reference to §466[bis].
18 What follows at this point in the original is simply a series of cross-references, thus: 'We [shall] discuss it in this regard in §§492, 493, 494, 495, and can for now only allude to those paragraphs.' The paragraphs thus cross-referred to all occur in chapter X 'Movement by leap', section II 'Detailed consideration of certain species of leaps', (C) 'Cross-relation'. The passages given in angle-brackets in translation are the relevant extracts from these cross-referred paragraphs, and are identified by individual footnote below.
19 The passage in angle-brackets is extracted from §§490–492 (vol. IV, pp. 28–31). In the original, it includes bb. 1–9 in short score (as Ex. 55), and concludes with a cross-reference to §466[bis].

[Instances of this] are the entries in the upper voice at b. 2 [a♮" against the a♭ in voice 3], and b. 6 [g♮" against the g♭ in voice 3].>[20]

<It is not infrequent to find [cross-relations that] disturb the smooth flow of the parts [. . .], while there are others, including so-called non-harmonic cross-relations, that under favourable circumstances sound not at all adverse.

Slightly less unobjectionable than these latter, at least to my way of feeling, are the cross-relations just discussed [i.e. bb. 2, 4 and 6].>[21]

<The cross-relation in bb. 4 and 5 [. . .] seems so foreign to the ear chiefly because there is only one quaver between the two notes; whereas the same progression [*Modulationen*] at a very slow tempo would be far more acceptable to the ear, as, for example, in the following:>[22]

Example 19

4 Parallel progressions between voices
§466[15]

The last feature that we consider worthy of note in the passage under discussion is {215} the fact that at two points a pair of voices proceeds in parallel motion at the interval of a second.[23]

<It never makes a particularly good effect to hear the bass proceeding, as it does in the transition from b. 2 to b. 3 of the passage concerned, from c to B♮ while voice 2 proceeds at the same moment from d' to c♯', and to hear similar pure parallel seconds again in the transition from b. 6 to b. 7, namely:[24]

```
              { d'    c♯'              { c'    b♮

bb. 2–3: {                  bb. 6–7: {

              { c     B♮               { B♭    A
                                                    . >
```

20   The passage in angle-brackets is extracted from §493 (vol. IV, pp. 31–2). The original cross-refers to Ex. 55 of the previous passage, and concludes with a cross-reference to §466[bis].

21   The passage in angle-brackets is extracted from §494 (vol. IV, pp. 32–3). The original cross-refers to Ex. 55 of the penultimate passage, and also to §§492 and 493, and concludes with cross-references to §§495 (the next passage) and 466[bis].

22   The passage in angle-brackets is extracted from §495 (vol. IV, p. 34). The original cross-refers to Ex. 55 of the earlier passage, and also to §494, and concludes with a cross-reference to §466[bis].

23   What follows in the original is merely a cross-reference, thus: 'In this respect, as before, we can only refer to our §500, particularly since it is a matter of no grave consequence.' The paragraph thus cross-referred to occurs in chapter XI 'Merits of different parallel progressions', section II 'Parallel progressions in seconds'. The passage given in angle-brackets in translation is the relevant extract from this cross-referred paragraph, and is identified by footnote below.

24   The passage in angle-brackets is extracted from §500 (vol. IV, p. 41). The original cross-refers to §492 and to Ex. 55 of that paragraph, and concludes with a cross-reference to §466[bis].

5 Review of the grammatical construction of the passage as a whole

§466[16]

Now that in each of the preceding [four] sections [of this analysis] we have examined the passage in question from an aspect which occupies an entire chapter of my theory of composition [*Tonsatzlehre*],[25] all that remains is for us now to go through it once again right from the beginning, bringing all these aspects *together* and seeing how they *operate in consort*.

§466[17]

As we listen to the passage, the first thing that strikes the ear as noticeably harsh is the chord [c g e♭' a"] in b. 2.

Example 20

What is disturbing in this arises from the interaction of several circumstances touched upon in the preceding paragraphs: the cross-related entry of the a" in the upper voice (§466[14]),[26] against which the unprepared passing note (§466[13]), struck at exactly the same moment as this a" and the c in the bass, and the chord [c g e♭' a"] that results from this, double the disturbing effect to the ear. (See 466[4-5] above.)

{216} The very fact *that* this disturbing effect results primarily from the interaction of these circumstances becomes apparent when we alter the passage so as to eliminate these circumstances, in ways such as the following:

---

25   i.e. chapters VI 'Tonal shaping of entire pieces', VIII 'Passing notes', X 'Movement by leap', and XI 'Merits of particular parallel progressions'.

26   In the following section, cross-references to §§466[13-15] given in parentheses take the form in the original of cross-references to paragraphs of vol. III and earlier paragraphs of vol. IV that have for purposes of this translation been incorporated into §§466[13-15] above.

Example 21

§466[18]

The second thing that strikes the ear as disturbing is the chord [B♮ g c♯' a"] at the very beginning of the next bar (b. 3).[27]

Example 22

The appearance of the ⑤ major chord in itself is more than welcome to the ear, conforming entirely to its expectations {217} (§466[6] above); and yet the ear's contentment appears to be disturbed once again by the c♯' in voice 2. It would have been happy for the neighbouring note a", itself prepared by the a" in the preceding bar, to introduce the root g" in the upper voice, while at the same time [against this a"] the root g itself is sounded in voice 3 (466[13]). It is not this, not the

27   Music example not in *Caecilia* version.

neighbouring note a", that disturbs the ear's contentment. Rather it is the c♯', as we shall see in just a moment, that causes the chord to lose all its harshness as soon as this neighbouring note is replaced by its own main note.

Example 23

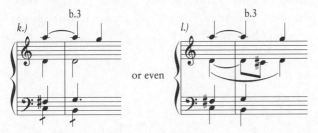

This c♯', as neighbouring note to the d', a constituent of the Ⓖ major chord, this upstart changing note that so rudely displaces its own main note, d', by a full crotchet-value and robs it of the stressed beat [. . .], and is in addition struck at the same moment as the harmony notes B♮ and g (§466¹³), reaches the ear out of place. So soon after its first turbulent encounter, the ear now yearns for a Ⓖ major chord simple and unadorned, or at most embellished by an a" suspension. But that this c♯' should forcibly displace the harmony note d', that it should mar its arrival, indeed subvert the entry of the long-desired Ⓖ major chord, on the first beat of the bar, and distort the chord into [B♮ g c♯' a"], which is not even a chord-semblance (§466¹³) – the likes of this it never expected.

§466¹⁹

In this same bar (b. 3), simultaneously with the fourth repeated {218} quaver B♮ in the bass (not the root, nor yet the fifth, but the third of the underlying chord, §466¹³), there sounds in voice 3 the neighbouring note a, a passing note to b, the two notes being struck at the same moment (§466¹³).[28]

Example 24

And at the selfsame instant, just as this a moves to its main note, the upper voice shifts again from the root g" to the passing note f♯"; and simultaneously with this

---

28   Music example not in *Caecilia* version.

f♯" the notes B♮ and b♮ (the third of the underlying chord) in the two lowest voices are struck anew (§466¹³).

The passing note f♯" is still sounding when, on the last quaver-beat of the bar, two more passing notes, c' and a', appear, the latter leading to b♮'. Against these three notes [c' a' f♯"], all foreign to the chord, the low third in the bass, B♮, is struck again (§466¹³), so that in the course of the last six quavers of this bar the ear hears the following succession of chords:²⁹

Example 25

Immediately after that, on the second quaver-beat of the next bar (b. 4), the passing notes a' and c" appear again together, the bass continually reiterating its low third, B♮.

§466²⁰

The second half of this bar (b. 4) has two further noteworthy features in store for us: the {219} transformation (already referred to in §§466⁷⁻⁹) of the Ⓖ major chord into a Ⓖ minor chord, brought about by the appearance of b♭" instead of b♮" in the upper voice – for no apparent reason – and at the same time by the cross-related entry of that same b♭" in the upper voice against the b♮' present in all the other voices up to this point. [. . .]

§466²¹

Finally, the transition from the fourth to the next bar, with the emergence of the dyad [B♭ d♭'''], brings with it the remote and unaccountable conjunction, already mentioned in §466¹⁰, of the keys of G minor and B♭ minor.

The fact that from this point on the entire phrase comprising bb. 1–4 is restated identically in the next four bars, but in the key one step lower, has already been noted (end of §466¹¹).

6 The rhetorical import of the passage

§466²²

Hitherto we have considered the passage solely as regards its *grammatical structure*. It remains for us now to examine it from the point of view of its inherent rhetorical disposition [*rhetorische Durchführung*], in terms of the rhetorical phrases that the

---

29   The following music example is given in letter-notation in the *Caecilia* version.

composer has deployed and the linkages that exist between them. This will instruct us as to *why* Mozart was unable to avoid – or perhaps spurned the avoidance of – some of the eccentricities that we have observed – some of them genuinely harsh, obtrusively so; why he might have had no use for any of the many excellent suggestions with which his critics so eagerly leap to his assistance, keen to advise him on how to improve the passage (no, not even those that I myself have suggested in §§466[17–18]).

{220}

§466[23]

The intention [*Intention*] behind this entire passage was unmistakeably the following pattern of *imitation*:

Example 26

in which the figure [*Gesang*] in the voice that enters at the end of b. 1 (viola) –

a♭ – a♭ – g – f♯ – g –

is *imitated note for note* an octave (double octave) higher by the upper voice (violin I) entering one bar later –

a" – a" – g" – f♯" – g" .

The only exception here is that the first note of violin I is not, as in the middle voice, a♭ but a♮". Thus the step from the first note, a", to the second, g", in the upper voice is a whole tone, whereas that in the viola, a♭–g, is a semitone, hence the imitation is *not entirely strict*. (The *reason* for a♮" rather than a♭" in the upper voice is easily stated: to give the upper voice a♭ at the very moment that the middle voice sounds f♯ would be to produce the far less satisfactory-sounding chord [c f♯ a♭"] – whether viewed as a chord-semblance or as a chord-reality ([. . .] 466[13]) – whereas the chord [c f♯ a"] suggests an entirely natural dominant of the dominant.

§466[24]

On looking more closely at the counterpoint reproduced in the preceding paragraph, we find it possible {221} to fit between the two imitative points [*Melodieen*] already working together yet a third voice in imitation, located one crotchet after the a♭ of the viola

ab – ab – g – f♯ – g

its imitative point pitched a fifth higher[30]

eb' – eb' – d' – c♯' – d'

the imitation entirely strict

Example 27

with the sole difference that this new entry by the middle voice (violin II) starts not on the final beat of the bar, as do the other two, then to be syncopated over the stressed first beat of the next bar, but the other way round: it starts on the stressed first beat and is held over the unstressed beat that follows (a difference which in technical terms is called *imitatio per thesin at arsin*,[31] but I will not burden my readers with a laborious explication [*Explication*] of that here.

§466[25]

The fact that interpolating this new imitative entry with its c♯ would entail the harshness already observed (§466[18-19]) in b. 3 must have seemed inconsequential to the composer, for {222} by one slight alteration to [each of] the imitative points he could have eradicated all traces of harshness:[32]

Example 28 here

30   The note symbols of the next example lack primes in the original.
31   lit. 'imitation by downbeat and upbeat': see Analysis 4 above for Sechter's use of the concept, and note 20 of that Analysis for Marpurg's description of the device in his *Abhandlung von der Fuge* (Berlin: A. Haude and J. C. Spener, 1753–4). The phrase *per arsin et thesin* was earlier used by Zarlino, Morley, Walther and others to signify inversion.
32   The following example in fact conforms with the first four bars of the celebrated 'improved version' produced by Fétis in 1830, which caused such a stir: see Vertrees, 'Mozart's String Quartet K.465', pp. 99–101.

§466²⁶

Thus, by the means described above, the composer contrived three voices in imitation. There remained, however, not only the fact, already remarked (§§466²³⁻²⁴), that the imitations were not totally strict and literal, but also the additional irregularity that the imitative point of violin II entered only a *single* crotchet after that of the viola, whereas the imitative point of violin I entered *two* crotchets after that of violin II. To put it another way, the entries of the viola and violin II are at *one* beat's distance (*one* crotchet-value), whereas those of violins I and II are at *two* beats' distance.

It might appear desirable to achieve greater regularity in the interval of these entries – to bring violin I in after violin II at the same distance as violin II after the viola.

To have effected this by introducing and continuing violin I's entire imitative point a crotchet earlier clearly would not have worked – but a *certain measure of* regularity was possible among the entries, or, if you prefer, a *semblance* of regularity, if just the first note, a", were advanced by a crotchet and its value prolonged [by that amount]:

Example 29

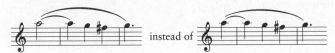

{223} As a result of this, *each* of the imitative voices at any rate *commences* its imitative [*imitirende*] point *one* crotchet after the previous one:

Example 30

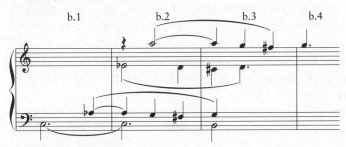

But this prolongation of the first note in the upper voice only serves to reduce in another respect the strict literalness of the imitation. What is more, the earlier entry of the a", immediately after the viola's a♭, only serves to create the harshness observed in §466¹⁷ – incidental effects³³ that the composer chose to overlook rather than to sacrifice his governing idea [*Idee*] of introducing each voice if at all possible one crotchet after the preceding one.³⁴

33 *Zufälligkeiten*: perhaps a faint hint here of Kirnberger's technical term, *zufällig*, for an 'inessential' dissonance – i.e. one produced by melodic operations rather than by intrinsically harmonic ones?

34 Weber interpolates a lengthy footnote at this point refuting Fétis's maxim that in imitation alternating at the fifth and fourth the distance between the second and third entries must always

§466²⁷

If we should want to go further and examine the continuation of the passage in question from the standpoint of imitation [*Imitation*] – which at this stage we could do only in concise form, however – then we can see the continuation of the imitative point in the viola

a – b♮ – c' – d'

closely followed in imitation one crotchet behind by violin II – now no longer at the fifth but instead at the octave

a' – b♮' – c" – d"

whereupon this figure is repeated two crotchets later in the upper voice, only now

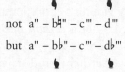

not a" – b♮" – c"' – d"'

but a" – b♭" – c"' – d♭"'

{225} The reason for this was that the composer wished to repeat the whole process, restating the phrase of the first four bars a step lower in the key of B♭ minor in the bars that follow (end of §466¹¹).

7 Conclusion

§466²⁸

These,[35] then, are the most choice idiosyncrasies that present themselves, close-packed within the space of so few bars, to our scrutiny.

No one with ears can deny that the piling up of so many unusual features at one time is disturbing – intensely disturbing – to the ear. Of what does the disturbing effect consist? Through what concatenation of circumstances is it effected? What were the intentions that lay behind it and prompted it? These things we have learned in the course of the foregoing analysis. All that technical theory could have done, it has here done.

But does this accumulation of simultaneities and successions of notes ever overstep the limits of harshness that can be tolerated by the ear? Or does it not? In all

be a beat or two, even a bar or two, greater than that between the first and second entries. Weber contends that, insofar as the maxim has any validity at all, it is inapplicable here, since equidistant entry points are a mere semblance in this case.

35 The *Caecilia* version has the next four paragraphs, but placed at the conclusion of the first 'instalment', at the end of section 5. In *Caecilia* at this point now appears the following paragraph:

Now that we have in the above enquiry also attempted to explore the rhetorical (or, as often said, the contrapuntal-imitative) intentions that the composer pursued in the oft-discussed passage, it must be left to the faculty of hearing and good taste of each individual to determine whether Mozart has done well or badly, or whether he ought to have foregone the harshnesses that confront our ears in this passage under the dictates of those intentions, or whether perhaps something else. To decide with apodeictic *assurance* which of the gentlemen who have been at loggerheads over the lawfulness or lawlessness of the passage has right on his side – is not decreed by *me*, or by *my* principles [. . .]. The verdict on this is reserved for the trained ear of every individual listener.

the preceding discussions this question has received no categorical answer, although it has been much illuminated. (I have stated on more than one occasion that I do not believe each and every one of the rules under which [. . .] one [commentator] can demonstrate the lawlessness of the passage while another can demonstrate its law-abiding quality.)

In the last resort, it is the *musically trained ear alone* that must be the judge, and in this respect a *supreme* judge has already decided *in favour* of the passage – I refer to *the ear* {226} *of a Mozart*, who dedicated this quartet, as the best that he was capable of, to his friend and mentor *Joseph Haydn*, as a token of grateful esteem.

As to what is acceptable to *my* ear, I freely admit that with tonal constructs such as these it does *not* feel comfortable. And this I can say openly and in defiance of those fools and jealous ones, because I believe I have the right to declare with pride: *I know what I like in my Mozart.*

Carl Czerny (1791–1857)
    'Harmonic Groundwork of Beethoven's Sonata Op. 53'

Antoine Reicha: *Course of Musical Composition*,
trans.   A. Merrick, ed. J. Bishop: Appendix by
Carl Czerny (*c.*1832–4)

The construing of a piece of music as a series of 'layers' goes back to the music theory of the Renaissance, even to that of the Middle Ages. *Conceptual* layers, that is, not actual ones – not like voices in a polyphonic texture (they could not with any meaning be performed simultaneously), nor like successive sections in a composition. Rather each layer in the series is a more elaborate version of a preceding layer, and so on until the first layer in the series is reached.

There are two distinct and opposite views that give rise to this conception. One is the view of music as organism (already much discussed above), whereby a piece of music expands in a continuous process of growth from initial cell or cells to fully developed life-form. If this process is truly continuous, then these 'layers' are like cross-sections taken through the growing organism at arbitrary stages in development – or like still photographs taken at selected points along the path of growth. The process, which can be called 'generative' and which has its theoretical origins in the fundamental bass analyses of Rameau discussed in the General Introduction, not to mention its even earlier practical semblance in the unmeasured lute pieces of the seventeenth century and the keyboard *préludes non mesurés* of Louis Couperin and others, is represented quintessentially by the methods of Heinrich Schenker, who deployed a succession of layers (*Schichten*): the background (itself a projection through time of the major triad, or 'chord of Nature', which was in turn a projection through tonal space of the single note), any number of middlegrounds and the foreground, beyond which lay the finished score. If on the other hand the process is seen as advancing by separate stages, as is the case with Lobe's portrayal of Bach's and Beethoven's working methods, then it is possible to claim these layers as real and tangible within the composer's creative process, rather than arbitrary.

The alternative view is the one whereby all musical utterances are susceptible of reformulation as more elementary musical utterances, just as, in language, statements are capable of reformulation as more elementary statements, and generally all complex entities capable of definition in terms of simpler entities. This view makes no assumptions as to how such utterances or statements or complex entities came into existence. It merely treats them analytically. The general term for such a procedure is 'reduction'.

Now Czerny did occasionally use organicist language. He spoke expressly of sonata form, for example, as making 'an organic whole'.[1] What is more, like Lobe, he took Beethoven's working methods as his paradigm of the compositional act – he had been, we should remember, a keyboard pupil of Beethoven from the age of ten, had worked as a copyist for the composer and remained an intimate friend thereafter. Nevertheless, Czerny envisaged composition still as the construction of thematic units ('ideas') into unified forms, not as the burgeoning of motifs into purposive wholes. Despite his quasi-organic language, he thought still in terms of *com-position*, that is, the assembling of thematic entities to form structures. Czerny was the first analyst to adopt a layered approach using musical notation, and to apply it to whole pieces of music – though one can see the antecedent of what he did in the figured-bass notation of the seventeenth and eighteenth centuries, and we have already seen that Vogler evolved a fully-fledged technique of 'reduction' using an admixture of bass figurings, root letters and scale-degree Roman numerals (Analysis 7). He developed a technique for extracting what he variously called the 'ground-harmony', the 'harmonic groundwork', the 'ground-melody', or the 'harmonic skeleton', from a piece of music by stripping away its surface matter, which he called its 'moving figure' or 'ornaments'. Although Czerny inculcated into his student-composers the practice of taking the 'harmonic groundwork' of a model composition and investing it with a new 'moving figure' of his or her own, this was seen as a purely synthetic exercise – in no sense as a replication of the true creative process. Hence Czerny's procedure has to be seen as reductive, not generative.

Writing somewhat later than the analysis given below, in his *School of Practical Composition*, in the 1840s or late 1830s, Czerny advocated the use of 'distinguished compositions' such as the sonatas, string quartets and symphonies of Mozart and Beethoven as models. There he described the reduction procedure in the following terms:[2]

> For this purpose, knowledge, care and a great penetration into the spirit of the music is required, in the case of complicated pieces, in order thus to divest the melodies and figures of all ornaments, and to reduce them to their *most simple* harmony. In so doing, particular care must be taken to write each chord in the position which perfectly answers to the melodic idea of the composer. He who is able correctly to draw up such an outline of a composition, thereby proves that he has thoroughly understood and entered into the work.
>
> By this procedure the pupil will with delight become acquainted with the internal structure of the most admirable compositions, and frequently remark, with surprise, on what a simple, though firm and symmetrical basis, the finest and most intellectual works of the great masters rest.

1   Carl Czerny, *School of Practical Composition: Complete Treatise on the Composition of All Kinds of Music . . .* , Op. 600, trans. John Bishop (London: Robert Cocks and Augener, *c.*1848, reprint edn New York: DaCapo Press, 1979; Ger. orig. ?1849), vol. I, p. 34.
2   ibid, p. 93. The italics are Czerny's. Also:

> the only means [for preserving moderation in Development Sections] . . . being – *the study of good models*. In the construction of the second part, Haydn, Mozart and Beethoven are pre-eminent; in which remark, we refer not only to their Pianoforte Sonatas, but also to their trios, quartetts, quintetts, symphonies and, generally, to all their great instrumental works. Clementi, Dussek, Hummel and some others, are also to be viewed as good patterns in this respect. (ibid, pp. 35–6)

In that later work, the chapter 'On the étude or study' puts the technique to work twice 'in order to illustrate the construction and the course of ideas of such pieces'. The first study from vol. IV of J. B. Cramer's *Studies for the Pianoforte* (1804–10), and the now much more famous first study from Chopin's *Studies* Op. 10 (1833) are presented entire in reduction, after each of which the first two bars are given in their original form. After both, there follows a verbal commentary which concludes:[3]

> this is, in a manner, the *anatomy* of the pieces, by which the pupil becomes acquainted with the plan, the construction, the melody, the harmony, the course of ideas, and, generally, with the particular thoughts of the composer, in essential points, and distinguishes them from all exterior embellishments calculated only for effect. A piece whose skeleton is unrhythmical or without meaning, must ever be ranked as a failure.

The implied analogy between corporeal skeleton and compositional 'plan' and 'construction', hence between anatomy and analysis, is plain. What is perhaps interesting is that Czerny considers the 'melody', the 'figures' and the 'course of ideas' still to be present in the finished reduction: all that is characteristic both of the piece and of the composer is preserved there; what has been stripped away belongs to a common stock of surface figuration that is subject to fashion[4] – a view belonging in a sense more to the Renaissance than to the nineteenth century.

Czerny used precisely the same technique as that for the Cramer and Chopin with the C major Prelude from Book I of Bach's *Well-tempered Clavier*,[5] and went a step further with the slow introduction to the Keyboard Sonata in D minor Op. 40 no. 3 by Clementi (1802) by reducing the thirteen-bar original to an unbarred series of seven essentially arhythmical chords, represented as minims.[6] Does this last case offer a clue to the undisclosed basis of Czerny's reduction? Consider: in Czerny's words, the Cramer study is 'built [. . .] on a kind of Choral-melody'; the reduction of the 'Waldstein' Sonata given below is 'pure and noble', and if arranged for choir could serve as a 'serious ecclesiastical composition'; the chorale as a genre in its own right has 'no rhythm [. . .], and the melody springs up, by a regular succession of chords, as it were of itself'.[7] Is there perhaps an only half-realized notion of the chorale as a musical archetype – as what Koch in 1787 called 'simple harmony' or 'primal substance' (*Urstoff*), which streams forth without effort in the composer's mind, but which the composer moulds to his own character and in which he embeds his ideas, and which can then be uncovered by analysis? If this speculation seems to conflict with Czerny's condemnation of 'unrhythmic' skeletons, then perhaps the rhythm that he has in mind is not detailed patterning at the level of notes (of which there is little either in the chorales that he cites or in his skeletons), but rather the rhythm of musical phraseology.

In the 'Waldstein' reduction given below Czerny inevitably falls into inconsistencies in scale of reduction, leaving some ideas intact, partly reducing others,

3   ibid, 91–4.
4   ibid, 88–9: 'Embellishments are an object and an offspring of fashion, and grow old, as soon as better or at least others of a pleasing kind are invented.' It is to the latest operas that Czerny referred the young composer for the latest in embellishment.
5   ibid, 114–15.
6   ibid, 53, 55.
7   vol. II, p. 195, chap. 10 'On the oratorio and the cantata'.

eliminating others altogether, even treating one formation differently in two different places (compare b. 12 with b. 147, for example). He frequently moves extreme register to middle register; and where one idea is stated successively in different registers, he normally reduces them at the same. By reduction, some of the most striking surface effects are lost – the pungent minor ninth followed by major ninth in bb. 70–72 and 231–3, for example, disappears, whereas the minor ninth in b. 290 is retained. It is important to realize that Czerny has omitted bb. 188–9, hence all bar numbers from 190 to the end are two less than their corresponding bars in the published score.

Carl Czerny (1791–1857) was born, and lived most of his life, in Vienna. He embarked on a brilliant career as a concert pianist in 1800, including early performances of works by Beethoven, but later withdrew from public performance, becoming one of the most influential piano teachers of the century, as well as one of the most prolific composers. He also produced many editions of early keyboard works (see the Introduction to Analysis 3 above, for his Bach editions) and numerous pedagogical works, as well as making contributions to music theory. Between about 1832 and 1834, he published in German translation in four volumes, under the composite title *Reicha's Theory of Composition*, or *Complete Textbook of Musical Composition*, the three treatises of Antoine Reicha on melody (1814), harmony (?1816–18) and counterpoint and fugue (1824–6), examples of which have already featured in the present volume (Analyses 2, 8, 9).[8] To vol. III of this translation, Czerny appended an essay of his own entitled 'Über die Formen und den Bau jedes Tonstückes [. . .] Zusatz des Übersetzers' ('Concerning the forms and construction of every piece of music [. . .] Addendum by the translator'),[9] and it is part of this essay, translated by John Bishop of Cheltenham, and appended to Arnold Merrick's translation of Reicha's *Course in Musical Composition*, that is given below.

Czerny subsequently translated Reicha's fourth major treatise, the *Art of the Dramatic Composer, or Complete Course in Vocal Composition* (1833), probably sometime in the late 1830s.[10] The dating of his own three-volume *School of Practical Composition* is a vexed question: published in English translation in about 1848, seemingly about a year before the German original, he may have written it earlier in the 1840s, or even in the late 1830s.[11]

---

8   *Reicha's Compositions-Lehre . . . / Vollständiges Lehrbuch der musikalischen Composition . . .*, trans. and ed. C. Czerny, in two-column bilingual arrangement (Vienna: Anton Diabelli, c.1832–34, reprint edn Amsterdam: Heuwekemeijer, [1974–?]). Simon Sechter's name appears in the subscription list.
9   vol. III, pp. 316–39.
10 *Die Kunst der dramatischen Composition; oder, Vollständiges Lehrbuch der vocal Tonsetzkunst . . .* (Vienna: Anton Diabelli, c.1835–40), trans. of Reicha's *Art du compositeur dramatique ou cours complet de composition vocale* (Paris: Farrenc, 1833).
11 See Communication by William S. Newman, *JAMS*, 20 (1967), 513–15.

'Harmonic Groundwork of Beethoven's Sonata [No. 21 in C] Op. 53 [("Waldstein")]'

Carl Czerny: Appendix to Antoine Reicha: *Course of Musical Composition*

Source:
'Harmonic Groundwork of Beethoven's Sonata Op. 53', Appendix by Carl Czerny:
'Concerning the forms and construction of every piece of music', trans. John Bishop,
in Antoine Reicha: *Course of Musical Composition, or Complete & Methodical
Treatise of Practical Harmony*, trans. Arnold Merrick, ed. John Bishop (London:
Robert Cocks, [1854]), pp. 329–37.

§18. It has already been stated, that the middle subject of the first part of a
musical composition must always be given in the key of the dominant.

   BEETHOVEN, however, and after him several modern authors, have sought
to enhance the effects of this modulation by departing from this rule; thus, for
instance, the above-named composer has modulated, in many of his Sonatas &c,
from the *Tonic* (major) into the *Mediant*, (that is, into the major third above, as
from C major into E major, or from G major into B major,) and in this key, apparently so remote, has introduced the middle subject and the close of the first part. In
like manner we find, in some of his other works, the modulation into the *Submediant*, (as from C major into A major, or from B flat major into G major &c.)

   It is natural that only a very experienced composer can be allowed such exceptions; and, indeed, only in those cases where the plan and ideas of his composition
freely admit of them. We here give the scheme of *BEETHOVEN*'S Grand Sonata
in C major, Op. 53, which is composed in this way, and advise the pupil to
compare it with the original, by which means he may review and study both the
harmonic construction and the order of the ideas of this noble work in a highly
instructive manner.

{330}

Harmonic groundwork of Beethoven's Sonata Op. 53.

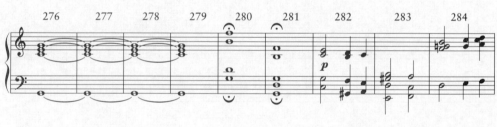

{336}

Remarks on the foregoing sonata

§19. This first movement, grand both in its ideas and their treatment, contains, inclusive of the repetition of the first part, 385 bars (in ℂ time), and, although meant to be played in a quick degree of movement, is of considerable length, which it would be rarely advisable to exceed, in a *Solo*-work. In order to avoid the serious fault of too great extent, and thereby of creating weariness among the hearers, it is very advantageous for the young composer to pay a due regard to the number of bars, and to the length of each movement calculated in minutes.

§20. Not less important is the following second general remark. The foregoing *Sonata* is, in the original, one of the most dazzling, brilliant and difficult of Beethoven. But when, on the other hand, the above real groundwork is calmly played through, how pure and noble is the whole harmonic structure! So that, if it were properly arranged for a choir, it would even be perfectly suitable for a serious ecclesiastical composition. On this classical foundation all Beethoven's works are based, and it would be difficult to recommend anything more useful to the student, than to write down the fundamental chords of a great number of them in this manner; and then, on such a ground-work, to compose pieces of his own, by way of exercise, preserving the same number of bars and the same harmonies: the melodies and passages, however, must be everywhere different from those of the original composition.[12]

§21. In the foregoing Sonata, after the highly significant theme has sufficiently excited the attention of the hearer by its continued interest through the first 21 bars, the modulation suddenly changes (bar 22) – and that, designedly, in a single bar lying beyond the rhythm – from the original key of C to the dominant of E minor, by means of the chord of the augmented sixth; whereupon the measured cadence introduces the beautiful *choral-like* middle subject in E major, which, *like so many of Beethoven's ideas*, derives its melody from the simple diatonic scale, namely:

Example 2

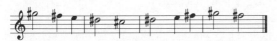

and which, on its repetition, is suitably varied in triplets. The subsequent harmonious imitation (bars 50 to 58) joins the brilliant concluding cadence without farther extraneous modulation; after which (bars 74 to 85), the transition to E minor naturally and agreeably prepares for the repetition of the principal theme.

§22. The development of the second part is founded on the principal subject (from bar 86 to bar 112), and on the imitation from the first part (from bar 112 to bar 141), in very interesting and yet natural modulations; after which, the constantly

12   [Bishop:] An interesting example of this kind, on a Sonata-movement by Mozart, is given by Czerny in his *School of Practical Composition* vol. I. page 43. [The model is Mozart's Sonata in D, K 381/123a for piano four hands, first movement, presented on pp. 37–40 and discussed on pp. 41–2, followed by a recomposition by Czerny of the harmonic skeleton of the movement on pp. 43–6.]

ascending passage on the dominant pedal most effectively leads back to the theme. From this point, the first part is again given in all its leading features, with the exception of some additions to the principal theme, designed to excite still greater attention, and of a quicker transition into the original key after the recurrence of the middle subject, which is here given in A major (consequently in the submediant). At bar 243, the concluding portion of the work begins, {337} which, after a fine development of the principal theme, followed by a brilliant final cadence and some gentle allusions to the middle subject, winds up the whole in an energetic and dazzling style.

The remarkable unity and symmetry of the whole of this movement depend on the following causes:-

1st It is not overladen with too many different melodies; for it consists only of four ideas, namely: the principal theme, the middle subject, the imitation following it, and the concluding subject.

2^{ndly} The ideas, which are judiciously chosen, are always beautifully connected with each other.

3^{rdly} The modulations are naturally and rhythmically conducted.

4^{thly} Each period is of suitable length.

5^{thly} The character of the whole, from beginning to end, is truthfully designed and preserved.

Johann Christian Lobe (1797–1881)
'Die erste Form des Streichquartetts'
Lehrbuch der musikalischen Komposition, vol. I (1850)

We saw in the Introduction to Part I that Marpurg's use of the analytical process in his *Treatise on Fugue* of 1753–4 could at times spiral round and become the process of the composer. The same is true of the passage from Lobe given below. In its discourse, analysis and compositional process mingle and fuse as they do nowhere else in the present volume. Lobe's text is Janus-faced: it is compositional instruction that incidentally employs analysis for illustrative purposes; at the same time, it is on-going analysis of a small pool of works that incidentally infers compositional precepts. There is, however, a difference between Marpurg's and Lobe's methods of working. Marpurg taught the invention of a fugue subject as a whole, and its retrospective fragmentation into reusable elements; Lobe teaches the creation of musical germ-cells, and their prospective formation into any number of themes. Lobe teaches the composition of *musical organisms* – and as we saw in the General Introduction above, the analytical tools that he uses in so doing stem from Marpurg and Riepel by way of Koch, Kirnberger and others. Lobe has, however, as Riepel never, and Marpurg only partially did, embedded analysis of pre-existent works deep within the learning process. The student is constantly assigned tasks (regretfully omitted from the passage below) to analyse movements by Haydn, Mozart and Beethoven, and extract from them structural plans or harmonic schemes on which to build his own rudimentary compositional exercises.

Lobe's *Textbook of Musical Composition* is a work of pre-eminently practical nature. Lobe homed in right at the outset on those fundamentals that would get the pupil composing as rapidly as possible – composing, what is more, in the nineteenth-century spirit of that word. To this end, he focussed on two genres, the string quartet and the piano composition, leaving the more polychrome media until after specialized instruction in instrumentation. This latter subject he incorporated into his curriculum in second place (vol. II). Finally, after treating fugue, canon and double counterpoint (vol. III), he addressed (as Reicha had done in 1833) the largest-scale and most complex form of all, opera (vol. IV).

The instrumentation volume shows what skills Lobe possessed as a teacher. It progresses from the unison line to homophonic and then polyphonic textures, dealing thoughtfully with sudden change (contrast at various structural levels) and gradual process (increase and decrease in density and volume), discussing overall design, orchestral accompaniment and virtuoso writing. It is thus radically different from its illustrious forerunner, Berlioz's *Treatise on Orchestration* (1843). The counterpoint volume reveals Lobe's inductive approach, starting with Contra-punctus I of Bach's *Art of Fugue*, laid out in score, with analytical annotations sig-nifying all occurrences of the subject, answer, countersubject and episodes, followed by verbal analysis and tabular 'disposition', and only then articulating a series of rules, using illustrations from the analysed example, finally consolidating all work so far by a re-analysis of Contrapunctus I, this time in single-line graphic form. This pedagogical procedure is then re-enacted with three fugues from *The Well-tempered Clavier*, whose analyses coalesce into a larger discussion. At that point, the method shifts from analysis to synthesis. The pupil is instructed in invention of ideas, in planning and design, in the finer details of construction, and the drawing-together of the whole fugue as a work of art. In this way, the first 162 pages sustain a single span of unfolding instruction, moulded and paced: exemplification–analysis–regulation–invention–design–completion.

This cycle occurs again and again in the *Lehrbuch*. The passage translated below from vol. I, comprising selected portions of a section spanning seventy-five pages (pp. 291–365, of which the first twenty-five pages, only partly summarized here, introduce the quartet in general; exemplify, analyse and synthesize a minuet; and then introduce first-movement form) is just such a cycle, and could be seen as continuing for a further fifteen pages in which the spiritual and emotional con-tent of the finished work are discussed. It is this mixture of analysis and synthesis, together with the author's interest in composers' working methods, that gives this passage its quite extraordinary depth of treatment, and makes it so prophetic of Schenker's concern with reconstructing the organic process of composition from analysis.

It is in two late chapters of the instrumentation volume, and the full expanse of the first volume, that Lobe's preoccupation with the music of Beethoven comes to the fore. In vol. I (entitled *From the First Elements of Harmonic Theory right up to the Finished Composition of the String Quartet and All Species of Piano Works*) Lobe can wait only ten pages before he begins to throw up motivic fragments from Beethoven's music. In the first nine pages he has simply primed the pupil with tonic, dominant and subdominant chords and rules of thumb for progressions between them, so that the student may start working with thematic material. He then builds up an apparatus for thematic expansion, at appropriate moments introducing new elements of harmonic language so as to allow the development of thematic work to flow on unhindered. Likewise, he introduces analytical symbols and techniques at the point at which he feels need of them.

Two other facets of his educationalist's approach show up. First, he uses his illustrative material with great thrift. Vol. I is copiously illustrated, to be sure, but the same material is used again and again, revealing each time yet another aspect of it. Thus the first movement of Beethoven's Op. 18 no. 2, analysed in full below, appears first no later than on p. 12, where the first five bars are analysed into five motifs. Second, he adopts what in the modern espionage world is called the 'need-to-know' principle. He leads his pupil on, feeding him information only when it is called for, and thus keeps the mind uncluttered, enabling it always to concentrate on what is central to Lobe's teaching: artistic purpose.

Lobe is a highly technical writer, using terms with care and precision. His terminology of processes characterizes his writing most conspicuously: *Erfindung*, the 'invention' of basic material (including *Keim*, 'germ-cell', *Motivmaterial*, 'motivic material', *Gedanke*, 'idea', which is evidently larger, and the *Modell*, 'model', usually a one-bar generating cell for a period); *Skizzirung*, 'sketching-out' (which includes *Umwandlungskunst*, 'transformation', *Sequenz*, which is strictly 'restatement', and a group of terms: *ausspinnen*, 'to extend' or 'derive', *fortführen*, 'to continue', *fortspinnen*, 'to extend', *Fortsetzung*, 'expansion') and *Ausführung*, 'execution' (which involves the filling-out of the texture, and the laying-out of the piece in score). This vocabulary is an interesting mixture of old and new: a rhetorical substructure, *Erfindung* and *Ausführung* (which entered music theory during the Baroque), upon which are superimposed terms (as was seen in the General Introduction) suggestive of organism: *Keim* and *Motiv*, also *fortspinnen* (redolent of *fortpflanzen*, 'to propagate'), the relative neologism, *Skizzirung* (a nineteenth-century coinage), and the Wagnerian-sounding *Umwandlung*.

One term needs particular attention: *thematisch* does not mean 'thematic' in the modern sense. *Thema* refers not to any theme whatsoever, but specifically to the first main theme of a movement, hence *thematisch* is 'derived from the theme', its opposite being *neu*, 'newly-invented'. As to structural units, *Abschnitt* generally refers to a 'two-bar unit', *Periode* to what is notionally an eight-bar unit but which can in practice be shorter or longer; *Satz* is a unit not long enough to qualify as 'period', and has here been rendered loosely as 'phrase'; *Gruppe*, 'group', designates a cluster of thematic entities that together perform a formal function (hence *Themagruppe*, etc. – an interesting anticipation of Tovey's usage), several groups making up a *Theil*, 'section'.

Form is a problematic word for the translator. It signifies 'form' not in the modern sense of a structural template, but the actual 'example of form' which is to hand. The influence of Goethe and the Nature Philosophers, as discussed in the General Introduction above, emerges clearly in this: a 'form' is the representative of an ideal form, an archetype, rather than the ideal itself, for which Lobe has to indulge in circumlocution. *Melodiefaden* has no satisfactory rendering. It signifies the stream of consciousness of the prevailing melodic material, running through the texture, the 'red thread' of the music. It is here given, imperfectly, as 'melodic strand'.

Johann Christian Lobe was a man of broad interests and skills who belonged to the circle of Goethe in Weimar and who knew Zelter, Weber, Hummel, Lortzing, Berlioz, Mendelssohn and Schumann. He published 'conversations' with several of these (a fascinating one with Hummel is quoted in the analysis below, but has had to be omitted here[1]), as well as Spohr, Marschner, Liszt and Meyerbeer. Important are his communications regarding Carl Maria von Weber, in particular *Der Freischütz*. Early in life he was a chamber musician at the ducal court of Weimar, and was widely known as a virtuoso flautist. Among his many compositions are seven operas, but he abandoned composition in 1844. In 1841 he had founded in Weimar an Institute for Instruction in Music Theory, and from soon thereafter he

---

1   Lobe's interview with Hummel, an excerpt from which appears on pp. 357–8 of the *Lehrbuch*, vol. I, was first published as 'Gespräche mit Hummel' in *AmZ*, 49 (1847), cols. 313–320.

concentrated on work as an educationalist, critic and writer on music. In 1846 he moved to Leipzig, where he founded a music institute and took over the editorship of the *Allgemeine musikalische Zeitung*.

Between 1844 and 1872 he published some nine books on music. Of the theoretical works, the *Catechism of Music* (1851) went through twenty-eight editions, then underwent revisions by Franz Eschweiler, Hugo Leichtentritt and Werner Neumann, and was continuously available at least into the 1980s, while English translations were issued in America (by Fanny Raymond Ritter [1867], later revised by Theodore Baker and J.H.Cornell) and Britain (Constance Bache [1885?]). His *Catechism of the Study of Composition* (1862) came close to matching this success story. The *Textbook of Musical Composition* (1850–67), from which the present passage is taken, was by far the most important of his theoretical works. The first of its four volumes apparently ran through six editions – the last two being revised by Hermann Kretzschmar.

2   Example 1 is reproduced here as corrected in the 2nd edn. This graphic analysis is also reproduced in Lobe's *Katechismus der Compositionslehre* (Leipzig: J. J. Weber, [P1862], 4/1887), pp. 146–53, and with translated annotations in the English translation by Fanny Raymond Ritter (New York: J. Schubert, [1867]; London: Augener, 2/1891), pp. 134–42.

'First-movement Form in the String Quartet [: Beethoven: Op. 18 no. 2 in G: Allegro]'

Textbook of Musical Composition

Source:
Lehrbuch der musikalischen Komposition, vol. 1 (Leipzig: B&H, 1850), chaps.27, 29, pp. 316–26, 332–52.

[Lobe begins (pp. 305–16) with a discussion of the motivic content of primary melodic strand and accompaniment, of period structure, and modulatory scheme, using Op. 59 no. 1 as his example.]

Here now is an analysis of a first-movement form of just this type: an opening Allegro. I have selected for these purposes the [String] Quartet [Op. 18] no. 2 by Beethoven; and in order to save space I have given only the principal melodic strand as it threads its way through the various instrumental parts, together with the special symbols introduced earlier.[2]

Example 1

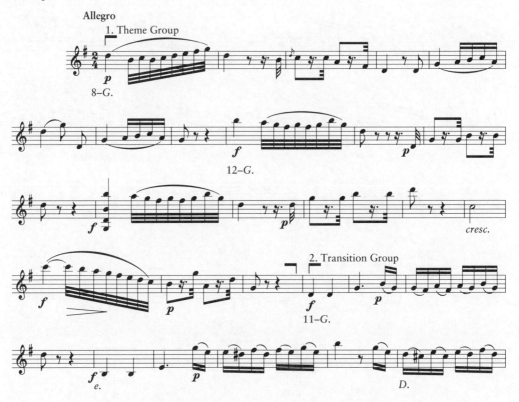

[See previous page for n. 2]

{321} **Commentary**

1. The melodic strand throughout has been extracted here from the instrumental lines as they in turn carry the thematic motifs, for it is in this form that the composer in general originally conceived them. The pupil is recommended now to take the score and examine for himself first the way in which the melodic outline [*Zeichnung*] given above is distributed among the different parts, and secondly the way in which it spreads into the accompaniment in the most diverse and interesting way. An example from the middle section may show what can be made of an apparently limited melodic outline by dispersal of thematic material in a variety of ways together with new figuration. It comes from the fourth, fifth and sixth periods of the middle section, and is based throughout on the third motif of the theme, namely:[3]

Example 2

Here the whole passage derived from that motif:[4]

Example 3

3   Reproduced in *Katechismus der Compositionslehre*, 158–61; Eng. trans., 146–51.
4   ibid.

{323} Note here, in addition, that the composer has not evolved this treatment solely as a single thematic strand working its way through the various parts, but has composed the *first four bars* contrapuntally in three parts, only then beginning to extend the melody which starts the period in violin I with harmonic support. The pupil may in due course try this for himself; but for his analytical studies in the tracing of melodic continuity he should always follow the method shown above, since it offers him the simplest and surest picture of the *constructional unity* of an entire composition.

2. A very good way of clarifying for oneself graphically the construction of examples of a form, and the ways in which they differ from one another, is to abstract them schematically by means purely of the special symbols that I have devised for the purpose. I give below just such an abstraction for the opening Allegro of Beethoven's [String Quartet Op. 18 no. 2] by way of illustration:[5]

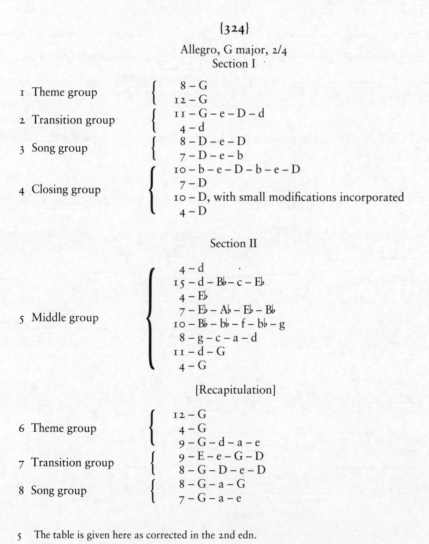

{324}

Allegro, G major, 2/4
Section I

1 Theme group { 8 – G
               12 – G

2 Transition group { 11 – G – e – D – d
                      4 – d

3 Song group { 8 – D – e – D
                7 – D – e – b

4 Closing group { 10 – b – e – D – b – e – D
                   7 – D
                   10 – D, with small modifications incorporated
                   4 – D

Section II

5 Middle group { 4 – d
                  15 – d – Bb – c – Eb
                  4 – Eb
                  7 – Eb – Ab – Eb – Bb
                  10 – Bb – bb – f – bb – g
                  8 – g – c – a – d
                  11 – d – G
                  4 – G

[Recapitulation]

6 Theme group { 12 – G
                 4 – G
                 9 – G – d – a – e

7 Transition group { 9 – E – e – G – D
                      8 – G – D – e – D

8 Song group { 8 – G – a – G
                7 – G – a – e

5   The table is given here as corrected in the 2nd edn.

9 Closing group	10 – e – a – G – e – a – G
	7 – G
	10 – G, with small modifications incorporated
	4 – G
10 Coda	8 – G – C – e – G
	8 – G

3. The third period of the closing group shows the melodic strand to be of very free construction, with new motivic material in almost every two-bar unit [*Abschnitt*]. A unifying force is, however, provided here in the form of a *single* motif running in turn through the other parts. This motif, albeit somewhat difficult to recognize, nonetheless derives from the theme, for it recalls the viola motif in the fifth bar of the theme. There it takes the form of:

{325}

Example 4

In the period concerned, it works its way diagonally through the various parts in the following formation:

Example 5

In the period concerned, it works its way diagonally through the various parts in the following formation:

Such constructs occur frequently, and increase the resources of variety while at the same time maintaining the greatest unity.

4. As already observed, the four groups that comprise section I of the above Allegro by Beethoven all bring into play new motivic material; this is the way in which many such forms are constructed. It is as if the whole of section I were to be considered as theme, and that section II carries that thematically forward. There are, however, also very many examples of this species of form in which material from the theme group is subject to elaboration even as early as the transition group and closing group. The pupil must gradually make himself completely familiar with the various types of [formal] treatment through diligent study of a great many scores by the major composers.

5. The purpose of the middle section group – and we are here concerned only with technical matters – is primarily to reveal the art of thematic development in its full glory. To their fullest capacity, the periods that comprise this group either present the principal theme itself in a variety of new and surprising combinations – 'situations', one might call them – or at least bring back ideas drawn from section I. Absolutely no new motivic material appears in this group. In compensation, the modulatory tonal scheme now goes further, reaching out into remoter keys, bringing with it new, bolder and more surprising harmonic progressions and changes.

6. The recapitulation, as is well known, brings back the whole of section I, with its four principal groups. However, these now all remain in the tonic. Consequently, the tonal scheme in the major must not revert to the dominant, and that in the minor must not revert to the mediant. Instead, in both modes it must lead to the tonic, in which key the song group and the closing group remain throughout. However, we have [already] seen that even at the level of construction of the individual phrase, an exactly literal repetition of earlier ideas fails to sustain interest. In just the same way, the {326} recapitulation has, at least in places, to be varied in a host of ways – melodically, harmonically and so on – and these variations bring a new charm to it. The recapitulation of the Beethoven Allegro offers an example of precisely this. The transition in this movement does not make use of the corresponding motivic material from section I, but for the most part comprises material from the theme group. Only at the end does it recall its original material.

7. The song group of section I of the Beethoven Allegro concludes not with a full close but only with a half close. This however happens rarely. Mostly it ends with a full close.

8. The transition group of section I is very short, consisting of only one period and one phrase [*Satz*]. Most groups in this species of form are extended to greater length. They often comprise three, four or even five periods./

> [Pp. 326–32 explain middle-movement and rondo finale form, giving for Op. 18 no. 2 a full melodic-strand analysis of the second, and tabular analysis of the fourth movement, pp. 295–305 having explained the structure of the minuet, using Op. 18 no. 4, third movement.]

{332}

Invention and execution: method of producing finished structures for the string quartet

There is no other way, as we said at the beginning of chapter 2,[6] in which a composer can invent his works than – bar-by-bar. One bar springs up in his imagination, a second adds itself to it, then a third and so on until the whole piece is born. But do not for a moment suppose that all this happens as a *single* process – the composer inventing an entire structure from first note to last, writing it straight into score, all in final form. Quite the contrary: he needs a great many separate processes, occurring one after another, for his creative inner workings. He does in fact have available to him certain mechanical procedures which assist the generation of his ideas and make it easier.[7] As with all artists, painters, sculptors and

---

6   *Lehrbuch*, vol. I, p. 9: 'There is no other way in which a composer can invent his works than – bar-by-bar. One bar springs up in his imagination, [Example] a second adds itself to it, [Example] then a third, [Example] and so on until the whole piece is born.' His examples are the opening three bars of the slow introduction to the first movement of the Beethoven Septet, Op. 20.

7   '. . . mechanische Mittel, welche seinen geistigen Operationen zu Hülfe kommen und sie erleichtern'. Cf. p. 258:

> Many will perhaps recall here the words of *Goethe*: 'To calculate is not to invent [*Rechnen ist nicht Erfinden*]'. – To counter that I recollect another remark by the same thinker: 'On the contrary, there are many mechanical procedures to assist etc. [*Es giebt vielmehr mechanische Hülfmittel u.s.w.*]', which is printed at the front of this volume as a motto.

so forth, the composer starts by searching for individual ideas and sketching them out, then assembles and combines them, and bit by bit draws the work together as a whole.

I shall now disclose to the pupil the way in which a composition is conceived and brought into existence, from very first and tiniest germ-cell right through to full development and execution; and I shall show him the separate processes {333} as they usually follow on one from another. He need do nothing more than work through each phase of production using material of his own, then at the end of my remarks, if he has any talent at all, he will have the larger forms of the string quartet ready in score before his very eyes. He will be able technically to fashion whole pieces out of minute germ-cells – this has been the sole aim of our course of instruction up to this point. Let us assume that the pupil wishes to compose the first-movement form, the Allegro, of a string quartet.

First process – Invention of the principal ideas (first sketch)

We know that no musical idea, no period, consists solely of [a string of] new motifs. We know, indeed, that there exist melodies that are extended by means of sequences out of a single motivic element [*Motivglied*] which is adopted as model. The invention, strictly speaking, thus resides purely in the model, for the extension is a continuation of what already exists. Such extension is something that can be acquired through teaching and practice, and if the student has followed the instructions of this book he will already in large measure find it within his capability.

> [Brief illustrations follow from Beethoven's Violin Sonata in A, Op. 12 no. 2, first movement, and String Quartet in E♭, Op. 74, third movement.]

{334} It hardly needs saying that, as a rule, the composer already has in his mind the underlying harmonies of such an idea, and at least a vague notion of the accompaniment style, when he comes to construct that idea.

The first sections of the larger forms usually have, in addition to the principal theme, several self-sufficient ideas – ideas, that is, which do not derive from the first theme but bring into play new and individual motivic material. *Such ideas, however, appear only in the first four period-groups.* The middle section group, the recapitulation in its entirety and the coda do no more than bring back, thematically reworked, material already present in section I.

The composer therefore invents the other self-sufficient ideas of section I at the outset as well, with as yet no regard for their continuation or combination, just as it were the models for the various period-groups. *This constitutes the first process of invention, the first plan or the first sketch.*

> The motto, taken from Goethe, reads as follows:
>> There is much more in art that is *positive*, hence that *can be taught* and *passed on*, than is generally believed. And there are a great many such advantageous technical devices [*mechanische Vortheile*] by which truly *artistic effects* can be produced (assuming of course the presence of a creative mind). Once these little artistic tricks of the trade are known, much is child's play which outwardly appears miraculous.

If we take the first-movement form of the String Quartet [Op. 18] no. 2 of Beethoven, which can be seen in Example 1, then the first plan of that would look as below:

Example 6

Sketch of the Theme Group

Example 7

Sketch, or Model for the second, or Transition Group

Example 8

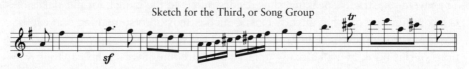

Sketch for the Third, or Song Group

Example 9

Sketch for the Fourth, or Closing Group
a. For the first of its periods

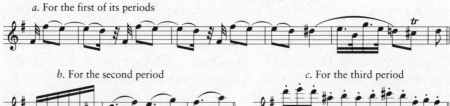

b. For the second period   *c.* For the third period

{335} or in place of *c*, the figure given below, which is present throughout the whole period:

Example 10

These may be seen as the newly invented ideas, all clearly differentiated from each other, which occur in this opening Allegro movement. Everything else that occurs

in the movement is thematic development and transformation of these. Accordingly, in the strict sense of the word, invention is by this stage over.

I have chosen this quartet because it offers the *greatest wealth* of new ideas or models. The basic sketches [*Grundskizzen*] of many quartets and works in similar forms have far less new fundamental material [*Grundmaterial*].

> [Illustrations of monothematic structure follow from Op. 18 no. 1, first movement, and Haydn Symphony No. 104, fourth movement. In response to scepticism that composers sketch discontinuously rather than as a single outpouring, Lobe cites and quotes in examples as absolute proof the four themes of the Finale of Mozart's 'Jupiter' Symphony, which must have been invented out of order since they fit together, and the disjointed ideas from Beethoven's supposed sketches for a Tenth Symphony and an Overture on B.A.C.H.[8]]

{339}

Second process (second sketch)

When the budding composer has assembled the principal ideas for a piece and is content with them, the hardest task, that of the actual invention, is over. *The entire piece will be derived from them through continuation of these tiny sketches and through elaboration – i.e. through the construction of new periods. No ideas occur in section II that do not have their origin in the above first sketch.*

In this process, what one composer makes out of so little material by means of elaboration and by transformation of ideas, whether he knows how to impart fresh charms to the existing material at its increasing recurrences or brings it back in more or less the same guise, makes him out as master or bungler.

[. . .]

[The transformation of a melody so as to achieve the greatest possible variety] is done first and foremost in the following fashion.

The pupil should take the first two-bar unit from the sketch for his theme and try to find as many ways as possible of presenting it, so that each one is different, sometimes by virtue of a new melodic turn of phrase, sometimes by virtue of new accompaniment, and so forth.[9] For example:

The melody of the first two-bar unit of the sketch for the theme group, thematically transformed in a variety of ways:

---

8   Lobe was writing fifteen years before Nottebohm's publications on the sketchbooks. These sketches had been published in transcription for the first time by Hermann Hirschbach, in *Musikalisch-kritisches Repertorium*, 1/1 (January 1844), 1–5. See on this analysis and the use of Beethoven's sketches Bent, 'The "Compositional Process" in Music Theory 1713–1850', *Music Analysis*, 3 (1984), 37–46, 51.

9   [Lobe:] The pupil can lay this out on a two-stave system, wherever it can be accommodated.

Example 11

{340} These are the ten different forms in which this one idea appears in the Beethoven string quartet. The pupil will appreciate from the {341} observations made above that the possibilities for transformation have not been exhausted, indeed cannot be wholly exhausted. Limitless hundreds of new forms could be evolved out of this one initial idea, for example:

Example 12

17.

{342} When the pupil has treated one two-bar unit of his theme in this way, then he should proceed to the second, third, etc. units that contain new motivic material. In the same fashion, he should then go on to perform thematic transformation on the sketches for the transition group, the song group and the closing group, pursuing each two-bar unit for as long as variant forms continue to occur to him. If he can think up twenty, then that will be sufficient; but if he can devise forty or fifty, then so much the better.

If the pupil will only follow this method of practising, *he will be astonished in a very short space of time how rich his imagination has become. For him there will never be an idea which fails to prompt his mind with the most interesting transformations. And every one of these variant forms can readily serve as a model from which to derive yet new periods.*

Third process (third sketch)

Let us suppose that the pupil has invented his first sketch for an Allegro, following the method given earlier, and has evolved models from these principal ideas according to our second process. At this stage he has far more raw material at his disposal than he can possibly use for constructing a complete movement.

Now the third process consists of selecting the best models from among this wide variety of sketches, of fashioning interesting periods out of them, of bringing these together to form satisfactory groups and of linking them smoothly so as to create the total form.

The first stage of this is as follows:

Finished sketching-out of section I

[Having invented the sketch for the first period of the first group or theme group, the composer must now determine (a) how many periods that group should include, and (b) the lengths of these periods. He also now needs to consider the harmonic join between the theme and transition groups.]

{343} Let us look again at the first sketch for Beethoven's String Quartet [Op. 18] no. 2; and let us consider the first period of the theme group. *As a rule, this entire period serves as the model for the other periods of the theme group.*

Very often, moreover, this group comprises only two periods. Since the sketch for the transition group begins with the dominant chord, the theme group may end on a tonic triad.

The schema for the theme group could thus simply be:

$$
\text{theme group:}
\begin{cases}
8 - G \text{ model period} \\
\\
8 - G \text{ sequence period}
\end{cases}
$$

The best way to execute the finished sketch is to lay out the melodic strand on one staff and to indicate the accompaniment and harmony underneath it on a second staff in the form of a bass line.

Accordingly, the sketch for the entire theme group following the above schema would look as follows:

Example 13

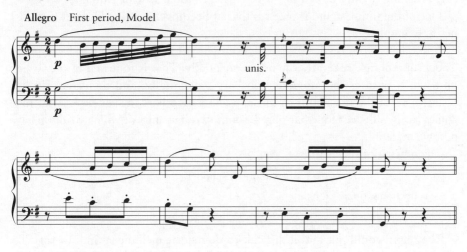

{344}The pupil could leave the sketch for the theme group as it stands in his first attempt, since this would allow scope to accompany the melody differently at its second appearance, to introduce a different tone-colour, to transfer it to another part, and thereby to avoid making it a literal repetition of the first period. Beethoven himself, however, fashioned his sequence more freely. Not only is the melody varied and the accompaniment differently configured, but also the extent of the period is increased to twelve bars. His schema for this group thus looks as follows:

$$\left\{ \begin{array}{l} 8 - G \\ 12 - G \end{array} \right.$$

The execution of the sketch according to this can be seen in Example 1.

> [Theme groups often have three periods. This is illustrated with Op. 18 no. 1, first movement.]

{345}

Finished sketching-out of the second group, or transition group

The first group, the theme group, is easy to sketch out. The second group, by contrast, the transition group, leaves the pupil with more creative work to do. In Beethoven's works, the construction of this group exhibits great variety; it also carries with it greater difficulties with regard to tonal scheme [*Modulation*].

One of the simplest and shortest is that of Beethoven's String Quartet [Op. 18] no. 2, Example 1.

Its model is a phrase of four bars, as can be seen in the first sketch, Example 7. The second phrase reiterates the first sequentially. That is followed by a two-bar unit which restates the previous two bars sequentially, and then by a further restatement of the first motif of those previous two bars in sequence. After that comes a self-sufficient four-bar phrase, both two-bar units of which work up new motivic material.

The schema of this is thus:

$$\text{transition group:} \left\{ \begin{array}{l} 11 - \text{new phrase as model} \\ \\ 4 - \text{new two-bar units} \end{array} \right.$$

The pupil would not find it difficult to sketch the melodic strand for this. To produce a satisfactory scheme for the tonal movement, on the other hand, is not so easy. Specifically, this must be so arranged that a half close on the dominant is reached at the end of the group, after which the third group, the song group, can follow on in the dominant.

Here, then, is an exercise in selecting harmonic progressions for the sequences so as to lead smoothly to the half close.

{346} At first, the pupil will get on best when constructing his sequences if he generally adheres closely to the harmonic progressions of his model, merely shifting them into other keys so that gradually and in accordance with the length of the period they arrive unhindered at a half close on the dominant. Since he has the melody of the model to hand, he can do this initially by indicating the tonal movement solely with our special symbols. Thus a harmonic sketch for the above transition group might be arranged in something like the following way:

Example 14

All groups, so far as their material is concerned, can be placed in one of three main categories, viz.:

(a)   groups whose periods are based entirely on thematically derived models[10];
(b)   groups whose periods are fashioned entirely out of newly invented models;
(c)   groups whose periods are worked up partly out of newly invented models and partly out of thematically derived ones.

The transition group given above belongs to category (b).

[An example of type (c) from Op. 18 no. 1, first movement is analysed. After a practice exercise, the finished sketching-out of section II [i.e. the development]: no new ideas are to be introduced; so he should draw from his existing stock of models, ordering with a view to (i) contrast of material, (ii) variety of period lengths. The recapitulation and coda are then discussed. Finally, the whole should be gone through for smoothness of continuity.]

{352}

Explanatory note

1. The model of a simple period – i.e. the idea, be it large or small, which is used in repeated and sequential form within the period – is *usually* to be found at the beginning of that period. *But this is not always the case.* Occasionally it does not appear until the later part of the period.

Example 15

In this example, the model does not occur until the fifth bar, and the sequence not until the seventh.

[A similar case from Op. 18 no. 1, second movement, is quoted.]

10   *nur aus thematischen Modellen gesponnen*: i.e. from models which are already present within the theme.

Never, however, as has often been said earlier, *does a single period occur without a model and its associated sequence or sequences.*

This holds good for every single period, taken in isolation.

2. Where, however, as often occurs, periods are repeated within groups, *a whole period may adopt the function of model, and the other period or periods may acquire the role of sequences to it.*

Consequently, a theme group usually contains a model period and one or two sequence periods.

> [Alternative strategies for invention are given. Finally, 'The Scoring-up of the Full Sketch' quotes a fascinating interview with Hummel on how to sketch out scoring, and his advice is demonstrated for Op. 18 no. 1, first the scherzo, then the first movement.]

Karl Mayrberger (1828–1881)

Die Harmonik Richard Wagner's an den Leitmotiven aus 'Tristan und Isolde' (1881)

August 1876 saw the first complete production of the *Ring of the Nibelung* in Wagner's newly constructed Festspielhaus at Bayreuth, for which occasion Hans von Wolzogen's guide (cf. vol. II, Analysis 6) was written. Two years later, in 1878, the first issue appeared of a journal that was to serve as the mouthpiece for Wagner's ideas: *Bayreuther Blätter*. Within three years, its editor, von Wolzogen, was bewailing his inability to recruit hitherto a theorist qualified to address Wagner's 'technique, and the laws of form and style that he has evolved especially for his musico-dramatic art, and the extension of current music theory that these entail' – the journal had been long on 'enthusiasm', short on 'deeper considerations'.[1]

Now, at last, such a man had come forward: Karl Mayrberger, an obscure Kapellmeister from Bratislava (then in Hungary, now capital city of Slovakia), who had produced in 1878 the first volume of a *Textbook of Musical Harmony*[2] and had submitted to the journal an article on Wagner's chromatic harmony that was to 'cause a sensation'. Wagner – contrary to the received impression that he forbade all discussion of his musical language[3] – had given his personal blessing to this article, hailing its author as 'the so-long-awaited theorist for our *Blätter*'. Mayrberger elucidated Wagner's harmonic style in this article only 'with respect to the leitmotifs of the *Prelude to* "Tristan and Isolde"' (my italics). Published in the May/June 1881 issue of the journal, it comprised a little under half of the present analysis. The remainder had been written as a sequel to that, dealing with the motifs of Act I (though in fact it strayed into Acts II and III). It had been scheduled for the October issue, and was set in type and corrected when news of Mayrberger's sudden death had arrived. Von Wolzogen tells us that in connection with a plan by the Vienna Academic Wagner Union to procure for him an appointment as 'Lecturer in New (Chromatic) Harmony' in that city, Mayrberger had planned to expand the two articles into something more ambitious. Death having frustrated this plan, von Wolzogen had removed the second article from the October issue, put the two articles together, and made minor adjustments in keeping with the pamphlet format in which it was finally published.

1 Foreword by von Wolzogen to *Harmonik*, pp. 3–4.
2 *Lehrbuch der musikalischen Harmonik in gemeinfasslicher Darstellung für höhere Musikschulen und Lehrerseminarien, sowie zum Selbstunterrichte*, vol. 1 *Die diatonische Harmonik in Dur* (Pressburg and Leipzig: Gustav Heckenast, 1878). Von Wolzogen erroneously gives the date as 1879.
3 See J. Deathridge: 'Wagner "Literature" and Wagner "Research"', in *Wagner*, 7 (1987; Ger. orig. in *Wagner-Handbuch*, ed. U. Müller and P. Wapnewski, Stuttgart: Kröner, 1986), pp. 92–114, esp. 102.

Mayrberger's analysis is highly technical in ways not readily comprehensible by the modern reader. It therefore merits some special explanation here. Indeed, he stressed in his *Textbook* the systematic nature of his approach to harmony:[4]

> Harmonic theory, as the grammar of the language of music, cannot afford either to neglect the logical formulation and scientific substantiation of its linguistic rules, or to stray into the realms of the aesthetic or the more broadly philosophical. [. . .] The present work, in giving precise definition to the concept of 'chord consonance' [. . .] and advancing it as the axiom from which all subsequent rules logically derive, adopts the scientific path.

Rejecting simplistic past definitions of consonance and dissonance, Mayrberger posits that the only 'real consonances' are those that form either a perfect octave, fifth or unison, or major or minor third, *with the fundamental of the chord*. An overlapping category of intervals (perfect fifth and fourth, major and minor third and sixth) may be 'consonant-sounding' in their own right and yet dissonant with the fundamental. From this 'fundamental law' stream all the rules of chordal formation and dissonance treatment.

Mayrberger was a pupil, at one remove, of the great Viennese theorist Simon Sechter (Analysis 4 above), and credited all the main tenets of his theory to either Sechter or Moritz Hauptmann (Analysis 3).[5] He claimed for himself only that he had treated in a more exhaustive and comprehensible way than other theorists the notions of suspension (*Vorhalt*), passing note (*Durchgangsnote*) and neighbouring note (*Wechselnote*). These three concepts play a large part in the present analysis, and therefore deserve closer examination. First, however, the notion of the 'extended minor' needs explanation. Mayrberger, in the course of the analysis, decries the reliance of many mid-nineteenth-century textbooks solely upon the harmonic minor scale, and advocates that harmonic and melodic minors should be taken together as the basis for melodic movement in the minor mode:

Example 1

In distinguishing between diatonic and chromatic notes and chords in the present analysis, Mayrberger implicitly adopted Sechter's mapping of harmony on to scale. Sechter, accepting both diminished and augmented triads as legitimate chord formations, and thinking of a scale as a 'ladder' on all the steps (*Stufen*) of which chords could be positioned, had constructed thirteen possible triads in any given minor key; thus, in D minor:[6]

---

4   *Lehrbuch*, vol. I, Foreword, p. vii.
5   S. Sechter, *Die Grundsätze der musikalischen Komposition*, vol. I *Die richtige Folge der Grundharmonien, oder vom Fundamentalbass und dessen Umkehrungen und Stellvertretern* (Leipzig: B&H, 1853; Eng. trans. C. C. Müller, 1871); M. Hauptmann: *Die Natur der Harmonik und der Metrik: zur Theorie der Musik* (Leipzig: B&H, 1853, 2/1873; Eng. trans. W. E. Heathcote, 1888).
6   *Grundsätze*, vol. I, p. 57.

Example 2

He did likewise in constructing chords of the seventh, yielding in principle sixteen possibilities. However, there were certain conflicts of function. The seventh of the chord (which must always fall) could never take the form of the raised sixth or seventh of the scale (which must always rise); the fifth of the chord could not be the raised sixth of the scale (because that must always ascend to the raised seventh and would have unacceptable consequences). This left eleven possibilities:[7]

Example 3

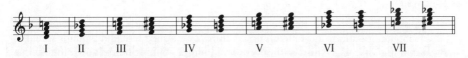

It is crucial to realize that none of these chords was chromatic for Mayrberger: all were *diatonic*. Together they provided the total diatonic collection of notes for melody, and of chords for harmony.

Thus, when Mayrberger describes the g♯' in b. 2 of the Prelude (bar c of motif no. 1/2) as coming 'diatonically from A minor' he means that it belongs to the total diatonic of A minor (A, B, C, D, E, F♮, F♯, G♮, G♯). The a♯' in the following bar is chromatic since it is part of the diatonic in neither A minor nor E minor or major; moreover, it 'belongs to the melodic-chromatic as distinct from the harmonic-chromatic' because the chord at that point (E–G♯–A♯–D♮) is neither a diatonic seventh chord (E–G♮–B–D♮ or E–G♯–B–D♮) nor a chromatic alteration of one of those.[8]

A 'free suspension' (*freier Vorhalt*: 'free' because it is acceptable in free composition but not in strict[9]) is a suspension that disobeys the rule requiring it to be prepared: thus the g' in bar d of motif no. 5 is a regular suspension, being prepared by the g' semiquaver in bar c, whilst the b' in bar b of motif no. 3 is a free suspension because it is not prepared at the end of bar a. Mayrberger permits a suspension to resolve upwards rather than downwards. Hence in bar c of motif no. 6, g♯' and d♯' are suspended rising seventh and eleventh;[10] but these are allowable only because (i) the seventh is raised, i.e. is the leading-note to A minor, and (ii) the situation arises where the fundamental falls by a fifth (V–I or I–IV).[11] On both accounts, the doubled f♯" in bar a of motif no. 3 does not qualify as an upward suspension; it is thus interpreted as a lower neighbouring note of g♯". Then what about the e♯" on the first beat of that bar? This fails to qualify as a suspension on an additional ground: suspended notes must be seventh, eleventh or

7 ibid, 57–8.
8 'The melodic-chromatic is that which merely decorates a melody note without thereby altering the chord.' (*Harmonik*, p. 34 'Anhang: Musikalische Aphorismen von Karl Mayrberger', Aphorism no. VIII).
9 *Lehrbuch*, vol. I, p. 223.
10 *Harmonik*, p. 13: a footnote cross-interprets the d♯' in E minor as a (diatonic) lower neighbouring note.
11 *Lehrbuch*, vol. I, pp. 197–8, 220–2.

thirteenth above the fundamental, whereas this is an augmented octave. Is it then a lower neighbouring note to f♯", as it was four bars earlier, in bar m of motif no. 1/2? No, because a neighbouring note may embellish by tone or semitone *only a constituent note of a chord* (i.e. root, third, fifth or seventh).[12] In bar m, F♯ was indeed a constituent of the triad B–D♯–F♯, whereas in bar a of motif no. 3 it is not so because Mayrberger does not acknowledge the chord of the ninth. The only way in which it can be interpreted here is as a passing note – and a chromatic one since E♯ does not exist as diatonic in A minor.

Two further technical concepts need explanation. Mayrberger reads the 'Tristan chord' (the first chord of bar c of motif no. 1/2: B–D♯–F♮–A, the last note being elaborated by a G♯ neighbouring note) as a 'hybrid chord' (*Zwitterakkord*). The concept of the hybrid chord is taken from Sechter, who portrays its derivation as follows:[13]

> If a seventh chord, or better a chord with seventh and ninth, is considered as II of a [. . .] minor scale, it must have a minor third, diminished fifth and a minor seventh; and, in the case of a chord with seventh and ninth, a minor ninth [also]. If now the minor third is made major without altering the diminished fifth, then such a chord is by nature hybrid, its major third being located in a key different from that of its diminished fifth. For, on the strength of its major third this chord ought to be on V, whilst on the strength of its diminished fifth it belongs on II. It is, as a result, a genuinely *chromatic* chord, which cannot be located in any one diatonic scale.

Taking the case in point – the chord of the seventh on B – this might be expressed diagrammatically as follows, yielding the 'Tristan chord':

Example 4

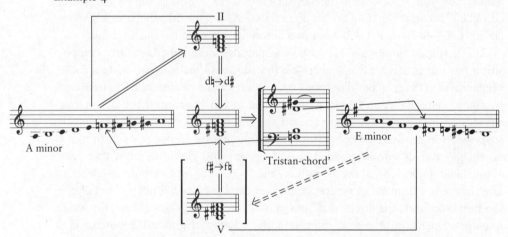

The second of these two concepts is the dual notion of 'intermediate fundamental' and 'substitute'. Both address the problem of successive fundamentals a second apart – a problem inherited from Rameau's 'fundamental bass', of which Sechter's harmonic system was in part a revival. We have encountered the first of these two notions (called by Sechter *Zwischenfundament*) in the fugal analysis by Reicha

12   ibid, 124–5.
13   *Grundsätze*, vol. I, pp. 146–7, see also 188–50, 186–93, 215–17.

(Analysis 2 above).[14] It is an interpolated root which splits the step of a second into two permissible leaps. Mayrberger places such a root in parentheses: see, for example, bar l of motif no. 1/2: 'A (F♯) B', converting the tone A–B into successive leaps of minor third and perfect fourth. In bar n of motif no. 10, the chord of C♭ major masks, so to speak, the true chord of E♭ minor, which lies behind it. In this case, the C♭ is a 'substitute' (*Stellvertreter*) for E♭ and Mayrberger unmasks it, citing E♭ as the true fundamental. A further, more sweeping manner of interpreting stepwise fundamentals is Mayrberger's notion of 'ellipsis' (*Ellipsis*), whereby not one chord but a succession of chords is deemed to have been 'elided' by the composer. Mayrberger gives a clear and illustrated account of this process with respect to motif no. 11.

This study of the leitmotifs of *Tristan* was a major contribution in its time to the understanding of Wagner's musical language. Mayrberger deployed Sechter's harmonic theory, which was essentially backwards-looking and interpreted chromatic phenomena in terms of diatonic processes,[15] in tackling the most extreme case of chromatic harmony known in its day. If the result was not wholly successful, and does not convince us today, then we should ask ourselves which explanation of the style since that time *has* entirely persuaded us. The harmony of *Tristan* remains one of those exceptional phenomena capable of being viewed from an infinite number of perspectives.

Karl Mayrberger was a pupil in Vienna of Gottfried von Preyer (1807–1901), the latter a former pupil of Simon Sechter. Thereafter, in 1864 he was appointed Kapellmeister at the cathedral of Bratislava. He was also Professor of Music at the Staatspräparandie, a teacher-training school in Bratislava, for which he in large part wrote his *Textbook* (its title-page states: 'for advanced schools of music and teacher-training seminaries, and for independent study').[16]

---

14   It is perhaps coincidence that Mayrberger's teacher, Gottfried von Preyer, is said to have used Reicha's theoretical works in translation in his classes at the Vienna Conservatory, 1839–48 (Robert W. Wason, *Viennese Harmonic Theory from Albrechtsberger to Schenker and Schoenberg* (Ann Arbor: UMI Research Press, 1985), p. 146n). As noted in Analysis 11 above, note 8, Sechter was on the subscription list of Czerny's French-German bilingual edition of Reicha's three main treatises.

15   Since fundamentals have their place exclusively in diatonic scales, be they major or minor, it follows that the diatonic is the sole basis for the chromatic and enharmonic. On these grounds, every chromatic or enharmonic construction [*Satz*], insofar as it lays claim to correctness, must be reducible ultimately to a correct diatonic major or minor construction. (*Harmonik*, p. 34 'Anhang: Musikalische Aphorismen von Karl Mayrberger', Aphorism no. VI).

16   Wason, *Viennese Harmonic Theory*, pp. 168n, 146n; *Lehrbuch*, vol. I, title-page, p. vii.

The Harmonic Style of Richard Wagner, Elucidated with Respect to the Leitmotifs of 'Tristan and Isolde'

Source:
Die Harmonik Richard Wagner's an den Leitmotiven aus 'Tristan und Isolde' erläutert
(Bayreuth: Bayreuther Patronatverein, [1881]), 7–33.

[Foreword][17]

The harmonic language of the present day is on a footing essentially different from that of the past. Richard Wagner has pointed the musical world along the path that it must henceforth travel. The sixteenth century knew only the realm of the diatonic. In the eighteenth century, the diatonic and the chromatic existed side by side, equal in status. The nineteenth century, in the work of Beethoven, Schubert, Weber and Spohr, gravitated more and more towards chromaticism. But with Richard Wagner an altogether new era begins: major and minor intermingle, and the realm of the diatonic gives way to that of the chromatic and the enharmonic.

If, however, we are to do more than just marvel at the master, and perhaps unconsciously ape him, we must study his music, and so make ourselves cognizant of the expressive means by which he is able to conjure up his lofty musical ideas in harmony of such wonderful luminosity. That current thinking in the world of music theory is ill-equipped for this comes as no surprise when we consider that the great majority of our more recent harmonic theorists flatly deny it any scientific basis. Even those few among them who exhibit a keener feeling for the advances of more recent music, thanks to a faulty understanding of Moritz Hauptmann's extended minor system,[18] to the various contradictory explanations of so-called altered chords, which Simon Sechter more accurately terms 'hybrid chords' [*Zwitterakkorde*],[19] and in general to the far too superficial and inadequate teaching of the resources of chromaticism, introduce more misunderstanding into the system of harmonic instruction than reigned in the time of Mozart and Beethoven.

---

17   Though untitled at this point, the opening section is referred to in the penultimate paragraph as 'the Foreword'. The [Foreword] and [Part I] were first published in *Bayreuther Blätter*, 4/5–6 (May/June 1881), 169–80.

18   *Erweitertes Mollsystem* is not a technical term in Hauptmann. Mayrberger may be referring here to Hauptmann's 'minor-key system' (*Molltonart-System*) in itself (*Die Natur der Harmonik und Metrik* [Leipzig: B&H, 1853, 2/1873], pp. 32–5), or perhaps to his 'minor-key series' (*Molltonart-Reihe*, ibid, 35), rather than to his 'major-minor system' (*Moll-Dur-Tonart*, ibid, 36–8).

19   See Introduction. In deploying hybrid chords of the seventh or ninth, Sechter offers a set of modulatory strategies, chromatically altering diatonic chords. In C major, their construction on VII, III, VI, V or II yields modulation to A minor, D minor, G major [or minor] or F major [or minor], or leaves the harmony in C major [or minor], respectively; in A minor, on II, V, I or VII it leaves the harmony in A minor, or yields modulation to D minor, [G minor,] C major, [C minor,] or F major respectively. Sechter has another role for the hybrid ninth chord (e.g. D–F♯–A♭–C–E♭): if its root is suppressed and the chord is re-ordered (A♭–C–E♭–F♯ = A♭–C–E♭–G♭) it simulates a dominant seventh chord on ♭II, hence functions as the so-called 'German augmented sixth chord'.

A mastery of the resources of chromaticism cannot be said to have been achieved until the student has gained a clear understanding of the diatonic in minor keys, and the modulatory relationship of that to the major.

It is not sufficient that the student be expected to learn by heart the various resolutions of dissonances that have arisen in past practice. A sense of their propriety must also be instilled into him, so that he comes to an understanding of direct resolution, interrupted resolution, and implicit but unstated resolution, the last of which has its basis in *harmonic ellipsis*.[20]

Furthermore, it must be a part of the teaching of chromatic resources to show not only *that*, but also *how* the legitimacy of chromaticism can be traced back to the relationships between keys; and to show that in addition to harmonic chromaticism there is also {8} a melodic chromaticism; and that these two can, as Richard Wagner demonstrates on practically every page of his scores, function very effectively side by side.

Full and equal attention must be given to the diatonic in the major key and that in the minor key, since chromaticism has its roots in the very union of the two. Failure to grasp this completely will leave chromaticism for ever unintelligible.

The view has recently taken hold in textbooks that only the so-called harmonic minor scale should be used when harmonizing in the minor key, without recourse to the melodic minor scale.[21] This view asserts, furthermore, that the chromatic scale belongs to no particular key, whereas in reality there exists precisely the same number of chromatic scales as diatonic scales. We must once and for all rid ourselves utterly of this view.

But enough of this tale of woe over present-day theory. The task of the studies that I have undertaken is quite simply to analyse the music of Richard Wagner according to scientific principles, at appropriate points to draw attention to a number of erroneous interpretations that have sprung up hitherto, and thus to render the music of the present day easier for the music lover to understand. I therefore now present as my first endeavour along these lines a study of the motifs of *Tristan and Isolde*, conscious of being of service to a good cause, and in the hope of perhaps convincing the theorists of our day that the statements they make and the doctrines they put forward contain many misconceptions.[22]

---

20   'implicit but unstated': *verschwiegen* (lit. 'withheld').

21   E.g. 'All other forms of the minor scale [than that of the harmonic minor] [. . .] rest upon melodic conditions which prohibit the *step of an augmented second* between the sixth and seventh degrees [. . .] In the abstract, these forms have no influence on the harmonic structure' (E. F. Richter, *Lehrbuch der Harmonie* (Leipzig: B&H, 1853; Eng. trans. 1896), pp. 43–4).

22   [Mayrberger:] The labels used for the motifs in this study are taken from the work by Hans von Wolzogen, *Richard Wagner's 'Tristan und Isolde': ein Leitfaden durch Sage, Dichtung und Musik* (Leipzig: L. Senf, [n.d.]). The harmonization of these motifs was adapted for piano by the present writer from the score, very kindly made available by the publisher B&H. [The full score of *Tristan und Isolde* was first published in 1860, the vocal score by Hans von Bülow later in the same year.]

[PART I]

1. *Tristan's motif of suffering* 2. *Isolde's motif of yearning (score, p. 3)*

Example 5

Fundamentals: or	A.	D.	B♭.
Scale-degrees in A minor	1.	4.	2.
" " E minor/major			5.

{9}

bar c   The opening chord is a *hybrid chord*, the F of which derives from A minor and the D♯ of which derives from E minor.[23]

    The G♯ with which the second motif begins is the lower neighbouring note of A and comes diatonically from A minor.

Example 6

Fundamentals: or	E.		B.	E.	A.
Scale-degrees in A minor	5.		2.	5.	1.
" " E minor/major	1.			in D minor	5.

bar d   The A♯ is the lower neighbouring note of B♮, and belongs to the melodic-chromatic as distinct from the harmonic-chromatic.

Example 7

Fundamentals: or	D.	G.
Scale-degrees in A minor	4.	
" " C minor/major	2.	5.
" " G minor/major	5.	1.

bar g The B♮ in the upper voice is the free lower neighbouring note of C, the formation as a whole being a hybrid chord, namely: the F♯ is borrowed chromatically from G minor/major as also is the A♭ from C minor.

bar h The C♯ is the lower neighbouring note of D and is also melodic-chromatic.

Bars e, f, g and h can be construed as an unbroken succession of dominant seventh chords, e.g.:

{10}

Example 8

Fundamentals:		A.	(F♯)	B.
or				
Scale-degrees in A minor		1.		
„ „ E minor		4.	(2.)	5.

bar l D is the freely suspended eleventh which, in order to ascend, describes a melodic-chromatic passing motion to D♯.

G♯ is the suspended upward-resolving seventh, which turns into the ninth of the implicit fundamental F♯[24] and later resolves on to the dominant seventh of the fundamental B♮.

F is the suspended thirteenth, which resolves in orthodox fashion.

bar m E♯ in the upper voice is the melodic-chromatic lower neighbouring note of F♯.

bars l and m These last two bars, rather complicated as they are for the layman, can be reduced to the following simple harmonic progression:

Example 9

Fund.:   A.   (F♯.)   B.

23 [Mayrberger:] By 'hybrid chord' the author intends what was earlier meant by 'altered chords' and is nowadays referred to as 'chords of the extended minor system'. The first of these is the most apt, as can be seen from the fact that such a chord belongs *purely* to neither the one key nor the other, hence has something genuinely hybrid about it. [See Introduction for a discussion of this chord.]

A different interpretation is offered by one of our more recent theorists and teachers, Cyrill Kistler, who can claim the undoubted distinction of having, among many estimable things, drawn the examples for his *Manual of Harmony* (Chemnitz: E. Schmeitzner, 1880)[25] in large part from the compositions of the master [i.e. Wagner], works of momentous importance for the music of the modern era. He accounts for the chord formations in bb. 2 and 6 (c and g) as diminished seventh harmonies with minor triads on {11} scale-degree VII of A minor and C minor respectively. However, the sheer naturalness of the succession of fundamentals in the above examples, and the unmistakeably melodic character of the neighbouring notes G♯ and B♮ in the upper voice of these two bars, bear out the correctness of our own analysis. It would require a separate essay to demonstrate that there are no diminished seventh chords with minor triad, nor ever could be, in our musical system. The hypothesis of such chord formations rests on an incorrect understanding of the extended minor system. The present author's interpretation given above, intelligible as it is to all, proves that it is not necessary even to believe in the existence of such chords.

3. *Tristan motif (score, p. 3)*

Example 10[26]

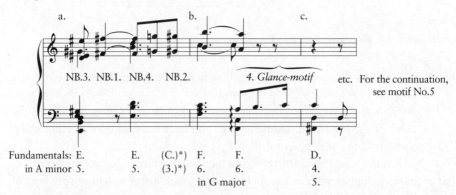

bar a   (NB 1 and 2) The F♯ is the lower diatonic neighbouring note of the leading-note G♯, while (NB 3 and 4) the E♯ and G♮ provide the melodic-chromatic passing motion to the F♯ and G♯.

bars b and c These two bars require no interpretation from the harmonic point of view.

The B♮ in the upper voice of b. 2 is the freely suspended eleventh of the fundamental F.

24 'implicit': *im Geiste gedacht* (lit. 'thought in the mind'). Following Sechter, Mayrberger rejects the conjunct root progression A–B, interpolating an unsounded root F♯ (on beat 6) and thereby creating an acceptable root progression of third–fourth. See Introduction.

25 Cyrill Kistler (1848–1907), German composer and music theorist. Mayrberger appears to have confused two of his publications, *Harmonielehre* (Munich: Schmid, 1879) and *Musikalische Elementarlehre* (Chemnitz: Schmeitzner, 1880).

26 [Mayrberger:] Parentheses round a fundamental denote that that fundamental must be mentally supplied in order to provide a correct relationship between two successive fundamentals one step apart. [See Introduction.]

When the first two bars are set out as a simple harmonic progression, the rightness of the above analysis emerges even more clearly.

Example 11

(The fundamentals or degrees as above)

{12}

5. *Development of the (principal) motif of yearning (score, p. 3)*

Example 12

Fundamentals:		D.	D.		D.	G.		C.		A.
or										
Scale-degrees in G major		5.	5.		5.	1.				
				in C major	5.			1.		
				in D minor				7.		5.

The [first] three successive fundamentals show the chordal connection as one of passing motion.

bars b and c These two bars are self-explanatory with the aid of the fundamentals and keys noted beneath the staff. The latter in particular show the interplay of the relationship.

Example 13

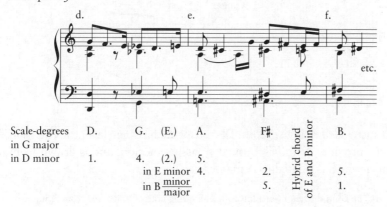

Scale-degrees in G major	D.		G.	(E.)	A.		F♯.	Hybrid chord of E and B minor	B.
in D minor	1.		4.	(2.)	5.		2.		5.
		in E minor	4.						
		in B minor/major	5.						1.

bar d   The G in the upper voice is a suspended eleventh of the fundamental D, the
        E♭ a suspended thirteenth of the fundamental G, deriving chromatically
        from G minor.

bar e   The D of the upper voice is a suspended eleventh of the fundamental A.
        The D♯ in the tenor is melodic-chromatic: as the lower neighbouring note
        of E it derives from E minor, as also, harmonic-chromatically, does the
        last C♮ in the alto. The D♯ in the tenor is a melodic-chromatic embellish-
        ment of E.

bar f   The E of the upper voice is a suspended eleventh on the fundamental B♮.

   {13} The simplified harmonic progression of the last two bars (e and f) bears
out the rightness of the above interpretation, namely:

Example 14

(Fundamentals as above)

From the harmonization of the last-but-one bar (e), and from countless other
similar constructions in Wagner's work, we can see what strength, what individual character the master brings to his polyphonic part-writing by combining
the *melodic*-chromatic with the harmonic-chromatic whenever he intends to bring
out a leitmotif or fragments of a motif. The student will see this at once if he will
compare the original with the simplified harmonic progression.

6. *Further development of the motif of yearning (score, p. 6)*

Example 15[27]

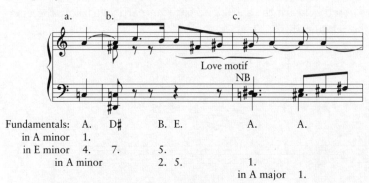

Fundamentals:	A.	D♯		B. E.		A.		A.
in A minor	1.							
in E minor	4.	7.		5.				
in A minor				2.	5.		1.	
in A major								1.

bar c   G♯ is a suspended rising seventh, D♯ a suspended rising eleventh. The E♯ in
        the tenor provides *melodic*-chromatic passing motion, and is drawn from
        F♯ minor, which is related to A major.

---

27   [Mayrberger:] The D♯ in the tenor [is] a lower neighbouring note of E, derived from E minor.

Example 16

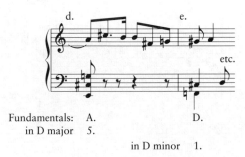

Fundamentals: A.   D.
  in D major   5.
                        in D minor   1.

{14}

bar d Here the F♯ is a lower neighbouring note of the dominant seventh G♮, leading in a moment to a close in the minor.

bar e The G♯ is a *melodic*-chromatic neighbouring note, and is drawn from A minor, which is related to D minor. The C♯ in the tenor is a suspended rising seventh of the fundamental D.

   The fundamentals in their own right, and the positions attributed to them in the respective keys with which they are associated, as suffixed in our examples, offer a sufficient interpretation of the chromaticism of the new musical system, inaugurated in the work of Richard Wagner, in which the diatonic is subsumed within the chromatic. This can be seen even more clearly from the following simplified harmonic progression:

Example 17

(Fundamentals as above)

7. Inversion of the Tristan motif (score, p. 5)

Example 18[28]

Fund.:		(G.)	C. (F.) B.	(G.)	C.		C♯	(A.)	D. (G.) C♯	(A.)	D.
in C $\frac{minor}{major}$	7.	(5.)	1. (4.) 7.	(5.)	1.						
in F $\frac{minor}{major}$		(2.)	5. (1.)	(2.)	5.						
in D $\frac{minor}{major}$						7.	(5.)	1. (4.) 7.	(5.)	1.
in G $\frac{minor}{major}$							(2.)	5. (1.)	(2.)	5.

bar a   The first chord, over the bass note D♭, is a hybrid chord in which the B♮ of the tenor [*recte* alto] points to C minor/major whereas the D♭ points to F minor/major.

{15}

bar b   The F♯ in the soprano is the melodic-chromatic lower neighbouring note of G.
         The second half of bar b and first half of bar c are a literal repetition of the foregoing, and are to be interpreted in the same way.

bar c   The chord formation over the bass note E♭ is a hybrid chord in which the C♯ points to D minor/major whereas the E♭ points to G minor/major.

bar d   The G♯ in the soprano is the melodic-chromatic lower neighbouring note of A. There then follows a repetition of this, which is to be interpreted in the same way.

Although the interpretation of the bars given above is sufficient in itself for an understanding of the rich chromaticism contained in them, a simplified harmonic progression is nonetheless supplied below, because reduction to simple diatonic form is the only way to make complicated chromaticism readily intelligible to the layman.

Example 19

pure C major   pure D minor enclosed within C major

(Fundamentals as above)

8. *Motif of the defiance of death (score, p. 7)*

– omitting the rushing demisemiquaver scales which, while giving impetus to this motif, have, as passing notes, no bearing upon the harmonic substance of our analysis.

Example 20

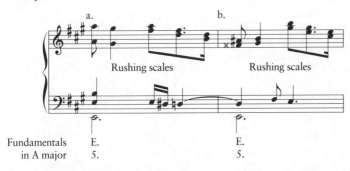

Rushing scales   Rushing scales

Fundamentals   E.   E.
in A major   5.   5.

{16}

bar a   The A at the beginning of the bar is a freely suspended eleventh.

       The A and F♯ are freely suspended eleventh and ninth.

       The F♯ and D are freely suspended ninth and dominant seventh.

       The D and B♮ are dominant seventh and fifth.

       The semiquaver D♯ on the lower staff is a melodic-chromatic passing note, and is borrowed from E major.

bar b   F𝄪 and A♯ in the upper two voices are the melodic-chromatic lower neighbouring notes of G♯ and B♮.

       The C♯ at the end of the bar can be seen as an anticipation of the suspended thirteenth in the bar that follows.

Example 21

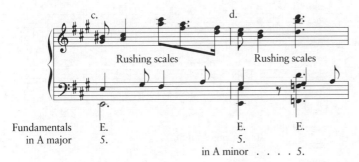

Rushing scales   Rushing scales

Fundamentals   E.   E.   E.
in A major   5.   5.
                   in A minor . . . . 5.

bar c   B♯ and G♯ are the melodic-chromatic lower neighbouring notes of C♯ and A.

       C♯ and A are suspended thirteenth and eleventh.

       A and F♯ are suspended eleventh and ninth.

       F♯ and D are suspended ninth with dominant seventh.

       The F♯ and A on the lower staff must be viewed as lower and upper[29] neighbouring notes of the G♯ which follows them.

28   The alto C♯–C♮ in bars c–d is editorially supplied.   29   *obere und untere.*

bar d The C♯ in the alto is a suspended thirteenth. The bass note F♮ in the second half of the bar is the harmonic embellishment of the bass note E and derives from A minor, whereas the A is a passing note leading thereafter to B♮, the fifth above the bass.

Example 22

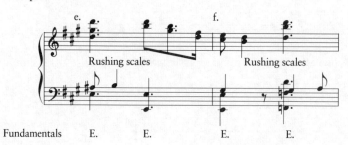

bar e The A♯ in the tenor provides melodic-chromatic passing motion between the diatonic passing note A and the fifth B♮.

The D and B♮ in the upper voice are dominant seventh and fifth.

The B♮ and G♯ are fifth and leading note, the F♯ and D are suspended ninth and seventh.

bar f The C♯ in the alto is a suspended thirteenth.

The F♮ in the second half of the bar is the harmonic-chromatic embellishment of the bass note E and derives from A minor, whereas the A is a passing note leading thereafter to B♮, the fifth above the bass.

Example 23

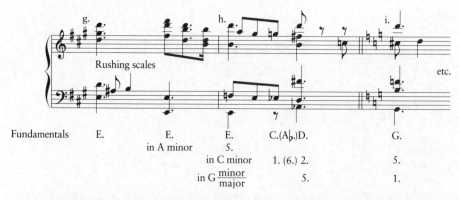

bar g The A♯ in the tenor provides melodic-chromatic passing motion between the diatonic passing note A and the fifth B♮.

The F♯ and D in the uppermost voice are the suspended ninth and dominant seventh.

The D and B♮ are dominant seventh and fifth.

The B and D are fifth and dominant seventh.

bar h The A in the upper voice and the F♮ in the tenor are suspended eleventh
and ninth that resolve in orthodox fashion on to the third and octave.

G♮ and E♭ in these same two voices provide harmonic-chromatic passing
motions drawn from C minor, which is related to A minor.

The chord A♭–D–F♯ is a hybrid chord, with A♭ drawn from C minor and
F♯ from G minor.

The B in the middle voice is a melodic-chromatic embellishment of the
seventh, C, of the fundamental D.

The D at the very top of the texture, assigned to flute in the score, should
be regarded as a pedal note.

{18}

bar i The C♯ in the upper middle voice is a melodic-chromatic lower neighbouring note of D, and is borrowed from D minor.

The above A major passage has as a whole the feel of a mighty and steadily
intensifying pedal-point, owing partly to the rushing demisemiquaver scales that
soar aloft, partly to the harmonic figuration of free suspensions and harmonic
neighbouring notes that drive downwards into the depths. To help the layman
understand this passage better, let me once again offer a simplified harmonic form
of it, in which the leaps are filled out with the intervening passing notes, as follows:

Example 24

(Fundamentals as above)

{19}

[PART II]

9. [Death motif]

A wonderful piece of harmony, but at the same time one which certainly taxes the understanding of many a musician, is that of the Death motif (Act I, Scene 2: score, p. 26):

Example 25

For clarity, bars e and f have been enharmonically rewritten, as follows:

Fundamentals:	D.	G.	(E♮)	A♭.	A♭.	D♭.	D♭.	F.	D.	G.

in G $\frac{minor}{major}$ 5.

in C minor 2.   5.   (1.)   6.

in D♭ $\frac{minor}{major}$ 5.   5.   1.   1. D♭ major 3.

in C minor ... 4.   2.   5.

in G $\frac{minor}{major}$ 5.

bars a and b The interpretation given for bars g and h of motif 1 applies also here.

bar b The B♭ and A♮ in the upper middle voice provide melodic-chromatic passing motion to the A♭ that follows them. This same A♮ replaces B♭♭ enharmonically, and serves as a forewarning of the approaching modulation towards the ominous key of D♭ minor.

bars c and d The fundamentals and keys noted beneath the staff provide all the explanation that is necessary of these two bars.

bars e and f The B♭♭ in the upper voice is a freely suspended thirteenth, except that rather than resolving over the fundamental D♭ it does so over the following fundamental, F, a device which is accounted for in theoretical terms as a simple retarded suspension (see the author's *Textbook of Musical Harmony* (Pressburg and Leipzig: Gustav Heckenast), 201, §89).[30] It is precisely because bars e and f can be construed as in D♭ minor that {20}

---

30 *Lehrbuch*, vol. I, pp. 201–03, §89 'Von der verzögerten Auflösung der Vorhalte' ('Retarded Resolution of Suspensions'). This clause deals first with the ninth, showing with examples 'how the ninth is resolved not over its own fundamental, but over some other', and then with the eleventh.

Wagner is able so effectively to depict the awesome power of death, the flesh-creeping impact of which is heightened by the *pianissimo* entry of the trombones to produce a shattering effect.

bar g That the F♭ in the preceding bar is able to move to F♮ rather than having to remain where it is arises out of the harmonic freedom of the minor key to cadence in the major; and since this movement takes place over the scale-degree not of D♭ but of F it must be seen as a retardation.

To provide an easier understanding of the harmonic substance in bars f and g, a simplified form of the chords is given below which shows the [implied] resolution of the suspended thirteenth over the fundamental D♭.

Example 26

Here the thirteenth resolves over the D♭ fundamental itself, whereas in the original the resolution does not take place until the F fundamental has arrived.

bar h The interpretation is the same as that of bar a.

bar i The E♭ in the upper voice is a freely suspended thirteenth.

10. *Further development of the glance motif (score, p. 27)*

Example 27

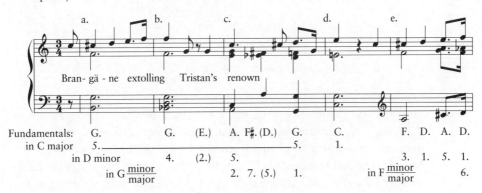

The fundamentals and keys suffixed to the above example account not only for the chromatic modulation but also for the chromatic-melodic material in the upper voice.

{21}

Example 28

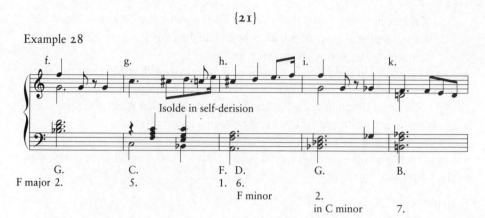

Isolde in self-derision

G.
F major 2.   C.   F. D.   G.   B.
                               5.   1. 6.

                                                    F minor   2.
                                                                          in C minor   7.

Here, too, the fundamentals and associated keys account for the modulatory coherence of the above bars.

bar g Attention need be drawn only to the fact that the F and A over the fundamental C are suspended eleventh and thirteenth. It is perhaps worth mentioning in passing that most theorists and teachers treat such formations as 6/4-chords of scale-degree I, hence in this case of the scale-degree F. This interpretation is totally false. The reason for this particular theoretical view lies partly in an ignorance of correct dissonance treatment and partly in a far too superficial treatment of suspensions in well-nigh all textbooks up to now.

Example 29

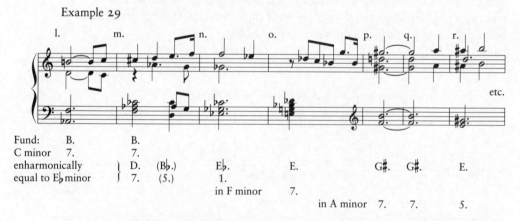

etc.

Fund:	B.	B.							
C minor	7.	7.							
enharmonically			D.	(B♭.)	E♭.	E.	G♯.	G♯.	E.
equal to E♭ minor			7.	(5.)	1.				
					in F minor	7.			
							in A minor	7.	7.	5.

bars l and m The chromaticism of these two bars points unambiguously to C minor. But because the ear in bar n above seems to perceive the sixth natural scale-degree in E♭ minor, that is to say C♭, brought about by the simple retarded resolution of the thirteenth, Wagner has changed the B♮ enharmonically to C♭ in advance in bar m, this in turn resulting in the enharmonic modulation from C minor to E♭ minor. From what has just been said, it is plain that the C♯ in the upper voice of bar m is to be thought of in melodic terms.

{22}

bar n. The F in the upper voice is a suspended ninth over the fundamental E♭, to which the fundamental C♭ appears as a substitute.

Anyone who wishes to learn more about such substitutions of fundamentals should consult the author's wall-charts, issued by C. Stampfel of Pressburg, showing the technique of modulation via diminished seventh chords.[31]

bar o   This bar would seem to require no interpretation. Its connection with bar p is another matter. Following the diminished seventh chord of F minor, the only harmony that should occur in ascent if the logical coherence of keys is not to be violated is that of the diminished seventh of C minor. However, since the latter is enharmonically identical with that of A minor, Wagner has promptly executed the enharmonic exchange. On this, too, the author's wall-charts, mentioned above, give all the information necessary. The fact that bars l, m and n point in reality to C minor, and that the modulation to E♭ minor became possible only after the enharmonic exchange in the original key, suggests the following simplified harmonic progression:

Example 30

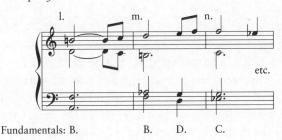

Fundamentals: B.   B.   D.   C.

11. *Motif of the ailing Tristan*

Example 31

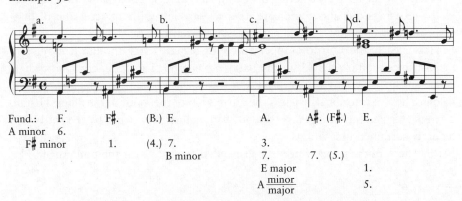

bar a   If it is possible to suppress the resolution of dissonances and then continue them as consonances, {23} perfectly feasible though their resolution would

31   I have been unable to locate a surviving copy of these charts.

have been – a process that I call harmonic ellipsis – then it is a logical extension of such ellipsis to apply it to those chords that function in a purely mediating capacity between two harmonies. This maxim provides the basis for the legitimacy of chromatically ascending successions of fundamentals such as that which we find in bar a (F♮–F♯).

The following example should make this maxim clear:

Example 32

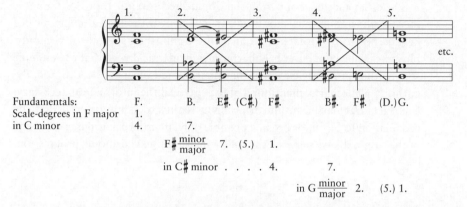

The legitimacy of the chromatic connection between the two chords A–C–F and B♮–D–F–A♭ (see bb. 1 and 2) must be admitted on the basis of harmonic theory, in which it is stated that the tonic triad of a major key may be followed equally well by the diminished seventh chord of the tonic minor key or by that of the dominant minor or that of the subdominant minor key. Hence the tonic triad of F major may be followed by the diminished seventh chord of F minor or of C minor or of B♭ minor. In the above example, that of C minor has been selected.

The enharmonic exchange within b. 2 needs no interpretation, nor does the connection of b. 2 with b. 3.

If we now excise the mediating bars 2, 4, etc., that is, leave them out altogether as the crossings-out above indicate, then we are left with a succession of first-inversion chords whose fundamentals ascend by chromatic steps.

How clearly the B♭ in the upper voice [of bar a], harsh though it may seem against the simultaneous A♯ [in the bass], advertises its melodic-chromatic character; and in providing a glance back towards the F major to which it actually belongs, how extraordinarily apt is the attribution of the motif to the ailing Tristan. The effect is perfectly capped by the orchestra's *pianissimo* and by the softly and tenderly sustained first violins.

bar b The A in the upper voice is a suspended eleventh over the fundamental E.

{24}

bar c The melodic-chromatic path of the upper voice via D♯ surely needs no further explanation at this stage.

Similar though the succession of fundamental A to fundamental A♯ in the present bar may appear to the situation in bar a, the interpretation given to the latter has no bearing whatsoever on the former. The present case has a rather different explanation. In any minor key it is permissible after the natural scale-degree VII chromatically to introduce the raised VII, since in any case the dominant scale-degree must be mentally supplied after the second of these, as the F♯ in parentheses shows here.

bar d   The proliferation of fundamentals and keys in this bar may put off the musician who is less well grounded in harmony, if not perplex him. However, since a full interpretation of the procedure involved in these fundamentals would demand more space than is possible in these pages, I must yet again refer the reader to my above-mentioned wall-charts, issued by C. Stampfel of Pressburg, where this very case is thoroughly explicated on chart II, no. 40.

Continuation of motif 11

Example 33

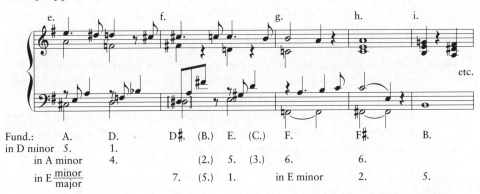

Fund.:	A.	D.	D♯.	(B.)	E.	(C.)	F.		F♯.		B.
in D minor	5.	1.									
in A minor		4.		(2.)	5.	(3.)	6.		6.		
in E $\frac{minor}{major}$			7.	(5.)	1.		in E minor		2.		5.

bar e   The upper voice is melodic-chromatic through and through. The B♭ in the lower middle voice is a freely suspended thirteenth, and resolves to A in orthodox fashion in the next bar.

bar f   The melodic-chromatic C♯ and C♮ in the upper voice constitute a suspended ninth over the fundamental B♮. Since before it resolves the C♮ is detained, turning into a suspended thirteenth over the fundamental [E], the result is an example of the doubly retarded suspension (see the author's *Textbook of Musical Harmony* (Leipzig: Heckenast), 202, §89).

{25}

bars g and h   The capacity of the raised scale-degree VI, F♯ in A minor, to follow directly on from the natural VI, F, has already been accounted for in connection with bar c. (What is more, this liberty is conceded by no less an authority than the contrapuntist Simon Sechter.)

12. *Brangäne's conciliation motif*

Example 34

Fundamentals:	B♭.	E♭.	B♭.	E♭. (C.) F.
in E♭ major	5.	1.	5.	1. (6.) 2.
in G minor	3.	6.	3.	6.

bar a The F♯ in the lowest voice is the augmented fifth of the scale-degree B♭, chromatically derived from G minor, but it can also be seen as a melodic-chromatic substitute for F. The E♭ in the upper voice and lower middle voice is an anticipation of the fundamental E♭ that comes next.

bar b The A♮ in the upper voice is melodic-chromatic, the D and F in the upper middle voice are neighbouring notes of E♭.

bar c The F♯ in the lowest voice has been accounted for under bar a. The F in the upper voice, as a diminished octave of the F♯ in the lowest voice, has the character of a suspension, as also does the C in the upper middle voice.

bar d The E in the upper voice is melodic-chromatic, the G and B♮ in the upper middle voice are the lower neighbouring notes of A♭ and C respectively, the D in the same voice is the upper neighbouring note of C.

Continuation of motif 12

Example 35

Fund.:	F.	(D.)	G. (C.) F.	B♭.	E♭.
in E♭ major	2.	(7.)	3. (6.) 2.	5.	1.

{26}

bar e This bar speaks volumes to anyone who has even a modest grasp of the beguiling power of passing notes and neighbouring notes. Equally explicit is the suspension-like quality of the E♭ in the upper and lower middle voices.

bar f The E♮–G in the upper and lower middle voices are neighbouring notes of the chord constituent F, likewise G and B♭ of the chromatic chord constituent A♮. The first D in the upper voice is a suspended thirteenth over the fundamental F, the second D is a passing note to the eleventh which follows over the fundamental B♭.

bar g This needs no comment for anyone with even a modicum of training in harmony.

bar h C and A♮ in the upper voices are free neighbouring notes of the chord constituent B♭, likewise D and F in the upper middle voice [of E♭].

We need only put together the gently rising conjunct lowest voice with the conjunct melody of the upper voice and the entreating line of the second violin and viola, to realize that Wagner has created in this a masterpiece of melodic as well as of harmonic writing.

The path traversed by the middle voice in this motif is proof enough that Wagner, in his inspired yet conscious use of passing notes, possessed a mastery which no composer before him can boast.

13. *Continuation of Brangäne's conciliation motif*

Example 36

| Fundamentals: | G♭. | G♭. (E♭). A♭. | A♭. | D♭. | D♭. | G♭. | G♭. |
| in G♭ major | 1. | 1. (6). 2. | 2. | 5. | 5. | 1. | 1. |

bar a The F in the middle voice is a lower neighbouring note of G♭.

bar b The F in the upper voice is a lower neighbouring note of G♭, the A♮ in the lowest voice a melodic-chromatic embellishment of B♭, deriving from the related key of B♭ minor.

bar c The D♮ and F in the middle voice constitute lower and upper neighbouring notes of E♭, the D deriving from the related key of E♭ minor.

{27}

bars d and e E♮ and C♮ in the upper two voices are melodic passing notes providing a more natural progression toward their goals, F and D♭. If nonetheless the C instead of moving to D♭ in bar e leaps to E♭, the suspended ninth over the fundamental D♭, then this suspension acts as a substitute for D♭, its resolution finally appearing, after a lengthy circumambulation, in bar h over the fundamental G♭.

The G♮ in bar e is a melodic-chromatic embellishment of the fifth, A♭.

bar f The upper voice adopts a harmonic role, while the middle voice first makes a detour from the seventh, C♭, to the ninth, E♭, and then resolves down towards B♭ in orthodox fashion in bar g.

bar g   The C♮ in the upper voice is a melodic-chromatic passing note leading to
D♭; the F in the middle voice is a lower neighbouring note of G♭.

bar h   This is to be interpreted exactly as was bar b.

14. *Hero motif*

Example 37

Fundam.:	F.	F. ——————— B♭.	B♭.	B♭.	(E♭.)	A♭.	A♭.	F.	F.	B♭.
in F minor	1.	1.								
in E♭ minor		2.	5. ———————————			4.	4.	2.	2.	5.
in A♭ minor			2.	2.	(5.)	1.				

The fundamentals and keys noted beneath the staff account fully for the above
passage from the harmonic point of view.

The A♭ sustained by oboes, cor anglais, horns and bassoons from bar b to the
end is to be seen as an upper pedal-point, portraying in a most expressive way the
steadfast character of Tristan, subduing powerful emotions, while the clipped harmonic motif so perfectly depicting Tristan's chivalry and valour is sounded by
the string chorus between and below[32] the pedal point.

{28}

15. *The sleep motif together with the death motif in new guise*

Example 38

Fundamentals:	G♭.		G♭.	C♭.	E♭.	(C♭.)	F.		C.	(A♭.)	D♭.
in G♭ major	1.		1.	4.	6.						
in A♭ $\frac{\text{minor}}{\text{major}}$					5.	(3.)	6.		3.		
in D♭ $\frac{\text{minor}}{\text{major}}$					. . . .		7.	5.	1.		
in G♭ major					. . . .			5.			
in E♭ minor					. . . .		7.		7.		

32 *über und zwischen* (lit. 'above and between'). Mayrberger's piano reduction faithfully reflects
the written registers of the score. The lowest line is doubled at the octave below in the sounding
register of the double basses, but this does not justify the chosen prepositions.

bar a   The E♭♭, A♮ and C♮ in the three middle voices are harmonic-chromatic embellishments of the chord constituents D♭, B♭ and D♭. The fact that they sound simultaneously with the G♭ in the lowest voice lends to this formation the aspect of a hybrid chord, as its three chromatic notes are derived from three related minor keys, namely:

> E♭♭ from G♭ minor
>
> A♮ from B♭ minor, and
>
> C♮ from D♭ minor.

This chord could just as well be notated as G♭, B♭♭, C♮, E♭♭, in which case its chromatic notes would derive from only two related minor keys, namely:

> E♭♭ from G♭ minor
>
> B♭♭ and C♮ from D♭ minor.

bar b   In their capacity as embellishments of B♭ and D♭, the A♮ and C♮ are tied over into this bar, but because they now occur on the strong beat they acquire the character of upward-resolving suspensions.

The C♮ in the upper middle voice here is purely melodic-chromatic.

The D♮ in the lower middle voice is a chromatic passing note to the chord constituent E♭, whereas the F is a diatonic passing note to the chromatic chord constituent G♮.

bar d   The G♭[33] in the upper voice is a suspended eleventh and does not resolve until the following bar. The remaining melodic material of the upper voice is partly embellishing, partly harmonic in function.

{29}

Continuation of 15

Example 39

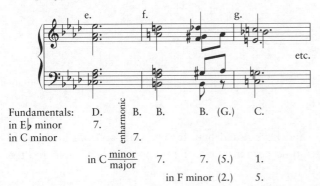

Fundamentals:	D.	enharmonic	B.	B.	B. (G.)	C.
in E♭ minor	7.					
in C minor			7.			
in C $\frac{minor}{major}$				7.	7. (5.)	1.
in F minor					(2.)	5.

---

33   *ad Takt c. Das g*: the double error ('bar c' for 'bar d', and 'The G♮' for 'The G♭') suggests an error of copying or typesetting at this point, since Mayrberger unaccountably offers no commentary on bar c, and since the G♮ in the upper voice would have been the first feature on which to comment in bar c, as the lower neighbouring note of A♭.

bar e The E♭ in the upper voice is a freely suspended ninth, which does not resolve
until the next bar over the fundamental B♮. As a result of the enharmonic
exchange that occurs between the diminished seventh chords of E♭ minor
and C minor, which is not visible to the eye but which must be mentally
supplied, the suspended ninth over the fundamental D♮ turns into a suspended eleventh over the fundamental B♮.

bar f The D♭ in the upper voice is chromatically derived from F minor, while
the B♮ in the lowest voice stems from C minor/major, hence the resulting
hybrid chord, of which the G♯ in the middle voice is the melodic-chromatic
lower neighbouring note of A♮. This does not, of course, belong to F minor,
and as such brings all the more astringent a quality both to the hybrid
chord itself and to what it expresses: Tristan's death wish.

16. *Song of death*

Example 40

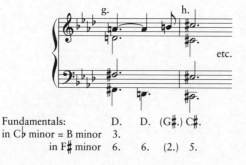

{30} The fundamentals and keys noted beneath the staff account adequately
on their own for the harmonic construction of this passage, and also for the
enharmonic procedure of bar g.

17. *Song of death, combined with the transfiguration motif*

Example 41

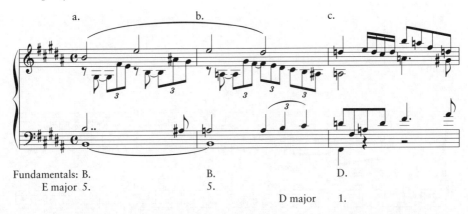

bars a, b and c The melodic motion of the individual voices in the above bars
needs no further interpretation in terms of the analytical method used here.
As for the fabric produced by the interweaving voices, here and in many
other places Wagner shows in practice the rule intuitively felt by theorists but
never yet formally articulated: *within the space of a single bar, even the most
dissonant vertical combinations of voices may be permitted so long as each
individual voice is in conformity with the harmonic spirit of its fundamental.*

It is this that makes possible those mysterious rustlings and whisperings,
half melody, half harmony, which transport the listener's mind magically
to faraway enchanted places.

So much for melodic part-writing.

There remains the chromatic modulatory connection between bars b and c. At
the bottom of this lies a harmonic ellipsis, as the following simplified progression
shows:

{31}

Example 42

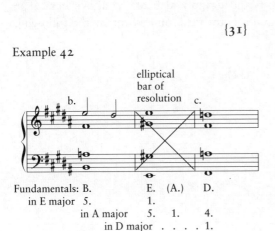

From this can plainly be seen that the seventh, A♮, over the fundamental B, would have been able to resolve normally, and that that is precisely how the harmonic ellipsis came about.

Continuation of 17

Example 43

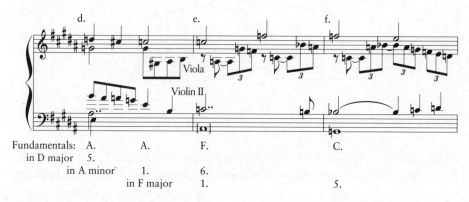

Fundamentals: A.   A.   F.   C.
    in D major   5.
            in A minor   1.   6.
            in F major   1.   5.

etc.

Fundamentals: E♭.
    in E♭ major   1.

The remarks made about bars a, b and c apply also to the above bars. The harmonic ellipsis between bars f and g is to be accounted for by the following simplified progression:

{32}

Example 44

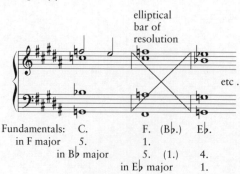

elliptical
bar of
resolution

etc.

Fundamentals: C.   F.   (B♭.)   E♭.
    in F major   5.   1.
            in B♭ major   5.   (1.)   4.
                    in E♭ major   1.

18. *Mark's motif*

Example 45

Fundamentals: Gb.   Bb.   Eb.   Ab.   Db.
  in Eb minor   3.   5.   1.   4.
            in Ab minor 1.   4.

bar b   The F in the upper voice is an upward-resolving ninth, the Db in the same
        voice a suspended eleventh. The G♮ in the upper middle voice is a sus-
        pended seventh that resolves upward. From the harmonic point of view,
        the remainder is self-evident.

[Conclusion]

From the analysis of the passages given above, and in particular from the fundamentals and keys suffixed to the examples and the way in which these interact
with one another can be seen very clearly how necessary it is to have a full grasp
of the laws of diatonic progression in major and minor.

How can the musician hope to find his way amid the manifold intricacies of
chromaticism if his knowledge of the diatonic is still shaky?

Does anybody really think he can master the fundamentals of this science from
the severely abridged harmony textbooks of today, with their seventy or fewer
pages? Just consider how many false assertions, how many specious arguments,
must be purveyed by these textbooks, in their cursoriness.

{33} Do we not require every instrumentalist and every singer to undergo long
years of training before he earns the right to be called an artist? Then how can it
be that according to the textbooks of the present day the study of harmony can be
encompassed in a shorter time?

What are the consequences of this cursoriness, this superficiality?

The consequences are that the whole theory of harmony has been brought into
discredit as a field of study, that one new system follows another, and that things
have come to such a pass that even good composers have begun to show scant
regard for harmonic theory.

If one is to understand the harmonic style of Richard Wagner, if one is to master
it for one's own creative purposes, it is essential that one grasp fully the laws of:

the realm of the diatonic in major and minor,
diatonic modulation,
chromatic modulation, and lastly
the realm of the enharmonic.

These must be studied *in the prescribed order*, since one grows out of another, and the music of the present day came into being in this way, as already expounded above in the Foreword.

Let me commend this course of study most heartily to young musicians, and let me close with the words of the master:[34]

Imbibe the master-rules right soon,
That they may be your constant boon.

---

34 *Die Meistersinger von Nürnberg*, Act III Scene 2 (Hans Sachs). The monograph is signed 'Pressburg, August 1880, K. Mayrberger'.

PART III:

The classification of personal style

Introduction

The literature of music abounds in classificatory systems. They can be found in the writings of the Greeks, of the medieval and Renaissance theorists, and of seventeenth- and eighteenth-century theorists and commentators. Thus Boethius, in the early sixth century, crystallized and amplified ancient concepts of the universal field of 'music' and fashioned a threefold classification: 'planetary', 'human' and 'instrumental'. Rejecting this division eight centuries later, Johannes de Grocheio grudgingly accepted a twofold classification into 'measured' (i.e. polyphony) and 'not precisely measured' (i.e. monophony), but categorized the Parisian music of the late 1200s in threefold manner as: 'of the people', 'measured' (or 'composed') and 'of the church' – a polyglot of function, technique and social group. Grocheio further subclassified these, eventually identifying genres such as the rondeau, the *estampie*, organum, hocket and motet.

Temporal and generational distinctions were created around such words as 'art' and 'practice'. With 'old art', 'new art' and later 'subtler art', theorists in the fourteenth century differentiated between types of metre, rhythmic pacing and patterning (features that were at least as visible in the notation as they were audible in performance). Two centuries later, Claudio Monteverdi's brother Giulio Cesare invoked 'first practice' and 'second practice', in 1607, when speaking of the primacy of counterpoint or harmony, the pre-eminence of music or text, the strict or free observance of dissonance rules. Diruta, reflecting the last of these three distinctions two years later, articulated two categories of 'counterpoint' as what might rather freely be translated 'law-abiding' (*osservato*) and 'lax' (*commune*).

The word 'style' appeared as a vehicle for such categories towards the middle of the seventeenth century. Thus Marco Scacchi, in about 1648, adumbrated a threefold classification of style whose categories were 'of the church', 'of the chamber' and 'of the stage or theatre'. Two of these styles were in turn broken down into substyles by the identification of genres, performance forces and stylistic features:[1]

> the church style into four types: masses, motets and other vocal pieces without organ for four to eight voices; the same with organ or with several choruses; similar vocal music *in concerto*, that is with instruments; and motets or concerti in the modern style, that is [. . .] in *stile misto* or *recitativo imbastardito* ('hybrid recitative'), in which the recitative is interrupted by ornate and melodious passages or sacred songs in aria style. The chamber style had three components: madrigals without instruments (*da tavolino*), vocal pieces with continuo, and vocal pieces with instruments such as violins, violas 'majores', theorbos, lutes and recorders. The theatrical style [was] a single style of 'speech perfected by song, or song by speech'.

1 Claude V. Palisca, 'Scacchi, Marco', in *NGDM*.

In about 1660, Christoph Bernhard offered two alternative twofold classifications, one descriptive, the other temporal: he himself chose to speak of 'counterpoint', and to categorize it as either 'solemn' (*gravis*) or 'luxuriant'; others, he
acknowledged, spoke of 'style', categorizing it as either 'ancient' (or *a cappella*,
or 'of the church') or 'modern'. Both systems were predicated on quantity of
dissonance, the former representing the Palestrinian style and recognizing only a
few dissonant devices ('figures'), the latter reflecting contemporary practice and
recognizing many more such devices. They therefore equated broadly with
Monteverdi's 'first' and 'second practice'. Obliquely recalling Diruta and Scacchi,
Bernhard subclassified luxuriant counterpoint into 'common-practice' (*communis*)
and 'comic' (or 'theatrical', or 'recitative', or 'oratorical'). Bernhard specified the
'figures' appropriate to each category in extraordinary detail, thus presenting a
true taxonomy of style.

Scacchi's threefold classification appeared in the work of his pupil Angelo Berardi
in 1681, its categories and subcategories attributed to a newer generation of composers; and Johann Joseph Fux was in turn indebted to Berardi in his discussion of
styles in the *Gradus ad Parnassum* (1725), and in his retention of Scacchi's three
categories, which are found also in Mattheson's first treatise (1713), and in his
chapter 'On the Categories of Musical Composition' in his encyclopedic *The Complete Capellmeister* (1739). At the same time, it was Mattheson who, in that first
treatise, with its Frenchified title,[2] established a new polarity between the 'learned'
style and the 'galant' style – a polarity that later echoed through the writings of
Quantz (1752, 1754), C. P. E. Bach (1753), Marpurg (1753–4) and others.

In all of the above medieval and Baroque systems, contemporary observers
identified boundaries that divided their own universes of music and sought to
articulate the differences that lay across those boundaries, and the similarities
among what lay within them. In each case, the differences and similarities were
features of musical style: types of rhythmic organization, syntaxes of consonance
and dissonance, varieties of texture, correlations of words to notes, deployments
of voices and instruments and so on. In every case, categories were linked to
external phenomena: time ('old' *versus* 'new'; 'ancient' *versus* 'modern'; 'first'
versus 'second'), context ('church' *versus* 'chamber' *versus* 'theatre'), behaviour or
character ('law-abiding' *versus* 'lax'; 'solemn' *versus* 'luxuriant'; 'learned' *versus*
'galant'). Increasingly during the Baroque, nationality became one such external
phenomenon. Scacchi himself, around 1648, was contributing to a long-running
controversy on Polish soil over the merits of Italian music as against those of other
countries' music. Awareness of the discontinuities between French, German and
Italian national styles intensified during the later seventeenth and early eighteenth
centuries. The differences between French and Italian styles within opera were
the subject of propagandistic quarrels and pamphleteering wars throughout the
early and mid-eighteenth century, though their products were less stylistic definitions

---

2   Which can be roughly translated as 'The Newly Established *Orchestre*, or *Universelle* and
     Thorough Introduction as to How a *Galant Homme* may obtain a Complete Understanding of
     the Loftiness and Worth of the Noble *Music*, *Formiren* His *Gout* According to It, Grasp the
     terminos technicos, and Skilfully *raisonniren* of this Excellent Science'.

than critical polemics. The base-terms of such differences in these various polarities and triangularities were several: 'music', 'counterpoint', 'opera', 'art', 'practice' and 'style'.

When we come to the early nineteenth century, the principal base-terms were two: 'style' and 'manner'. 'Style' and 'manner' are terms very much related to the *doing* of art. 'Style' derives, through French *stile*, from Latin *stilus*, a pointed instrument used for incising lines on parchment, or writing on wax tablets. 'Manner' comes, through Italian *maniera* and French *manière*, from the Latin adjective *manuarius*, literally 'belonging to the hand'. 'Style' and 'manner' had existed side by side in eighteenth-century vocabulary, in part performing parallel functions. In French, *manière* provided behavioural modes of self-conduct, bearing, speaking, thinking and perceiving; *maniéré* signified 'affected', 'unnatural' and 'having exaggerated features'; while *style* provided modes of presentation, of conceptualization, of acting or proceeding (including that in government, finance and justice), *stylé* signifying 'used to' and 'skilled in'.

In the metalanguage of the arts, however, if the dictionaries of the time are to be believed, each term had its own preserve, as is shown by the following two subentries, reproduced untranslated from a French-English dictionary of 1796:[3]

> MANIÈRE (goût) de peindre, *style in painting*. La manière de Raphaël diffère de celle du Titien. *Raphael's style differs from that of Titian.*
> STYLE (manière de composer, d'écrire) *style, manner of writing*. Style familier, *familiar style*. Style bas, *low style*. Style populaire, *vulgar style*, such as is used by the common people.

The two terms were coupled in mutual definition, and both concerned the activity of *composer*, which meant equally 'to arrange a [visual] composition' in painting and 'to compose one's thoughts' in verbal communication. Thus 'STYLE signifies the manner of composing, of writing' (1744),[4] shows *manière* in a defining role to *style*, and *composer* as meaning 'to order one's ideas' in a speech or oration.[5] (Compare this with Buffon's 'Style is the order and movement that one puts into one's thoughts'.[6]) Correspondingly, '"The manner of a painter" is the term given to the way of composing and painting peculiar to that painter. It is style in painting'

---

3   Abel Boyer, *Le dictionnaire royal, françois-anglois, et anglois-françois / The Royal Dictionary, French and English, English and French*, ed. P. M. Fierville (London: Thomas Davison, 1796), vol. I, gath. Pp, f.2ʳ, col.3; vol. I, gath. 3O, f.4ʳ, col.1. The subentry 'Manière' first appeared in the 1748 edition; the beginning of the subentry 'Style' was already present in the 1702 edition, without compound phrases.

4   *Le dictionnaire de l'Académie Françoise* (Paris: Coignard, 1744), vol. II, p. 553; likewise, 'Style is the term given to the manner of composing, of writing' (Abbé Féraud, *Dictionaire critique de la langue française* (Marseille: Jean Mossy, 1787–8), vol. III, gath. liii, f.1ʳ, col.2); 'STYLE . . . manner of writing' (P.–C.–V. Boïste, *Dictionnaire universel de la langue française* (Paris: Verdière,' 1829), p. 651, col.2).

5   Cf. 'Style: the manner, way of writing or conducting a discourse, peculiar to each individual' (François Antoine Pomey, *Le dictionnaire royal*, expanded edition (Lyon: Molin, 1677), p. 896).

6   Georges-Louis Leclerc, comte de Buffon in his inaugural address to the Académie Française on the theme of language and style, commonly known as the *Discours sur le style*, on 25 August 1753 (*Buffon: Discours sur le style: a facsimile of the 1753 12ᵐᵒ Edition, Together with the Text of the First Draft of the Discours . . .* , ed. Cedric E. Pickford (Hull: Hull French Texts, 1978), p. vi). The famous remark, *le style est l'homme même* (p. xvii), was not in the original address; it implies that the subject-matter of a discourse is external to the author, and may come and go, whereas style is the author himself, and remains unchanged.

(1788),[7] shows *style* as defining *manière*, and *composer* as 'arranging the visual elements on the canvas'.[8] The Italian term *maniera* was allegedly first applied to visual art in 1442, in praise of Pisanello's work,[9] and came to denote the quality of stylishness.

The definitions given so far assert a demarcation in French usage, *manière* being applied to painting, *style* to speech and writing. Both applications are amplified in an admittedly late Italian dictionary: '*Maniera*, mode, guise, form of working, in painters, sculptors, architects . . .', '*Stile*, quality, and mode of literary composition [*dettare*], whether in prose or in verse . . .'.[10] The end of this demarcation is signalled as early as 1787–8:[11]

> 'Style' and 'manner' are but one and the same thing under different names. Custom has assigned the term 'manner' to painting, and 'style' to the art of verbal expressions [*bien dire*]. Thus one says 'This picture is *in the manner of* Raphael', just as one says 'This speech for the defence is *in the style of* Cicero. –For some time now, changes being as popular in language as in fashion, people have spoken of 'style' in painting, and 'manner' in literature.

There existed, however, in the eighteenth century, an asymmetrical relationship between the two terms. Far from performing the same function within their respective artistic spheres, they behaved remarkably differently. 'Style' was associated with an array of vivid descriptive adjectives denoting non-personal styles of writing, of which the following is only a brief segment: 'Dry and emaciated style. Full and copious, rounded and well-balanced style. Lofty style. Virile, terse style. Prolix style. Asiatic, or slack style . . .'.[12] By contrast, 'manner' functioned only weakly for non-personal categories: 'grandiose manner' and 'beautiful manner' were stock phrases, but were the exceptions that proved the rule. It was associated mostly with proper nouns and their adjectival forms, and with personal pronouns, as in: 'the manners of Rubens, of Da Ponte; the early or recent manner of one and the same painter; the Flemish or Italian manner; [. . .] the manner of Michelangelo or

---

7   *Dictionnaire de l'Académie Françoise*, new edition (Nîmes: Beaume, 1778), vol. II, p. 553; the 1744 edition has '"Manner" is used for short to signify the manner of a painter, his way of painting' (vol. II, p. 10).

8   Cf. '"Manner" relates equally to invention, design [*dessein*] and colouration [*coloris*]' (Antoine Furetière, *Dictionnaire universel, contenant généralement tous les mots françois tant vieux que modernes* (The Hague and Rotterdam: Arnoud et Reinier Leers, 1701), gath LllII, f.2ᵛ, col.2). This triad is reminiscent of the rhetorical triad Inventio–Elaboratio–Executio. It is foreshadowed in Vasari's *The Lives of the Painters*: 'improving its design, colouration and invention' (*Le vite de'più eccellenti pittori, scultori e architettori, nelle redazioni del 1550 e 1568*, ed. R. Bettarini and P. Barocchi, *Testo*, vol. IV (Florence: Scelte, 1976), p. 204).

9   By Agnolo Galli or Ottaviano Ubaldini in Urbino (*Encyclopaedia Britannica*, vol. II, p. 567 'Mannerism'). John Shearman attributes it to a sonnet of 1442 that lists *maniera* as one of the heaven-sent gifts of Pisanello (*Mannerism* (Harmondsworth: Penguin, 1967), p. 17).

10   Paolo Costa, *Dizionario della lingua italiana* (Bologna: Fratelli Masi, 1819–26), vol. IV (1822), p. 650; vol. VI (1824), pp. 520–21, giving etymology as 'Lat. *forma dicendi, stylus* . . .'. The demarcation is not absolute: a 1701 definition reads '"Manner" refers [. . .] to that particular character that painters, poets, and other people who work by art possess [. . .]' (Furetière, *Dictionnaire universel*, vol. II, gath. LllII, f.2ʳ⁻ᵛ, giving as examples 'This historian has written in the Greek, or Latin, manner. This poet has adopted the manner of Pindar, of Horace').

11   Féraud, *Dictionaire critique*, vol. II, p. 603.

12   *Dictionnaire de l'Académie Françoise* (1778), vol. II, p. 553: 'Style sec & décharné. Style plein & nourri, périodique & nombreux. Style soutenu. Style mâle, nerveux. Style diffus. Style asiatique ou lâche . . .'

Raphael can be detected in their pupils; [. . .] a painter who has formed his manner under good teachers; [. . .] these statues, these buildings, are in the Gothic manner'.[13]

The use of 'manner' for personal designation was especially strong: it was 'that particular character that painters [. . .] possess, by which can be recognized their brushwork [*pinceau*], their style [*stile*], their locality [*païs*]'.[14] 'Raphael had had several manners. [. . .] Rembrandt developed a manner specially for producing grand effects; it is dangerous to imitate his manner'[15] reminds us that manner was something acquired by emulation, rather than itself developing by growth and maturity. Nowhere does this view emerge more clearly than in *The Lives of the Artists* of Giorgio Vasari (1511–74). Vasari tells us that Raphael, having mastered the style of Pietro Perugino in his apprenticeship around 1500, found it an encumbrance, so 'purged himself of the manner of Pietro, and used it as a stepping-stone to mastering that of Michelangelo'; but, realizing that he would never equal the latter, subsequently borrowed what he needed from the manner of Bartolomeo di San Marco and others, 'making from many manners a single one, which came then to be considered always as his own . . .'.[16]

Vasari's portrayal is far from the organic evolution of style that was to become the nineteenth-century paradigm of inner artistic development. In its course are adumbrated three, possibly four, manners; they are never through-numbered, however, only presented as binary pairs, old/new. In the *Encyclopedia* of Diderot and d'Alembert, we find a scheme for stylistic progression (1765) that is every bit as calculated, but is also through-numbered and normative. Manner in painting 'is a particular way whereby each painter achieves his design, composition, expression and colouration'.[17] Whether it is good or bad depends on the extent to which it conforms to 'nature, or whatever is adjudged beautiful'. It then continues:

> Any one painter has three successive *manners*, sometimes more. The first arises from the practice of imitating that of his master. Thus it is that from the works of a given [painter] one can tell that he comes from the school of this or that master. The second [*manner*] takes shape from his discovery that there are beauties in nature, and then the change is much for the better. But often, instead of substituting nature for the *manner* that he took over from his master, he opts for the *manner* of some other [painter] that he considers better. Finally, of the various defects by which his different *manners* have been marred, those of the [painter's] third [*manner*] are always still more exaggerated, and his last *manner* is always the worst.

13 Furetière, *Dictionnaire universel* (1701), vol. II, gath. Lllll, f.2ᵛ, col.2. An early nineteenth-century Italian list reverses the relationship, mapping the matrix of style on to that of manner: 'Beautiful and grand, luxurious, mellow, good, strong, vigorous, emphatic, developed, sweet, harsh, insipid, stingy, languid, wooden, dry, pungent, over-refined, excessively detailed manner' (Costa, *Dizionario*, vol. IV (1822), p. 650).

14 Furetière, *Dictionnaire universel* (1701), vol. II, gath. Lllll, f.2ᵛ, cols. 1–2.

15 *Dictionnaire de l'Académie Françoise* (1778), vol. II, p. 60.

16 *Giorgio Vasari: Le vite, Testo*, vol. IV, pp. 154–214, esp. 205–07. The 1550 edition describes Raphael's development of a 'smooth manner', and his subsequent emulation of Leonardo's sublimity and Michelangelo's grandeur, referring to the results as *prima* and *nuova maniera* (p. 176). The 1568 edition, from which the above quotations are taken, expands the stylistic account, giving it a concluding overview.

17 *L'Encyclopédie ou Dictionnaire raisonné des sciences, des arts et des métiers, par une société de gens de lettres* (Paris: Le Breton, 1751–72, suppl.1776–7, index 1780), vol. XII (1765), p. 37. (D'Alembert had given up his editorship in 1758.) This opening statement is an expansion of the invention–design–colouration triad.

Diderot was himself an art critic of considerable importance. This strangely cantankerous outburst may perhaps relate to Michelangelo and Raphael, to whose late works 'mannerist' tendencies have been attributed, or perhaps to the next generation of painters in Florence and Rome, in disparagement of whose self-consciously artificial, even bizarre style the architectural theorist Roland Fréart de Chambray had coined the term *maniériste* in 1662.

The representation of Raphael's stylistic changes was transmuted by the nineteenth century from Vasari's portrayal of calculation and opportunism to a seamless continuum. Denying that Michelangelo had a denaturing impact on the character or taste of Raphael's work, Quatremère de Quincy declared in 1824 that the latter 'never deviated from the line that his own genius traced out for him, he did not even hurry its course. There is a discernible progression, but a slow one, a graduated one; there is no sudden change, no gap in continuity'.[18] De Quincy recognized three manners in Raphael's output, the first simple, clear, fresh and passionless, the second bolder, more vigorous, more masculine, and the third combining the purity and candour of the first with the firmness and breadth of the second, but with an additional grace.[19]

Of the art historian's interest in charting the stylistic development of individual artists there is really no counterpart among writers on music in the sixteenth, seventeenth or eighteenth centuries. To be sure, Berardi in 1681 cited composers whose styles represented each of his categories (Josquin, Palestrina, Nanino and Carissimi the church style, Marenzio, Monteverdi and Rossi the chamber style, and Peri, Monteverdi and Cesti the theatrical style); but these citations were to a composer's output as a whole. It was not until the early nineteenth century that the musical equivalents of Vasari and Giovanni Pietro Bellori (c.1615–96) arose.

These writers were a new breed. Up to 1800, the charting of the universe of music was carried out by men whom we nowadays call music theorists. From 1800 on, that universe itself became the totality of a single composer's output; and the writers were biographers and bibliographers – men engaged in tracing the lives and careers of major composers, and men occupied in cataloguing composers' *oeuvres*. To say that from now on the definition of style was in the hands of historians rather than theorists would be to use modern professionalisms where they do not apply; it is broadly true, however, that those who wrote about styles were now more interested in historical processes than in the fundamental nature of music. In their writings, music and personality became fused, artistic development inextricably bound up with the unfolding of a career. That Vasari served as a model for these writers is beyond question: Baini and Wilhelm von Lenz both knew his *Lives of the Artists*, and were acquainted in particular with his account of Raphael's career. Raphael was held up as the paradigm for the great artist.

It was at this point that biographical dictionaries of composers began to appear, beginning with Choron's and Fayolle's *Historical Dictionary of Musicians*

18   Quatremère de Quincy, *Histoire de la vie et des ouvrages de Raphael* (Paris: Charles Gosselin, 1824), p. 40. However, Raphael exhibits an 'equilibrium'; the various styles are 'not properly changes, passages from one genre to another, but only new combinations of these genres' (p. 407).

19   ibid, 431, 434–5, 124–5, 149–50. De Quincy delineates the third much less sharply than the first two.

(1810–11), followed by Ernst Ludwig Gerber's *New Historical-Biographical Lexicon of Composers* (1812–14, itself a revision of a *Lexicon* published in 1790–92), John Sainsbury's *A Dictionary of Musicians* (1824), and a host of others, pre-eminent among which was François-Joseph Fétis's *Universal Biographical Dictionary of Musicians and General Bibliography of Music* (1833–44). Music history itself underwent significant organizational changes at this time. Raphael Georg Kiesewetter advocated in 1834 that each of the 'epochs' into which music history was divided 'should be named after one of the most celebrated men of his time – of him, for instance, who possessed the greatest influence over the taste of his contemporaries in their cultivation of the art, and who [. . .] may have demonstrably promoted the art to a higher degree of perfection'.[20] In these terms, it was genius, the genius of the individual composer, that was seen to drive music history. In order to chart such history, the works of the geniuses needed to be available; thus it was that long-term projects were initiated to publish the complete works of the greatest masters. The earliest of these, often never completed, began in the late eighteenth century: Handel (1787–97), Mozart (1798–1806), Beethoven (1828–45) and others; and later there appeared the monumental series that were in many cases to remain unreplaced until after the Second World War: J. S. Bach (1851–99), Handel (1858–1902), Palestrina (1862–1903), Beethoven (1862–88), Mozart (1877–83) and so forth.

Contemporaneous with these lexicographical, historical and editorial enterprises was a succession of early biographies of composers: Forkel's *Life, Art and Works of Johann Sebastian Bach* (1802), Baini's *Historical and Critical Memoirs of the Life and Works of Giovanni Pierluigi da Palestrina* (1828: Analysis 14 below), Winterfeld's *Johannes Gabrieli and His Age* (1834), Schindler's *Biography of Ludwig van Beethoven* (1840), Ulïbïshev's *New Biography of Mozart* (1843: Analysis 15) and *Beethoven, His Critics and His Glossators* (1857: Analysis 16d), A. B. Marx's *Ludwig van Beethoven: Life and Creative Output* (1859: vol. II, Analysis 12), Jahn's *W. A. Mozart* (1856–9), and Spitta's *Johann Sebastian Bach* (1873–80: vol. II, Analysis 5). Taken together, these biographies provide the principal forum for the new discussion, not just of a composer's style, but of the stage-by-stage development of that style according to the organic model.

In Baini's account of the stylistic development of Palestrina's music we see an earnest attempt to wrestle with the difficulties of chronology. Like Vasari, Baini had access to privileged information; but whereas Vasari – close friend of Michelangelo, able to interview Titian personally and talk with the northern Italian artistic community of his day – was in direct touch with his subjects, Baini – although surrounded by Palestrinian source-materials at the Vatican – was separated from his subject by 250 years. What occupies thirty-five pages in Baini's book, occupies no fewer than 627 pages in Ulïbïshev's. First come eighty-five pages of stylistic overview, then a chapter devoted to each of the seven principal

20 Raphael Georg Kiesewetter, *Geschichte der europäisch-abendländlischen oder unsrer heutigen Musik* (Leipzig: B&H, 1834, 2/1846, reprint edn Wiesbaden: Sändig, 1971), quoted from the Eng. trans. (London: Newby, 1848, reprint edn New York: Da Capo, 1973), pp. 26–7. Note the subtitle, 'Presentation of its Growth and its Development [*Entwicklung*] from the First Century AD to the Present Time'.

operas and the Requiem, in chronological order. Interleaved between these are chapters on instrumental and vocal works. The whole thus moves in a majestic chronological sweep against two main phases, each with a brief culminating period. The first phase extends to 1787, 'a single ascendant progress towards *Don Giovanni*, masterpiece of masterpieces', with a brief high plateau including the C major and G minor string quintets and symphonies, all from 1787-8. The second phase extends from late 1788 to mid-1791, during which period Mozart's artistic powers 'began to decline, [and] his physical sufferings began bit by bit to aggravate the mental disorder that manifested itself when he was about thirty years of age', such that each of the subsequent operas 'bore witness to this decadence'; but this phase was terminated by a final six months of 'superhuman fecundity and angelic inspiration'.[21] Part III of the present volume concludes with the charting of Beethoven's stylistic growth successively by Schlosser in 1828, Fétis in 1837, von Lenz in 1852 and Ulïbïshev in 1857, the tripartite classifications of the first three of these authors mirroring in some ways the three stages of child, man and old age put forward by Victor Hugo in the Preface to his *Cromwell* (1827), and the 'law of three stages' of development of the human intellect postulated in Auguste Comte's *Course of Positive Philosophy* (1830–42).

21   *Mozart*, vol. III, pp. 206, 452.

Giuseppe Baini (1775–1844)

Memorie storico-critiche della vita e delle opere di Giovanni Pierluigi da Palestrina (1828)

To have attempted in the 1820s a close account of the stylistic development of a Renaissance composer without benefit of either of those scholarly tools that we now regard as essential to such an enterprise, a catalogue of works and a complete critical edition, was surely a hazardous undertaking. Palestrina's output, moreover, was gigantic: 104 masses, more than 375 motets and 140 madrigals, sixty-eight offertories, sixty-five hymns, thirty-five Magnificats and four or five sets of Lamentations, to speak only of authenticated works.[1] Prerequisite to such a task was a chronological framework. In Baini's day, the only significant sources of such a framework were Palestrina's publications. However, a publication date was in itself no reliable indicator of the time of composition, for composers often assembled for publication works that they had composed months or even years earlier. What is more, over forty percent of Palestrina's output was published for the first time after his death, so providing no basis at all for chronology.

What Baini achieved in 1828 was a pioneering accomplishment. If his historiography had its antecedent in that of La Borde (1780), Burney (1776–89) and others, and his biography its precursors in Mainwairing's *Memoirs* of Handel (1760) and Forkel's *Life, Art and Works* of Bach (1802), his description and classification of personal style was without precedent. He was from the age of twenty himself a member of the papal chapel, the one institution that had an unbroken tradition of *a cappella* singing from Palestrina's own time. As a bass singer, and later the chapel's archivist and administrator, he not only steeped himself in the Palestrinian style but also used his access to early editions, manuscripts and documents to conduct serious research, of which the *Memorie* is the chief result – 'a vast mixture of erudition and hero-worship' (Lockwood). He also planned an edition of the composer's works, but this apparently came to nothing.

In the course of the passage given below, Baini takes his reader through Palestrina's compositional output twice, first summarily, then schematically. However, the latter presentation does not always map on to the former. Underlying the former is a tripartite scheme whereby Palestrina first imbibed the style of his alleged teacher, Claude Goudimel (*c.*1515–72), a style that was 'artificial' despite the assertion that Goudimel extolled the virtues of nature to his pupils; then dramatically discarded that artificial style ('he broke his shackles and his chains, overthrew art, and restored the command to Nature'); and finally evolved

---

1   I take these figures from the fine article on Palestrina by Lewis Lockwood in *NGDM*. I am greatly indebted to Leeman Perkins and Jerome Roche, both of whom aided me greatly in interpreting Baini's meanings. There remains much that I have had to leave unexplained.

a grandeur and sublimity that was still in keeping with nature, a grandeur and sublimity the seeds of which had been sown, Baini elsewhere says, by Josquin and Costanzo Festa, and was characterized by 'long-held notes and pauses [*coronate*]'.[2] The move from assimilated artificiality to a self-acquired naturalness ('The imitator of various manners not his own is now the imitator of nature') obeys the dictates of Diderot's and d'Alembert's *Encyclopedia* quoted in the Introduction to Part III above ('substituting nature for the *manner* that he took over from his master'). It also has much in common with the career of Raphael as portrayed by Vasari – and we know that Baini was familiar with Vasari's *Lives of the Artists* (1550 and 1568), and in particular with his life of Raphael[3] – save that Raphael was said to have failed in his quest for grandeur and sublimity and resorted to an amalgam of styles, whereas Palestrina is said to have succeeded.

Interwoven with this theme of passage from art to nature, and then to the sublime, is a second theme: that of suffering. Baini speaks of Palestrina's 'afflictions' and 'cruel wound' without specifying their nature. In the biographical section of the *Memorie*, Baini speaks of Palestrina's wife when he says:[4]

> With her, Giovanni shared the pleasure of seeing himself elected head of the *maestri* at the Vatican [. . .]; with her he suffered the most trying privations of his life, with her he endured the cruellest afflictions of his spirit, and with her he also tasted the bitter gall of sorrow, as we shall see in the remaining chapters of this Section [covering the period 1555–61]; but with her he still basked in the flashes of light that lit up from time to time to his glory and to his credit; the faithful married couple having been together almost 30 years . . .

Palestrina had married Lucrezia Gori in 1547 and subsequently been admitted to the Sistine Chapel by Pope Julius III in 1555, in violation of the rule of celibacy. Julius had died three months later. Five months after that, with two other married singers he had been summarily expelled from the Chapel by the counter-reformation zealot Pope Paul IV as a matter of 'utmost scandal', after which Palestrina was to enjoy little favour with the papacy ever again. It is clearly to these events that Baini is referring, despite the puzzling retrospective allusion to thirty years of marriage, which might otherwise be seen as referring to his second period at the Cappella Giulia (1571–94), during which plague claimed the lives of his brother Silla and first son Rodolfo in 1572, his second son Angelo in 1575, leaving him only one surviving child, and finally his wife Lucrezia in 1580 after more than thirty years of marriage. Indeed, Baini makes nothing at all of the deaths of the brother and sons. Instead, he chooses the agony of conflict with papal authority as the affliction that romantically drove Palestrina to change his style, 'the flint, the sparks from which lit up his intellect, heated his imagination, and put in motion the creative spirit which bountiful Nature had given him in an inexhaustible supply', dramatically heightening the contrast between the five masses in the first

---

2 *Memorie*, vol. II, p. 415.
3 Giorgio Vasari: *Le vite de'più eccellenti pittori, scultori e architettori, nelle redazioni del 1550 e 1568*, ed. R. Bettarini and P. Barocchi (Florence: Sansoni, Scelte, 1966–87). For Baini and Vasari, see, e.g. Baini's comparison of Raphael's immoderate love life and early death with Palestrina's timely marriage and long life (vol. I, p. 36 and notes 47–8).
4 *Memorie*, vol. I, p. 36.

style dedicated to Julius III in 1554 and the Lamentations that Baini dates 1555–61 and attributes to the second style.

Vasari enumerated five qualities lacking in artists of the first period of his *Lives*, including Giotto, but present in those of the second period, including Piero della Francesca and Botticelli: 'good rule, order, proportion, design and manner'. Speaking in the past tense of that second period, he characterized the last of these, *maniera*, in the following way:[5]

> Then the highest perfection of manner came from the practice of frequently copying the most beautiful things, and by combining the most perfect of these, whether hands, head, torso, or legs, and producing a figure of the greatest possible beauty, and using that in every work, for all figures; it is in this that *la bella maniera* is said to consist.

Even then, artists fell short; only Leonardo da Vinci was to create figures 'that moved and breathed', only Michelangelo's work was to be 'superior to nature'. Superiority to nature lies at the heart of what Sir Joshua Reynolds called 'the grand style' and 'the great style'. In his third *Discourse on Art* (1770) he quoted Proclus: 'the works of Nature are full of disproportion, and fall very short of the true standard of beauty'; grandeur arises in art, Reynolds declared robustly, when the artist's eye can 'distinguish the accidental deficiencies, excrescences and deformities of things, from their general figures', and make out 'an abstract idea of their forms more perfect than any one original'.[6] The concept of grandeur was of central importance in art theory: the art historian Giovanni Pietro Bellori, for example, advocate of classicism and critic of mannerism for its departures from nature, said of Annibale Carracci's paintings for the Gallery of the Farnese Palace: 'No one could imagine seeing anywhere else a more noble and magnificent style of ornamentation, obtaining supreme excellence in the compartmentalization and in the figures and executed with the grandest manner in design'.[7]

Baini made use of *maniera grandiose*, *stil grandioso tratti grandiosi* and, in its own right, *grandiosità*, to describe a certain monumentality that featured in Palestrina's fourth style and epitomized the seventh (which includes the Mass *Papae Marcelli*) and eighth styles, being retained as an element in the ninth and tenth styles. That grandeur has, however, been filtered through the aesthetic of Romanticism. No longer superior to nature, the grandiose is now coupled with the sublime (*il sublime; sublimità*). Baini, after all, was the exact contemporary of Turner and only one year older than Constable, and though he was doubtless ignorant of those artists' work he was evidently influenced by ideas such as those of Edmund Burke's *Philosophical Enquiry into the Origin of Our Ideas of the Sublime and Beautiful* (1757) and Kant's *Critique of Judgment* (1790), in which irregularity, disproportion, indeterminacy, limitlessness, even ugliness and

5 *Le vite*, Preface to Part III, *Testo*, vol. I (Florence: Scelte, 1976), p. 4.
6 *Discourses on Art*, ed. R. R. Wark (New Haven: Yale University Press, 1975), Discourse III (14 December 1770), pp. 41–53, esp. 42, 44. Michelangelo and Raphael are cited as the highest exponents of the great style (Discourse V (10 December 1772), pp. 84–5).
7 G. P. Bellori, *Le vite de'pittori, scultori et architetti moderni* [1672], Part I, ed. E. Battisti and E. Caciagli (Genoa: University of Genoa, [1969]), p. 69; *The Lives of Annibale and Agostino Carracci by Giovanni Pietro Bellori*, trans. Catherine Enggass (University Park and London: Pennsylvania State University Press, 1968), p. 33.

repulsiveness, are accepted as part of nature, and as inspiring admiration, respect, awe and fear in the beholder. In this way, the grandeur of Michelangelo's *Last Judgment* in the Sistine Chapel, which Baini knew at first hand as well as from Vasari's words, was short-circuited in his mind by the grandeur of the Alps as seen by artists around the beginning of the nineteenth century. It is also coupled with the 'surprise' (*sorpresa*) that it arouses: it is not only the grandiose and the sublime style but also the 'surprising style' (*lo stil da sorprendere*).

Baini's essay abounds in deliberate antitheses, of which three are primary: rhetoric *versus* philosophy, art *versus* nature and science *versus* art. The first two of these antitheses are, so to speak, in parallel. *Rhetoric* has to do with a musical surface devoid of meaning – both meaning as embodied in the text being set to music, and meaning in the larger sense of human life. *Philosophy*, by contrast, has to do with a musical surface that embraces meaning, that responds to its own text and that resonates with humanity. Rhetoric is thus the deployment of technical devices: contrapuntal intricacies, canonic ingenuities, notational sophisms and such like. Contrary to Ciceronian rhetoric, it fails to communicate – it is esoteric and impenetrable, its effect is one of 'masses of harmony, meaningless notes'.

Art, when opposed to nature, is the artist's 'weaponry' owned to no extrinsic purpose; his technical apparatus unapplied to the world and the living reality of nature. *Art*, in this antithesis, is 'trivial', 'cold', 'meaningless', 'effortful and laborious'; whereas *nature* is 'serious', has 'fire, soul, truth', and 'runs and flows without any impediment or difficulty'. When art is opposed to science, on the other hand, its value reverses. Now *science* is the sum total of artistic theory, and in particular (where music is concerned) the proportional note-value system of fifteenth- and early sixteenth-century polyphony, whereas *art* is the humane use of that theory in musical composition.

Art, then, as Baini uses the word, has two faces to it. However, the picture is complicated by a further antithesis: artificial style *versus* simple style. The *artificial style*, 'rigorous, spare, austere, spacious', is a style born of technicalities. The *simple style* is 'soft, easy, natural', 'light and melodious', with 'graceful ideas' and 'clear texture'.[8] And yet, while (as we saw earlier) Palestrina abandoned the artificial style, he by no means foresook 'artifice'. *Artifices* were in themselves desirable, though they must be used in moderation: they constituted 'arguments and reason', necessary in convincing the listener's intellect. Hence, in his second style Palestrina employed 'few and well-placed artifices', in the fourth style his artifices were 'transparent', and so forth.

The concept of *imitazione* and its adjective *imitativa* dominates Baini's essay, and yet the author never fully explains to us how what we can understand for the visual arts may be translated into musical terms. It has nothing whatsoever to do with imitation in the technical sense of voices echoing one another in what we speak of as 'imitative polyphony'; nor with the emulation within one work of another work's design and structure, nowadays commonly referred to as *imitatio*. *Imitazione*, as Baini uses it here, relates in general terms to what we might call verisimilitude. Since the works of nature are 'products rather of neglect than of

8   *Memorie*, vol. II, p. 416.

careful attention', the imitation of nature in music entails an appearance of effort-lessness, an ease, a smoothness. 'Imitative music', then, is music that feels natural, that holds no puzzles or distractions. Yet there is another aspect of musical verisimilitude – one that can evidently bring *imitazione* into conflict with *natura*. Baini is presumably alluding to word-painting when he says of the fifth style: 'if [Palestrina] used imitations with more frequency, he always clothed them master-fully according to nature'. While acting mimetically upon the text, word-painting, because of its specificity, can disrupt the flow of the music – an effect that must be counteracted by some smoothing process. And yet, in his closing words Baini associates Palestrina's artistic perfection with 'the exact imitation of words and meanings'. 'Imitative music' is equated with musical 'philosophy'; its antithesis is equated with musical 'rhetoric'. The latter is what Palestrina learned in his youth from Goudimel, the former is what he imbibed subsequently from Festa, Morales and others.

Ultimately, Palestrina achieved not what Vasari had seen as the amalgam of styles of Raphael's late work, but what Baini saw as the unified style of late Palestrina: a style of great flexibility, in which grandiosity coexists with simplicity and artifice; a style in which all antitheses are resolved: nature is wed to art, rhetoric and philosophy are reconciled, and art and science join forces.

Baini's notion that Palestrina studied with Goudimel stems from a late seventeenth-century reference to one 'Gaudio mell flandro' as having taught several Roman composers. The French composer Goudimel is not known ever to have been in Italy, and the supposed teacher-pupil relationship has long been discredited. To this day, we do not know with whom Palestrina studied, and scholars can only surmise that he was trained by senior men at Santa Maria Maggiore, among whom Robin Mallapert and Firmin Lebel, both Frenchmen, were in post at about the right time (*c.*1537–44). Thus, if indeed his first masses, motets and madrigals are in an apprenticeship style, we have yet to identify whose style they emulate.

Baini's *Memorie* comprise two volumes, some 850 quarto-size pages. Straddling these two volumes are three principal sections (each of twelve chapters), the first (vol. I, pp. 1–73) covering Palestrina's life and work up to his appointment at Santa Maria Maggiore in 1561, the second (vol. I, pp. 74–370) examining at length the church's desire to prohibit elaborate polyphony, the Council of Trent, and Palestrina's defense of liturgical music during the decade 1561–71, the third (vol. II, pp. 1–434) covering the remainder of his life, the posthumous publications and the works surviving only in manuscript, a chronology of the life and works and, finally, an attempt to set Palestrina in the context of music history.

It is the closing pages of this latter attempt, chapter 12 of Section 3 (vol. II, pp. 387–434), that are given below. This final chapter provides a history of musical style from the tenth century, through Palestrina to his 'followers'. The first three-quarters of the chapter (vol. II, pp. 387–421) outline the history of music from the tenth century to the end of the fourteenth, and then chart four generations of composers from 1400 to the time of Palestrina, the final quarter comprising the essay on Palestrina's ten styles, which concludes with Cavalieri, Peri and others, exponents of the *seconda prattica* and the age of *basso continuo*, with its 'groping organ' and 'simpering soloist'. (Did Baini get his idea for this chapter from the structure of Vasari's *Lives*, with its survey of art from the Chaldeans to the thirteenth century, striding through three epochs spanning *c*.1250–1500, culminating in the massive essay on Michelangelo, then concluding with Titian, others, and Vasari himself?) In describing these four generations, Baini enumerates many substyles and features: *prima epoca*, Dufay, Dunstable, Binchois, Busnois and their contemporaries (vol. II, pp. 400–03), with twenty-six features, the style summarized as 'always uniform, always ponderous, always abstruse, with gloomy sonority, with tenor notes immensely long and tedious'; and likewise, *seconda epoca*, Ockeghem, Obrecht, Caron and others (vol. II, pp. 403–07); *terza epoca*, above all Josquin, also Isaac, Agricola, De la Rue, Mouton, Verdelot, Gombert, Clemens, Janequin and others (vol. II, pp. 407–13); and *quarta epoca*, Willaert, Arcadelt, Festa, Rore, Goudimel, Claudin de Sermisy, Vicentino, Morales and others (vol. II, pp. 413–21).

'[The ten styles of Palestrina]'

Historical and Critical Memoirs of the Life and Works of Giovanni Pierluigi da Palestrina

Source:
Memorie storico-critiche della vita e delle opere di Giovanni Pierluigi da Palestrina . . . detto Il Principe della Musica (Rome: Dalla Societa Tipografia, 1828), 420–34.

translated by Jonathan Shiff

To summarize the advances made by music in this fourth generation [of composers since 1400], it must be said that the public conceived the highest hopes of soon seeing both the art and the science of music brought to the desired perfection – hopes, however, which went unfulfilled, as, in the end, both the one and the other were simply improved, not perfected. And as for the art of music, certainly the majority of composers wrote solely in the barbaric style [*stil*] of the three preceding generations, themselves adding as many enigmas, difficulties and mysteries as they could. Unquestionably, even the most excellent composers made quite frequent use of this manner [*maniera*]. Nevertheless to these men we owe the cultivation of two new styles. The first – *artificial*,[9] yes, but rigorous, spare, austere, spacious: and in this they wrote motets, madrigals, canticle settings, ricercars and *terzi*:[10] they even wrote masses in it sometimes, but there the fray of competing syllables and words was ever more noticeable, damaging [to intelligibility] as it was. The other style – simple,[11] even, free of artifice – was cultivated in various ways and with varying degrees of success. The informal masses [*messe familiari*] written in this style did not please.[12] When a little variety was added to its ornamentation [*figure*], the style served for lamentations and for requiem masses: but it was no more acceptable in this form. In the same style, but with more melodic bass lines, two- and three-choir psalm-settings were written, which did receive praise.[13] This

9 'artificial': i.e. characterized by the contrapuntal 'artifices' of Franco-Flemish polyphony, such as strict imitation, the notating of music by proportional time signatures (especially simultaneous, different signatures), the use of complex canonic structures and of cryptic verbal instructions for performance.

10 *terzi*: In his earlier description of the *quarta epoca*, he refers to 'sacred and secular ricercars, intabulations, *terzetti* and *duetti*, known as *terzi* and *duo*' (vol. II, p. 414). By these last two terms, Baini probably implied *tricinia* and *bicinia*, i.e. three- and two-part music, whether vocal or instrumental, perhaps of a studied, didactic nature.

11 'simple': i.e. music lacking notational obscurities, and relatively free from contrapuntal complexity with a greater tendency to homophonic movement.

12 *familiare*: the term, as *familiere*, seems to have been used first by Loys Bourgeois with reference to his *Le premier livre des [24] pseaulmes* (1547). Baini cites five composers who wrote such masses, though of them only Gasparo Alberti did in fact do so. Such note-against-note, mostly equal-value, music 'held rather more difficulties than were apparent, hence these masses were born and died in the same instant, as deformed, abortive monsters' (vol. II, p. 415). (Cf. discussion of 'monstrosities' in the General Introduction, above.)

13 Baini may perhaps have been aware of the settings of psalms, hymns and other texts for two answering three- or four-part choruses by Johannes Martini and Johannes Brebis at the Ferrarese

same style, in a somewhat exaggerated form, was used by those seeking to revive the ancient *genera* of Greek music.[14] Embellished with graceful melodies, this style brought fame to the writers of villottas, arias, barcarolles, mascheratas, etc.[15] And finally those composers who dared to write in up to fifty parts must have made use of this style.[16] As for the science of music, the same composers, aside from those few who added harmony to villottas, arias, etc.,[17] all deserved the bitterest reproaches. They knew the effect of *imitative* music [*musica imitativa*]: they knew the beauty, trivial and light though it was, of simple, melodic music: they knew the imposing quality of the grandiose manner, and the surprises that one could produce with it. They felt themselves, almost without being aware of it, spurred {421} or rather obliged by nature to use now the grandiose [style], now the humble, now the tender, the happy, the sad, in imitation of the words and meanings which they were setting to music. But more firmly attached to the prejudices of their school than the limpet to the rock, they never lifted pen from motet, madrigal, hymn or canticle, however full of feeling its words, if they had not besmirched it – whether at beginning, middle, or end – with artificial difficulties, with conglomerations of harmony, with irrelevant notes.

Musical affairs were in this state when Giovanni Pierluigi, around 1544, at the age of twenty, entered the school which had recently been opened in Rome by Claude Goudimel.[18] This fine master did certainly teach his new disciple the practice of the day, and what should be avoided or followed. Thus it is, that never in the works of Pierluigi does one find irregularities of counterpoint: never does one see more than one flat in the key signature; never a part for low bass

court in the 1470s, of a mass and psalms by Ruffino d'Assisi for double chorus in eight parts at Padua somewhere between 1510 and 1532, and of psalms by Francesco Santa Croce at Treviso between 1520 and 1550, all in manuscript; and of the double-choir vesper psalms in eight parts by Adrian Willaert first published in *Di Adriano et di Jachet: I salmi . . . a uno et a duoi chori . . .* (Venice: Gardano) in 1550, of which eight are true *cori spezzati* works for eight voices. Andrea Gabrieli's two-, three- and four-choir works began to appear in print in 1587.

14   i.e. the chromatic and enharmonic genera. Baini has Ghiselin Danckerts's treatise (*c.*1551) and Nicola Vicentino's music primarily in mind (vol. II, p. 418).

15   All four terms may have been associated with monophonic genres of music with secular texts in the later fifteenth and early sixteenth centuries: the villotta as a popular or street song, associated with Padua and Venice, the aria and barcarolle associated particularly with Venice, the mascherata with Florentine carnivals. They may, however, be associated also with the lighter forms of Italian polyphony that emerged in parallel with the madrigal from *c.*1520.

16   Two works survive in forty parts: Tallis's *Spem in alium* and Striggio's *Ecce beatam lucem*. Baini's source for this remark (vol. II, p. 418) is Zarlino, *Sopplimenti musicali* (Venice: Franceschi, 1588; reprint edns New York: Broude Brothers, 1966; Ridgewood, NJ: Gregg Press, 1966), p. 18: 'Composers not content with three or four voices have redoubled that number, some going as far as fifty voices; the result is a great racket, a mighty din, and almost as much confusion.'

17   Four-part settings of monophonic villottas, e.g. by Francesco Patavino, Michele Pesenti, Sebastiano Festa and Alvise Castellino, date from the period 1520–50; Giovanni Croce (1590) set mascherate for four, six and eight voices, but there were probably earlier settings.

18   Baini (vol. I, pp. 21–7) earlier rejects three possible identities for Goudimel, yet asserts 'The latter had recently been the first to open a public school of music in Rome, and to the selfsame was entrusted little Giovanni Pierluigi's instruction' along with that of alleged fellow-pupils Giovanni Animuccia, Steffano Betti ('Il Fornarino'), Alessandro Merlo ('Della Viola') and Giovanni Maria Nanino, for none of whom clear evidence is adduced. Michel Brenet [Marie Bobillier] dismissed his hypothesis as 'dubious, indeed improbable', speaking of his 'grave errors, and the extraordinary slipshodness of his methods' (*Claude Goudimel: essai bio-bibliographique* (Besançon: Jacquin, 1898), vol. II, pp. 123–5). Palestrina is now thought to have been trained at S Maria Maggiore in Rome from at least 1537 until at latest 1544.

parts;[19] never in all of his works an A♭; never enigmas or mysteries in the canons, but only the most customary and well-known types of resolutions; the parts of the polyphonic texture [*concento*] always restricted to the precise extension of the respective scale; dissonances always treated according to the appropriate rules; the method always varied, and delighting with new inventions, never bound to predetermined manners, since Goudimel used to reiterate to his pupils (*Memorie a penna*[20]): 'Variation is what makes creations seem beautiful; as the old proverb says, "Nature is beautiful for its variety"'. In short, one finds even in Giovanni's earliest works the most regular and learned fashion of composing that was then known.

Just as Goudimel, however, had never condescended to use the simple style of the villotta, aria and mascherata, as his contemporaries did, neither did Pierluigi ever work in this style. As Goudimel had never learned to savour the effect of the grandiose passages that had sometimes left the pen of Josquin or of Festa, neither was Pierluigi at first familiar with this manner. Goudimel was quite taken with matters of Time, Prolation, proportions, hemiolas;[21] and Pierluigi did his master proud in this science. Finally, Goudimel never knew imitative music, or the philosophy of music; and Pierluigi came out of his school a pure rhetorician.

{422} Nature, however, had given Giovanni talents far superior to those of his master. He was furnished with a vast, fertile, inexhaustible mind, a great and noble soul, a sensitive heart, a vivid imagination, a genius for music, an indefatigable will: he could not write contrary to reason for long, he could not remain the servant of an unrefined master: he broke his shackles and his chains, overthrew art and restored the command to Nature; and following her lead, or rather side by side with her, he was the first to imitate all manner of her works, simple and complex, large and small, exalted and humble. Seeking first in his studies a balm for his afflictions,[22] he perfected, with Nature's help, the simple style of the Lamentations, which his immediate predecessors had discovered but used without finesse. He then set himself to polishing and embellishing the artificial style coupled with Gregorian

19   *contrabbassi*: Baini presumably means that Palestrina did not use any combination involving the F5 clef – i.e. anything below *chiavi naturali*; but Baini's understanding of the abstrusenesses of high and low clefs must have been incomplete.

20   '*Memoires from the pens* <*of various composers*>: manuscript leaves of information concerning the chapel and the apostolic chaplain-cantors, once belonging to <my predecessors> [Gregorio] Allegri [1582–1652], <disciple of Giovanni Maria Nanino [1543/4–1607], who was at the school of Goudimel,> [Antimo] Liberati [1617–92], [Giovanni] Biordi [1691–1748], [Pasquale] Pisari [c.1725–78] <and my Roman *maestro* Giuseppe> Jannacconi [1741–1816], and put in order for me by the last-named' (vol. II, Index, p. xiii, the material in angle brackets taken from vol. I, p. 23). Since Nanino may have been a pupil of Palestrina, Baini evidently considered these papers, which were 'passed to me by *maestro* Giuseppe Jannaconi' (vol. II, p. 126), to transmit authentic information in an unbroken chain of members of the papal choir (including Baini himself). They apparently no longer survive.

21   'Time' (*tempi* = Lat. *tempus*): the relationship (triple or duple) between breve and semibreve in the mensural notational system of the fourteenth, fifteenth and sixteenth centuries; 'Prolation' (*prolazioni* = Lat. *prolatio*): the relationship between minim and semibreve; 'proportions': a complex fifteenth- and sixteenth-century system relating the note values of a passage of music notation to those of adjacent passages, and to their realization in sound, by means of mathematical ratios; 'hemiola': the use of three notes (breves or semibreves, imperfect) in place of two (perfect).

22   The 'deep afflictions that oppressed Giovanni after the publication of his first volume of masses [1554]', alluded to below under the second style, are hinted at in the biographical section of the book; see the Introduction, above.

chant: and what good manners his governess taught him in the species of both modulations[23] and imitations! From this he passed on to a style that was still artificial, but free; and here, with Nature as his guide, he broke through to the immense variety of his ideas: he retraced meanwhile the uncertain footsteps of his predecessors, reducing all to that regular form of which their ideas were capable. He then devised a system of verisimilitude [*imitazione*]; and on the model of those most common of Nature's works, which seem to be products rather of neglect than of careful attention, he enriched art with a perfect, concise, easy, running style. From this imitation he advanced to a style that was all neatness, elegance and precision, like that which Nature herself uses in the various seashells and flowers, and in the plumage of birds. After this he ascended with Nature herself to the grand, the sublime and the surprising, and he smoothed all the roads for his followers, even those steep and difficult paths that lead to the highest peaks. Finally, in his gratitude towards her, he decided to espouse Nature, who had shown herself to him unveiled for the first time in order to cure with her loving cares his cruel wound, and from then on had revealed to him the most deeply hidden secrets, as to a faithful friend; and his love, his attentions, her adornments, her beauty, his remorse for his transgressions before he met her, all this he painted with the vivid colours of a new style; a style however not simple, humble, abject, mediocre, temperate; but so noble, {423} sublime and full of ideas, that never in my opinion has anyone been able continuously to sustain one so elevated.

This said, I divide the works of Pierluigi into the following ten styles.

First style of Giovanni Pierluigi

The first manner, or style of Giovanni Pierluigi is extremely artificial, studied, laborious, effortful. Everything in it is polished and finished, and each note serves an evident artistic purpose. It suffers from a superfluity of rich harmonies, but less so than in the hands of his predecessors. From time to time one finds a judicious echo of Josquin in the repetitions of the same melody at different pitch levels, and in the ways in which parts clash with one another. The words are always placed exactly below the notes, even in the masses. The vocal writing of the parts is always natural. The ideas [*concetti*], phrases and melodies are so closely related to the themes as to seem their daughters. The product is a sonorous music, always resplendent with harmonic colour; but never does it allow the listeners to understand the words, or the meaning of what is being sung.

In this style, little different from that of the best of his immediate predecessors and contemporaries, Giovanni wrote various masses, several motets and quite a few madrigals. And in that three years had meanwhile passed since he had had the incomparable honour to be chosen the first *maestro* of the Julian Chapel at the Vatican,[24] he felt obliged to give once and for all a public display of his talents,

23   Baini used *modulazione* not in the Renaissance sense of *modulatio*, but in the modern sense of 'modulation'. He thus interpreted the introduction of E♭, B♮, F♯ and C♯ in the context of a one-flat signature, and of B♭, F♯, C♯ and G♯ in the context of an open signature, as modulation to keys such as B♭ major, G major, D major and A minor, though never speaking in terms of keys. He notes modulation in the Lamentations, hymns, Magnificats, and late motets and madrigals.
24   Palestrina was appointed *maestro* on 1 September 1551.

and to appear with glory in his rightful place among the greatest artists. To this end he chose five masses, his best and most worthy of publication, and those most likely to establish his reputation; and, gathering them in a volume, he dedicated them to Pope Julius III.[25] What then were the singular beauties which, in the judgment of the young Pierluigi, distinguished these five masses from his other numerous works? It was the combination of new words with those of the mass; the use of differing Time and Prolation;[26] and the canons.

In the first and most solemn mass, one of the parts (usually the soprano) constantly sings the notes and words of the antiphon, *Ecce sacerdos magnus, qui in diebus suis* {424} *placuit Deo, et inventus est justus;*[27] there is a *Hosanna* in imperfect Time and major Prolation;[28] and an *Agnus* in which the soprano and contralto simultaneously have perfect Time and minor Prolation, the tenor has perfect Time and major Prolation, and the bass has imperfect Time and major Prolation:[29] its *Dona nobis pacem* closes with the clash of frequent instances of minor hemiola against imperfect Time and minor Prolation.[30] The second mass, *O Regem coeli,*[31] has a *Hosanna* in perfect Time and major Prolation.[32] The third, *Virtute magna,*[33] has a *Hosanna* in imperfect Time and major Prolation, joined several times by the triple major proportion, so that some voices are singing in duple metre, others in triple;[34] in the Agnus it has a canon at the fifth.[35] The fourth, *Gabriel Archangelus,*[36] has in the *Benedictus* a canon at the unison,[37] and in the *Hosanna* perfect Time without proportion,[38] the latest fashion recently introduced by several composers, for which they were harshly rebuked by Ghiselin Danckerts in his manuscript treatise.[39] The last, *Ad coenam Agni providi,*[40] for five voices, has a constant canon in the soprano at the fifth below;[41] the first *Hosanna* in perfect Time without proportion; and the second *Hosanna* in perfect Time and major Prolation, with dots of alteration and division.[42] These are the

25 *Missarum liber primus* (Rome: Valerio & Aloysius Dorico, 1554).
26 See note 21, above.
27 *Le opere complete di Giovanni Pierluigi da Palestrina,* ed. R. Casimiri [=C], vol. I (Rome, 1939), pp. 1–34, based on the plainsong antiphon *Ecce sacerdos magnus.*
28 *Hosanna* II: C, vol. I, pp. 26–7.
29 *Agnus* III: C, vol. I, pp. 33–4.
30 i.e. a three-against-two cross rhythm involving (in terms of original note values) three semibreves in the time of two imperfect semibreves in a wholly duple context.
31 C, vol. I, pp. 35–61, based on a four-part motet by Andreas De Silva (c.1475–?) dating from 1532.
32 *Hosanna* II: C, vol. I, pp. 56–7.
33 C, vol. I, pp. 62–92, based on a four-part motet by Mathieu Lasson (died before 1595) dating from 1532.
34 C, vol. I, pp. 86–7, resulting in cross rhythms of three against two, and also three against four.
35 *Agnus* II: C, vol. I, pp. 89–92.
36 C, vol. I, pp. 93–124, based on a four-part motet by Philippe Verdelot (c.1475–before 1552) dating from 1532.
37 C, vol. I, pp. 116–18.
38 *Hosanna* II: C, vol. I, pp. 118–19.
39 Ghiselin Danckerts (c.1510–1565). There are thought to have been three redactions of this unpublished treatise, c.1551, c.1555–6 and c.1559–60: see J. de Bruyn, 'Ghiselinus Danckerts', *Tijdschrift van de Vereniging voor Nederlandse muziekgeschiedenis,* 16/4 (1946), 217–52; 17/2 (1949), 128–57.
40 C, vol. I, pp. 125–63, based on a plainsong hymn.
41 i.e. canon in all movements with one of the two alto parts.
42 C, vol. I, pp. 153–4, 156–8; *punti di alterazione, e di divisione;* the *punctus alterationis* and *punctus divisionis* were notational dots clarifying local rhythmic organization.

fine subtleties which added beauty and decorum to the music of the day! This is
what constituted the sublime for those minds completely devoid of philosophical
ideas! Even Pierluigi, *maestro* of the Vatican basilica, flew in the face of reason!

Second style of Giovanni Pierluigi

The deep afflictions that oppressed Giovanni after the publication of his first
volume of masses, afflictions we have already mentioned in recounting his life
story,[43] were the flint whose sparks kindled his intellect, heated his imagination
and put in motion the creative spirit that bountiful Nature had given him in an
inexhaustible supply. At the same time his voluntary retreat to a lonely little house
on Monte Celio, near the Lateran Palace, gave him the opportunity to consult at
his leisure the works of Festa and of the other most skilful composers, and to extract
from them that essence which he had missed under Goudimel's tutelage. So that
when, unable to resist the compulsion of his genius, or the force of his natural
inclination to write, he chose as the subject {425} of his labours the Lamentations
of the Prophet Jeremiah, as being full of the ideas best corresponding to his present
state, he painted the mournful portrait of his anguish in a style completely different
from any he had used before.[44]

   Oh! how different is the Pierluigi of the Lamentations from the Pierluigi of the
five above-mentioned masses! What was then all art is now all nature; what was
full of trivialities is now all seriousness. The cold and meaningless is now fire,
soul, truth. No longer effortful and laborious, it now runs and flows without any
impediment or difficulty. The imitator of various manners not his own is now the
imitator of nature, in fashions of his own invention. As to its art, the style of these
and the two later books of Lamentations is simple, clear, easy, with few and well-
placed artifices, with even figures now in semibreves, now in minims; with varied
harmonies, timely retards and modulations that are new and quite natural. As to
its science, it is a profoundly philosophical style, now grandiose, now supplicating,
now sublime, humble, angry, tender: all told, there is no passion in Jeremiah's words
that is not made proportionately sweeter or harsher by Pierluigi's music. I know
that these first Lamentations were not made public through the press; in fact to this
day they have remained unpublished. But what does that matter? Around 1559,
while he was *maestro* at the Lateran,[45] Pierluigi was the first one after the rebirth
of music to become a composer-philosopher, faithful imitator of nature: all of his
works from then on would be seasoned with this salt.

43   See Introduction.
44   C, vol. XIII (1941), presents four sets of Lamentations and an appendix of single items. The only
     one of these sets to be printed in Palestrina's lifetime was probably the last to be composed:
     Lamentationum Hieremiae prophetae liber primus (Rome: Gardano) with dedication to Sixtus V
     (pontificate: 1585–90), published first in 1588 and again in 1589. The other three sets exist in
     manuscript, as does a fifth set identified since, and their chronology is unknown. Baini knew
     only three sets, and states that the set described here is one of those in manuscript. Elsewhere, he
     states that among the works from 1555–61 'preserved unedited in the Archive of the Proto-
     basilica because composed in the service of the same, deserve particularly to be recalled a volume
     of Lamentations of the Prophet Jeremiah set to music for four voices, and a volume of
     Magnificats for five and six voices' (vol. I, pp. 63–4; also vol. I, pp. 193–201). The three manu-
     script sets of Lamentations edited in C all require more than four voices.
45   Palestrina was appointed *maestro di capella* of the church of St John Lateran on 1 October 1555.

Third style of Giovanni Pierluigi

No sooner had he put to sleep that cruel passion that had been devouring his heart, with the drugged sop of the Lamentations, than Giovanni, in the service of his proto-basilica, turned to the cultivation of a musical manner for the canticle *Magnificat*, on the melodies of the church psalmody.[46] Costanzo Festa, and especially Cristobal Morales, had distinguished themselves in setting this work in what we have called the 'second style'. Pierluigi followed the same style, but he improved it with more natural melodies, more concise phrases, more sensible ideas, more spacious harmonies: and here is where he began to cause the basses to sing in a truly new manner, {426} the result being a grave, melodious and noble vocal line; the virtues of which are not commonly found in the unfortunate, unnatural bass lines of his predecessors. The many artifices that he used in this style did not at all prevent him from following faithfully in Nature's footsteps: in fact, having recently bound himself to her with the sweet ties of the most tender friendship, he eloquently magnified with her help the glories of the omnipotent and merciful arm of the Lord. I consider Pierluigi's hymns to be in this same style: only that in them the use of modulation is more varied, refined, strong, and the melodies are of a totally new character.[47]

Fourth style of Giovanni Pierluigi

In his fourth and most common [*più commune*] style, Giovanni wrote the majority of the masses and motets for four, five, six and seven voices, and several sacred and profane madrigals for four and five voices. It is an artificial style, but quite natural, easy, pretty, full of soul and sentiment. In it he used to great profit Josquin's odd practice of unaccountably stopping all the parts at once on a consonance, and then having them sing several syllables and words on this consonance. In each of his compositions, though, Pierluigi chooses the words of greatest sentiment, however artificial: and on these words he unites all the parts, not only at the beginning, but also at various points in the middle, and at the end; and with harmonic strokes of the greatest force above a majestic bass, he produces a wonderful effect, philosophically. After these grandiose passages he lets us enjoy his new, transparent artifices, and from such artifices he may return to the grandiose, always with admirable art and naturalness. He seasons all this with a manner so fertile with novelty, that each of the hundreds of compositions written in this style has a particular character that is so distinctive, that I can only compare them to the individuals of the human species, each one different as to body, physiognomy, mind, heart, wishes and passions. To this style belong those

46 Palestrina composed at least thirty-five Magnificat settings, of which two sets – sixteen, for four voices – were published as *Magnificat octo tonorum* (Venice: Gardano) in 1591. Two further sets surviving in manuscript were probably earlier, though their precise chronology is unknown. All are given in C, vol. XVI. The passage quoted in note 44 above points clearly to the third (C, vol. XVI, pp. 190–302) as the set that Baini had in mind.

47 Palestrina composed at least sixty-five hymn settings, of which forty-five, published as *Hymni tocius anni* . . . (Rome: Torniero and Donangelo) in 1589, and given in C, vol. XIV, may possibly have been written by 1582.

compositions in which Giovanni imitated the most extravagant manners of his predecessors, while correcting them according to the dictates of philosophy and extracting from them the best that they were {427} capable of: as for example the mass *L'homme armé*, in differing Times, and differing proportions and Prolations, which can be sung also in duple Time;[48] or the motet *Tribularer si nescirem*, one part of which states the words *Miserere mei Deus* over and over again at five different pitch levels;[49] the masses and motets with canons at the second, third, fourth, etc., normal and inverted, with the same or opposite metre;[50] artifices which are treated with a wonderful and inimitable delicacy, which belongs only to the Prince of Music. In this style finally the words and meaning of what is being sung can be sufficiently understood, provided one waits for that union of the parts which is often found between the artifices.

Fifth style of Giovanni Pierluigi

The fifth style is concise, running, sober, expressive, of such exquisite naturalness that it seems born more of nature than of art, whereas it is the product of the most refined art, a most difficult facility. In this style, Giovanni wrote his litanies for four, six and eight voices;[51] and also some masses, such as *Aeterna Christi munera, Iste confessor*, the Missa Brevis,[52] etc., in which if he used imitations with more frequency, he always clothed them in masterly fashion according to nature. In this style one hears the words distinctly.

Sixth style of Giovanni Pierluigi

Giovanni's sixth style is one which can in some ways be likened to the art of illumination. In this style he composed many motets for four voices, several verses of his *Magnificats*, various stanzas of his hymns and some passages of the masses for three or four like voices. How beautiful this style is! The vocal writing is sweet and natural; the artifices clear, well-arranged, timely, transparent, neat; the harmonies most delightful; the chords from time to time new and unexpected; little modulation; inexhaustible variety; a perfect imitation of nature. And while this

48   *di varii tempi, e di varie proporzioni e prolazioni, la quale si può cantare anche in tempo pari:* C, vol. VI, pp. 97–129, for five voices, published in 1570: *Missarum liber tertius* (Rome: Dorico). The pre-existent *L'homme armé* tune is in triple rhythm, and Baini's formulation may refer to the tune's being introduced under differing mensural and proportional conditions, sometimes triple, sometimes duple, culminating in the cantus of the Benedictus, when it is stated three times successively under different time signatures.

49   C, vol. VII, pp. 107–116, in both halves of which the phrase *Miserere mei Deus* is stated nine times, beginning successively on d', e', f', g', a', g', f', e' and d' (cf. Josquin's own *Miserere* ostinato).

50   The intervals of the canons in the Mass *Repleatur os meum*, for example, published in *Missarum liber tertius*, 1570 (C, vol. VI, pp. 136–74), reduce successively from octave (Kyrie) to unison (Agnus I), the last of these in augmentation, with two simultaneous canons in the Agnus II.

51   C, vol. XX, presents nineteen Litanies (fourteen of the BVM, three of Christ, two of the Blessed Sacrament), of which two sets of five (plus a motet) each were contemporaneously published as *Litaniae deiparae virginis . . .* (Rome: Coattino) in 1593. The remaining nine survive in manuscript.

52   C, vol. XV, pp. 1–19, 72–88, published in *Missarum liber quintus* (Rome: Coattino) in 1590; C, vol. VI, pp. 62–83, in *Missarum liber tertius* (Rome: Dorico) in 1570.

style at times also becomes invigorated and uplifted by following closely the ideas of the sacred text, so knowingly is this done, so pleasing {428} its new dignified aspect, that rather than producing in the listeners a sense of surprise, it draws them in and pleases them all the more. To this style belong the exercises on the scale for four equal voices.[53]

Seventh style of Giovanni Pierluigi

Who would believe it, if he saw the hand of Fra Angelico produce the Last Judgment of the Sistine Chapel in the Vatican, or Buonarotti [i.e. Michelangelo] apply himself to the illumination of the frontispiece of one of the books in our apostolic chapel, drawing in miniature a beetle, a butterfly, a leafy branch? And yet so it is. Pierluigi's pen, which in the preceding style was the faithful imitator of the most delicate forms in nature, is in this seventh style cut to gigantic proportions; it writes the Mass *Papae Marcelli* with simplicity, clarity, naturalness, nobility, grandeur and a sublimeness never again imagined.[54] This Mass is Pierluigi's only production in such a style. As the first and only one of its kind it is on a par with the *Iliad*.

Eighth style of Giovanni Pierluigi

Even though Pierluigi was never able to retrace his own steps to the preceding style, he nevertheless tried as much as he could to blaze a mountainous trail, so as to clear for others a safe road to a high summit opposite the inaccessible peak. His eighth style is clear, easy, grandiose and majestic, like the style of his Mass *Papae Marcelli*. In this mass, however, the character of the whole is always sustained, severe, stern, inimitable: in the new style the character varies according to the words and meanings; it is thus more malleable, and adapts with dignity and preciseness to any form. Giovanni used this style in his masses for eight voices,[55] in various motets and sequences also for eight voices, and in some compositions for three choruses.[56] In order that the imitation of nature would not be lacking in this style and (when

53   *Esercizi XI sopra la scala*, ed. F. X. Haberl in *Ioannis Petraloysii Praenestini: opera omnia* (Leipzig: B&H, 1863–94), vol. XXXI, pp. 99–111, of doubtful authenticity.

54   C, vol. IV, pp. 167–201, first published in *Missarum liber secundus* (Rome: Dorico) in 1567. Baini instigated the idea that this mass was composed for a trial of textual intelligibility in polyphony conducted by the post-Tridentine Commission of Cardinals on 28 April 1565 (e.g. vol. I, p. 278: '. . . the mass by means of which church music was saved'). Haberl, rejecting this idea in 1892, posited a composition date as early as 1555, for the election of Pope Marcellus II; Jeppesen (*MGG*, 1962) argued for a date closer to 1562; current opinion does not altogether rule out its use in the trial. For a selection of contemporaneous documents, see L. Lockwood, ed., *Giovanni Pierluigi da Palestrina: Pope Marcellus Mass*, Norton Critical Score (New York: Norton, 1975), pp. 6–36, Baini's comments on the mass (vol. I, pp. 215–16, 228–9), 34–6, and an essay by Jeppesen (1930, 1944–5), 99–130.

55   All for two four-part choirs: Mass *Confitebor tibi*, published in *Una messa a otto voci . . .* (Venice: Scotto) in 1585 (C, vol. XXX, pp. 163–227, Baini, vol. II, pp. 155–9); Mass *Laudate dominum*, Mass *Hodie Christus natus*, Mass *Fratres ego enim* (C, vol. XXX, pp. 1–58, 59–109, 110–62), all four posthumously published in *Missae quatuor octonis vocibus concinendae* (Venice: Amadino) in 1601.

56   Palestrina wrote sixty-two eight-voice motets, only eleven contemporaneously published (1572, 1575, 1581, 1592); most can be found in Haberl, vols. II, III, VI, VII, XXX and C, vols. VII, VIII. He wrote eleven motets and one hymn for three four-voice choirs (Haberl, vols. VII, XXVI, XXX, XXXII; C, vol. XXXII), and the Mass *Tu es Petrus* for three six-voice choirs (C, vol. XXXI), none contemporaneously published.

necessary) the shock of surprise in the listeners would be {429} stronger and more irresistible, he invented in both masses and motets the difficult manner of writing for two choirs, one of high voices and the other of middle voices, supported by two different bass lines.

Premise to the ninth and tenth styles

With the two preceding styles Giovanni perfected the grandiose style, the surprising style; he stormed the human heart by taking by surprise its most noble, elevated and sublime feelings. In the two following styles he changed weapons, and took possession of the intellect and the will, by calmly allowing his listeners to taste the truth, thus putting them in such a state that they could not defend themselves against his attempts to move their tender passions.

The following two styles are not so free of artifice as the two preceding ones; because while the soul accepts truth in its simplest garment, the intellect will not concede unless it is convinced by arguments and reason.

The following two styles always proceed at a slow pace; and no matter how heated the musical ideas, they still keep their sense of repose: because the truth has no need for vehemence and noise; in fact, a good cause can be undermined by a loud argument.

The following two styles are often cloaked in grandeur and provoke surprise, but in a manner all their own. They start off with two, three, or four blows to shake the hardest hearts; but a softening soon follows: for man's heart refuses to admit that it acts because it has been convinced of the truth; it must always show that it acts out of its own goodness.

The following two styles are always used with passionate and very forceful words and ideas; for music does not work in isolation – she is not an Amazon, but a peaceful Muse, despite her rich panoply of weapons formed of melodies and harmonies; but her weak arm cannot wield these weapons, only at the most display them. Nevertheless, she supplies these weapons to the words and ideas in proportion to their strength, and these words and ideas do combat with the human intellect and heart; and in this way, with her own weapons and the strength of others she triumphs, crowned with laurel. But let us now describe the differences between these two styles.

{430} Ninth style of Giovanni Pierluigi

The ninth style was distinguished by Pierluigi himself with the term *alacrior*;[57] in it he set to music Solomon's *Song of Songs*,[58] several spiritual madrigals and a

---

57 *alacrior*: lit. 'brisker', 'more eager', by extension 'more spirited'. Baini (vol. I, p. 140) quotes from Palestrina's Latin dedication of the published edition of the Song of Solomon (see note 58) to Pope Gregory XIII: 'I have used a somewhat more spirited style [*genere aliquanto alacriore*] than I am accustomed to using in other sacred works, for it seemed to me that that is what the [Song of Solomon] called for.' Baini discusses the style in detail (vol. I, p. 142).

58 Palestrina wrote twenty-nine settings of texts from the Song of Solomon, all published as *Motettorum quinque vocibus liber quartus <ex canticis Salomonis>* (Rome: Gardano) in 1583/84, and in later editions (C, vol. XI, pp. 89–200: material in angle brackets in later editions only).

good portion of the mass *Assumpta est.*[59] Nature and art coined its form: plain, easy, natural, simple; full of strength, and of sweetness; now higher, now lower, now flattering, now thundering, but always dignified. The artifices do not complicate it, but rather add bright splendour to it. The frequent union of the parts does not weaken it, but rather adds power and strength. In this style, art is always covered over with nature. Nature is always wed to art; and the words and meanings, which can be understood distinctly, acquire in this style that insinuating quality which delights and persuades.

Tenth style of Giovanni Pierluigi

The tenth style is a blend of the second, eighth and ninth. It is used mainly in setting words that express grief, pain, repentance, supplication, fear, death – as in the motets *Peccavimus cum patribus nostris, Peccantem me quotidie, Paucitas dierum meorum–Manus tuae, Domine, Peccavi: quid faciam tibi, etc.*,[60] and in the madrigals *Io son ferito: ahi lasso!, Se amarissimo fele, o mortal tosco, etc.*[61] This style has each of the qualities of the preceding ninth style. Since, however, the words in that style were more charming, tender, confiding, more about love, desire, delight, and here, on the other hand, the words are about pain, suffering, sadness, and weeping, it thus contains many traits of the second style, all full of laments; and it borrows from the eighth style, in order to give vent to its grief, modulations that are more carefully chosen, more concentrated, of greater power, of immense strength, unforeseeable and unforeseen, although unbelievably natural: and thus a new style is formed, serious, severe, dark and profound, {431} very different from the preceding one because it combines the beauties of that style itself with those of the second and eighth styles. As a result, the words and meanings, though still distinctly intelligible, acquire that penetrating quality which persuades and moves as it delights, armed only with melody and harmony, and not needing stage, scenery, gesture, costumes and illusion.

With these different styles Giovanni perfected every manner of music, both as an art, and as a science, in other words both the rhetoric and the philosophy of music; so that he deserved the title of 'Homer of music' given him by Dr Burney (*History of Music*, vol. III, p. 198): 'Palestrina the Homer of the most Ancient music that has been preserved, merits all the reverence and attention which it is in a musical historian's power to bestow.' In the words of this respected historian,

59 Of Palestrina's sacred madrigals, all for five voices, twenty-six occupy his *Il primo libro de madrigali a cinque voci* (Venice: Gardano) of 1581 (C, vol. IX, pp. 1–116), and thirty his *Delle madrigali spirituali . . . libro secondo* (Rome: Coattino) of 1594 (C, vol. XXII). Baini (vol. II, pp. 129–31) questions the reputation of nos 1–8 (to Petrarch's sonnet to the Virgin Mary, stzs.1–8) of 1581 on grounds of slavish imitation of nature, childish moments, lack of sublimity. He assigns the Mass *Assumpta* (C, vol. XXV, pp. 209–45) to 1585 (Baini, vol. II, pp. 162–5, 171).

60 *Peccantem* (C, vol. VII, pp. 98–101) was published in *Motettorum . . . liber secundus* (Venice: Scotto) in 1572; the others (C, vol. XII, *Peccavimus* pp. 96–9 (Part II of *Tribulationes civitatum*), *Paucitas* pp. 9–15, *Peccavi* pp. 36–9) in *Motettorum quinque vocibus liber quintus* (Rome: Gardano) in 1584.

61 *Io son* (secular) (C, vol. II, pp. 161–5), published in the collection *Il terzo libro delle Muse a cinque voce . . .* (Venice: Gardano) in 1561; *Se amarissimo* (sacred) (C, vol. XXII, pp. 31–4, Baini, vol. II, pp. 251–2), published in *Delli madrigali spirituali . . .* in 1594.

the most trustworthy and impartial one there is, 'All the parts have an equal share of importance, and hardly a note appears in them without some peculiar intention and effect' (p. 196). And yet faced with the amount of care and effort that Giovanni had to devote to each one of his works, what an immense number of them he drew from his inexhaustible mind, and with what success! 'We are as much astonished, at the number of his productions, as pleased with their effects. Indeed the works of Aristotle, Cicero, or the elder Pliny were hardly more numerous. With the union, indeed, of great erudition and great industry we are not surprised; but Genius is not often so voluminous' (p. 195). Pierluigi having therefore raised this type of music to the highest level of perfection, and smoothed the way for musical imitation, it should come as no surprise that his successors held his productions in such esteem, that all their works for voices alone {432} can be traced back to his prototypes, and bear the technical designation of music *alla Palestrina*: 'Palestrina having brought his style to such perfection, that the best compositions which have been produced for the church since his time are proverbially said to be *alla Palestrina*, it seems as if this were the place to discuss its merit.'

[. . .]

{434} Let all manner of praise, then, be heaped on this Homer, Prince of music: *Laudemus virum gloriosum, et parentem nostrum* ['Let us now praise a famous man, and our father'] (*Ecclesiasticus*, 44.1),[62] who with the great talents which Nature had lavishly bestowed on him, was able to bring the Art and Science of music to the highest perfection, in the exact imitation of words and meanings: *in peritia sua requirentem modos musicos* ['Seeking out, in his mastery, the musical means'].[63] And let grateful posterity continue to preserve throughout future centuries, as in those that are past, the imperishability of his glorious name, which has become synonymous with the purest music for unaccompanied voices: *Musica alla Palestrina*.

---

62   The Vulgate reads in the plural: *Laudemus viros gloriosos, et parentes nostros in generatione sua* ['Let us now praise famous men, and our fathers that begat us.'] (*Authorized Version*: Apocrypha).
63   *Ecclesiasticus*, 44.5; Vulgate again reads in the plural: *requirentes*.

Alexander Dmitryevich Ulïbïshev (1794–1858)
Nouvelle biographie de Mozart (1843)

Forkel's *Life, Art and Works* of Bach (1802), Baini's *Historical and Critical Memoirs of the Life and Works* of Palestrina (1828: Analysis 14 above), Winterfeld's study of *Giovanni Gabrieli and His Age* (1834) – these monuments of early nineteenth-century biography differ from their contemporary 'necrologies' by displaying an awareness of historical context and stylistic milieu that was new for their time. Ulïbïshev's biography of Mozart, complete with *A Survey of the History of Music, and Analysis of Mozart's Principal Works*, of 1843, followed in this line. In three fat volumes, over 1,100 pages in all, only its first volume was pure biography. Mozart biography had well and truly established itself by that time, through the contributions of Schlichtegroll (1794), Niemetschek (1798), Arnold (1803), Stendhal (1814), Lichtenthal (1816) and others. Such a biography, by Georg Nissen (1828), which made many important documents public for the first time, came into Ulïbïshev's hands in 1830.[1] 'There is nothing of him [Nissen] in the work that bears his name', complained Ulïbïshev, only ' . . . a mortally tedious recitation' of minutiae. Even worse: about music there is nothing but facts: 'Idea, unity, plan, sketching process [*rédaction*], style, logic – you search in vain for any of these things.'[2] Ulïbïshev filled his hours of solitude in remote Nizhni-Novgorod by rewriting Nissen in readable form, believing that Mozart's compositions were 'the principal actions of his life', and so providing in vols. II–III a *partie analytique*.[3] The task took him ten years; one of its results was a genuine attempt to create a stylistic classification of Mozart's output as a totality.

The second half of vol. II and the whole of vol. III form a series of chapters on the works. The Requiem and each of the major operas from *Idomeneo* to *La clemenza di Tito* has its own chapter, as does the Overture to *The Magic Flute*. The instrumental works are treated collectively in three chapters: the string quartets, the string quintets, the symphonies.[4] The string quintets, emotionally more

---

1 Georg Nikolaus Nissen, *Biographie W. A. Mozarts: nach Originalbriefen, Sammlungen alles über ihn Geschriebenen, mit vielen neuen Beylagen, Steindrucken, Musikblättern und einem Facsimile* (Leipzig: B&H, 1828, suppl. 1829). Nissen (1761–1826) was Danish Chargé d'Affairs in Vienna, 1793–1820. In 1809 he married Mozart's widow, Constanze; in 1820 they retired to Salzburg, where the biography was compiled. It was completed posthumously, and Constanze saw it through the press.

2 *Nouvelle biographie*, vol. I, pp. iv–vi. Ulïbïshev wrote in French because Russian was 'deficient in almost all its technical terminologies, including musical vocabulary', and so as to reach a more knowledgeable readership (ibid, xvi–xvii).

3 ibid, vi–ix, xiii, xv.

4 ibid, III, 1–27, 206–32, 233–70. Von Lenz criticized him for ignoring the works for piano, those with piano accompaniment and others. See *Beethoven et ses trois styles* (St Petersburg: Bernard, 1852; new edn, ed. M. D. Calvocoressi, Paris: Legouix, 1909; reprint edn New York: Da Capo, 1980), 27–8.

tangible than the quartets, their melodies more generous and ostentatious, and the symphonies, still more vehement, harmonically audacious, even eccentric, their thematic treatment more arresting, exist on a stylistic continuum the extremes of which are the operas, *musique appliquée*, and the string quartets, *musique pure*.[5] In 'applied music', harmonic and thematic development is governed by 'the demands of a text, of action, or of the *tableau* that constitutes its programme', functioning by translation, by analogy. In 'pure music', it proceeds by its own internal logic, dictated by the absolute sense of its musical ideas, all its elements inevitable and interrelated.

Of 'pure music', Mozart's quartets were for Ulïbïshev the truest examples – but only the six quartets dedicated to Haydn that Mozart composed between 1782 and 1785 and published in 1785. The earlier quartets preceded the onset of Mozart's 'classical' phase; the three later 'Prussian' quartets were stylistically compromised by the prominence of the cello part. The chapter given below devotes space to placing these quartets within a broader taxonomy. It first carefully discriminates between, on the one hand, the operatic vocal quartet and other music in four parts, and, on the other hand, the 'quartet proper', and subsequently distinguishes between the types of string quartet to be found in the late eighteenth and early nineteenth centuries. While never naming directly the *quatuor concertant*, Ulïbïshev several times speaks of the incursion of *musique concertante* into the quartet, and of the *style concertant*. The concertante quartet was an essentially amateur genre enormously popular in Paris from about 1770 to 1800, in which all four instruments shared the solo melodic material by turns. Examples are those by Jean-Baptiste Davaux, Opp. 9 (1779) and 17 (*c*.1800), Boccherini, Op. 24 (1776–8), and Giovanni Battista Viotti from the 1780s and 1817. Haydn's quartets Opp. 20, 50 and 64 were all published in Paris under this title. Ulïbïshev does speak directly of the *quatuor brillant*, a genre that blossomed about 1800, comprising a virtuosic first violin part accompanied by string trio. Spohr produced many sets between 1808 and 1838. Ulïbïshev also speaks of the *quatuor dramatique*.

These various genres of quartet he distinguishes sharply from the *véritable quatuor* or *vrai quatuor*. The distinction recalls Spohr's comment in his *Violin School* of 1832:[6]

> In recent times a genre of quartet has arisen in which the first violin takes the lead as solo instrument while the other three instruments merely provide accompaniment. These are called 'solo quartets' (*quatuors brillants*), to distinguish them from the real quartets. Their purpose is to afford the solo player the opportunity of displaying his virtuosity with smaller-scale musical forces.

Spohr's distinction is between *Soloquartett* and *wirkliches Quartett*. Forty years earlier, Heinrich Christoph Koch had cited precisely Mozart's 'Haydn' Quartets as 'those that, among all modern four-part sonatas, correspond most closely to the concept of a genuine quartet [*eigentliches Quatuor*], and that are unique of their kind by virtue of their distinctive mixture of the strict and free styles, and their treatment

---

5   ibid, III, 208, 249–50; II, 160–62.
6   L. Spohr, *Violinschule: mit erläuternden Kupfertafeln* (Vienna: Haslinger, 1832), p. 246.

of harmony'.[7] Ulïbïshev's technical term for this latter type is *quatuor travaillé*, equivalent of the German *gearbeitetes Quartett*, literally 'worked quartet'. Quantz, in 1752, had presented *gearbeitet* as the antithesis of *galant* – elaborate and contrapuntal, as against the light, clear style that was currently in vogue.[8] Its distinguishing character for Ulïbïshev, as for Koch, is its combining of the 'melodic style' (*style mélodique*) with the 'contrapuntal style' (*style contrapontique*, or *style thématique et fugué*).[9] The former is the musical language of feeling, of expression, of sensuality; the latter, its psychological opposite, austere, ineffable, equalizing the parts, injecting harmonic tension and providing thematic development and the means of unity.[10] The special quality of the quartet *travaillé*, as articulated in the present chapter, is that its thematic materials are to be chosen so as to function under both styles. Ulïbïshev goes so far as to exhort that the unity, the organic quality (he too, like Hoffmann (vol. II, Analysis 9), uses the image of a tree) procured by this process be extended to the four movements as a whole.

As pure music *par excellence*, the quartet is food for the connoisseur. It 'ought not to respond to any psychological state of mind, definite or indefinite'.[11] Asked what it signifies, Ulïbïshev responds: 'Signifies! I have simply no idea. I appreciate it perfectly well [*je le sens bien*]; but to put it into words – I would not know how to do that. *Das lässt sich eigentlich nicht sagen* ['It defies putting precisely into words'].'[12] The present chapter offers us a bonus. In its own right, it is an analysis of style and genre. Embedded within its final section is a gentle parody of the hack music critic and his 'sterile analysis', contrived so as to demonstrate the futility of verbalizing musical abstraction. Another bonus of this chapter is Ulïbïshev's attempt to portray the compositional process of an abstract work: a fascinating attempt at psychological formulation, and worth comparing with that by Lobe (Analysis 12).

Ulïbïshev was the son of a Russian diplomat posted in Dresden, hence he benefitted early in life from a German musical education. From 1810, when he moved to Russia, he became, like von Lenz after him, a civil servant. He was active as a music critic in the *Journal de St. Pétersbourg*. The polemical material against Beethoven that appeared in the symphony chapter of his biography of Mozart drew him into

---

7   *Versuch einer Anleitung zur Composition* (Leipzig: Böhme, 1782–93; reprint edn Hildesheim: Olms, 1969), vol. III (1793), pp. 326–7; see Nancy Kovaleff Baker: *Heinrich Christoph Koch: Introductory Essay on Composition: The Mechanical Rules of Melody, Sections 3 and 4* (New Haven: Yale University Press, 1983), p. 207. Schulz and Kirnberger delineate *Quatuor* as 'three solo [*concertirend*] parts and a bass, itself sometimes playing solo [. . .] one of the most difficult of all types of composition, dem‑nding a composer with mastery of counterpoint [. . .] the parts must differ from each other, and yet form a whole' (J. G. Sulzer, *Allgemeine Theorie der schönen Künste* (Leipzig: Weidmann, 1771–4, 4/1792–9; reprint edn Hildesheim: Olms, 1967–70), 'Quartet; Quatuor').

8   *Versuch einer Anweisung, die Flöte traversière zu spielen* (Berlin: Voss, 1752): p. 294, 'Trios are either, as one says, *gearbeitet* or *galant*'; p. 94, 'well *gearbeitet* duets and trios, including fugues'; 95, 'music that is called *gearbeitet*, especially fugues'.

9   Ulïbïshev offers an extended discussion of these two styles in the eighteenth century (vol. II, pp. 133–75).

10 ibid, II, 152–5, 170–71.

11 ibid, III, 208.

12 ibid, II, 162.

controversy and eventually prompted his second book, *Beethoven, His Critics and His Glossators*, in 1857 (Analysis 16d). A need to master the art of score reading before writing his book on Mozart is ambiguously implied by the preface. Ulïbïshev was an amateur violinist, and he tells how in his retirement he played with other amateurs 'besides the brilliant and concertante pieces' the quartets and quintets of Haydn, Mozart and Beethoven, Onslow and Boccherini, and the quartets of Cherubini, Spohr, Ries, Mendelssohn and others.[13]

13   ibid, I, xvii, xx.

'[Mozart's] String Quartets Dedicated to Haydn'
New Biography of Mozart

Source:
'Les quatuors de violon dediés à Haydn', *Nouvelle biographie de Mozart, suivie d'un aperçu sur l'histoire générale de la musique et de l'analyse des principales œuvres de Mozart* (Moscow: August Semen, 1843), vol. III, [chap. 1], pp. 1–27.

We often hear it said, and see it written, that nothing is more difficult to accomplish than the writing of a quartet. The quartet, it is said, is the touchstone of the composer's craft [*science*].[14] For the trained musician, this remark needs no proof; but for those who lack adequate instruction it is surely anything but self-evident. Indeed, in the minds of most people it must seem rather contradictory. How could it possibly be that a maestro who is at home when combining twenty parts, vocal as well as instrumental, in a piece for full orchestra, could come to grief when combining four parts in a quartet? The only way in which to answer this question will be to explain the stringent demands that the genre makes on the composer; and such an explanation seems to us the only way of demonstrating how Mozart met these demands.

It is vital first to define the very precise sense in which 'quartet' is to be understood in this context, for the word has several markedly different usages, some of them wholly inappropriate. Thus, in opera we call a 'quartet' a combining of four vocal parts sung by principal characters, together with a number of extra {2} orchestral parts. Likewise, we give the name to a piece composed for harpsichord and three other instruments. Yet since the harpsichord alone plays in three or four parts the result is bound to be not just a quartet, but rather more than a quartet. Let us then begin by declaring, as does M de La Palisse,[15] that a genuine quartet never has more than four parts. Is that all that is needed to establish it as an independent genre, sufficient unto itself? Just think. Imagine yourself consigning a melody to one main part, one predominant line, and distributing your chords among the remaining three parts. Hey presto! You have an aria, a ballad, a song of some sort, a fantasy, a few variations, or some such, accompanied by three instruments. You share out the main melody so that each of the parts in turn comes to the fore and then recedes, and what you get is a concerto grosso, or a sinfonia concertante in miniature. But you know better than that: you know how to depict feelings. At the creative inspiration of your genius, love or hate, pleasure or displeasure, will breathe life into four devices made of resonant wood. Now the violin will utter cries of pathos, the viola will issue a muffled groan, the cello will lift tearful eyes to heaven. Splendid! What we will have is the dramatic instrumental

14 Cf. Quantz, 'A quartet [. . .] is really the touchstone of a true contrapuntist' (*Versuch einer Anweisung*, p. 302).
15 I have been unable to identify M de La Palisse, who is alluded to also without citation in *Beethoven, ses critiques et ses glossateurs*, pp. 161, 162, 308.

quartet[16] – in other words, opera without the action, without the words, without the singers and without even the orchestra. To put it another way, we will have the frog who tries to puff himself up until he is the size of the ox.

All that we have done so far, then, is to substitute an instrument for the human voice, or to produce a small-scale version of concertante music [*musique concertante*] or a very imperfect surrogate of operatic music [*musique de théâtre*], hence an inferior genre, {3} an understudy for use when the star performer is indisposed. The quartet proper, on the other hand, deserves to be a distinct and independent branch among the higher realms of instrumental music.[17] It must be self-motivating and self-sufficient, and not exist as a substitute for something better, something more complete than itself. Assuredly, the quartet as we understand it cannot function wholly within the confines of the melodic style, for on all fronts it would be condemned to a subordinate role. It could not survive without the imitative, fugal style.[18] This immediately confronts the idolized composer of opera, used as he is to filling up the staves of the most massive scores, with a first difficulty which would stop him dead in his tracks. True, there is no era in which good contrapuntists have been totally lacking. Would being one of them qualify one to write a good quartet? We think not. In the system of composition that Haydn and Mozart have created, expressive melody is inseparable from counterpoint. Today's greater emphasis on technique [*science*] risks starving music of the very melody which is its soul.[19] Thus if one is to compose a quartet one must know how to create melody that sings – sings just as well as in opera, but in a totally different way from opera. And there lies the second difficulty, which is even less surmountable than the first.

Thus far, we have brought to bear on the quartet only the general requirements of pure music. However, there are other rules, specific rules, rules no less important, and in our view even more difficult to observe, rules without which the quartet would not exist at all as an independent genre. How are we to distinguish it from the quintet, from the sextet, from the septet, indeed from the symphony for full orchestra? By the number of instruments, you may say. But if there were no other difference than this, the quartet would be a substitute for the symphony and for any instrumental composition {4} with more than four parts, just as in other cases we have seen that it could become a substitute for concertante music and for operatic music. On what qualifications, therefore, are we to base its independence? The qualifications are as follows.

16   [Ulïbïshev:] String quartets have already appeared under this very title. [Editor: I have failed to trace works with this title.]

17   *de la haute musique instrumentale*: reminiscent of Reicha's title *Traité de haute composition musicale* (Paris: Zetter, 1824–6), a treatise that deals not with melody, simple harmony or single counterpoint, but with the elevated world of invertible counterpoint, canon, fugue, musical form, and the development of musical ideas, the implied distinction is parallel to that established below between the 'melodic style' and the 'imitative, fugal style'.

18   *le style mélodique* and *le style thématique et fugué*: *thème* in this context is to be equated not with 'melody' but rather with 'subject', as in a fugue.

19   This sentiment allies with those of Reicha (see Analysis 9 above, note 3). The allusion is presumably to, among others, François-Joseph Fétis (see Analysis 16b below), in particular his *Traité de contrepoint et de la fugue* (Paris: Janet et Cotelle, 1824), and Luigi Cherubini, notably his *Cours de contrepoint et de fugue* (Paris: M. Schlesinger, 1835).

There exists between musical ideas and the practical resources needed to realize and convert them most effectively into sound a natural relationship of which connoisseurs are very much aware. There is a certain kind of idea which is fittingly realized at the keyboard of the piano or on the fingerboard of the guitar; any greater noise would be detrimental. And there is another kind of idea, which calls for all the might of chorus and orchestra. Four hundred performers, a thousand if you like, will not be too many for Handel's Halleluia Chorus or the final chorus of Part I of *The Creation*.[20] As a general rule, the more overtly expressive a composer's ideas are, and the more powerful and impassioned the feelings they bring into play, the more vividly will they convey what is needed to give them definition, and the less can they do without the support that sheer numbers of instruments and diversity of tone-colours bring to melody and harmony. The power of sound [*la force tonique*] which the realization exerts should always be in proportion to the musical ideas, just as the intonations of the orator's delivery should be in keeping with the words. It follows from this that the motifs that are closest in nature to characters in opera [*la musique dramatique*] are specially suited to the overture and the symphony, and that in order to maintain the logical relationship of ideas to resources of performance the composer should distance himself ever more greatly from subsidiary characters the more spartan are his practical resources, his sound-materials. By this reckoning, the instrumental septet or sextet {5} will be less overt than the symphony, the quintet less than the sextet. On this scale of regression the quartet, which is musical thought reduced to its simplest expression and narrowed down to its barest essentials as regards material effect, the quartet emerges not as the substitute for the symphony, but on the contrary as the genre most diametrically opposed to it in its psychological tendencies. Let us put it this way: the quartet is the musician's thought reduced to its simplest expression. Decrease beyond four parts, and you no longer have the notes with which to complete the harmony without resorting to arpeggios and double-stops, which are devices inappropriate to the melodic style and almost nugatory in the fugal style. The string duo and trio do not constitute genres in their own right. There are some beautiful examples, I know; but because the addition of an extra part or two, thereby completing the harmony, would render them even more beautiful, one is forced to recognize them, in every case, as a last resort for when a gathering of amateur players is not enough to make up a quartet.

The most essential, and the most difficult thing in the genre with which we are concerned is therefore the choice of ideas. The problem that the composer of a string quartet is called upon to resolve is thus: to banish from his work all traces of dramatic expression – the very thing that has the greatest power over the mind of the listener; to renounce the brilliance of virtuoso concertante writing; to create melody that sings, without ever suggesting vocal performance; to operate only with themes whose psychological character is of the least definable and most abstract – for to these must the composer restrict himself, according to our theory, and always to arouse our profound interest in the work, to give us such satis-

---

20   Part I no. 13, Chorus with Soli: 'Die Himmel erzählen die Ehre Gottes' ('The Heavens are telling').

faction that we could wish for nothing beyond what reaches our ears, neither in the music itself nor in the fitness of its resources of performance. {6} Here, more than ever, the composer is thrown back on his own inner resources. Gone are all the props, all those secondary elements to which credit is often due for most of his success. As to virtuosic display, in the quartet proper there scarcely is any, since the musical ideas, bound up as they always are with the workings of the ensemble as a whole, cannot and must not stand out too much in any one part. As to the resultant sound quality, the acoustical end product: that is limited to the sounds produced by four homogeneous instruments. And finally, as to the visual element, all that you have before you is four players, seated around a table as if for a whist drive, and who can be seen, during their rests, busily taking a pinch of snuff, blowing their noses or polishing the lenses of their spectacles on their cravats, when they are not rosining their bows.

Quite apart from avoiding explicit and over-assertive displays of expression, it is also necessary in the quartet to abstain from using too many stock figures, or conventional turns of phrase in melody or harmony and to eschew obvious cadences and rowdy endings such as are acceptable in opera and the symphony. That sort of thing is all well and good there; it can even occasionally make a big splash, and can contribute to the desired effect. Consider, for instance, the celebrated 'Fiat lux' of Haydn's *Creation*, so simply achieved by a chord of C major played *ff* by full orchestra.[21] If played by four instruments of the violin family, this dazzling representation of light universal would cast no more light than a dim lamp. It would be less than nothing – altogether lost as an effect.

All that remains now is to say a few words about the technical difficulties of the genre. All quartets – the good ones, that is – include sections written in melodic style and {7} others written in fugal style. The best are those whose musical motifs do service for both melodic material and contrapuntal working-out. They are the best, we say, but they are also the most difficult to write, and this is why. In the fugal sections of these works, with subjects operating strictly [*strictement thématiques*], each note has a double function [*double emploi*]:[22] it supplies a vertical interval in a chord, and contributes to the design of the figures and to the points of imitation, as in a regular fugue. There is one difference, however. Instead of operating on fugue subjects chosen expressly according to the demands of the fugal style, the composer is obliged to subject to these same erudite, fragmenting processes [*aux mêmes analyses savantes*] the melodies that supply the lyrical sections of the work – and this is a task of incomparably greater difficulty. This inner structure [*structure intérieure*], possessed by the quartet, rests on an order of musical analogies which it is important to recognize and to define precisely.[23]

21   The reference is to the words 'Es werde Licht, und es ward Licht' at the end of Part I no. 1, 'Und der Geist Gottes schwebte'.
22   *double emploi*: this phrase recalls Rameau's and d'Alembert's use of the term to denote the property whereby a given chord has two different harmonic functions. Ulïbïshev, however, may be using it in a common-parlance sense as 'doing double duty'.
23   For Ulïbïshev, 'applied music' rests on musical analogy to external phenomena (text, action, scene, programme); 'pure music' rests on internal analogy among absolute themes and motifs.

The composer of a quartet does not deal in implied action, in covert narrative, in an emotional state conjured up by a surface activity [*mobile extérieur*], or a *tableau pittoresque* of some sort. Action, narration, story-telling, depiction of tangible objects: these are all pursuits which may lead a composer to become a practitioner of opera, of the dramatic overture or the programmatic symphony; in other words, lead him to inevitable inferiority by comparison with other branches of the art of music. The composer of a quartet must respond purely and simply to any spontaneous state of mind that arises, to any flight of the free-wheeling, independent imagination transmitted through the dreams to which it gives rise, entirely dissociated from external things. He must be sensitive to whatever feeling arises, capable of taking on its character to some degree while never being motivated actively by that feeling itself. You {8} start out, I suppose, in a melancholic or sad or downhearted frame of mind, or in a state of conflicting feelings, or with whatever else you care to name. Then a motif springs to mind, taking shape at first simply and uniquely – that is, in melodic form. The idea-cum-feeling gathers momentum. It traverses the psychological mode within the realm of its inception. On the way, it encounters other thematic ideas [*thèmes*], which assume roles as principal or auxiliary ideas [*idées principales ou accessoires*] in proportion to the compatibility they display with the original idea [*idée-mère*],²⁴ or sometimes in proportion to their very incompatibility, which gives them a semblance of opposition to that idea. After these various aspects, modifications, nuances, commentaries, episodes or contradictions of the underlying psychological impulse [*donnée*] have passed successively before the mind, the mind associates them and compares them. From that moment on, recourse must be had to the contrapuntal style. Musical unity is from now on no longer simple. The four parts take on individuality; they begin to engage each other in discourse. Sometimes they are cordially of one mind, each making its own contribution to the general accord. Sometimes they argue: two against two, three against one, all against each other. There is no music that better resembles a conversation than the quartet proper; but to achieve that effect it is essential to choose ideas that appear to flow naturally from one another; it is essential that the subject-matter of the discourse be perfectly comprehensible to the mind, and that where sharp disagreements occur the reader can see that all are talking about the same thing; it is essential that the combination and fragmentation [*analyse*] of the musical ideas demonstrate the truths of feeling with as much coherence, precision and clarity as does rational dialectic those of the mind.

We have {9} already spoken, in our Introduction,²⁵ of the striking analogy by which the contrapuntal style reproduces in the sphere of sensations the logical

---

24 *idée-mère*: see above, Analysis 9; *idée mère* and *idée accessoire* are both crucial terms in Reicha's theory of thematic development and taxonomy of larger musical forms. See *Traité de haute composition musicale*, vol. II, pp. 234–320 *passim*, esp. 234–5, 296–300.

25 'Introduction', i.e. vol. II, pp. 1–205, in large part a survey of the history of musical style from the ancient Greeks to Mozart, which he claims to have written ten years earlier (p. 185, note). It contains an extended discussion of fugal style (pp. 143–69), in the course of which Ulïbïshev asks: 'What, then, is a fugue?', replying, 'A musical thesis, which is discussed straightforwardly or contradictorily . . .' (p. 162).

It might be said that the contrapuntal genre transports, by analogy, the faculties and laws of comprehension into the domain of feelings. Thus, the motif-based order and succession of

forms that govern the development of thought-processes. Moreover, we saw there how the greater the extent to which a work simulated a proposition discussed straightforwardly or contradictorily, sustained, attacked, and ultimately demonstrated as true, the more did the meaning of that work resist definition in words. This is of special relevance to the quartet. More than any other genre in the world of music, the quartet appears to address itself to our faculty of intelligence. This is why there is no genre that calls for a more motif-based choice of thematic materials, for a more logical sequence of events, for a more severe discipline of style and for such an abundance of melodic and harmonic invention, in order to compensate for the inevitably spartan nature of its resultant sound quality on the one hand and lack of powerful, emotive and impassioned outpourings to which the quartet cannot and must never aspire on the other. But let us not misunderstand ourselves. There are of course passages in Mozart's quartets dedicated to Haydn that are powerful, emotive, impassioned in the extreme. But never do they form principal themes; in no case do they represent the overall character of a quartet. They pass by rapidly like one of those surges of happiness that sometimes takes us totally by surprise when we are in the calmest frame of mind, or like one of those sudden and acute pangs of conscience that occasionally strike us to the core without apparent rhyme or reason. Such *unaccountable* flarings-up of passion (not arising out of the thematic materials) are allowed to occur in the quartet, since their brilliance radiates, as is appropriate, in the psychological realm, the domain to which we have assigned the quartet.

Such, in a word, is the theory of that type of quartet {10} known as *travaillé* (*das gearbeitete Quartett*)[26] in order to distinguish it from the many other instrumental compositions in four parts: a genre of which Haydn takes the credit for being the founder, and which Mozart carried to the highest imaginable, the highest possible degree of perfection; a genre which is, by virtue of its stringent arguments and special qualities, and as the world is coming to recognize it, in process of becoming the touchstone of the composer's true skills, the favourite music of the experts and at the same time the bugbear, the bane of the ladies, be they musicians or no. This is not a theory that we have dreamed up; as with any theory of art which contains a grain of truth, ours stems directly from practice. It has been deduced and abstracted, piece by piece and word by word, from existing models of the genre, above all from the quartets of Mozart, the most perfect that there are. We have done no more than verify empirically, and attempted to unify in a single system, rules that would not have been discovered had example not preceded them. If there is any truth in these observations, it will be an easy task for us to demonstrate the superiority of Mozart's quartets over those of all other composers; not so much by comparing their beauties with the perhaps equal beauties that distinguish other composers' works – a line of enquiry that would

---

musical ideas, the beauty of thematic development, correspond to the inferences, proofs and corollaries that the skilled logician is able to deduce from some fruitful proposition. (p. 163)

26   See Introduction for Quantz's use of *gearbeitet* to mean 'elaborate', 'contrapuntal' (1752). While applying it to duets, trios, and the main theme of overtures yet not to the quartet, Quantz did include 'correct and short imitations', and ideas that will combine contrapuntally as requirements for the quartet, and allowed for inclusion of fugue (*Versuch einer Anweisung*, p. 302).

lead us nowhere at all, for musical beauties cannot be weighed by the pound or the ounce – but to demonstrate it by negative means, drawing attention through examples to the way in which the most skilful composers have sometimes deviated in one way or another from the fundamental theoretical requirements of the genre, whereas our hero has never at any time gone astray.

When we speak of Mozart's rivals, in the realm of the quartet there are but two to invoke: Haydn–{11}–Mozart–Beethoven! –the three greatest names in all music, the names that are most frequently on our lips, and that we most gladly hear spoken.

In other times, the general preference was for Haydn and Mozart; nowadays it is Beethoven who is most in favour. Haydn has a kind of sprightliness or good humour that renders him approachable to people of mediocre intelligence. He loves to jest and laugh with his listeners, which goes down well with his audience. This endearing playfulness, this amicability, Mozart replaces with a loftiness and profundity. Mozart breathes life again into Bach, but this is Bach with the benefit of an extra half-century, Bach turned great melodist, yielding up from the depths of his grave, or perhaps we should say from the celestial heights above, novel harmonies, the likes of which our poor planet took a long time to assimilate. Therein lie the very different fates of the two great composers. The one, the idol of his contemporaries, no doubt looked upon with special favour by God as the bard who sang of his creation, Haydn still today counts among his admirers all trained and discriminating musicians. The other saw his quartets hounded out of Italy for copying errors that did not exist.[27] He was criticized by one professor for faults in composition that were, with one exception, in reality novel and original beauties,[28] exposed to public criticism in concert for errors that were initially blamed on the players! All of this because they were too perfect. You will see what I mean.

[First,] in the majority of Haydn's quartets, *cantabile* sections and decorative passage-work alternate with a regularity that simply cannot be tolerated in the genre, an effect which gives to thematically constructed works a false air of con-certante music and enfeebles the work of the composer in the interests of the first violinist. In the case of Mozart, these features are kept apart, {12} and are less prominent. They derive more closely from the thematic material, and they work together with it in contrapuntal combinations that lead to the use of fugal style. In

27 *AmZ*, 1 (1799), col. 855:

> These quartets suffered a singular fate at times. After the late Artaria had sent them to Italy, he received them back – 'because the engraving was so full of errors'. People took the many strange chords and dissonances for engraver's errors. True, in time people came to think better of it. But this work of Mozart's fared no better at times in Germany. The late Count Grassalkowich, for example, once had some of his court musicians play these same quartets. Again and again, he shouted: 'You're not playing it right!', and when they convinced him to the contrary he tore up the parts on the spot.'

No date is given for either anecdote, nor is there evidence to support their veracity (the quartets were first released in 1785, and again in 1787 and 1797; Pasquale Artaria died in 1785).

28 The reference is presumably to Fétis, who rewrote passages of the String Quartet in C K465 ('Dissonance') that he found contravened the rules of his own counterpoint treatise (see introduction to Analysis 16, below) (F.-J. Fétis, 'Sur un passage singulier d'un quatuor de Mozart', *La Revue musicale*, 5 (1829), 601–02, and 6 (1830), 25–32); for an excellent account of this controversy, see J. A. Vertrees, 'Mozart's String Quartet K.465: The History of a Controversy', *Current Musicology*, 17 (1974), 96–114.

that way, they become closely wedded to the original idea and acquire a significance, an import, that mere ornamentation of the melody, or bravura passage-work, interspersed throughout a thematically constructed composition so as to enhance the status of the player, could never have attained. It is a delight to the ear and to the spirit at one and the same time to hear how a simple melismatic turn of phrase, a light *fioritura*, accompanied almost imperceptibly, changes a moment later into a contrapuntal figure of great elegance, logic and vigour, as in Example 1.[29]

Example 1

{13} Secondly, in many places, the melodic style of Haydn's quartets comes distinctly close to vocal music. He harks back to *The Creation* and *The Seasons* even when he is not actually working with such archaic melodic forms. Many of Haydn's adagios and andantes are veritable cavatinas from beginning to end, the first violin reduced to being a substitute for a singer. The only thing missing is the text – as in Example 2.[30]

Example 2

Scour the pages of Mozart's quartets. You will be hard put to to find anything – let me not say a whole movement, but just an isolated phrase – that smacks of opera, or that would even sound well if sung. But what aristocratic grace, what indescribable elegance, what psychological profundity shine through these impossible-to-sing melodies, how clearly they bear the stamp of immortality! And what makes them vocally unsingable? The fact that they could never carry text. And why could they never carry text? Because the things they say to you are so difficult to express and recount that there is not a language in the whole world in which the words would do other than a disservice, would be other than an absurd contradiction, at best a gross approximation, would ever convey a faithful translation of the music.

Thirdly, we showed earlier how, for perfectly obvious reasons, conventional turns of phrase that are acceptable in orchestral works – where they would in fact be difficult {14} always to avoid – must strenuously be eliminated from quartets. True, Haydn let them creep in, though rarely and as it were inadvertently. Example 3 in a case in point.[31]

---

29   Mozart: Quartet in G major, K387: mvt 4, Molto Allegro, bb. 23–39.
30   Haydn: Quartet in C Op. 50 no. 2, Hob. III/45: mvt 2, Adagio cantabile, bb. 8–16.
31   Haydn: Quartet in E♭ Op. 71 no. 3, Hob. III/71: mvt 1, Vivace, bb. 300–15.

Example 3

The first four bars present the very same notes, and in almost exactly the right rhythm, as Almaviva's tune from his duet with Susanna: 'Mi sento dal contento, pieno di gioja il cor'.[32] Mozart must surely have stolen the tune from Haydn – unless, that is, Haydn stole it from Mozart. What then follows is one of the best known and most hackneyed rhetorical devices in all opera. Search as you may through Mozart's output, you will find not the slightest trace of a conventional turn of phrase of this sort, or of any other.

More conspicuous passage-work, i.e. a propensity for concertante music; more singable melodies, i.e. a tendency to vocal music; a more popular style, i.e. less highbrow; more accessible ideas, i.e. less exalted and less profound; –these explain the preference that people used once to feel for Haydn's quartets over those of our hero, and that many music lovers have continued to harbour up to the present without always admitting it.

Just as Haydn responded to the best and most enlightened taste of his time, so Beethoven is today the composer {15} of the moment. However, it is not our purpose here to judge him by the standards of present-day trends and preoccupations. Our task is to compare his string quartets with those of Mozart, in particular as regards the theoretical principles that we have adduced.

On one issue there is general agreement: that Beethoven, in his instrumental music, is the only man to be compared with Mozart for transcendency of ideas and melodic invention. On one other issue there is no need of proof, since it is a matter of fact, not of opinion or taste: that Beethoven did not reach the same heights as his two illustrious predecessors when it came to counterpoint. The fugal sections of his works are habitually the weakest sections; they are quite often lacking in euphony and clarity. Up to now many people have confused harmony with counterpoint. It is an error which gives rise to countless misunderstandings. There have been skilled contrapuntists ever since the fifteenth century, at which time harmony as such scarcely existed, and when no clear notion of the chord had yet dawned. Sublime harmonist, sublime melodist as he is, it has to be admitted that Beethoven has not distinguished himself in the craft of Josquin, Bach and Handel, all three of whom were surpassed by Mozart, who is to my mind the greatest contrapuntist the world has ever known. But as we have remarked

32   'dal': 'di'; Mozart: *Le Nozze di Figaro*, Act III Scene 2 No. 17, Duettino 'Crudel perchè finora', bb. 33–4. It is true that there is a difference of only one pitch, and that the rhythm (though 4/4 rather than 2/4) only slightly displaces the corresponding pitches. *Figaro* was completed in 1786; Haydn's 'Aponyi' Quartets, Opp. 71 and 74, were written in 1792–3.

again and again, counterpoint, the element that brings strength and durability to music, represents our faculty of intelligence in musical works of art; it is logic in music. Moreover, we can see immediately that the works of Beethoven do not display to the extent that those of Mozart do that quality of aesthetic inevitability whereby the work of the contrapuntist appears to take shape of its {16} own accord, as if there were no other way in which it could be done. Even the most partisan of Beethoven's advocates are bound to concede this brand of superiority to our hero because it would be difficult to contest it among musicians. But they will undoubtedly add that this quality, paramount as it was in the scholastic era of music, ranks no higher than second place in our own day. Genius, they will contend, transcends technique; very few listeners bother their heads about logic in music; most of them have no idea what it is, whereas all of them want to be overcome with emotion. Now, the quartets of Beethoven have something about them that is more moving than those of Mozart. If they *prove* less, they *are* more *moving*, and that is at least sufficient compensation, you will claim, when it comes to music. I accept the premise, and I repudiate the consequence. True enough, several of Beethoven's quartets, among them those in C minor [Op. 18 no. 4] and F minor [Op. 95], have a more impassioned character than any of Mozart's; and according to our principles what follows from this is nothing but a second species of relative inferiority. The composer of *Don Giovanni* has every bit as much passion in his soul as the composer of *Fidelio*; but since it is instrumental music of which we are speaking, let us take the Allegro, Minuet and Finale of Mozart's G minor Symphony [No. 40, K550]. I put it to you: can you recall a piece of music, can you even conceive of a piece, more filled with pathos, more alive with vitality, more profoundly incisive than this, especially the Finale?[33] [This is] proof that Mozart could show as much sign of emotion, and could become as excited as anyone else, if not more, when he wanted to. If he never exhibited such great passion in the quartet, this is because *non erat hic locus* ['this was not the place for it'].[34] He did not want his quartets – masterpieces equal in their genre to the most perfect things that he ever wrote – to become symphonies for two violins, viola and cello [*base*], a {17} very incomplete instrumentation for a symphony, as anyone will tell you. Beethoven is far from having understood the principle with the same reflective and intuitive clarity of mind. First and foremost a great symphonist, he is sometimes able to bring to chamber music the feel of orchestral music – the genre which was his highest calling, his most unmistakeable vocation. In one place, you may hear a shapely and distinctive melody, smooth and mellifluous phrases, which would sound natural on flute, bassoon or clarinet, if only there were a bassoon, a clarinet or a flute to hand. In another, an impressive-sounding thematic idea seems to cry

33 Ulïbïshev's discussions of *Don Giovanni* and the G minor Symphony occur in vol. III, pp. 67–208 and 255–60. Eduard Hanslick cited passages from these two discussions as corroborating 'Oulibicheff's mistaken opinion that a piece of instrumental music cannot be a product of genius [*geistreich*] because "genius [*Geist*] in a composer consists purely and simply in a certain applicability of his music to a direct or indirect program"' (*Vom Musikalisch-Schönen* (Leipzig: Barth, 1854, 17/1971), pp. 74–5; trans. G. Payzant (Indiana: Hackett, 1986), p. 36). Bujić, 26, translates *Geist* and *geistreich* as 'ingenuity' and 'ingenious'.
34 Horace, *Ars poetica*, line 19: *Sed nunc non erat his locus* ('But now there is no place for them'), speaking of 'purple patches' in poetic style. I am indebted to James Zetzel for this identification.

out for the might of assembled strings and wind,   brave and loyal troops whom
no one has commanded better that Generalissimus Beethoven,[35] troops with whom
he is always sure to vanquish, never to die. But this time the bulk of the army has
stayed behind the lines. To carry out all of his orders, to realize the grandiose schemes
that his genius has conceived, the maestro is left with nothing more than four
wretched instruments, blushing in shame at their weakness. Something tells you
that such ideas do not belong to the quartet: there is a lack of proportion between
the end and the means. Consider, for example, the closing Allegro of the Quartet in
C major (no. 3 of those that the composer dedicated to Count Razumovsky [Op.
59]), a movement patently conceived for full orchestra and lacking only the
orchestra with which to perform it. It needs the body of sound not of four but of
eight at the very least, and then only when they make enough noise for fifty. It is
pure symphony from beginning to end.

If the creative faculty, the genius [*génie*], of the two composers whom we are
comparing seems roughly {18} equal, the same is not true of the critical faculty, or
taste, the concurrence of which is every bit as essential as genius itself to the
creation of perfect masterpieces. An old adage, which has stood the test of time:
genius contributes the ideas, taste makes the selection. The ideas that Mozart has
put together always seem to have been meant for each other. Their interaction as
well as their development have an organic quality about them. They interrelate as
do the leaves on a tree to the branches of that tree, and the branches themselves to
the trunk from which they sprang. This is the aesthetic inevitability to which I
referred earlier, and which, we may say, did not always appear in Beethoven's
case in equal measure, not even in the most pure of his masterpieces, before the
onset of the double sickness, moral and physical, which was to divert him unawares
from the paths of the beautiful along which he had followed in Mozart's footsteps.
There is perhaps nothing among his chamber music for strings more imposing
than the Quintet in C major, Op. 29. What dilettante who has ever heard it could
forget the mystical opening of the initial allegro, with its theme vacillating uncer-
tainly, trembling in righteous horror, like the mind of a prophet in the throes of
some mighty revelation! It is sublime. But what can we say of the triplet figure
that directly follows it [bb. 17ff], and which constitutes a principal theme. You
have only to hear these two motifs one after the other to realize that they are
unsuited to one another. Their incompatibility becomes all the more apparent at
the beginning of section II, where the composer has combined them according to
the dictates of the contrapuntal style [bb. 95ff, especially bb. 129–78] – a conflation which I have to confess has never pleased me, either in live performance or in
reading from the score.

{19} By the principles that we have enumerated, the standard subdivisions of a
quartet or quintet – opening allegro, andante or adagio, minuet or scherzo, and
finale – if not always stamped by a single unified character, albeit with diversity,
ought at least to present a succession of states which follow naturally one from
another. It should be possible to discern a wholeness among these fragments, an
intelligible thread which links these various psychological *tableaux*. If not, then

35 [Ulïbïshev:] A title that he gave himself in jest in his private correspondence.

every movement would be a work in its own right. Whatever difference of character exists between these, the main subdivisions of the work as a whole, each one must remain faithful to itself. That is to say, it must, through the working-out and combination of its motifs, be comprehensible in its own terms from beginning to end, eschewing anything that might need justification in other terms. According to this, any unprepared change of tempo or time signature, of key or character in the course of a single movement is inadmissible in theory because such a change calls for a programme, and pure music prohibits the use of a programme, explicit or implicit [*programme direct et indirect*]. The practice belongs solely to dramatic music. Beethoven used it several times in his instrumental music; Mozart never did so. The quintet already cited provides an example of just one such change, sudden, unexpected, unaccountable, lacking justification from within its thematic material, and suggesting some ulterior motive on the part of the composer. In the midst of the finale, which is a presto 6/8 in C major, splendid music, you are suddenly confronted with an andante 3/4 in A major. It is full of grace and originality. It is altogether charming. But what does this andante ask of us?[36] Since there is no way in which the listener can trace even the least connection in musical logic between this untexted arietta {20} and the electrifying effects of the presto, he is driven back on to his own imagination to seek some link which will bring unity to such disparate ideas. And this is what I mean by an implicit programme, or an imaginary programme. When the composer decides to spare us the trouble, and sets down on paper what the music signifies, then that is an explicit programme. And so it is that we find among the Beethoven quartets a movement entitled *La malinconia*.[37] An andante [adagio] 2/4, highly chromatic, alternates with an allegretto quasi allegro 3/8 almost jocular in manner turning just before the end into a prestissimo. Melancholy has flown right out of the window. Recapture it if you can.

In identifying the respect in which we find Beethoven inferior to Mozart, we have set forth the very reasons why the composer of the Pastoral Symphony, the *Eroica* and the Choral Symphony commands the approval of a majority of people nowadays. By the sheer calibre of his genius, and by his very faults, Beethoven today is more topical than Mozart, just as was Haydn at the end of the last century and beginning of our own. The man for all ages cannot be the man for one particular age.

Let the reader not misinterpret the aim of our remarks. Searching under the microscope, so to speak, for blemishes that are both rare and minor in the finest quartets of Haydn, and in those that Beethoven wrote before his decline, we have had no desire to exalt Mozart at the expense of his rivals. The genius of each man, the particular beauties of his work, remain beyond question in the parallel that we have drawn. It was our purpose simply to reinforce and illuminate the theory by way of illustrations, to point up the prodigious {21} difficulties of the genre, to make known the almost unavoidable pitfalls that surround it on every side, and lastly to prove that of the three masters of the quartet Mozart deserves recognition

36   ... *cet* Andante, *mais que nous veut-il?*: perhaps a conscious echo of the remark 'Sonate, que me veux-tu?', widely but untraceably attributed to Bernard le Bouvoir de Fontenelle (1657–1757) – which Ulïbïshev himself quotes in connection with the symphonies (vol. III, p. 241).

37   Beethoven: Quartet in B♭ major Op. 18 no. 6, mvt 4.

as first among equals for having understood and overcome these difficulties the most effectively, for having avoided the pitfalls more consistently and more successfully, than anyone before or after him.

Since men such as Haydn and Beethoven, equals of Mozart as they are, are not always beyond reproach when it comes to the principles [of style],[38] what are we to say about, or rather what do those principles tell us about some of the most celebrated musicians who cultivate this same branch of art today? –Exhibit 1: the dramatic quartet, in which the violin sings you a recitative, but a recitative so expressive that it seems to form words, to speak to you, it as good as tells a story. Very well, then: why not put it into the mouth of a prima donna, and the words might come over even more clearly? –Exhibit 2: the quintet with explicit programme: 'Fever', 'Delirium', 'Convalescence', 'Recovery'. Call a conference of doctors and they will unerringly recognize in the music the symptoms, the tell-tale signs of these various conditions. Doctors, maybe. But for each of these states there would be a far clearer way of issuing a medical bulletin: for fever, an actor tucked up warm in a blanket; for delirium, in a night gown or *in naturalibus*; for convalescence, in a dressing gown; and for recovery, in fancy dress. –Exhibit 3: the quartet *brillant* without pretensions: a solo with simple accompaniment. Principles have nothing to tell us about this one. When a soloist plays with limited resources [*en petit comité*], having no orchestra at his disposal, he needs something to provide the chords for him; whether it is three instruments of the violin family or a harpsichord is neither here nor there. –And now Exhibit 4: {22} the quartet *brillant* with technical pretensions, that is to say, with a leading violin part even more difficult than a concerto, together with an accompaniment heavy with erudition, overloaded with chromatic and enharmonic passage-work. 'Two husbands! – That is more than custom permits', as the notary said in *Femmes savantes*.[39] Two genres of music in one and the same composition? –too much for the ear, our principles tell us. You have forgotten, they say to the composer, that the contrapuntal style and the concertante style are mutually exclusive: they make diametrically opposite demands and hence are totally antipathetic. The one achieves its effect by the disciplined combination of contrapuntal parts, the other by the wholesale isolation of one part from others. Obviously, you have begun by writing your *violino primo*; and in so doing you have thought in purely melodic terms. At some point you decided to dabble a little in technique; and so, observing the rules of musical arithmetic, you tried to find short phrases [*dessins*] and points of imitation [*imitations*] that could be worked into the other parts so as to impart a little rigour. Being the patient fellow that you are at figures, you have achieved what you set out to do. But let us remind you, my dear sir, that this is technique after the fact. True contrapuntists do not compose in this way. They think all-of-a-piece. They work with fire and inspiration; they do not first surrender their ideas to the demands of virtuosity – demands totally alien to their purpose. To them,

38   *principes*: 'of style' has been inferred from the succeeding discussion.
39   Molière, *Les femmes savantes*, Act V Scene 3, lines 1623–4: 'Deux époux! | C'est trop pour la coutume' (quotation-marks not given by Ulïbïshev) (*Molière: Oeuvres complètes*, ed. G. Mongrédien, vol. IV (Paris: Garnier-Flammarion, 1965), p. 366).

the arithmetic is second nature, they are scarcely aware of it. To you, on the other hand, it is the laborious result of fretful trial and error, of tortuous mental effort. It looks right on paper, for the rules of harmony are tolerant, and paper is long-suffering. But the ear is more stringent in its requirements. And what do we find after all? Something apparently strange but in reality quite natural, namely that your {23} quartet often sounds better when played by first violin on its own than when played by all four instruments.

From all that has now been put forward we can make the inference, established in theoretical terms and demonstrated in practice, that the two branches of the art of music formally the most antipathetic to one another are opera and the string quartet *travaillé*. This is true to the extent that the moral temperament and artistic faculty demanded by one of these two genres seems the absolute negation of the temperament and faculties required by the other. And yet, is there any musician more tragic than the composer of *Idomeneo*? Merrier, more loving, more lyrical than the composer of *Die Entführung*? Would not so dazzling a vocation for works of the theatre, *seria* and *buffa*, of necessity exclude all other pursuits? Yet at the same time, of all instrumentalists, this is the composer who has also risen to the highest level of musical abstraction, who has in his quartets most consistently excluded all trace of vocal melody and all hint of a programme; who has most successfully resisted the power of opera (resisted himself, that is) by renouncing more adamantly than any other composer those never-failing devices of dramatic music: vehement passion, narrative, the *tableau pittoresque*, action, vocal melody, virtuosic display, reliance upon sheer volume of sound to make an impact. As ever, the best explanation of the musician lies in the man himself. Was not Mozart, that merry companion, of a thoughtful disposition; was he not given to a dreamy imagination and predisposed to melancholy? Was not the poet-musician who exuded epic and tragic grandeur in the choruses of *Idomeneo*, and who poured out such glowing passion in the arias of {24} Belmonte [in *Die Entführung*], able to carry out in his head the most complicated musical calculations? Did not all the contrasts of human nature converge within this one man!

Of all the quartets dedicated to Haydn, the first three were written in 1783, the fourth in 1784 and the last two in 1785.[40] They mark out the twenty-seventh year of Mozart's life decisively as the beginning of his classical period. These master-pieces of instrumental music no longer display, as do the works [*opéras*] that led up to them, a mixture of the beautiful and the mediocre, nor do they betray the vestiges of contemporary taste that time was to transform into spots of rust. Nothing in the quartets even hints at the date of their composition. Everything in them is as fresh as if written yesterday, and will remain so for evermore. All criticism is reduced to a stunned silence before these works: there is nothing that can be said about them in words, and they resist all attempts at factual analysis. All the same, I would know perfectly well how to circumvent this resistence if, as a

40 These are the quartets published in 1785 as Op. 10 nos 1–6. Their Köchel numbers and current dating are: K387 (G major), 31 December 1782 [Op. 10 no. 1]; K421/417*b* (D minor), June 1783 [Op. 10 no. 2]; K428/421*b* (E♭ major), June-July 1783 [Op. 10 no. 4]; K 458 (B♭ major, 'Hunt'), 9 November 1784 [Op. 10 no. 3]; K464 (A major), 10 January 1785 [Op. 10 no. 5]; K465 (C major, 'Dissonance'), 14 January 1785 [Op. 10 no. 6].

contributor to some musical journal paid so much a page, I had to give a detailed account of the quartets of Mozart. There is a formula for the production of such articles. First comes the key of the movement, then the tempo and time signature; then its aesthetic character, indicated by an epithet or two, selected at random if suitable words do not come to mind; a phrase of melody here, a bit of the bass line there are picked out and quoted. Then, if the *maestro critico* has a touch of the learned about him, he identifies for your benefit the species of double counterpoint by which the thematic materials are combined and inverted in the course of the composition, he pinpoints for you the pairs of suspect fifths, the questionable octaves, any badly constructed chords, any awkward intervallic movement and so forth.[41] None of this is at all difficult to write; {25} but of what value is it to the reader? What does it say to him that he cannot learn just as well, indeed infinitely better, for himself by a simple inspection of the music? What is there in common between the grammatical framework that is presented to him and the intimate meaning conveyed by the work itself? It is as if in examining a poem one were to limit oneself solely to the mechanics of the verse structure, leaving aside subject-matter, ignoring the ideas in the poet's mind. Confronted with many a piece of music, criticism could do no better; it is reduced to choosing between sterile analysis and silence, unless it prefers to resort to the style of nonsense verse.

Let us open at random the pages of the quartets that we are supposed to be looking at in detail. Chance has served us well, for what lies open before us is the Andante of No. 4 in E♭ major [K428/421b]. What will criticism make of this? It will say that it is an Andante con moto in A♭ major, 6/8; that it is full of syncopations, suspensions and points of imitation; a skilfully constructed movement, with a tinge of mysticism, surprising in effect – and that is all that could be said factually. But to what state of mind, real or imagined, mirroring the present or portending the future, is one to attribute the impression that the movement gives? To a dream, a trance, a state of ecstasy? Does it come from some irresistible clairvoyance which has the power to alter our perception of things and to take over our senses? Or is it the beginning of some regeneration in which the dimensions of time and space are about to disappear? An elusive theme, devoid of phrases or contours, floats in the harmony, percolating through it like a fluid stream of melody. Slipping from one voice to another, it leaves a long misty trail behind it as it forsakes a voice; and in so doing it constantly renews itself, engendering as it combines with other figures a {26} succession of opalescent images, of drifting shadow-plays, in which the mind thinks to see portrayed all manner of unknown things that it has dreamed or sensed in some confused way. From the heart of

---

41 If Italian, maybe Giuseppe Sarti (1729–1802) is intended: he criticized the quartets in C, K465, and D minor, K421/417b, for their barbarities in an undated and now lost manuscript allegedly entitled *Esame acustico fatto sopra due frammenti di Mozart*, referred to in 'Nachrichten von Manuscripten' (*AmZ*, 26 (1824), col.540), and excerpted as 'Auszug aus dem Sarti'schen Manuscripte, worin Mozart bitter getadelt wird' (*AmZ*, 34 (1832), cols. 373–8), the same material appearing in 'Sarti *versus* Mozart', *The Harmonicon*, 10 (1832), 243–6; see W. J. Mitchell, 'Giuseppe Sarti and Mozart's Quartet K421', *Current Musicology*, 9 (1969), 147–53; and Vertrees, 'Mozart's String Quartet K.465', 96–8, 107–09. However, the formula that Ulïbïshev sets out here hardly matches the surviving fragments of Sarti's criticisms, nor the analyses of Gottfried Weber (Analysis 10) or Fétis (see note 19 above). These remarks seem closer to criticisms made later by Kretzschmar: see vol. II, General Introduction, §8.

this twilight harmonic world, peopled with arcane ghostly apparitions, a profound questioning surges upwards from time to time, accompanied by a sort of moaning, as if the soul were struggling mightily to break the spell that binds it and prevents it from reaching a conscious perception of what it sees indistinctly. The underlying metre conflicts with the displacements in the surface rhythm. The slurred and accented quavers on the lower strings of the cello [*basse*] murmur in the ear like silence itself; the numerous suspensions which deprive the melody of its characteristic contours and detract from the natural clarity of the chords have the effect of obliterating visible objects. All is calm and peaceful; outwardly all is at rest. The vision is sheer intuition. What a movement! Beethoven, the great explorer of the soul's enigmas, could never himself have conceived of anything more supernaturally true, more divinely mystical.

I like to think that the reader will have understood me. In trying to analyse music that is pure and transcendent I have sought to prove the impossibility of such an analysis. I wanted to show how with the best will in the world the humble critic risks lapsing into nonsense when he tries to put into words feelings and images that are by their nature for ever inexpressible. Moreover, it has always seemed to me that the arsenal of literary ultra-romantic jargon was powerless in the face of musical effects, a sterile and ill-conceived attempt on the part of verbal language to say something without the assistance of logical ideas, as the language of sounds succeeds in doing. But how can we, who as a matter of course translate this untranslatable idiom that is called music, {27} always avoid the balderdash [*galimatias*] so freely used by our esteemed novelists and poets, no need though they have to resort to it? Having said that once and for all, we dare to pride ourselves on the stylistic difficulties inherent in music criticism, as if we had a rightful claim to clemency on the part of the reader.

It would be as well to remind ourselves that what has been said in the present article concerns specifically the six string quartets dedicated to Haydn. Those that Mozart composed earlier in his life do not belong among his classical works; and those that were commissioned from him in 1789 by the King of Prussia,[42] beautiful as all three are, notably the first in D major which is sheer delight, depart somewhat from the theoretical requirements of the quartet *travaillé*. We no longer find in them music that is utterly pure. A cello part that sings in the alto register and plays in concertante style with the first violin, leaving the viola to provide the function of the bass line in its absence, introduces into these works an ingredient contrary to the laws of the genre that we have been at pains to define. The solo element subverts the ensemble, the brilliant cantilenas and passage-work run counter to the psychologico-rational development of the thematic materials. In this way, the primary purpose is at time sacrificed to secondary concerns; and as a result the quartets dedicated to His Majesty the King of Prussia appear weak in style and harmonically a little thin when compared with the masterly and sublime works with which Haydn alone was worthy to be paid homage. For it was he alone, among all living people, who was sufficiently in advance of his time to appreciate his young rival, and magnanimous enough to admit himself vanquished.

---

42   K575 (D major), June 1789; K589 (B♭ major), May 1790; K590 (F major), June 1790.

Four essays on the styles of Beethoven's music

(a) Johann Aloys Schlosser (c.1790–?)
     'Urtheile über Beethoven's Werke'

     Ludwig van Beethoven: eine Biographie (1828)

(b) François-Joseph Fétis (1784–1871)
     'Beethoven (Louis van)'

     Biographie universelle des musiciens (1837)

(c) Wilhelm von Lenz (1809–1883)
     'Les trois styles de Beethoven'

     Beethoven et ses trois styles (1852)

(d) Alexander Dmitryevich Ulïbïshev (1794–1858)
     'Les trois manières de Beethoven'

     Beethoven, ses critiques et ses glossateurs (1857)

The notion that Beethoven's musical output forms three distinctive, largely consecutive temporal categories is one that we find in many writers over a period of some thirty years after Beethoven's death, notably Schlosser in 1828, Fétis in 1837, Schindler in 1840, von Lenz in 1852 and Ulïbïshev in 1857. We might suppose that these men shared a single method of classification, based on a common view of the composer's career. The truth is somewhat more complex. There are three distinct paradigms at work in the writings of these five men, represented in purest form by Schindler, von Lenz and Ulïbïshev.

Anton Felix Schindler (1795–1865) had been Beethoven's amanuensis and friend for many years, and at the composer's death had acquired conversation books and letters which, together with his own reminiscences, formed the basis of his *Biography of Ludwig van Beethoven*, the first edition of which was published in 1840.[1] Schindler had opted to divide this work into three 'periods' (*Perioden*), the first extending from Beethoven's birth to 1800, the second from the onset of troubles with his brothers and the early signs of deafness to October 1813, and

---

1   Anton Schindler, *Biographie von Ludwig van Beethoven* (Münster: Aschendorff, 1840, 2/1845; Eng. trans. Ignace Moscheles, London: Colburn, 1841).

the third from the scandal over Maelzel to his death in 1827 – uneven time-periods which, perhaps by chance, produced roughly equal numbers of opuses.[2] Schindler made no attempt to analyse Beethoven's musical style, or to categorize it by intrinsic criteria: 'I follow here', he declared, 'a scheme of division derived not from the course of [Beethoven's] spiritual development, but purely from the various phases of his life as Beethoven himself had observed them'.[3] The association of individual works with 'first period', 'second period' and 'third period' (the labels most commonly used nowadays to classify Beethoven's output) was therefore purely mechanical, and the result an entirely clean compartmentalization of the works into three exclusive periods which presented no problems of stylistic definition.

Wilhelm von Lenz's *Beethoven and his Three Styles* of 1852 represents the second of our paradigms in its purest form. Von Lenz relegated external biography to a passive role, assigning himself a very specific task: 'To orient the music lover within Beethoven's *œuvre*, complex as it is'.[4] His is a developmental account of Beethoven's output: the works are treated as manifestations of a dynamic inner growth. He charted this growth in three phases, calling them, significantly, not 'periods', but 'styles' or 'manners'. He was careful to detach these phases as far as possible from temporal categories. As he said of the composer: 'There are within him three Beethovens, very different from one other.' Von Lenz conceptualizes these as 'the different directions that his mind took' and 'the *layers* [*assises*] of his output' – both epithets that avoid strictly temporal associations. Not that the three manners are completely synchronous: the word *assise* denotes a 'course of bricks' in bricklaying, and so conveys an image of successive construction (as it does too of upward and cumulative progression); an *enchaînement* ('linkage') exists between the manners, which 'influence' one another and in themselves constitute 'major transformations of his genius'. However, the sequentiality that these epithets imply is not purely one of chronological time. It exists as an independent construct – a construct that occupies Beethoven's life-span and yet does not precisely match the series of external events that constitute his career.

It matches, rather, the life of the mind and spirit. It should not surprise us, then, that the Sonatina in G Op. 79, though written in 1809, is assigned to the first style, or that, whereas the *Eroica* Symphony Op. 55 written (in von Lenz's view) in 1802–04, is a late manifestation of the first manner, the Piano Sonata in A♭ Op. 26 and the String Quintet Op. 29, written (again in his view) in 1802, were pure instances of the second manner. Nor were works necessarily to be assigned wholly to a single style: as we see in the analysis of the Sonata in F Op. 10

2   Schindler rewrote his biography in the late 1850s (Münster: Aschendorff, 1860; trans. and ed. D. W. McArdle as *Beethoven as I Knew Him*, London: Faber, 1966). Shifting his period divisions by a few months, the first back, the second forward, resulted in markedly unbalanced reallocation of works to periods (now in the form of lists): I, Opp. 1–15; II, broadly Opp. 16–93; III, broadly Opp. 90–127. By this time, he was familiar with the work of Fétis, von Lenz and Ulibishev, and betrays influence from their notions of style (e.g. pp. 110–11). Several works (notably the Seventh and Eighth Symphonies and the 'Archduke' Trio) now appeared in both the second and the third periods, so blurring his original compartmentalization.
3   *Biographie* (1840), pp. 9–10.
4   Wilhelm von Lenz, *Beethoven et ses trois styles*, ed. M. D. Calvocoressi (Paris: Legouix, 1909; reprint edn with Foreword by Joseph Kerman, New York: Da Capo, 1980), p. 4.

no. 2, dating from 1796/7 and given as Analysis 3 in vol. II of the present collection, the first and third movements are in the first manner, whereas the second movement 'belongs already to the second manner, the grand manner'.

Whereas Schindler's tripartite division of the works, then, is governed by biographical events, and is chronologically contained, that of von Lenz charts the inner life of the composer and invokes intrinsic criteria, the first manner recording Beethoven's apprenticeship, the second the achievement of independence, the third his reaching of full maturity – or from a Romantic perspective, the first representing his dependency upon Mozart's compositional world, the second his emancipation from that world and achievement of liberty, naturalness and individuality, the third his emancipation from the human compositional world as a whole and the attainment (reinforced by his deafness) of a transcendent, mystical state.[5]

The third paradigm is exemplified by Ulïbïshev. It embodies two counteractive processes: ascent and decline, or growth and decay. To Ulïbïshev, Beethoven achieved perfection with the String Quintet Op. 29, the Second Symphony, the Third Piano Concerto and a small handful of other works – 'ravishing or sublime creations in which Beethoven's genius reaches its apogée'. From 1804 (by Ulïbïshev's chronology), decadence began to set in: with the Kreutzer Sonata Op. 47, the 'Waldstein' Sonata Op. 53, the *Eroica* Symphony Op. 55 and above all the 'Rasumovsky' Quartets Op. 59, as the first to be tainted. In these, over-indulgence of ideas led to disproportionate musical forms, originality tended to the bizarre, and the rules of harmonic and rhythmic grammar were transgressed. For several years more, Beethoven produced 'the finest models of instrumental music'; but, while the symphonies remained 'melodious throughout, clear-textured, and free and grandiose in style' as far as the Eighth, the sonatas and quartets exhibited 'ever more complicated construction, increasingly frequent use of the polyphonic style [. . .] and the impoverishment of melody'. Beyond Op. 90, these became endemic, leading to the drying-up of melody, and to procedures so obscure as to amount to a state of enigma.[6]

Thus, the two counteractive processes that Ulïbïshev perceives ultimately describe three periods: the first, in which the initial process of growth, governed by the style of Haydn and Mozart, held sway; the second, a ten-year period during which the two processes competed, with decay gradually taking hold; the third, a period of decadence in which Beethoven surrendered himself to an ideal music that lost touch with all reality, and to 'mystical ideas fused with the hallucinations of deafness', save for rare moments of lucidity, as in the instrumental movements of the Ninth Symphony and the Sonata Op. 111. At the same time, Ulïbïshev adumbrates a *fourth* period, comprising the late quartets alone, a music of pure chimera, or rather a 'non-music'.[7]

In the light of these three paradigms, the classifications of Schlosser and Fétis – for all that they precede the three examples in time – emerge as hybrids. Unlike

5   ibid, 235–6.
6   Alexander Ulïbïshev, *Beethoven, ses critiques et ses glossateurs* (Leipzig: F. A. Brockhaus; Paris: Jules Gavelot, 1857), pp. 132, 160, 163–4.
7   ibid, 277, 284–5, 288.

Schindler's treatment of the creative output, that of Schlosser is centred on the music, and is style-critical in nature. Nevertheless, its place lies within a biography (a 'worthless and error-filled' one, according to Solomon[8]), it follows directly on from the life, and it is itself based on chronology, speaking in terms of 'periods' as much as of 'styles'. It envisages 'critical moments' at which changes in the prevailing style occur; periods are thus discrete compartments of time, hence artistic life is seen as a linear progression. However, while coexistence of styles is consequently not allowed for, nor even transitional phases introduced, 'reversion to an earlier period', because mentally linear, is conceded. The entire process is teleological in that it moves towards the organic wholeness that Schlosser finds in the third period, and as a result, there is no question of late-period decadence.

Fétis's discussion is also coupled with a biographical account. Whether Fétis knew Schlosser's biography when writing his article on Beethoven is not clear, though he furnished a biographical article on him later in his *Universal Biographical Dictionary of Musicians*. That Fétis's account was familiar to von Lenz and Ulïbïshev is undoubted, and his influence on both of them is manifest.

His treatment of Beethoven's works embraces elements of all three paradigms. It is chronologically framed, in that no work is assigned to more than one manner. On the other hand, works are said to look forward to the next period or manner (notably the String Quintet Op. 29, the Violin Sonatas Op. 30 and the Piano Sonatas Op. 31 to the second manner, and the Seventh Symphony and the 'Archduke' Trio to the third), and the course of Beethoven's development is said to be a 'continual transformation'. Unmistakeably overlaid upon this is the growth–decay paradigm. In one sense, Beethoven found his own voice in the second period, freeing himself from the model of Haydn and Mozart; in another sense, however, Beethoven's artistic development advanced healthily and constructively until, from 1811 onwards, the composer's tendency to shut himself off from the outside world brought a mysticism and excess to his music that incurred an irreversible loss of coherence.

The conservative French critic Pierre Scudo (1806–64), noting that all of Beethoven's biographers had divided the composer's works into three categories, gave paradigmatic status to Fétis's hybrid model, in a broad-ranging essay from 1850 that took as its starting-point the 'Moonlight' Sonata Op. 27 no. 2 in C♯ minor:[9]

> These three *manners*, so the learned [biographers] tell us, can be observed in all men of genius save those who, like Tasso, Raphael and Mozart, died too young. They are the outward manifestation of the three broad periods incessantly traversed by the human spirit before reaching the fatal bourne: youth, maturity and decline [*décadence*]. During the first period, man gets up his courage, and makes his first sorties into the battles of life under the watchful eye of his mother; then he blossoms gloriously, lit by the fire of his passions; finally he diminishes and dies. These are the three ages of the world, of which the poets speak. For men dedicated to the pursuit of beauty, of the golden age, it is the age of love, of sublime and holy passion, that attains its full flood only *nel mezzo del cammin di nostra vita*.

8   Maynard Solomon, *Beethoven* (New York: Schirmer, 1977), p. x.
9   Pierre Scudo, 'Une sonate de Beethoven', *Revue des deux mondes*, 20/8 (1 October 1850), 77–97, esp. 92. The final phrase 'vers le milieu *di nostra vita*' is patently a reference to Dante's *Divine Comedy*, Inferno, 1.1.

Of other writers who adopted a threefold categorization, including an anonymous writer as early as 1818,[10] that by C. T. Seiffert is perhaps worth quoting for its concern with form.[11] Seiffert, in 1843, classified the sonatas and symphonies each into three 'divisions' (*Abtheilungen*), defining the sonatas as follows:[12]

FIRST DIVISION
Sonatas in which the conventional form is mostly adhered to, the first movement thus remaining fiery and dazzling, the second movement gentle, plaintive, etc., the third jesting [*scherzend*], the fourth cheerful and engaging. [Opp. 2 nos 2 and 3; 7; 10 nos 2 and 3; 14 nos 1 and 2; and most of the violin sonatas]

SECOND DIVISION
Sonatas in which, again, the form is adhered to, but a certain underlying feeling is present that runs through the whole, and so binds the individual sections together. [Opp. 22; 31 nos 1 and 3; 27 no. 2; 28; 53; 26; 81a; 90]

THIRD DIVISION
Sonatas in which is expressed exclusively longing for the infinite, inner strivings and struggles with one's lot, states of mind similar to those that Goethe has portrayed poetically in his *Faust*. [Opp. 2 no. 1; 10 no. 1; 13; 31 no. 2; 57]

Seiffert regarded Op. 90 as 'to all intents and purposes the end of Beethoven's sonatas. The later ones no longer breathe the wealth of poetry; they are more the results of premeditation and cogitation.'

For Adolf Bernhard Marx, whose *Ludwig van Beethoven: Life and Creative Output* was published in 1859, the classification of Beethoven's styles was a creation of an essentially French attitude of mind. Schlosser and Seiffert were unknown to him or disregarded; that Fétis was Belgian, and von Lenz and Ulïbïshev were Russians, was immaterial: all three had imbibed the intellectual attitudes of the Romance countries epitomized by France in the age of rationalism. Underlying his remarks is the Germanic perception of the Frenchman as elegant, witty, articulate and ultimately superficial, and the German, for all his relative inarticulateness, as profound, and as possessing 'culture'.

To Marx, the progressive advancement of Beethoven's artistic development was axiomatic, but it derived from the deeply felt consciousness of the artist's high calling, rather than from any notion of styles being outgrown and others acquired. Marx delivered a tirade against all who divided Beethoven's advancement into 'periods'. He disparaged Fétis in particular for 'viewing Beethoven from the narrow-minded perspective of the French, like trying to apply logarithms as if they were regular numbers' and the 'Frenchified' Ulïbïshev for endorsing Fétis's ideas 'while not knowing the first thing about German character or art'. Of Ulïbïshev's

10 'Ludwig van Beethoven', *Janus*, 2 (1818), 10, reported in Jean Boyer, *Le 'romantisme' de Beethoven* (Paris, 1938), pp. 191–2. The second period corresponds to Opp. 40–60.
11 Joseph Kerman and Maynard Solomon have studied the classification of Beethoven's styles in greater detail than can be done here (Kerman, Foreword to the 1980 edn of von Lenz, pp. v–xiv; Solomon, 'The Creative Periods of Beethoven', *Music Review*, 34 (1973), 30–38; reprinted in *Beethoven Essays* (Cambridge, MA: Harvard University Press, 1988), pp. 116–25, 323–6; also Kerman and Alan Tyson, 'Beethoven, Ludwig van', §11 'The "Three Periods"', in *NGDM*, reprinted as *The New Grove Beethoven* (London: Macmillan, 1983), chap. 2/1, pp. 89–91).
12 C. T. Seiffert, 'Characteristik der Beethoven'schen Sonaten und Symphonien', *AmZ*, 45 (1843), cols. 417–20, 433–8, 449–52, 465–9.

superimposition of three styles upon two, he remarks: 'the French outlook, bereft of idealism as it is, could not think otherwise'. Von Lenz, for all his higher sense of purpose, failed to divest himself of an outmoded view of musical form as 'something opposed to content, as at best a framework [*Spalier*], with the aid of which the teacher trains would-be infant composers to run for the first time'. Marx concluded:[13]

> Ironically, von Lenz's failure to probe more deeply [into the nature of form] proves a handicap, for his periodization is just so many lifeless compartments, forced barbarically and intrusively into a flow of life that is constant and unbroken, just as he himself visualizes art forms. Any other periodization would have met the same fate: life resists (as Lenz should have learned from the theory of form) every external intervention.

Of Schlosser, nothing is known save Fétis's report that he was born in Lann, in Bohemia, *c*.1790, and that in the same year as his Beethoven biography, 1828, he also wrote a biography of Mozart.

François-Joseph Fétis is remembered today mostly by music historians, and largely for one work: his *Universal Biographical Dictionary of Musicians and General Bibliography of Music*. First published in eight volumes between 1833 and 1844, enlarged and revised by Fétis himself in 1860–65 in the form that remains a standard reference tool to the present day; and subsequently reissued many times and supplemented by other writers, it is commonly dubbed 'unreliable' and 'biased', yet remains an indispensable source.[14] It is from the article on Beethoven in this work that the passage below is taken. As librarian of the Paris Conservatory between 1826 and 1830, and owner of a personal library of fabulous proportions, Fétis was well placed to amass the information that he needed for his dictionary. Moreover, as founding director of the Brussels Conservatory from 1833 to 1871, he exerted a powerful influence upon the world of music education. Historians of music theory know him as a thinker of considerable originality. His *Treatise on Counterpoint and Fugue* (1824) was commissioned as the textbook for the Paris Conservatory alongside Simon Catel's *Treatise on Harmony* (1802).[15] In his *Outline History of Harmony* (1840), Fétis adumbrated a new theory of 'tonality' (*tonalité*), which he then developed in his *Complete Treatise on the Theory and Practice of Harmony* (1844),[16] in which he defined the stylistic phases

13 Adolf Bernhard Marx, *Ludwig van Beethoven: Leben und Schaffen* (Berlin: Janke, 1859), vol. I, pp. 34–5.
14 *Biographie universelle des musiciens et bibliographie générale de la musique* (Brussels: Leroux; Paris: H. Fournier, 1833–44; enlarged 1860–65, 1873–75, suppl. 1878–80, ed. A. Pougin; reprint edn Brussels: Editions Culture et Civilisation, 1972).
15 By Cherubini, then its director (1822–42). *Traité du contrepoint et de la fugue, contenant l'exposé analytique des règles de la composition musicale* (Paris: Ozu, 1824; enlarged 1846). Catel's *Traité de l'harmonie* (Paris: Conservatoire de Musique, 1802), adopted in 1802 as a bulwark against Rameau's theories, was replaced by Antoine Reicha's *Cours de composition musicale ou Traité complet et raisonné d'harmonie pratique* (see Analysis 2 above) in 1817, but reinstated by Cherubini (see Renate Groth, *Die französische Kompositionslehre des 19. Jahrhunderts*, Beihefte zum Archiv für Musikwissenschaft, vol. XII (Wiesbaden: Franz Steiner, 1983), pp. 7–11).
16 *Esquisse de l'histoire de l'harmonie considérée comme art et comme science systématique* (Paris: Bourgogne et Martinet, 1840; Eng. trans. M. I. Marvin, PhD diss., Indiana University, 1972); *Traité complet de la théorie et de la pratique de l'harmonie contenant la doctrine de la science et de l'art* (Paris: Schlesinger, 1844; enlarged 1849). The term *tonalité* was previously used by Alexandre Étienne Choron (1771–1834) in his *Méthode élèmentaire de composition . . .* (Paris: Courcier,

of Western music history as 'unitonic', 'transitonic', 'pluritonic' and 'omnitonic', and offered many keen insights into the nature of tonality.

Wilhelm von Lenz, born and educated in Riga, was by profession a civil servant, based in St Petersburg; but his consuming passions were the music of Beethoven and the world of pianism. He claimed acquaintance with many of the major piano virtuosi of his day: Moscheles and Liszt (with both of whom he studied), Field, Hummel, Kalkbrenner, Chopin, Tausig and Henselt. He published a set of verbal portraits of four of these in 1872.[17] Cosmopolitan, multi-lingual, he espoused the musical culture of Germany while disparaging that of France (with the exception of Berlioz). It was Ulïbïshev's *New Biography of Mozart*, of 1843 (see Analysis 15 above), with its attack on Beethoven's symphonies for their exaggeration, incongruities and harmonic transgression and their immoderate length, that prompted von Lenz, after nine years of careful preparation, to produce his second and most important book, *Beethoven and his Three Styles* (1852), in which he launched a reasoned counter-attack, tracing the history of Beethoven's mind and artistic thought, for the first time through the medium of the music rather than through a fabric of reminiscences and reports. Berlioz praised the book in fulsome terms perhaps tinged with irony.[18] Von Lenz did what he had chided Ulïbïshev for failing to do with Mozart. He painstakingly gathered factual information concerning the music and compiled a 100-page critical catalogue of all Beethoven's works as a basis for the proper study of the music. The fact that he was upstaged by Breitkopf and Härtel's published catalogue of 1851, and that it was soon to be superseded by Thayer's catalogue of 1865 and Nottebohm's thematic catalogue of 1868 does not dimish the stature and intelligence of his achievement. He later expanded his book into a five-volume work in German.[19]

When he saw von Lenz's counter-attack, Ulïbïshev (for biographical information, see the Introduction to Analysis 15 above), inflamed by von Lenz's remarks, threw himself into the five-year task of producing *Beethoven, His Critics and His Glossators* in 1857. He imputed to von Lenz a less than perfect knowledge of both French and music – 'two things which are not without value when one is analysing the works of a composer in French', and hinted at von Lenz's technical incompetence.

1814) and was included in F. H. J. Castil-Blaze's *Dictionnaire de musique moderne* (Paris: Magasin de musique de la Lyre moderne, 1821); see Groth, *Die französische Kompositionslehre*, pp. 58–63, and Bryan Simms, 'Choron, Fétis, and the Theory of Tonality', *JMT*, 19 (1975), 112–28.

17   *Die grossen Pianoforte-Virtuosen unserer Zeit aus persönlicher Bekanntschaft: Liszt, Chopin, Tausig, Henselt* (Berlin: Behr, 1872; Eng. trans., New York: Schirmer, 1899, reprint edn London: Regency, 1971).

18   Hector Berlioz, *Les soirées de l'orchestre* (Paris: Lévy, 1852; Eng. trans. J. Barzun, New York: Knopf, 1956, 2/1973), pp. 315–26.

19   *Beethoven: eine Kunststudie*, vols. I–II (Kassel: Balde, 1855); III–V: *Kritische Katalog sämtlicher Werke Ludwig van Beethovens mit Analysen derselben* (Hamburg: Hoffmann & Campe, 1860).

(a) Johann Aloys Schlosser
'Critical Assessment of Beethoven's Works'

Source:
Ludwig van Beethoven: eine Biographie desselben, verbunden mit Urtheilen über seine Werke (Prague: Buchler, Stephani & Schlosser, 1828), pp. 79–85.

I shall refrain here from enumerating Beethoven's[20] works individually, since they are to be found cited in the catalogues of the various music dealers. More to my purpose here is to make a critical assessment of these works and to gauge their value.

In the life of every great artist certain periods can be discerned through which of necessity that artist must pass, drawn along as he is by the flood-tide of a natural force which evolves immutably in accordance with fixed laws. To be sure, great artists occasionally do emerge apparently fully formed from the very beginning; but in reality such men have kept themselves to themselves during their formative period, and in this way their true beginnings have been hidden from public view. Then there are those whose style alters with the {80} materials at hand,[21] in such a way that the process of change is always linked to their spiritual development. This last is especially true of Goethe,[22] whose artistic career has proceeded in an unbroken circle, describing the entire circumference of one individual's human creative powers.

Thus we confront the task of charting for Beethoven's[23] career the critical moments through which he inevitably had to pass if he was ultimately to emerge fully formed in his own individual perfection. The establishment of the periods of his life cannot rest solely on the successive numbering of his works, for many a work was composed early in life which was not published till much later. Nor can such a categorization aspire to mathematical precision, for that would be to place music, which is an outpouring of artistic freedom, into an alien and injurious environment.

Beethoven's[24] genius manifested itself for the first time in three Trios [Op. 1] for fortepiano, violin {81} and cello. There is about these trios a pleasing quality which is extraordinarily deeply inspired but which has not yet quite found its true and right outlet. It is precisely on this account that some have complained – and not without justification – of disorder in this work and that which followed it. This music, as well as that of the later works, gives ample evidence of the inexhaustible surging of Beethoven's heart towards that new world which he was subsequently

---

20 *Beethoven*: spaced type.
21 *mit dem Stoffe*: lit. 'with the raw material'. It is unclear whether this refers to the musical substance or to the circumstance and subject-matter of a piece.
22 *Goethe*: spaced type.
23 *Beethoven*: spaced type.
24 *Beethoven*: spaced type.

to conquer. At first, by his very nature he was incapable of working with ideas on other than a grand scale [*in grossen . . . Massen*], ideas which were not always clearly delineated or sharply distinguished. Nevertheless, he aroused great expectations in the minds of the connoisseurs, especially on grounds of the sustained melody [*Gesang*] to be found in his allegros and also in his exquisitely beautiful adagios. In view of the sublime and passionate style of his works, requiring as it does a sense of grand proportions and a high degree of involvement on the part of the performer, it was only natural that he should demand more than the usual from his instruments. The style of keyboard writing had {82} by his time been extended through the addition of several happy effects, and to these Beethoven[25] in turn contributed – for instance, through the unconventional use of widely spaced harmony[26] with spread chords in his keyboard writing, to cite but one instance. For the rest, the works of this and the following period are reminiscent of the form made pre-eminent by Haydn and Mozart, albeit Beethoven,[27] although under the influence of these composers, was striving continuously to attain independent clarity of thought. To this period belong his world-famous Sextet,[28] and also the two symphonies [No. 1] in C and [No. 2] in D and the six[29] String Quartets Op. 18. At the same time, all manner of foretastes of the later period abound, as is inevitable with so tirelessly questing an artistic development.

The works that span Opp. 40–60 form a sort of transition. This is not wholly without digression, of course – {83} there are occasional reversions to the earlier period – on the whole, however, it is the later period which predominates to a telling extent. The *Eroica* Symphony[30] will serve to represent this period and to endorse the view just expressed. In general, the period is marked by a profound seriousness which is nonetheless capable of turning into boisterous jollity now and then as the composer, overtaken by an irresistible impulse, erupts into brilliant and mischievous mockery. One might almost call it musical humour. The character of several works from this time seems to point, if conjecture may be allowed here, to a condition of mind marked by something quite exceptional [. . .]

The Fifth Symphony resoundingly proclaims Beethoven's[31] arrival at the threshold of the third period. Indeed, in its blend of {84} retrospective and prophetic tones it chronicles the inner life of the composer. It begins with an

25 *Beethoven*: spaced type.
26 'of widely spaced harmony': *der zerstreuten Harmonie*.

> When [. . .] the notes of the chords comprising the harmonic fabric lie so far apart from each other that between the upper voice and the inner voices lie notes that are fundamental to the chords [. . .], the harmony is said to be *zerstreut*, or the chords are said to be in *zerstreuter Harmonie*. If, by contrast, the notes of the chords [. . .] lie so close to one another that no chord constituents can occur between them, then the chords are used in *enger Harmonie*. [. . .] In thoroughbass, the chords are usually taken in *enger Harmonie*, since the span of the hand does not permit the use of chords in widely spaced harmony. (H.C. Koch, *Musikalisches Lexikon* (Frankfurt a/M: Hermann, 1802; reprint edn Hildesheim: Olms, 1964), 1757–8)

27 *Haydn, Mozart, Beethoven*: spaced type.
28 It is unclear whether the E♭ Sextet for two horns and strings, Op. 81b (?1795), is intended, or the E♭ Wind Sextet Op. 71 (1796) – neither published until 1810; or even perhaps the E♭ Septet for wind and strings, Op. 20 (1799–1800) – published in 1802.
29 six: 16.
30 *Eroica Symphony*: Roman type.
31 *Beethoven*: spaced type.

impetuous Allegro, the seriousness of which, full of foreboding, sets the underlying tone of a life of energetic purpose. The wistful sorrow of the Andante which
follows is relieved, as the music turns its gaze full of hope out into infinity. In the
ensuing Allegro, fate's storm can be heard breaking in, until at the onset of the
Finale all earthly burdens fall away and the victorious spirit soars into the sun-
filled transparent ether of eternal freedom.

The works of this last period are characterized by an inner compulsion. Features
that arise are always intrinsically prepared and determined by those that precede
them, such that any possibility of fortuitous, wayward or alien elements is excluded,
and the whole, in its well-regulated inner coherence, achieves a vigorous unity. In
just the same way, the fruit springs {85} from the blossom, and the blossom itself
from the burgeoning, totally controlled germination of the tree. Herein lies the
secret, the law of every single life-form, be it in nature or in art. Beethoven obeys
a controlling force which regulates right down to the smallest detail; and precisely
because of this he exhausts the possibilities of a theme – even sometimes a conventional and perfectly trivial theme – in the production of what many people
who have neither the intelligence nor the sensibility to appreciate readily overlook:
purely and simply, an artistic form fully articulated in its own right. Beethoven is
to be likened to Goethe[32] in that the latter, too, sometimes follows[33] the inspiration
of a less-than-portentous moment, and that he like Beethoven brings to bear on
the realization of the work that selfsame primal guiding spirit,[34] right down to the
very last detail.

So much for Beethoven's[35] works as a whole.

32 *Goethe*: spaced type.
33 At the time that Schlosser was writing (1828), Goethe (1749–1832) was still alive; *Wilhelm
Meisters Wanderjahre* was not quite complete, and Part II of *Faust* was yet to be published,
posthumously, in 1832.
34 'primal guiding spirit': *Urgeist*.
35 *Beethoven*: spaced type.

(b) François-Joseph Fétis
[The three periods of Beethoven's music]

'Beethoven (Louis van)', *Universal Biographical Dictionary of Musicians*

Source:
Biographie universelle des musiciens et bibliographie générale de la musique, vol. II (Brussels: Meline, Cans, 1837), pp. 109–12.

{109b} The works of Beethoven can be classified into several categories, each marking a phase in the continual transformation of his genius. At first, as an enthusiastic admirer of Mozart, he could not free himself from the consequences of this admiration – consequences which are always apparent in the most original of men and those best equipped for creativity. I refer to the young artist's propensity for imitating the forms that he has chosen, consciously or unconsciously, as his model of perfection. Originality of ideas, when accompanied by judgment and integrity, cries out for self-expression in intelligible forms. Now, the ability to create new forms and to apprehend them effortlessly comes only as the fruit of {110a} experience, whereas the conceiving of an idea is a product of instinct. Such intuitive invention can never result in a lasting work if form does not lend its support and thus experience turn it to good account. If personal experience is not there, then one has to avail oneself of the experience of a master. That is what Mozart did when he took C. P. E. Bach as his model in his earliest piano compositions and Hasse in his dramatic music. And this is what Beethoven, in his turn, did when he trod in the footsteps of Mozart.

Consequently, despite the undeniable originality of his ideas, the Piano Trios Op. 1, the solo piano sonatas Opp. 2, 7 and 10, the Violin Sonatas Op. 12, the string trios Opp. 3, 8 and 9, and the String Quartets Op. 18 are reminiscent of the style of Mozart in their form and construction, although signs of individuality do make themselves increasingly felt as Op. 18 approaches. In the C major Symphony [No. 1] Op. 21 this individuality comes alive. Already the Scherzo of this symphony has an imaginative quality that is pure Beethoven. The richness of the composer's imagination, asserting itself even more energetically, shines through the String Quintet Op. 29 and the lovely Violin Sonatas (Op. 30).[36] The Symphony [No. 2] in D Op. 36 is a work less noteworthy for its originality of

36   2/1860 interpolates at this point:

> Beethoven has expanded the solo piano sonata to immense proportions. He has brought to it the genius of the symphony, and has made an orchestra out of the one instrument. From among the finest sonatas of these three periods [*époques*] – sonatas for piano, either solo or with violin – the following can be singled out as works of the very highest stature: the Sonata in D major Op. 10 [no. 3], the Sonata *Pathétique* in C minor Op. 13, those in C♯ minor Op. 27 [no. 2] and in D minor Op. 31 [no. 2], the Violin Sonata in A major Op. 47 (dedicated to Kreutzer), the solo sonatas in C major Op. 53, in F minor Op. 57, *Les adieux* in E♭ major Op. 81[a] and finally in B♭ major Op. 106.

ideas than for the quality of its construction, which is on a very grand scale. It is
in this symphony that there can be detected for the first time that marvellous
feeling for the placing of instruments which from then on gives his symphonies a
colouring [*coloris*] so varied, so vigorous and so brilliant.

But it is especially in the Third Symphony, the *Eroica*, Op. 55, that the composer's genius is revealed through the sheer absoluteness of its creativity. Here, all
trace of inherited forms disappears. The composer is himself, {110b} his individuality asserts itself majestically; his work becomes the embodiment of an epoch in
the history of music. The time of conception of this work goes back to 1804.[37] It
is thoroughly German in spirit, and owes its allegiance at heart to the government
of Austria. But as a poet, as a man of imagination, Beethoven could not help
himself admiring the genius of Napoleon. He visualized him as a republican hero;
and the power vested solely in him, the disinterestedness, the unalloyed love of
homeland and liberty, made him in Beethoven's eyes a model man for modern
times. It was in this frame of mind that we believe he began his heroic symphony.
He had decided to give it the name *Bonaparte*, whatever the danger of doing such
a thing in a country where that name surely evoked memories of humiliation.[38] It
is even said that the second movement of the work was finished, and that it was
none other than the colossal opening of the last movement of the C minor
symphony, when one of his friends,[39] coming into his study one day newspaper in
hand, announced that the First Consul had just declared himself Emperor.
Stupified, Beethoven was at first struck dumb, then he shouted: 'So he is ambitious
just like the rest of them.'[40] His ideas then took a new direction. In place of the
heroic movement he substituted the funeral march which today forms the second
movement of the symphony; and instead of the simple inscription *Bonaparte* he
entered: *Sinfonia eroica per festeggiare il souvenire d'un grand uomo*. It was as if his
hero had already descended into his grave, and in place of a hymn of glory a dirge
was in order. The massive movement in C was soon to awaken in Beethoven's mind
the plan for his Symphony [No. 5] in C minor.

Beethoven's second period [*époque*], so clearly signalled by the *Eroica* Symphony,
encloses a span of about ten years {111a} during which he also wrote the symphonies in B♭ [No. 4] and C minor [No. 5] and the Pastoral Symphony [No. 6],
the lovely String Quartets Op. 59, the opera *Fidelio*, the overture to *Coriolan*, the
splendid piano sonatas in F minor [Op. 57], F♯ [Op. 78] and E minor [Op. 90],
the piano concertos in C [minor, No. 3], in G [No. 4] and in E♭ [No. 5], the Violin
Concerto, the Sextet [Op. 81b][41] and the first Mass [in C, Op. 86]. In general, all
of this music springs from a free-ranging imagination and is full of daring; but it
remains within the limits set by good taste, a true sense of fitness in harmony,
and the need for clarity of thought. The oratorio *Christus am Oelberge* belongs to

37 The drafting of the *Eroica* goes back at least well into 1803. For the arguments that it goes back
    into 1802, see R. Wade, 'Beethoven's Eroica Sketchbook', *Fontes artis musicae*, 24 (1977), 254–89.
38 2/1860 interpolates at this point, 'He wished to dedicate it to the First Consul of the French
    Republic: his dedication was already inscribed.'
39 Ferdinand Ries, who reported it in F. G. Wegeler and F. Ries, *Biographische Notizen über Ludwig
    van Beethoven* (Koblenz: Bädeker, 1838), p. 87; Eng. trans. (Arlington: Great Ocean, 1987), p. 68.
40 2/1860 continues, 'He seized the score, ripped out the first page and flung it on the floor.'
41 This was probably written much earlier, *c*.1795, but not published until 1810.

this same period, but there is a kind of awkwardness about it – an awkwardness that is often to be found in Beethoven's vocal works when he tries to use the scientific forms, and that gives this work an intangible coldness, detracting from it despite the lovely ideas with which it abounds. [. . .][42]

Beethoven apparently lived more of his time in the country after 1811 than hitherto, and gave himself over in this period to solitary walks, or to the silence of his room, and to the study of history and philosophy, with which he had had no more than a nodding acquaintance until then. He devoted himself frequently to his reading; and increasingly as time went on the artist in him felt the need to shut himself off from all contact with the outside world in an idealized state of self-sufficiency. Unconsciously, unknowingly, his philosophical[43] studies gave a faint tinge of mysticism to his ideas – a mysticism that crept into his music, as can be seen in the late quartets. Without his being aware of it, his originality lost something of its spontaneity, becoming systematic. The limits within which he had so far operated were turned inside out. He carried to excess the reiteration of the same ideas. Occasionally he pursued the development of a {111b} chosen subject to the point of incoherence. His melodic thought gradually lost its clarity as it became more and more dream-like. His harmony acquired a certain hardness [dureté], and seemed day by day to show increasing signs of a decline in his memory of how things sounded. Lastly, Beethoven affected to discover new forms, less as a result of sudden inspiration than in order to satisfy some premeditated scheme. The works that show these tendencies of mind make up the third period of his life, and his late manner.

This manner can be detected as early as the Symphony [No. 7] in A, the ['Archduke'] Piano Trio in B♭ Op. 97 and the last five piano sonatas – fine works whose qualities outweigh their defects. It reaches its culmination in the *Missa solemnis* in D, in the late overtures, in the Choral Symphony, and above all in the string quartets Opp. 127, 130, 131, 132 and 135.

As we have come to see, Beethoven's output falls into three categories, each one exhibiting its own particular tendencies of his mind. Beethoven had a low opinion of the works in the first category. He disliked people enthusing over them and genuinely believed that those who spoke highly of them were his enemies, intent only on disparaging his other works. This is a not unprecedented attitude of mind among great artists as they grow older. Whatever his opinion on this, it is nonetheless true that there are lovely things in many of the works of this first period of his artistic output.

The works of the second period are those in which the composer shows his greatest power of invention allied to the fullest possible familiarity with the perfection[44] of music. This period extends from Op. 55 [the Third Symphony] to Op. 92 [the Seventh].

At the onset of the third period, his {112a} thinking underwent a final transformation, a process which continued right through to the very last work. The

---

42   For interpolation in 2/1860 at this point, see Analysis 16d below: 'His three manners, when
       compared . . . more and more unequal as time went on'.
43   'philosophical': deleted in 2/1860.
44   'the perfection': 2/1860: 'the elegant forms'.

more he advanced along this new path, the more did he strive to introduce into music things that lie outside his domain, and the more did his sense of the essential intimacy of his art fade in his mind. From my own careful analysis of Opp. 127–135,[45] it is clear to me that in these last works the requirements of harmony had diminished in his mind in the face of considerations of a different sort. He was occasionally reproached for this towards the end of his life in criticisms that came to his notice. Allegedly he cried, wringing his hands: 'Yes, yes. They are astonished, but they understand nothing because they can find none of it in a treatise on figured bass!' At another part of his life he had energetically defended the teachings of his textbooks, and his studies[46] are full of expressions of confidence in their rules. These two totally contrary opinions stand for two opposite systems of thought, and encapsulate the entire history of the transformation of Beethoven's genius. [. . .][47]

What gives the compositions of this great man their distinctive quality is the spontaneity of the episodes by which he suspends the interest that he has aroused in these works, substituting for it another which is as vital as it is unexpected. This ability is his alone, and it is to this that his finest achievements can be attributed. These episodes, apparently alien to the first idea, initially command our attention by their originality. Then, as the effect of surprise diminishes, the composer knows just how to draw them into the unity of his plan and so bear out the fact that within the totality of a composition variety is subordinate to unity. To this rare quality Beethoven brought also his unique feeling for instrumental sonority, unlike that of any other composer. No one has the ability as well as he to *fill* the orchestra {112b} with sound, and to contrast one sonority with another. It is through this that the impact of his great works outstrips in power all that has been written before him.

Whatever differences of opinion may exist on the works of the various periods of Beethoven's life, there is one point on which everybody will eternally agree: that the works of this composer are to be counted among those of the very greatest artists, those who by their talents have contributed the most to furtherance of their art.[48]

45   'Les derniers quatuors de Beethoven', *Revue musicale*, 7 (= 2nd ser., 1), 279–86 (3 April 1830), 345–51 (17 April 1830).

46   Reference here is presumably to Beethoven's studies with Albrechtsberger in 1794–5, the exercise books of which had been edited by Ignaz Ritter von Seyfried in *Ludwig van Beethovens Studien im Generalbasse, Contrapunkt und in der Compositions-Lehre* (Vienna: Haslinger, 1832, 2/1853; reprint edn 1967; Eng. trans. 1853).

47   2/1860 continues:
       M Ulibïshev, whose taste was revulsed by the works of the last period of the great composer's life, and who provides, in his book, an analysis that is just, albeit harsh, of certain passages, does not shrink from offering an alternative cause for the aberrations of his genius. According to this, they are the product of a weakening of his faculties brought on by domestic unhappiness, and preoccupation with business matters that drove him to extreme neuroticism. Undaunted, he declares that Beethoven became prey to hallucinations. In the account that Rellstab of Berlin gives of a visit to this extraordinary man in his final years, he too expressed the opinion that his stability had been gravely undermined, and was nothing short of the degeneration of his mental equilibrium [*état primitif*].

48   2/1860 continues:
       He possessed one of those rare geniuses which dominates a whole era; and gives it a bearing which comes to characterize that art-form for that time. His attributes are grandeur, poetic

(c) Wilhelm von Lenz
'Beethoven's Three Styles'

Beethoven and his Three Styles

Source:
Beethoven et ses trois styles: analyses des sonates de piano suivies d'un essai d'un catalogue critique, chronologique et anecdotique de l'œuvre de Beethoven (St Petersburg: Bernard, 1852; Brussels: Stapleaux, 1854; Paris: Lavinié, 1855; new edn, ed. M. D. Calvocoressi, Paris: Legouix, 1909; reprint edn New York: Da Capo, 1980), pp. 52–67.

You must at some time or another have heard remarked what a composer Beethoven was, to have had the three Piano Trios Op. 1 as his first work! But we must make a distinction here. These trios are Beethoven's first *published* work, but not his first composition [. . .]. Quite the contrary: it is highly likely that with the exception of the String Quartets [Op. 18] the bulk of the compositions that comprise Opp. 1–18 were already in existence by the time that the trios were published. We exclude the string quartets from this because if Beethoven had indeed produced these works – works of major importance which ushered in a new era of chamber music – one might imagine that he would have launched his publications with them. Together with the string trios [Opp. 3 and 9], the First and Second Symphonies, the Septet [Op. 20] and certain of the sonatas for piano solo and for piano with one other instrument (*avec accompagnement*),[49] they represent in purest form the style that constitutes his first manner. No doubt Beethoven selected the piano trios as his first publication because they were the works to which, of all his output so far, he attached the greatest importance. {53} By so doing, in one leap he proved himself the equal of Haydn and Mozart, whose piano music contained nothing remotely like these trios, where everything was new, and still is to some extent. Beethoven himself did not surpass them so long as he worked in this style – a style that embodied a hallowed respect for the traditions that Haydn and Mozart brought into the world of music while exhibiting a

strength. He did not have Mozart's abundant flow of ideas, flooding in all directions. His thought processes matured slowly, laboriously; his themes, even those themes that seem simplest and most natural, were revised by him again and again before arriving at their definitive form. But once it was fixed, his mighty intellect grasped the overall shape of the composition. One of the most remarkable examples of this long gestation period which could precede the begetting of a theme, a theme which he envisages subjecting to extensive development, was that of the main melody of the great choral Finale of the Ninth Symphony. He drafted, erased and redrafted the phrases of this tune time and time again, and many days went by before he reached the final form. At long last he cried enthusiastically: "I have it! I have it!" True, this melody, which sent him into such transports of joy, is really quite vulgar. But he was looking at it not from the musical point of view, but from that of the emotion that he was striving to express. In his preoccupation with this theme there was more of Germanic reverie than of aesthetic conception.

49   Von Lenz gives a more specific version of this list of cited works later.

richness of ideas hitherto unknown. To elevate the piano (which was still little more than a harpsichord at that time) to such a lofty status, to display an abundance of ideas so plentiful that every piece seems almost to regret ever having to end (whereas the end of a piece in Haydn, and more often than not in Mozart too, and most especially in the finales of their chamber works, surrenders whatever life is left in it to the mechanical aids of repetition, imitation, canon, modulation and transformation) – to do all this was to create a revolution in art and to proclaim himself its dictator. 'Style is the man himself', as the Haydn of the naturalists said.[50] Applied to music, style is the mode of usage of the means that work together to express the composer's idea.

The intervening work in Haydn and Mozart – in brief, their way of taking up an idea and showering upon it all the resources of melody, harmony and rhythm – is not without its wearisomeness, and it betrays from time to time a certain monotony which is the inevitable companion of any taught precept, even if the precept is perfect and the teaching impeccable. By contrast, in Beethoven the idea never succumbs: it is form that proves to be impotent because the idea overflows. It is from this that the new forms of the second and third manner arise. M Fétis (*Universal Biographical Dictionary of Musicians*: 'Beethoven') has put his finger on one of the most characteristic aspects of Beethoven when he observes that what distinguishes him 'is the spontaneity of the *episodes* by which he suspends the interest that he has aroused, substituting for it another which is as vital as it is unexpected'. 'This ability is his alone,' says M Fétis. 'These episodes, apparently alien to the first idea, {54} initially command our attention by their originality. Then, as the effect of surprise diminishes,' Beethoven 'knows just how to draw them into the unity of his plan and so bear out the fact that within the totality of a composition variety is subordinate to unity.'[51]

To take Mozart's piano works, you would think that despite his being (or perhaps because of his being) a pianist, Mozart saw the piano as a poor object, a mediocre repository unfit to house his most precious treasures. Mozart thus preferred to concentrate on the quartet, the symphony, the ecclesiastical style and opera. Only fortuitously did he bestow his most beautiful things for performance on the piano – only by accident, when required to write something for piano. Beethoven laid bare the most intimate secrets of his soul lovingly to the piano, judging the symphony too large-scale an undertaking to attempt more than nine times in a life-span of fifty-seven years. Haydn and Mozart composed symphonies just as they composed anything else. For Beethoven the symphony was the central concern of his existence, the triumph of the style to which he for ever put his name. By virtue of his symphonies – leaving aside the music, and considering them only as edifices of ideas – Beethoven ranks equal with the greatest minds that the

---

50 *Le style c'est l'homme*: the comte de Buffon, 'Ces choses sont hors de l'homme, le style est l'homme même', *Discours sur le style*, address to the Académie française, 25 August 1753. Georges-Louis Leclerc, comte de Buffon (1707–88), was a naturalist, keeper of the Jardin du Roi and museum, author of, among other works, the *Histoire naturelle, générale et particulière* (Paris: Imprimerie royale, 1/1749–88). This aphorism soon became distorted as 'Le style, c'est l'homme', and is usually quoted in that form. See the Introduction to Part III, above, note 6.

51 See Analysis 16b above.

history of humanity has ever known. Like Napoleon, Beethoven has already acquired a legendary air – he sometimes seems more myth than reality. To grasp the full import of his genius one would need to be able to put oneself in the shoes of a composer whose contemporaries are Haydn and Mozart. How difficult it would be in that position to blaze a third trail! How difficult to avoid being enslaved by those prevailing influences, which must have seemed the only possible truth. What a phenomenal period the eighteenth century was, seeing in close succession the births of Gluck (1714), Haydn (1732), Mozart (1756), Beethoven (1770) and Weber (1786) in Germany; Grétry (1741) and Méhul (1763) in France; Pergolesi (1710), Cherubini (1760) and Rossini (1792) in Italy![52]

{55} Song, melodic idea, was the dominant force in music up to the instrumental music of Mozart. Think only of the latter's incomparable Quintet for Piano and Wind [K452]. This work has something very special about it, a grandeur, a taste of such purity, it has feelings of such nobility, exudes a conviction so profound as to the power of its genius, displays a sense of proportion so sure in all things; clearly Beethoven wrote his own Quintet for Piano and Wind [Op. 16] under the influence of this established masterpiece. It has the same basic shape: introduction–allegro–andante–finale:[53] no scherzo – it must have rankled with Beethoven that there was no place for what he excelled in; for in this form more than any other he could hope to draw attention to himself; he had, after all, already produced the very models of the genre, models that remain to this very day (those of the Piano Trios [Op. 1] and the String Trios Op. 9).

Beethoven seems to have put so much of himself into the String Trios Op. 9 that, after their polish, their classic elegance,[54] the very earliest piano works might be taken for hurriedly-done holiday products. The trios could be called his *Sposalizio*: they have all the grace, all the colour, all the sweet melancholy of that celebrated painting by Raphael,[55] attributes only to be abandoned later by Beethoven for the large canvasses and bold lines of his second manner, in which his style is assimilated into the exuberant invention, the reckless brush-strokes of the galérie Médicis of the Louvre.[56]

The String Trio Op. 3 in E♭ major, composed in 1796, two years before the Trios Op. 9,[57] is not of the same quality. It conforms to the String Trios [K563] of Mozart in its subdivisions, its formal structure and even its keys: both contain

52   'Haydn (1731)', 'Pergolesi (1707)', 'Rossini (1789)'.

53   K452: largo–allegro moderato–larghetto–[rondo:] allegretto. Op. 16: grave–allegro ma non troppo–andante cantabile–rondo: allegro ma non troppo.

54   *atticisme*: 'the peculiar style and idiom of the Greek language as used by the Athenians; *hence*, refined, elegant Greek, and *gen.* a refined amenity of speech, a well-turned phrase' (*OED*).

55   *Sposalizio*: Raphael's *Sposalizio*, or *Marriage of the Virgin*, was painted at Città di Castello in 1504 for the Church of St Francis. It is now in the Brera Museum, Milan. It is in a tradition of paintings on this subject, and is itself modelled on the painting (1503–04) by Raphael's master, Perugino, but goes beyond its model in its treatment.

56   Von Lenz is presumably alluding to the great cycle of twenty-one allegorical paintings by Rubens, one of two cycles commissioned by Marie de Médicis for her return as Queen Mother in 1620 and intended for two long galleries in the Luxembourg Palace, painted 1622–25 and exhibited in its own gallery in the Louvre, in Paris.

57   1796 and 1798 are the publication dates of Opp. 3 and 9. Op. 3 was composed sometime before 1794 and Op. 9 in 1797–8.

two minuets, an andante, an adagio and two allegros.[58] It was Beethoven's fate to live for a while under the sway of Mozart's style; he is indeed, in his earliest compositions, the most complete expression of that style rather than a copy of it: the First and Second Symphonies, the Septet [Op. 20], the first six string quartets [Op. 18], the four string trios [Opp. 3 and 9], the first four piano trios [Opp. 1 and 11], the first three {56} violin sonatas Op. 12, the first two cello sonatas Op. 5 and the first ten solo piano sonatas [Opp. 2, 7, 10, 13 and 14].

History repeatedly shows us that the man who is called to further his art and to set it enduringly on its destined path begins by summing up the genius possessed by the greatest of his predecessors, and sets out as the culmination of that before embarking on the course that will lead him to higher ground. But there is one thing above all else which we must realize about Beethoven, one thing which alone will enable us to understand him: namely, that there are within him three Beethovens, very different from each other. Like Raphael and Rubens, Beethoven has a first, a second and a third manner, each one with its own distinctive characteristics. The different styles that these represent, the different directions that his mind took, the major transformations that his genius underwent, are the *layers* of his output. It is important to study them as a continuity, and to trace the influences that they exert upon one another, if we are to have any hope of distinguishing them and of understanding them. The task that we have set ourselves in this essay is thus to analyse these layers, and so make the study of this great composer more widely possible.

Though a work of Mozart's youth may be inferior to a product of his genius at its height and full maturity, that is not to say that the man himself has changed in the meanwhile – only that his talent has become augmented. Beethoven's earliest works may indeed radiate the genius of Mozart, as if they were some temporary guest of the immortal composer taking up residence for a while in his household. But if you look more closely you will detect the stirrings of discontented melancholy, the embryonic plans of a conqueror, just where you would expect to find the gentle tones of Mozart. This remains true as late as the Third Symphony, the seventh string quartet [Op. 59 no. 1], dedicated to Count Rasumovsky; the three Violin Sonatas [Op. 30], dedicated to the Emperor Alexander [I]; and the solo Piano Sonata Op. 22,[59] the work which in our analysis of the sonatas takes us to the furthest remove of this, the first phase of the composer's genius, his first manner. From {57} this point on, the 'giant of music', as M Berlioz called him,[60]

58

K563	Op. 3
Allegro (E♭)	Allegro con brio (E♭)
Adagio (A♭)	Andante (B♭)
Menuetto (Allegro) (E♭)	Menuetto (Allegro) (E♭)
Andante (B♭)	Adagio (B♭)
Menuetto (Allegretto) (E♭)	Menuetto (Moderato) (E♭)
Allegro (E♭)	Finale: Allegro (E♭)

59   *opéra* 22. The works listed here date respectively from 1803, 1805, 1801 and 1800. Although von Lenz considered Op. 22 'composed in 1802', it is clear from his catalogue that he was aware of the relative chronology of these works.

60   '. . . only with one of the giants of poetry can we find anything to compare with this sublime page of the giant of music' (Berlioz, analysis of Beethoven's Fourth Symphony, *Revue et gazette musicale de Paris*, 5/4 (28 January 1838), 34); reprinted in *A travers chants* (Paris: Lévy, 1862), p. 28.

was to set about building a city unlike any other, a city without a name, too vast for habitation by anyone other than himself, a city which alone would not immure the treasures of this lofty intelligence, burning as it was to demolish and yet every bit as eager to rebuild. Beethoven was to write six symphonies in all, those colossal works that the reader has already named: from the Third Symphony on, not counting the Ninth; he was also to write the three String Quartets Op. 59, dedicated to Count Rasumovsky, and the String Quartet in E♭ Op. 74. The eagle's flight was to reach the F minor String Quartet [Op. 95], the furthest limit of the style of the second manner, a position occupied also by the two Piano Trios Op. 70, the ['Archduke'] Piano Trio in B♭ – that 'Farnese Bull' of the piano![61] – the Violin Sonata [Op. 47] dedicated to Kreutzer, who could make neither head nor tail of it,[62] the pastoral Violin Sonata in G Op. 96, and the three Violin Sonatas [Op. 30] dedicated to the Emperor Alexander [I],[63] of which no. 2 in C minor seems to glow with the chivalric spirit that inspired the great epoch of the wars against Napoleon: 'I recognized those resplendent heroes, those sons of the gods; – Alexander and Friedrich Wilhelm!'[64] Sixteen solo piano sonatas, starting with Op. 26 and going through to Op. 90,[65] complete this rich feast.

When we reach Beethoven's second manner, gone will be the leafy bowers tucked away in shady spots; gone will be the formal avenues of trees planted alternately in textbook fashion. The master despises formal gardens. For him the open parkland, the language of the forest's silence. Houses will have become mansions, the musician's life a checkered existence schooled in the potent forces of the earth. Beethoven will turn his gaze to the higher realms of human thought. He will become a law unto himself: *princeps legibus solutus est* ['The emperor is above the laws'].[66] Duple time, hitherto reserved almost exclusively for finales, will from now on feature in opening allegro movements (the Symphony in C minor, the Pastoral Symphony, {58} the Choral Symphony). Gone will be the andante with repeated sections, its elements all made up of so many bars. Gone will be the minuet with unvarying formal scheme. In short, gone will be any semblance of a grid imposed on musical construction.[67] In its place will be a new creation: the

61   The *Farnese Bull*, or *The Punishment of Dirce*, shows Dirce tied to a bull by Zethus and Amphion. It is one of the ornaments of the Baths of Caracalla in Naples. Dating from the second century BC, it is the largest sculpture surviving from classical antiquity. Von Lenz presumably has in mind the powerful turbulence of its pyramidal composition.

62   Von Lenz says in his catalogue (p. 336): 'Kreutzer could make nothing of this colossal work . . .' Berlioz reports that Kreutzer 'could never bring himself to play this outrageously unintelligible composition' (*Voyage musical en Allemagne et en Italie* (Paris: Labitte, 1844), vol. I, p. 264).

63   Von Lenz has assigned these earlier in the paragraph as late representatives of the first manner.

64   E. T. A. Hoffmann, *Die Vision auf dem Schlachtfelde bei Dresden*, in *Dichtungen und Schriften . . . Gesamtausgabe*, vol. XI (Weimar: Lichtenstein, 1924), p. 7: 'Ich erkannte die strahlenden Helden, die Söhne der Götter: – Alexander und Friedrich Wilhelm!'. Von Lenz gives the passage in French translation.

65   Von Lenz evidently counts Op. 49 nos 1 and 2 among these; they in fact date from 1795–7, but he attaches no date to them in his catalogue.

66   Apparently from a lost work by the Roman jurist Ulpian (born 228 AD). It appears in Justinian's *Digesta*, I, title 3, 31: 'Princeps legibus solutus est: Augusta autem licet legibus soluta non est, principes tamen eadem illi privilegia tribuunt, quae ipsi habent' (see *Corpus Juris Civilis*, ed. Theodore Mommsen (reprint edn Dublin/Zürich: Weidmann, 1973; orig. edn 1872), vol. I, p. 34; Eng. trans. Alan Watson (Philadelphia: University of Pennsylvania Press, 1985)). I am grateful to Wolf Liebeschuetz and James Zetzel for this identification.

67   *plus de cadastre en un mot*: *cadastre* lit. 'land registry' or 'Ordnance Survey'.

Beethoven allegretto (the C♯ minor Piano Sonata [Op. 27 no. 2], the String Quartet in F minor [Op. 95] and the piano sonatas in F Op. 10 [no. 2] and E Op. 14 [no. 1]). No longer will the scherzo be, as it still is in the six String Quartets Op. 18, a substitute minuet. For Beethoven alone, the scherzo is a genre in its own right, no longer automatically entailing a trio. True, there will still be a distinguishable third section; but this *tertia pars* will no more bear the designation 'Trio' than it will observe the rigorous restrictions imposed by convention. The trio of the Haydn or Mozart minuet is an obligatory component. Like some miniature garden, set within the time-honoured formal plan of the minuet, and which composers often adorned with their liveliest flowers, the trio not only adapted itself to the proportions of the minuet but also took over its tonal centre. Minuet and trio exchanged courtesies of various sorts in *major* and *minor*. If the minuet came forward in the *major*, the trio would consider it only proper to take up the *minor*. If the minuet adopted the minor, then the trio would dwell a while in the *major*. The minuet of Haydn's C♯ minor Piano Sonata [Hob.XVI:36] is a striking example of these niceties in the trio.

Since adopting the style of his second manner, Beethoven made up his mind that this intimate relationship had been going on long enough. Of the Scherzo in F from the A major Symphony, the third section is in D; of the Scherzo of the Pastoral Symphony, the third section is in duple time; and of the Scherzo in F from the last string quartet (Op. 135), it is in A major. We need think only of the much ampler proportions now accorded to this third section (e.g. the String Quartet Op. 74), the duple cross-accents superimposed on the triple-time minuet and scherzo (e.g. the Fourth Symphony, the appearance of the minor in the Scherzo from the ['Archduke'] Piano Trio in B♭), the undisguised duple time of the scherzos from the Piano Sonatas Op. 31 no. 3 and Op. 110, the duple-time episodes in the scherzos of the string quartets Opp. 127 and 132 and of the *Eroica* Symphony (four bars of *alla breve* [bb.381–4]), or the quadruple-time episode in the {59} astounding Scherzo of the Choral Symphony – all these examples are the achievements of a new rhythmic style, the results of a total emancipation from the formal scheme of the minuet of old. Beethoven did not relinquish such a trusty friend lightly in order to achieve these things. More than once he gave the minuet its head again before he finally abandoned it (for example, in the String Quartet in C with fugue [Op. 59 no. 3], the Eighth Symphony, the piano sonatas Op. 22 and Op. 31 no. 3, or the Violin Sonata Op. 30 no. 3). The allegretto will take on all manner of different guises – at times tender, at others stern, passionate or timid – with equally good effect. It will, for example, take the form of a fervent prayer in the F minor String Quartet [Op. 95], passing uninterruptedly from seraphic contemplation into a movement which takes the place of a scherzo; but this is a scherzo the heroic tone and concentrated intensity of which have as yet no name in music, a scherzo for which its marking, *Allegro assai vivace ma serioso*, will have henceforward to stand as designation, because there is nothing, there cannot be anything like it.

To say that the allegretto is a familiar order of ideas known until then by another name is valueless. Beethoven's allegretto is a realm of new ideas cast in new forms.

It will be both andante and scherzo in the Piano Trio in E♭ Op. 70 [no. 2], an andante in the Seventh and Eighth Symphonies[68] and in the F minor String Quartet [Op. 95]. How are we to comprehend this Proteus?[69] In the C minor Symphony and the Pastoral Symphony, the scherzo abandons its name but does not for a moment abandon its essential nature. No longer will it serve to paint some fabulous and fanciful picture without predictable subdivisions (cf. the Scherzo of the F major Rasumovsky String Quartet [Op. 59 no. 1] and of the String Quartet Op. 74). It will lead unerringly yet unassumingly towards an order of ideas altogether vaster and more lofty: it will lead towards the finale for which it has laid the groundwork so splendidly. The scherzo will be the phoenix rising from the ashes of the old school and launching itself in liberation toward the skies! The engravings of Della Bella, nowadays a rarity, are charmingly and simply entitled 'Facetious Inventions of Love and War'.[70] Beethoven's scherzos, too, are a thousand 'inventions of love and war' – two ingredients which go together far too well for us not to rejoice at {60} seeing them united. The extra life-span that Beethoven brought to the scherzo opened up such vistas to the imagination that it all seems obvious to our eyes now whereas in reality it was one of the most important conquests made by instrumental music. How far removed the Beethoven scherzo is from the minuet of Haydn and Mozart! It is completely new territory, the discovery of which should be heralded in the annals of music. At first, the Beethoven scherzo ventured little; it fell into the role of younger brother to the minuet (e.g. the String Quintet in C [Op. 29], the Piano Trios Op. 1 and the String Quartets Op. 18). For a long time it preserved the same formal scheme, before eventually unveiling to the world the emancipated style and bearing of the scherzo of the second and third manners. To appreciate in detail the metamorphoses undergone by the scherzo at the hands of Beethoven would require special investigation. We can do no more here than point to the need for such an investigation. But we can recommend the amateur pianist to make his own personal selection of scherzos from the piano works, irrespective of the sonatas to which they belong; to carve out for himself a repertory of scherzos within the reach of the amateur. These will teach him more about the great master than any number of études, for which he will have neither the time nor the technique. Equally well, for anyone who feels more sympathy for adagio movements, the adagios of the piano sonatas would make up a repertory every bit as interesting. The pianist has much to gain from the old adage about having a stab at something now and tackling the rest later. *Non omnia possunt omnes* ['Some limit must there be to all man's faculties'].[71]

---

68 Op. 70 no. 2 has two such movements. Von Lenz presumably sees the second movement, Allegretto, as a scherzo, and the third movement, Allegretto ma non troppo, as an andante. The Allegretto of the Eighth Symphony is actually designated *Allegretto scherzando*.

69 The sea-god Proteus was capable of assuming many different guises.

70 Stefano Della Bella (1610–64) was a Florentine engraver, prolific and highly successful in his day. The *Facétieuses inventions d'amour et de guerre pour le divertissement des beaux esprits* is a set of thirteen items designed by Della Bella but engraved by Colignon and printed in 1634, picturing dwarves and soldiers. See Alexandre de Vesme, *Steffano Della Bella: catalogue raisonné*, ed. P. D. Massar (New York: Collectors Editions, 1971), pp. 162–3, 197.

71 Virgil, *Eclogues*, VIII, p. 63. *Apprendre quelque chose et y rattacher le reste*: source unknown.

The sonata's constituent forms will lose their rigidity in the style of the second manner. What is in essence a single movement will become the whole sonata (Op. 90), and a very lovely sonata at that. From now on the adagio will take the shape of a colossal lament (as in the String Quartet in F Op. 59 [no. 1]), or of a plangent entreaty from the whole of suppliant humanity (as it does in the Fourth Symphony), or of a scene of Paradise in which lovers here below will meet again in ultimate bliss (the String Quartet in E minor [Op. 59 no. 2]). The adagio will no longer always reach a conclusion: its last note will be at the same time the first of the finale (as in the String Quartet in F Op. 59 [no. 1], the ['Archduke'] Piano Trio in B♭, {61} the Piano Sonata in F minor Op. 57 – cf. the Allegretto of the F minor String Quartet [Op. 95] and the coda of the Minuet in the C major String Quartet with fugue [Op. 59 no. 3]). In one case, a finale will blaze forth its new ideas in a magnificent stream at the very threshold of the movement (in the C minor Symphony). Another will resemble a banquet at which poison is slipped into the cups so that the guests, overtaken by death, adorn themselves with flowers for the very last time (A major Symphony). And so it is with the sonatas, too; for nothing in Beethoven's output is so small and yet at the same time in the absolute sense so great. Each is self-contained, each is but *one* thing: *man in his struggle with the world.*

No one will deny Beethoven the right to treat the world outrageously, or to outdo other men when they are in his company. He is after all a millionaire in the realm of ideas. It is this exuberance of ideas which has caused people to suspect he is reproaching them (Tieck: *Musikalische Freuden und Leiden*).[72]

But if one had all the treasures of this world, would the happiness that they brought leave nothing further to be desired? Is there not an element of the unattainable in everybody's life? It is out of this that the third and final transformation of Beethoven's genius sprang: the Choral Symphony, to which the inscription on Herschel's telescope might apply: *coeli munimente perrupit* ['It has pierced the walls of the heavens'];[73] the Adagio of this symphony, which might be called the *agapes*[74] of his instrumental music; and the late quartets, which are nothing less than a portrayal of the life of the just man, recording memories of his journey through earthly life – and these memories are just as confused as the memories of anything so fragile and so many-faceted as human existence once it has fallen by the wayside. Beethoven will write his last five sonatas in this style of mystic revelation which is the essence of his third manner. Beethoven's ideas, as they are presented in this wholly exceptional style, are always complex. They are the outward manifestation of his innermost thoughts – thoughts of an abnormal life which was by then running its course remote from the real world. Total deafness

72 Ludwig Tieck, *Musikalische Leiden und Freuden* (1824), see *Werke in vier Bänden*, vol. III *Novellen*, ed. M. Thalmann (Darmstadt: Wissenschaftliche Buchgesellschaft, 1965), pp. 75–128.

73 Sir William Herschel (1738–1822), musician, and a leading astronomer of his day. I have been unable to determine which of the many telescopes that he manufactured, now surviving worldwide, bears this inscription. A plaque to his memory in Westminster Abbey reads *Coelorum Perrupit claustra*, and a similar phrase occurs on his gravestone. I am grateful to Alan V. Sims of the William Herschel Society for this information.

74 *les agapes: agape* (Gk), 'love', in the New Testament the reciprocal love between God and man. Von Lenz uses the word in the plural with terminal -s.

shut him off from all exterior impressions. He no longer perceived mankind and the world about him {62} as they really were, but rather as he wished them to be, or as he supposed them to be. Sole inhabitant of the vast city at which he laboured unceasingly, surrounded by the towering cliffs of his deafness, at the foot of which the commotions of the world faded from his consciousness, his thought processes must have been complicated by the conflict between his memories and the fantastic world of his soul. Beethoven's third manner, product of incomparably profound contemplation, no longer possesses the spontaneity of the first and second manners, but it possesses instead, and always will possess, the fascination of genius seen grappling with reality. While still depending on what our realm of impressions conveys to him, Beethoven transcends that realm and drives it beyond the limits which it has for us mundane beings. This existence beyond human apprehension does have a certain glamour to it. But we seem to see Beethoven searching for the way of life of ordinary mortals, of which he has lost sight, and crying out to it in tones which you would have thought would have melted the heart of fate herself. The sheer number of notes that Beethoven imagined he could hear was bound to increase for the very reason that he could no longer hear any notes at all. Do we not all yearn *with immoderate passion* for that which we have *lost for ever*? Put another way, the third manner is teeming with notes precisely because for Beethoven notes are no more. There is no other reason for the jarring harmonic progressions that occur constantly, the sudden jolts that we have come to associate with him. In place of the spontaneous eruption of ideas we now have a kind of questing, the perpetual questing of genius, an obsessiveness, springing from deep introspection, reminiscences of youthful affairs of the heart. Hearing must have meant more to Beethoven than the whole gamut of sensations for any other human being. He had once possessed all his faculties, but they had been plundered. *Che faro senza Euridice?* – such is the cry that comes through the late works. And so, uncertainty took hold of his mind. He explored unknown paths. He saw himself moving towards the ecclesiastical style (as in the Mass in D). The output of his third manner contains, as if in a vague and overwhelming desire on the part of the composer to surpass himself, less frequently used keys (e.g. the String Quartet in C♯ minor [Op. 131]), a greater use of {63} transitions (as in the Gloria from the Mass in D), strange juxtapositions of ideas which appear to be mutually irreconcilable. The increased interest that he brings to his episodes begins to detract from the force of the initial idea, and to overbalance the work as a totality. Gone is that appealingly limpid quality in his ideas. Beethoven carves his late works out of the living flesh of his tortured memories, but never without sacrificing them before God as a burnt offering. He revels in the technical resources of his art, deploying them more formidably than ever before. There is now the occasional touch of Paracelsus about him.[75]

All his biographers report that he concealed his infirmity as far as he could, unfortunately seeing it as a cause for shame, instead of recognizing it as the will of God that he, the most perfect genius in the realm of instrumental music, should

---

75 Paracelsus: Philippus Aureolus Theophrastus Bombast von Hohenheim (1493–1541), Swiss chemist, physician and alchemist. Von Lenz is alluding to the popular image of him as a man of magical powers combined with immense learning. His outspokenness, controversial methods and visionary sense of enquiry all invite analogy with the Romantic image of Beethoven.

have to rise above the afflictions of human nature and so lead men back to the path of true destiny.

Beethoven occupies a place in the history of mankind alongside those of Shakespeare and Michelangelo. He exhibits a severity of mind like that of Buonarotti's 'Moses'; a mind which, for all that, does not lack the grace of Sanzio;[76] a mind which believes in the separateness of individualities, yet, tinged with pantheism, is able to declare also 'All is true!'.[77] Beethoven's spirit is a chasm that grows ever deeper as time passes. Among emotions, it is love which predominates: 'Beethoven was never out of love; and love almost always deeply moved him' (Wegeler, p. 42).[78]

After all, he had to love greatly in order to understand.

To the majority of his works can be applied the medieval legend in which the Devil accosts a painter, as he is drawing a tree, with the remark: 'You are a lover, Signor Pittore; if you were not, you could not see that tree in the way you do'.[79]

Youth and beauty have advantages that cannot be overlooked. The heart, with its richer hues – knowledge – genius: all are powerless in the face of them. All his life, Beethoven suffered unhappy love {64} because he fell for ladies in the upper classes of society. This is the real key to his complex output, the true breeding-ground of his sublime ideas. Rejected because they were misunderstood, the impassioned entreaties of his music were from then on conceived as if for some less earthly ladylove.

The object of his love was transformed into a passionate mirage, which was always receding (e.g. the *Appassionato* section of the Finale of the A minor String Quartet [Op. 132]).

M Scudo, in the *Revue des deux mondes*, 1 October 1850, confuses, among other things [. . .], the metamorphoses of Beethoven's style with the periods of his life established by Schindler, p. 9. M Scudo likens these three periods to youth, maturity and decline as they 'can be observed in all men of genius'; he adds, 'save those who, like Tasso, Raphael and Mozart, died too young'.[80]

It is a strange sort of decline that is represented by the Choral Symphony, the Mass in D, the late quartets and the late sonatas! Raphael, despite his death at the age of thirty-seven, did in fact have *three* manners. No critical study can afford to be unaware of this. Did he not start as a continuator of Perugino before becoming the painter who effected a fusion of the styles of da Vinci and Buonarotti? Is not this third manner represented by his *Spasimo* and by his *Transfiguration*?[81] We

76 Buonarotti (i.e. Michelangelo): his sculpture *Moses*, for the tomb of Pope Julius II at S Pietro in Vincula, Rome, dates from 1545 and displays the *terribilità* which is a feature of Michelangelo's work. Sanzio (i.e. Raphael).

77 'All is true!': von Lenz quotes in English.

78 F. G. Wegeler and F. Ries, *Biographische Notizen über Ludwig van Beethoven* (Koblenz: Bädeker, 1838), p. 42 (footnote to a letter from Beethoven to Wegeler of 16 November 1801): 'Ignaz Ritter von Seyfried . . . [contended]: "Beethoven never married, and oddly enough was never involved in a love-affair." The truth, as I gathered it from my brother-in-law Stephan von Breuning, from Ferdinand Ries and from Bernhard Romberg, and as I came to learn it for myself, is that Beethoven was *never out of love*, and was mostly consumed by a passion of great intensity.'

79 I have been unable to identify this quotation.

80 For Schindler and Scudo, see the Introduction, above.

81 Raphael's *Spasimo di Sicilia*, or *Christ bearing his Cross*, was painted for the monastery of S Maria della Spasimo, Palermo, in 1517, and is now in the Prado Museum in Madrid. The *Transfiguration*, Raphael's last work, was painted for the cathedral church of Narbonne in 1517–c.1520 and left unfinished at his death; it is now in the Vatican.

draw attention to this error on the part of M Scudo because we have ourselves referred to the three manners that are recognized in Raphael's work, when talking about the subject of our own study. [. . .]

{65} M Fétis is the first writer to have established a threefold categorization of Beethoven's works [. . .][82] It is to be regretted that he did not go into the subject in much greater detail.

For M Fétis, the second period extends from the *Eroica* Symphony Op. 55 to the [Seventh] Symphony in A Op. 92 exclusively. As can be seen, this grouping contains nothing but the symphonic style. The String Quintet in C Op. 29, the three Piano Sonatas Op. 31, and the three Violin Sonatas Op. 30, dedicated to the Emperor Alexander, all of them compositions that came *before* the *Eroica*, are no less manifestations of this style of the second manner, but simply located in another sphere of action. They reflect just as fully an increasing liberation from the received style to which belong the early trios Opp. 1, 3, 9 and 11, the first six string quartets, the First Symphony, and even the Septet and the Second Symphony, which stand right on the borderline between the styles of the first and second manners.

M Fétis finds in the Piano Trio in E♭ Op. 97 and the [Seventh] Symphony in A Op. 92 the *first* symptoms of the third manner. These symptoms are just as detectable, if not more so, in a {66} work that predates them: the Piano Sonata Op. 54 [and also] in the F minor String Quartet Op. 95, which plainly bears one of the characteristic signs of the style, the absence of [double bar and] repeat in the allegro, which is cast as a single span. The Symphony in A is undoubtedly very much more the fullest expression from within Beethoven's symphonic style of the second, or more grand manner, than it is a constituent of the third manner, of which we can recognize in it no symptoms other than the complacency with which Beethoven lingers over the welter of harmonic and rhythmic developments in section II of the allegro and in certain passages in the finale. The Symphony in A is the very last outpost of the symphonic style of the second manner, just as the Septet and the Second Symphony are the keystone of the arch of the first manner. It is the bridge that links the second manner to the third. The astonishing ['Archduke'] Trio in B♭ occupies the same place. It is one of the loftiest peaks of the second manner, and yet the appearance of the minor in the scherzo gives perhaps a first glimpse of the yawning apocalyptic chasms of the style of the third manner: *abyssus abyssum invocat.*[83] Alone among the symphonies, the Choral Symphony is a true product of the third manner, as are the five late string quartets, the five late piano sonatas, the Mass in D, the Overture [*The Consecration of the House*] Op. 124, but not the very latest overtures, as M Fétis says, because the Overture *The Ruins of Athens* Op. 113, the Overture to *King Stephen* Op. 117 and the [*Name-day*] Overture Op. 115 belong to the late works and yet show not the slightest trace of this style.[84] We plan to write a whole chapter on the

82 See Analysis 16b above.
83 Vulgate, Ps.41.8 = Authorized King James Version, Ps.42.7: 'Deep calleth unto deep'. See *Biblia sacra iuxta latinam vulgatam versionem*, vol. X (Rome: Vatican, 1953), p. 117.
84 Von Lenz gives no composition dates for these three works in his catalogue. The dates of publication of their scores were 1823, 1826 and 1825 respectively; but they are now known to have been composed in 1811, 1811 and 1814–15, facts which support von Lenz's judgment.

errors in M Fétis's cataloguing of Beethoven's output, and shall prove our point item by item. M Fétis depicts the character of the third manner as follows:

> He carried to excess the reiteration of the same ideas. Occasionally he pursued the development of a chosen subject to the point of incoherence. His melodic thought gradually lost its clarity as it became more and more dream-like. His harmony acquired a certain hardness, and seemed day by day to show increasing signs of a decline in his {67} memory of how things sounded. Lastly, Beethoven affected to discover new forms, less as a result of sudden inspiration than in order to satisfy some premeditated scheme. The works that show these tendencies of mind make up the third period of his life, and his late manner.

We shall take issue with M Fétis's verdict, mixing as it does fact with fiction. To judge ideas by the forms they take on, by the baggage they drag behind them, is to lose sight of the central question and to get drawn into the narrow and inevitably exclusive point of view of one particular school.

> Good sir, these things you view indeed,
> *Just as by other men they're viewed*;
> We must *more cleverly* proceed,
> *Before life's joys our grasp elude.*
> *Faust*[85]

---

85   Goethe, *Faust*, Part I, lines 1816–19, in *Goethe's sämtliche Werke*, vol. XIII (Stuttgart and Berlin: Cotta, n.d.), p. 72; *Goethe's Faust*, trans. A. Swanwick (London: Bell, 1902), p. 58.

(d) Alexander Dmitryevich Ulïbïshev
'Beethoven's Three Manners'

Beethoven, His Critics and His Glossators

Source:
Beethoven, ses critiques et ses glossateurs (Leipzig: F. A. Brockhaus; Paris: Jules
Gavelot, 1857), pp. 105–08.

Fétis was I believe the first, in France at least, to draw attention to the transformations undergone by Beethoven's style, and to classify the latter's output as a
whole into three categories of works [*productions*]. Our learned professor delineates
these transformations with his characteristic shrewdness; but while indicating their
outward effects he does not allow himself to touch on their causes, since this would
have taken him beyond the scope of a dictionary article.

Since Fétis, there has been a spate of commentaries on the three manners of
Beethoven, viewing them independently and in their chronological relationships.
To the best of my knowledge, not one of these critiques has addressed the possibility of a relationship of coexistence. Transformations of style are to be observed
in the output of a host of composers, {106} indeed of all who have produced enough
and lived long enough to make a name for themselves. These changes signify
nothing more than the stages of the artist's development – or his decline, should
he have suffered such a thing. Sometimes the change of manner occurs consciously,
premeditated, even calculated, as in the cases of Gluck, Cherubini, Spontini and
Meyerbeer who, having wrought their Italian operas, then embraced the opposite
system as being more profitable to their interests or as bringing them greater
glory, and became one after another the leading proponents of the French school.
However, there is one thing in common among musicians who subject themselves
to transformation, whether of their own volition or out of an inability to do otherwise: they all have in common that they divest themselves of the old manner and
adopt the new one as a permanency.

But none of this is true of Beethoven. His three manners, when compared with
each other, do indeed exhibit a kind of succession which bears out what Fétis main-
tains as their reality. However, a careful examination proves to us equally well that
none of these three systems of composition, which ultimately come down to two,
ever existed exclusively of the others in Beethoven's artistic personality. He used
them at all stages of his artistic career, mingling them, albeit in proportions that
became more and more unequal as time went on.[86] Once we have established

86   The passage from 'His three manners, when compared . . .' to this point is quoted in Fétis,
     2/1860, after the latter's words 'despite the lovely ideas with which it abounds'. It is prefaced by

     M Ulïbïshev, in his book entitled *Beethoven, His Critics and His Glossators*, of which more
     will be said later, acknowledges (p. 105) that I was the first to draw attention to the transfor-

reliable and practicable criteria for determining the chronology of Beethoven's output, we shall see beyond all shadow of doubt [in the chapter that follows, 'Beethoven's Output', pp. 109–297] that the first manner leads ultimately into the third, and that the second manner is nothing more than an admixture of the two others, albeit an admixture with an ever increasing propensity for the features of the late works. I should point out in passing that if the division of Beethoven's works into three categories had not already taken hold so firmly, there would be nothing now to prevent our positing four or five, or even more. Without a doubt, the string quartets Opp. 127, 130, 131, 132 and 135 {107} are an infinitely greater advance upon the [Seventh] Symphony in A Op. 92 with which according to Fétis the third manner begins, than that symphony could ever be upon the Trios Op. 1. Fétis himself seems to suggest that when composing Beethoven followed two opposite systems *in alternation*, one based on the principles of harmony and the demands of the ear, and common to all musicians, the other lying outside the dictates of grammar, and known only to himself. He exploited the two contrary systems side-by-side, blending them in different proportions according to whether the work under construction lent itself to normal artistic means, or its mode of thought demanded that he call on some degree of his novel resources. The more exalted the moral tone, or the deeper the metaphysical cast of the work, the more significant did the role of the third manner become, and the greater the extent of its application. This accounts for two things: first, the disdain that the composer came eventually to feel for the works written during the period 1795–1814 and second, the impossibility of putting a date to precisely how far back the third manner goes, given the way in which the second manner gradually merges with it.

To sum up, then, my contention is that the metamorphoses through which Beethoven's style went resulted much less from the natural development of the artist than from the spiritual aberrations of the man. At this stage, the assertion is no more than conjecture, proposition. Full corroboration must await the processes of a critical assessment of the music. When we come to examine the works of this great composer more closely, I shall demonstrate by way of musical examples – the best and most conclusive sort of proof for those who know their music – that the late works of Beethoven mark the end of the progressively more and more unequal struggle of *truth* against *error* – two words that must be understood here in their absolute sense, with all due rigour. {108} The error of the great man has never been illustrated in this way before; nor has it ever been explained to my entire satisfaction. It was primarily my desire to cast light on a subject of such considerable interest as this – let me confess it, my hope of being able to do so – that impelled me to embark on the present book. [. . .]

mations of Beethoven's style and divide his output as a whole into three categories of works (in the first edition of the *Universal Biographical Dictionary of Musicians*). He adds (p. 106) . . .

Fétis concludes with:

To this critical observation there is a reply that rings strikingly true: it is that the artist's genius, his propensities, and his habits, do not change on one specific day, such that at a given moment nothing of the past remains. The transformation takes place bit by bit, in the direction that his ideas are leading, and in his style. Moreover, I believe I have quite adequately established in the paragraphs that follow the causes that gave rise to the last manner of the illustrious composer.

Appendix

(a) Handel: Suite No. 6 : 3. Allegro (Fugue)
(b) G. J. Vogler: Prelude No. 8
(c) Reicha: Andante for Wind Quintet
     (keyboard reduction)

Appendix

(a) Handel: Suite No. 6 : 3. Allegro (Fugue)

Appendix

(b) G. J. Vogler: Prelude No. 8

Appendix

(c) Reicha?: Andante for Wind Quintet (keyboard reduction)

Bibliographical essay

Bibliographical essay

Introductions to the field of music analysis can be found in Ian Bent with William Drabkin, *Analysis* (London: Macmillan, 1987), and Hermann Beck, *Methoden der Werkanalyse in Musikgeschichte und Gegenwart* (Wilhelmshaven: Heinrichshofen, 1974), both with a strong historical orientation; also in Jonathan Dunsby and Arnold Whittall, *Music Analysis in Theory and Practice* (London: Faber, 1988), and Nicholas Cook, *A Guide to Musical Analysis* (London: Dent, 1987). Leo Treitler's '"To Worship that Celestial Sound": Motives for Analysis' (*Journal of Musicology*, 1 (1982), 153–70) is thought-provoking on the nature of analysis. In its coverage of the music theorists of the seventeenth, eighteenth and nineteenth centuries, but exclusive of critical writers and historians (men such as Spitta and von Lenz), David Damschroder and David Russell Williams, eds., *Music Theory from Zarlino to Schenker: A Bibliography and Guide* (Stuyvesant: Pendragon, 1990) is excellent, though far from exhaustive. Heavily biased, and now out of date, Hugo Riemann's *Geschichte der Musiktheorie im IX.–XIX. Jahrhundert* (Leipzig: Hesse, 1898), available in translation as *History of Music Theory, Books 1 and 2: Polyphonic Theory to the Sixteenth Century*, trans. Raymond H. Haggh, and *Hugo Riemann's Theory of Harmony, with a Translation of Riemann's 'History of Music Theory', Book 3*, trans. William C. Mickelsen (Lincoln: University of Nebraska Press, 1962, 1977) is still unreplaced. Its successor in German is the long-term project *Geschichte der Musiktheorie* (Darmstadt: Wissenschaftliche Buchgesellschaft), ed. Frieder Zaminer, planned in fifteen volumes, in which coverage of the nineteenth century has made a magisterial beginning with vols. X *Die Musiktheorie im 18. und 19. Jahrhundert*: Part I *Grundzüge einer Systematik* (1984) by Carl Dahlhaus and XI Part II *Historischer Teil I: Deutschland* (1989) by Carl Dahlhaus, ed. Ruth E. Müller, with XII, a further historical volume, to be issued. Vol. I, *Ideen zu einer Geschichte der Musiktheorie: Einleitung in das Gesamtwerk* (1985), is of general interest.

Many volumes of the series *Studien zur Musikgeschichte des 19. Jahrhunderts* (Regensburg, Bosse, 1965–) are relevant; for example vols. IV, *Beiträge zur Musiktheorie des 19. Jahrhunderts*, ed. Martin Vogel (1966); V, *Beiträge zur Geschichte der Musikkritik*, ed. Heinz Becker (1965); XII, *Musiktheoretisches Denken: Versuch einer Interpretation erkenntnistheoretischer Zeugnisse in der Musiktheorie*, ed. Peter Rummenhöller (1967); XIV, *Die Ausbreitung des Historismus über die Musik*, ed. Walter Wiora (1969); XVIII, *Das Zeitalter der thematischen Prozesse in der Geschichte der Musik*, ed. Karl Wörner (1969); XXV, *Hegels Musikästhetik*, ed. Adolf Nowak (1971); XXIX, *Wagner und Beethoven: Untersuchungen zur Beethoven-Rezeption Richard Wagners*, ed. Klaus Kropfinger (1975), Eng. trans. Peter Palmer (Cambridge: CUP, 1991); XXXIII, *Anfänge institutioneller Musikerziehung in Deutschland (1800–1843): Pläne, Realisierung und zeitgenössische Kritik . . .*, ed. Georg Sowa (1973); XXXVIII, *Die Harmonielehren der ersten Hälfte des 19. Jahrhunderts*, ed. Manfred Wagner (1974); XLIII, *Beiträge zur musikalischen Hermeneutik*, ed. Carl Dahlhaus (1975); and XLIV, *Musikästhetik und Musikkritik bei Eduard Hanslick*, ed. Werner Abegg (1974).

Histories of, and monographs on, music of the nineteenth century are too numerous to list here. Of those in English, two classics are Gerald Abraham, *A Hundred Years of Music* (London: Duckworth, 1938), and Alfred Einstein, *Music in the Romantic Era* (New York: Norton, 1947). Excellent more recent products are Carl Dahlhaus, *19th-Century Music*, Eng. trans. J. Bradford Robinson (Berkeley: University of California Press, 1989; Ger. orig. 1980), and Leon Plantinga, *Romantic Music: A History of Musical Style in Nineteenth-Century Europe* (New York: Norton, 1984). An authoritative charting of historical concepts is Friedrich Blume, *Classic and Romantic Music: A Comprehensive Survey* (New York: Norton, 1970; London: Faber, 1972), which derives from articles in the encyclopedia *Die Musik in Geschichte und Gegenwart* (1949–69).

Comparable in nature to the present volume, but very different in content, are five other works: two companion volumes in the series Cambridge Readings in the Literature of Music (CUP), *Music and Aesthetics in the Eighteenth and Early-Nineteenth Centuries*, ed. Peter le Huray and James Day (1981), and *Music in European Thought 1851–1912*, ed. Bojan Bujić (1988) – to both of which the present volume refers frequently; also, in the series Aesthetics in Music (Stuyvesant: Pendragon), *Musical Aesthetics: A Historical Reader*, ed. Edward A. Lippman, vol. II: *The Nineteenth Century* (1988), and *Contemplating Music: Source Readings in Musical Aesthetics*, ed. Ruth Katz and Carl Dahlhaus (1987–); and finally the time-honoured *Source Readings in Music History from Classical Antiquity through the Romantic Era*, ed. Oliver Strunk (New York: Norton, 1950), Parts XVII 'Literary Fore-runners of Musical Romanticism' and XVIII 'Composer-Critics of the Nineteenth Century' (available as a separate volume, 1965). In addition to these five readers, there is an excellent study of aesthetics from the eighteenth century to the present day: Edward A. Lippman, *A History of Western Musical Aesthetics* (Lincoln: University of Nebraska Press, 1992).

General introduction

The reference to Locke is to his *Essay Concerning Human Understanding* (1690), especially Part I, 'Innate Ideas': see the edition by Peter Nidditch (Oxford: Clarendon, 1975). For Condillac, see *An Essay on the Origin of Human Knowledge: being a Supplement to Mr Locke's Essay . . .* (1746), Eng. trans. Thomas Nugent (London: Nourse, 1756; reprint edn Gainesville: Scholars' Facsimiles & Reprints, 1971); *Treatise on Sensations* (1749), Eng. trans. Geraldine Carr (Los Angeles: University of Southern California Press, 1930). Mid- and late eighteenth-century German works referred to are Joseph Riepel, *Anfangsgründe zur musikalischen Setzkunst*, in five separately-titled volumes published variously in 1752, 1755, 1757, 1765 and 1768; Heinrich Christoph Koch, *Versuch einer Anleitung zur Composition*, 3 vols. (Leipzig and Rudolstadt: Böhme, 1782–93), of which the aesthetic portion of vol. II will soon be available in *Aesthetics and Music: Selected Writings of Johann Sulzer and Heinrich Koch*, ed. Nancy Baker and Thomas Christensen (Cambridge: CUP), and the thematic and formal material of vols. II–III is available in *Introductory Essay on Composition: The Mechanical Rules of Melody, Sections 3 and 4*, ed. and trans. Nancy Baker (New Haven: Yale University Press, 1983); and Johann Philipp Kirnberger, *Die Kunst des reinen Satzes in der Musik aus sicheren Grundsätzen hergeleitet . . .* (Berlin: Voss, 1771–9), of which vol. I and part of vol. II are available as *The Art of Strict Musical Composition*, ed. David Beach and Jürgen Thym (New Haven: Yale University Press, 1982).

For a penetrating study of the theories of Rameau from the perspective of intellectual history, see Thomas Christensen, *Rameau and Musical Thought in the Enlightenment* (Cambridge: CUP, 1993). For later eighteenth-century theory in social-historical context see Cynthia Gessele, 'The Institutionalization of Music Theory in France 1764–1802' (PhD diss.: Princeton University, 1989).

An excellent, detailed survey of French theory in the nineteenth century is given by Renate Groth in *Die französische Kompositionslehre des 19. Jahrhunderts* (Wiesbaden: Steiner, 1983). See also Bryan Simms, 'Choron, Fétis, and the Theory of Tonality', *JMT*, 19 (1975), 112–38. The authoritative study of Momigny is Albert Palm, *Jérôme-Joseph de Momigny: Leben und Werk* (Cologne: Volk, 1969); on the dialectical basis of Momigny's analyses, see his 'Mozarts Streichquartett D-moll, KV421, in der Interpretation Momignys', *Mozart Jahrbuch 1962/3* (1964), 256–79; on acoustical origins, see Ian Bent, 'Momigny's "Type de la Musique" and a Treatise in the Making', in *Music Theory and the Exploration of the Past*, ed. Christopher Hatch and David Bernstein (Chicago: Chicago University Press, forthcoming). On Fétis's theory, see Mary I. Arlin, 'Fétis' Contribution to Practical and Historical Music Theory', *Revue Belge de musicologie*, 26–7 (1972–3), 106–15; Robert Nichols, 'François-Joseph Fétis and the Theory of Tonalité' (PhD diss.: University of Michigan, Ann Arbor, 1971); and David Lewin, 'Concerning the Inspired Revelation of F.-J. Fétis', *Theoria*, 2 (1987), 1–12. The best study of the philosophical background to Fétis's theory is Rosalie Schellhous, 'Fétis's "Tonality" as a Metaphysical Principle: Hypothesis for a New Science', *Music Theory Spectrum*, 13 (1991), 219–40.

On medieval antecedents of rhetorical theory in music, see Rudolf Flotzinger, 'Vorstufen der musikalisch–rhetorischen Tradition im Notre-Dame Repertoire?', in *De ratione in musica: Festschrift Erich Schenk* (Kassel: Bärenreiter, 1975), pp. 1–9. Early stages of the incorporation of rhetoric into written music theory can be seen in Nikolaus Listenius, *Musica* (Wittenberg: Rhau, 1537), available in translation by Albert Seay (Colorado Springs: Colorado College Music Press, 1975), and Gallus Dressler's *Praecepta musicae poeticae* (1563–4), as discussed by Bernhard Engelke in 'Einige Bemerkungen zu Dresslers "Praecepta musicae poeticae"', *Geschichts-Blätter für Stadt und Land Magdeburg*, 49–50 (1914–15), 395–401. On Burmeister's three treatises and analyses, see Claude V. Palisca, '"Ut oratoria musica": The Rhetorical Basis of Musical Mannerism', in *The Meaning of Mannerism*, ed. F. W. Robinson and S. G. Nichols (Hanover: University Press of New England, 1972), pp. 37–65 (which contains a complete translation of the Lassus analysis, with reconstructed music examples and commentary); and 'Towards an Intrinsically Musical Definition of Mannerism in the Sixteenth Century', *Studi musicali*, 3 (1974), 313–46.

Further information on the growth of natural science in the seventeenth and eighteenth centuries, and in particular on early theories of generation and heredity, is to be found in Thomas L. Hankins, *Science and the Enlightenment* (Cambridge: CUP, 1985); *The Forerunners of Darwin: 1745–1859*, ed. Bentley Glass, Owsei Temkin and William L. Straus (Baltimore: Johns Hopkins Press, 1959); and Elizabeth B. Gasking, *Investigations into Generation 1651–1828* (Baltimore: Johns Hopkins Press, 1967) and *The Rise of Experimental Biology* (New York: Random House, 1970). The proponents of organic particle theory alluded to here are Pierre-Louis-Moreau de Maupertuis (1698–1759) (*Vénus physique* (1745) and *Système de la nature* (1757) in *Oeuvres de Maupertuis: nouvelle édition* (Lyons: Bruysset, 1768), vol. II, pp. 1–133, 135–84) and George-Louis Leclerc Comte de Buffon (1707–88) (*Histoire naturelle* (Paris: Sonnini-Dupont, 1749)).

On Mattheson, see *New Mattheson Studies*, ed. George J. Buelow and Hans J. Marx (Cambridge and New York: CUP, 1983); Peter Kivy, 'Mattheson as Philosopher of Art', *The Musical Quarterly*, 70 (1984), 248–65; Mark E. Bonds, *Wordless Rhetoric: Musical Form and the Metaphor of the Oration* (Cambridge, MA: Harvard University Press, 1991), pp. 82–90. The work by Simon Sechter is *Die Grundsätze der musikalischen Komposition*, in 3 vols. (Leipzig: B&H, 1853–4), of which vol. I was translated by Carl C. Müller (New York: Pond, 1871) as *Order of Fundamental Harmonies: A Treatise on Fundamental Basses, and their Inversions and Substitutes*. For Bruckner's teachings, see *Vorlesungen über*

Harmonielehre und Kontrapunkt an der Universität Wien, ed. Ernst Schwanzara (Vienna: Österreichischer Bundesverlag, 1950), and Dika Newlin, 'Bruckner the Teacher', *Chord and Discord*, 2 (1960), 35–8. Oettingen's treatise is *Harmoniesystem in dualer Entwickelung: Studien zur Theorie der Musik* (Dorpat and Leipzig: Gläser, 1866). Riemann's accounts of his functional theory are too numerous to cite here, but see especially *Vereinfachte Harmonielehre oder Die Lehre von den tonalen Funktionen der Akkorde* (London: Augener; New York: Schirmer, 1893), English translation by Henry Bewerunge (London: Augener, [1895]) as *Harmony Simplified or The Theory of the Tonal Functions of Chords*.

On biological developments in the nineteenth century, see L. J. Jordanova, *Lamarck* (Oxford: OUP, 1984); Charles C. Gillispie, 'Lamarck and Darwin in the History of Science', and Jan Oppenheimer, 'An Embryological Enigma in the Origin of Species', in *Forerunners of Darwin: 1745–1859*, pp. 265–91, 292–322; also Gasking, *The Rise of Experimental Biology*, chaps. 5–7; and Arthur O. Lovejoy, *The Great Chain of Being: A Study in the History of an Idea* (Cambridge, MA: Harvard University Press, 1936). On Goethe, see Rudolf Magnus, *Goethe as a Scientist*, Eng. trans. Heinz Norder (New York: Schumann, 1949); H. B. Nisbett, *Goethe and the Scientific Tradition* (London: Institute of German Studies, 1972); George A. Wells, *Goethe and the Development of Science, 1750–1900* (Alphenaan den Rijn: Sijthoff and Noordhoff, 1978); Walter Kaufmann, *Discovering the Mind* (New York: McGraw-Hill, 1980).

On organicist views of music, see Ruth Solie, 'The Living Work: Organicism and Musical Analysis', *19th-Century Music*, 4 (1980/81), 147–56; Brian Primmer, 'Unity and Ensemble: Contrasting Ideals in Romantic Music', *19th-Century Music*, 6 (1982/83), 97–140; William Pastille, 'Heinrich Schenker, Anti-Organicist', *19th-Century Music*, 8 (1984/85), 29–36, 'Music and Morphology: Goethe's Influence on Schenker's Ontology', in *Schenker Studies*, ed. Hedi Siegel (Cambridge: CUP, 1990), pp. 29–44, and 'The Development of the *Ursatz* in Schenker's Published Works', in *Trends in Schenkerian Research*, ed. Allen Cadwallader (New York: Schirmer, 1990), pp. 71–85; Jamie Croy Kassler, 'Heinrich Schenker's Epistemology and Philosophy of Music: An Essay on the Relations between Evolutionary Theory and Music', in *The Wider Domain of Evolutionary Thought*, ed. D. Oldroyd and I. Langham (Dordrecht: Reidel, 1983), pp. 221–60.

On Gottfried Weber's view of the theories of Rameau and his other predecessors, see Janna K. Saslaw, 'Gottfried Weber and the Concept of Mehrdeutigkeit' (PhD diss.: Columbia University, 1991), p. 23. On those of Fétis, see Rosalie Schellhous, 'Fétis's "Tonality" as a Metaphysical Principle: Hypothesis for a New Science', *Music Theory Spectrum*, 13 (1991), 219–40. On fundamental bass in Sechter, Bruckner, Mayrberger, Riemann, Schenker and others see Robert W. Wason, *Viennese Harmonic Theory from Albrechtsberger to Schenker and Schoenberg* (Ann Arbor: UMI Research Press, 1985), pp. 31–143.

Part I : Analysis of fugue

The two principal books in English on the history of fugue and its theory are Alfred Mann, *The Study of Fugue* (New Brunswick, NJ: Rutgers University Press, 1958; reprint edn Westport: Greenwood, 1981), which includes extended passages from fugue treatises by Fux, Marpurg, Albrechtsberger and Martini in translation; and Imogen Horsley, *Fugue: History and Practice* (New York: Free Press, 1966). To these should be added Warren Kirkendale, *Fugue and Fugato in Rococo and Classical Chamber Music*, trans. Margaret Bent (Durham, NC: Duke University Press, 1979; Ger. orig. 1966), and John Cockshoot, *Fugue in Beethoven's Piano Music* (London: Routledge & Kegan Paul, 1959). Of considerable interest in the light of the development of organicist thought in the nineteenth century is Heinrich Schenker,

'Das Organische in der Fuge', *Das Meisterwerk in der Musik*, vol. II (Vienna: Drei Masken Verlag, 1926; reprint edn Hildesheim: Olms, 1974), pp. 55–95, of which an English translation is available in Sylvan S. Kalib, 'Thirteen Essays from the Three Yearbooks "Das Meisterwerk in der Musik" by Heinrich Schenker: An Annotated Translation' (PhD diss.: Northwestern University, 1973), vol. III, pp. 92–113. A new translation by Hedi Siegel is forthcoming as part of a complete translation of *Das Meisterwerk*, ed. William Drabkin (Cambridge: CUP).

On the terminology of fugue, see Peter Cahn, 'Repercussio' (1981), Michael Beiche, 'Dux–Comes' (1986), and Siegfried Schmalzriedt, 'Durchführen, Durchführung' (1979), 'Episode' (1978) and 'Exposition' (1979) in *HwMT*. On terminology, history and theory, see Roger Bullivant, 'Fugue', in *NGDM*. On the tradition of fugal analysis extending back to Kirnberger and Rameau, see David Beach, 'The Origins of Harmonic Analysis', *JMT*, 18 (1974), 274–306.

1 Momigny/Handel

The authoritative work on Momigny is Albert Palm, *Jérôme-Joseph de Momigny: Leben und Werk: ein Beitrag zur Geschichte der Musiktheorie im 19. Jahrhundert* (Cologne: Volk, 1969). On Momigny's *Cours complet*, see Birgitte P. Moyer, 'Concepts of Musical Form in the Nineteenth Century with Special Reference to A. B. Marx and Sonata Form' (PhD diss.: Stanford University, 1969), pp. 30–35, 248–9; Groth, *Französische Kompositionslehre*, pp. 88–90, 165–6, 192–6; Bent/Drabkin, *Analysis*, pp. 20–25; Bent, 'Momigny's "Type de la Musique"'.

On Momigny and Handel, see Albert Palm, 'Händels Nachwirkung in Frankreich: Ein Beitrag zu Momignys Händelverständnis', *Händel-Jahrbuch*, 13/14 (1967–68), 61–82.

2 Reicha/Anon.

See Maurice Emmanuel, *Antonin Reicha* (Paris: Renouard/Laurens, 1937); Noel H. Magee, 'Anton Reicha as Theorist' (PhD diss.: University of Iowa, 1977); Groth, *Französische Kompositionslehre*, pp. 134–8 on fugue, also 41–4, 90–93; Adrienne Simpson, 'An Introduction to Antoine Reicha', *Consort*, 40 (1984), 13–19; Bent/Drabkin, *Analysis* (1987), pp. 17–20.

3 Hauptmann/Bach

A survey of Hauptmann's life and theoretical works is provided by Dale Jorgensen in *Moritz Hauptmann of Leipzig* (Lewiston, NY: Mellen, 1986). Studies of the theoretical ideas include Peter Rummenhöller, *Moritz Hauptmann als Theoretiker: eine Studie zum erkenntniskritischen Theoriebegriff in der Musik* (Wiesbaden: B&H, 1963), 'Moritz Hauptmann: Der Begründer einer transzendental-dialektischen Musiktheorie' in *Beiträge zur Musiktheorie des 19. Jahrhunderts*, ed. Martin Vogel (Regensburg: Bosse, 1966), pp. 11–38, and 'Der dialektische Theoriebegriff: Zur Verwirklichung Hegelschen Denkens in Moritz Hauptmanns Musiktheorie', in *Gesellschaft für Musikforschung: Bericht über den internationalen musikwissenschaftlichen Kongress: Leipzig 1966* (Kassel: Bärenreiter; Leipzig: VEB Deutscher Verlag für Musik, 1970), pp. 387–91; Wilhelm Seidel, 'Moritz Hautpmanns organische Lehre: Tradition, Inhalt und Geltung ihrer Prämisse', *International Review of the Aesthetics and Sociology of Music*, 2 (1971), 243–66; William Caplin, 'Moritz Hauptmann and the Theory of Suspensions', *JMT*, 28 (1984), 251–69; Mark McCune, 'Moritz Hauptmann: ein Haupt Mann in Nineteenth Century Music Theory', *Indiana Theory*

Review, 7/2 (Fall 1986), 1–28. On Hauptmann's harmonic theory, see Robert Wason, 'Progressive Harmonic Theory in the Nineteenth Century', *Journal of Musicological Research*, 8 (1988/89), 55–90.

Of Bach's *The Art of Fugue*, see the edition with commentary by Peter Williams (London: Eulenberg, 1986) and the keyboard edition with commentary and reconstruction of the final fugue by Davitt Moroney (Munich: Henle, [1989]). For analysis and discussion of the work, see Donald Francis Tovey, *A Companion to 'The Art of Fugue' (Die Kunst der Fuge) J. S. Bach* (London: OUP, 1931); and Christoph Wolff, 'Bach's "Art of Fugue": An Examination of the Sources', *Current Musicology*, 19 (1975), 47–77. See also Walter Kolneder, *Die Kunst der Fuge: Mythen des 20. Jahrhunderts* (Wilhelmshaven: Heinrich-shofen, 1977); Christoph Wolff, 'Zur Chronologie und Kompositionsgeschichte von Bachs Kunst der Fuge', *Beiträge zur Musikwissenschaft*, 25 (1983), 130–42.

4 Sechter/Mozart

On Sechter's theory of harmony, see the excellent discussion in Wason, *Viennese Harmonic Theory*, pp. 31–64 ('Simon Sechter and the Fundamental Bass'), and *passim*. See also Walter Zeleny, *Die historischen Grundlagen des Theoriesystems von Simon Sechter* (Tutzing: Schneider, 1979); Alfred Mann, 'Zur Kontrapunktlehre Haydns und Mozarts', in *Mozart und seine Umwelt: Bericht über die Tagung des Zentralinstituts für Mozartforschung . . .* (Kassel: Bärenreiter, 1979), pp. 195–9; and William Caplin, 'Harmony and Meter in the Theories of Simon Sechter', *Music Theory Spectrum*, 2 (1980), 74–89. More generally on Sechter as the source of a tradition, see Dika Newlin, *Bruckner, Mahler, Schoenberg* (New York: King's Crown Press, 1947, 2/1978), esp. pp. 47–53; and Alfred Mann, 'Schubert's Lesson with Sechter', *19th-Century Music*, 6 (1982/83), 159–65.

On Mozart's 'Jupiter' Symphony, see Johann N. David, *Die Jupiter-Sinfonie: eine Studie über die thematisch-melodischen Zusammenhänge* (Göttingen: Deuerlichsche Verlagsbuch-handlung, 1953, 4/1960); Gerd Sievers, 'Analyse des Finale aus Mozarts Jupiter-Symphonie', *Die Musikforschung*, 7 (1954), 318–31, reprinted in *Zur musikalischen Analyse*, ed. Gerhard Schuhmacher (Berlin: Merseburger, 1974), pp. 72–95; William Klenz, '*Per Aspera ad Astra* or The Stairway to Jupiter', *Music Review*, 30 (1969), 169–210; Rose Rosengard Subotnik, 'Evidence of a Critical World View in Mozart's Last Three Symphonies', in *Music and Civilization: Essays in Honor of Paul Henry Lang*, ed. Edmond Strainchamps, Maria Rika Maniates and Christopher Hatch (New York: Norton, 1984), pp. 29–43; Ellwood Derr, 'The `Deeper Examination of Mozart's 1–2–4–3 Theme and its Strategic Deployment', *In Theory Only*, 8/iv–v (Jan 1985), 5–43; Neal Zaslaw, *Mozart's Symphonies: Context, Performance Practice, Reception* (Oxford: Clarendon, 1989), pp. 532–44. A study by Elaine Sisman appears in the series Cambridge Music Handbooks: *Mozart: The 'Jupiter' Symphony* (Cambridge: CUP, 1993).

5 Dehn/Bach

Articles in *MGG* and *NGDM* are the only items devoted to Dehn. See also Wason, 'Progressive Harmonic Theory', 55–90.

On Bach's *Well-tempered Clavier*, see Ludwig Czaczkes, *Analyse des Wohltemperierten Klaviers* (Vienna: Kaltschmid, 1956); and Hermann Keller, *The Well-Tempered Clavier by Johann Sebastian Bach*, Eng. trans. Leigh Gerdine (New York: Norton, 1976; Ger. orig. 1965).

6 Riemann/Bach

On Riemann, see Hellmuth C. Federhofer, 'Die Funktionstheorie Hugo Riemanns und die Schichtenlehre Heinrich Schenkers', in *Bericht über den internationalen musikwissenschaftlichen Kongress Wien: Mozartjahr 1956* (Graz/Cologne: Böhlaus, 1958), pp. 183–90; Elmar Seidel, 'Die Harmonielehre Hugo Riemanns', in *Beiträge zur Musiktheorie des 19. Jahrhunderts*, ed. Martin Vogel (Regensburg: Bosse, 1966), pp. 39–92; Moyer, 'Concepts of Musical Form', 191–243; Carl Dahlhaus, 'Terminologisches zum Begriff der harmonischen Funktion', *Die Musikforschung*, 28 (1975), 197–202; and 'Harmony', in *NGDM*; Hellmuth Federhofer, *Akkord und Stimmführung in den musiktheoretischen Systemen von Hugo Riemann, Ernst Kurth und Heinrich Schenker* (Vienna: Österreichisches Akademie der Wissenschaft, 1981); William Caplin, 'Hugo Riemann's Theory of "Dynamic Shadings": A Theory of Musical Meter?', *Theoria*, 1 (1985), 1–24.

Part II: Technical analysis of form and style

The manuals of musical form referred to in the Introduction are Ernst Friedrich Richter, *Die Grundzüge der musikalischen Formen und ihre Analyse als Leitfaden beim Studium derselben* . . . (Leipzig: B&H, 1851; Wigand, 1852); Benedikt Widmann, *Formenlehre der Instrumentalmusik nach dem System Schnyder's von Wartensee* . . . (Leipzig: Merseburger, 1862, 2/1879); František Zdeněk Skuherský, *O formách hudebních* (Prague: Mikuláš and Knapp, 1873, 1879; Ger. trans. 1879); Ludwig Bussler, *Musikalische Formenlehre in dreiunddreissig Aufgaben mit zahlreichen* . . . *Muster-, Uebungs- und Erläuterungs-Beispielen, sowie Anführungen aus den Meisterwerken der Tonkunst* (Berlin: Habel, 1878, 9/1942); J. H. Cornell, *The Theory and Practice of Musical Form on the Basis of Ludwig Bussler's 'Musikalische Formenlehre'* (New York: Schirmer, 1883); Salomon Jadassohn, *Die Formen in den Werken der Tonkunst, analysirt und in stufenweise geordnetem Lehrgange* . . . *dargestellt* (Leipzig: Kistner, 1885, 6/1923; Eng. trans. E. M. Barber as *Manual of Musical Form* (Leipzig: B&H, 1892)); Hugo Riemann, *Katechismus der Kompositionslehre (Musikalische Formenlehre)* (Leipzig: Hesse, 1889, 3/1905 as *Grundriss der Kompositionslehre*; Eng. trans. n.d.; Span. trans. 1929); Ebenezer Prout, *Musical Form* (London: Augener, 1893; Russ. trans., 1896), and *Applied Forms: A Sequel to 'Musical Form'* (London: Augener, 1895; Russ. trans. 1910); Percy Goetschius, *Complete Musical Analysis: System designed to Cultivate the Art of Analyzing and Criticising* . . . (Cincinatti: Church; Chicago: Root, 1889), *Models of the Principal Musical Forms* (Boston: New England Conservatory, 1894), and *The Homophonic Forms of Musical Composition* (New York: Schirmer, 1898); Hugo Leichtentritt, *Musikalische Formenlehre* (Leipzig: B&H, 1911, 4/1948; Eng. trans. *Musical Form* (Cambridge, MA: Harvard University Press, 1951)). On the concept of development, see Siegfried Schmalzriedt, 'Durchführen, Durchführung' and 'Exposition', and Peter Cahn, 'Repercussio', in *HwMT*.

On harmony and harmonic theory in the eighteenth and nineteenth centuries, see *Die Harmonielehren der ersten Hälfte des 19. Jahrhunderts*, ed. Manfred Wagner as vol. XXXVIII of Studien zur Musikgeschichte des 19. Jahrhunderts; Carl Dahlhaus, 'Harmony', in *NGDM*; Wason, *Viennese Harmonic Theory*; Beth Shamgar, 'Romantic Harmony through the Eyes of Contemporary Observers', *Journal of Musicology*, 7 (1989), 518–39. The primary texts cited are Ernst Friedrich Richter, *Lehrbuch der Harmonie: Praktische Anleitung* . . . (Leipzig: B&H, 1853; Eng. trans. 1864, 1867, 1873, 1896, 1912; Russ. trans. 1868; Dan. trans. 1883; Fr. trans. 1884; Span. trans. 1892; Dutch trans. 1896; Ital. trans. 1935); Carl Friedrich Weitzmann, *Der übermässige Dreiklang* (Berlin: Trautwein, 1853), *Der verminderte*

Septimen-Akkord (Berlin: Peters, 1854), and *Die neue Harmonielehre im Streit mit der alten . . .* (Leipzig: Kahnt, 1861); Salomon Jadassohn, *Lehrbuch der Harmonie* (Leipzig: B&H, 1883; Eng. trans. 1884, 1893; Fr. trans. 1893; Ital. trans. 1898; Dutch trans. 1898), and *Melodik und Harmonik bei Richard Wagner* (Leipzig: B&H, 1899); and Cyrill Kistler, *Harmonielehre für Lehrer und Lernende* (Heilbronn: Schmidt, 1879, 2/1898; Eng. trans. as *A System of Harmony* (London: Haas, 1899)); Karl Mayrberger, *Lehrbuch der musikalischen Harmonik . . .*, Part I *Die diatonische Harmonik in Dur* (Pressburg and Leipzig: Heckenast, 1878).

For a discussion of Hynais and Schalk, see Wason, *Viennese Harmonic Theory*, pp. 100–111. Wason cites Cyrill Hynais, 'Die Harmonik R. Wagner's in Bezug auf die Fundamentaltheorie Sechter's', *Neue Musikalische Presse*, 10 (1901), 50–52, 67–9, 81–2, 97–100; Josef Schalk, 'Das Gesetz der Tonalität', *Bayreuther Blätter*, 11 (1888), 192–7, 381–7; 12 (1889), 191–8; 13 (1890), 65–70. The two early twentieth-century works cited are Rudolf Louis and Ludwig Thuille, *Harmonielehre* (Stuttgart: Grüninger, 1907), and Ernst Kurth, *Romantische Harmonik und ihre Krise in Wagners 'Tristan'* (Bern: Haupt, 1920; Berlin: Hesse, 1922, 1923; reprint edn Hildesheim: Olms, 1968).

7 Vogler/Vogler

See Margaret H. Grave, 'Vogler, Georg Joseph', in *NGDM*, and Floyd K. and Margaret H. Grave, *In Praise of Harmony: The Teachings of Abbé Georg Joseph Vogler* (Lincoln: University of Nebraska Press, 1987). See also Floyd K. Grave, 'Abbé Vogler's Revision of Pergolesi's *Stabat mater*', *JAMS*, 30 (1977), 43–71, 'Abbé Vogler and the Bach Legacy', *Eighteenth-Century Studies*, 13 (1979/80), 119–41, 'Abbé Vogler and the Study of Fugue', *Music Theory Spectrum*, 1 (1979), 43–67, and 'Abbé Vogler's Theory of Reduction', *Current Musicology*, 29 (1980), 41–69; Jane R. Stevens, 'Georg Joseph Vogler and the "Second Theme" in Sonata Form: Some Eighteenth-Century Perceptions of Musical Contrast', *The Journal of Musicology* 2 (1983), 278–304.

8–9 Reicha/Mozart–Reicha

See Emmanuel, *Antonin Reicha*; Moyer, 'Concepts of Musical Form', 35–58; Noel H. Magee, 'Anton Reicha as Theorist' (PhD diss.: University of Iowa, 1977); Groth, *Französische Kompositionslehre*, pp. 134–8 on fugue, also 41–4, 90–93; Simpson, 'An Introduction to Antoine Reicha', 13–19; Bent/Drabkin, *Analysis* (1987), pp. 17–20.

10 Weber/Mozart

On Gottfried Weber in general, see Arno Lemke, *Jacob Gottfried Weber: Leben und Werk: ein Beitrag zur Musikgeschichte des mittelrheinischen Raumes* (Mainz: Schott, 1968); Brigitte Höft, 'Gottfried Weber (1779–1839): ein Porträt', *Mitteilungen der Arbeitsgemeinschaft für mittelrheinische Musikgeschichte*, 42 (1981), 45–62.

Weber's *Versuch* was translated from the third edition (1830–32) into English by James F. Warner, as *The Theory of Musical Composition, treated with a View to a Naturally Consecutive Arrangement of Topics* (Boston: Wilkins & Carter; London: Novello, [1842–6]). This translation was later reissued under the same title, edited by John Bishop, with modifications to the translation, and with restoration of passages excised by Warner (London: Cocks, 1851). On Weber's theoretical writings, see Beach, 'The Origins of Harmonic

Analysis'; Lars U. Abraham, 'Die "Allgemeine Musiklehre" von Gottfried Weber im Lichte heutiger Musikdidaktik', in *Festschrift für Arno Volk*, ed. Carl Dahlhaus and Hans Oesch (Cologne: Gerig, 1974), 102–06; Elizabeth W. Marvin, '*Tonpsychologie* and *Musikpsychologie*: Historical Perspectives on the Study of Music Perception', *Theoria*, 2 (1987), 59–84; Janna K. Saslaw, 'Gottfried Weber and Multiple Meaning', *Theoria*, 5 (1990), 74–103, 'Gottfried Weber and the Concept of Mehrdeutigkeit' (PhD diss.: Columbia University, 1991), and 'Gottfried Weber's Cognitive Theory of Modulation', in *Studies in Music from the University of Western Ontario: Proceedings of the Third Canadian Music Theory Conference* (forthcoming).

On the dispute over Mozart's 'Dissonance' Quartet, see the fascinating account by Julie Anne Vertrees, 'Mozart's String Quartet K.465: the History of a Controversy', *Current Musicology*, 17 (1974), 96–114.

11 *Czerny/Beethoven*

Czerny's *School of Practical Composition, or Complete Treatise on the Composition of All Kinds of Music . . . Together with a Treatise on Instrumentation* Op. 600 seems to have been published in English (3 vols. (London: Cocks, [1848]; reprint edn New York: Da Capo, 1979)) before the German original appeared. Of great interest to the theorist as well as the historian and performer, his *Systematische Anleitung zum Fantasieren auf dem Pianoforte* Op. 200 is available in English translated by Alice L. Mitchell (New York: Longman, 1983) as *Systematic Introduction to Improvisation on the Pianoforte*. Czerny is perhaps best known for his manual of pianoforte playing, Op. 500, of which a contemporary English translation was issued by James A. Hamilton (London: Cocks, [1842–6]); excerpts from Op. 500 significant for the history of Beethoven performance practice are reproduced in *Carl Czerny: Über den richtigen Vortrag der sämtlichen Beethoven'schen Klavierwerke* (Vienna: Universal Edition, 1963), pp. 24–113.

Concerning Czerny's theoretical writings, see William S. Newman, 'About Carl Czerny's Op. 600 and the "First" Description of "Sonata Form"', *JAMS*, 20 (1967), 513–15; Moyer, 'Concepts of Musical Form', 58–68, 250–55; Malcom S. Cole, 'Czerny's Illustrated Description of the Rondo or Finale', *Music Review*, 36 (1975), 5–16; Alice L. Mitchell, 'A Systematic Introduction to the Pedagogy of Carl Czerny', in *Music and Civilization: Essays in Honor of Paul Henry Lang*, pp. 262–9; Peter Cahn, 'Carl Czernys erste Beschreibung der Sonatenform (1832)', *Musiktheorie*, 1 (1986), 277–9; see also Bent/Drabkin, *Analysis*, pp. 24–8.

On Beethoven's 'Waldstein' Sonata Op. 53 see Donald F. Tovey, *A Companion to Beethoven's Pianoforte Sonatas (Bar-to-Bar Analysis)* (London: Associated Board, 2/1948), pp. 156–68.

12 *Lobe/Beethoven*

There is little access to Lobe's work through the English language. His *Katechismus der Musik* (Leipzig: Weber, 1851) was issued twice in translation, by Fanny R. Ritter (New York: Schubert, [1867], and several other editions) and by Constance Bache (London: Augener, [?1885]), both as *Catechism of Music*, and thirdly by Oscar Coon (New York: Fischer [?1905]) as *A New Catechism of Music on the Plan of J. C. Lobe*. For discussion of his work, see Moyer, 'Concepts of Musical Form', 145–57, 265–70; Ian Bent, 'The "Compositional Process" in Music Theory 1713–1850', *Music Analysis*, 3 (1984), 29–55.

On the Beethoven String Quartets Op. 18, see Philip Radcliffe, *Beethoven's String Quartets* (London: Hutchinson, 1965; reprint edn 1978); Joseph Kerman, *The Beethoven Quartets* (New York: Knopf, 1967).

13 Mayrberger/Wagner

Mayrberger is a neglected figure. The only substantial treatment appears in Wason, *Viennese Harmonic Theory*, chaps. 4–8, 10. Of interest is Georg Capellen, *Ist das System S. Sechters ein geeigneter Ausgangspunkt für Wagner Forschung?* (Leipzig: Kahnt, 1902).

On Wagner's *Tristan and Isolde* there is a secondary literature too vast to cite here. Important is *Der Tristan-Akkord und die Krise der modernen Harmonielehre* (Düsseldorf: Verlag der Gesellschaft zur . . . Musikwissenschaft, 1962); also William J. Mitchell, 'The Tristan Prelude: Techniques and Structure', *Music Forum*, 1 (1967), 162–203; and William Kinderman, 'Das "Geheimnis der Form" in Wagners "Tristan und Isolde"', *Archiv für Musikwissenschaft*, 40 (1983), 174–88. For a selection of important essays on *Tristan* (not including that of Mayrberger), see *Richard Wagner: Prelude and Transfiguration from "Tristan and Isolde": Authoritative Scores, Historical Background, Sketches and Drafts, Views and Comments, Analytical Essays*, Norton Critical Score, ed. Robert Bailey (New York: Norton, 1985), pp. 179–303, with a useful short bibliography, 305–07. For a selection of Wagner's own comments on *Tristan*, see *Richard Wagner über Tristan und Isolde: Aussprüche des Meisters über sein Werk* (Leipzig, 1912).

On Wagner's harmonic language, two classic works are Salomon Jadassohn, *Melodik und Harmonik bei Richard Wagner* (Berlin: Verlagsgesellschaft für Literatur und Kunst, [?1899]); and Ernst Kurth, *Romantische Harmonik*, from which substantial passages are translated in *Ernst Kurth: Selected Writings*, ed. Lee A. Rothfarb (Cambridge: CUP, 1991), pp. 97–147; see also Cyrill Hynais, 'Die Harmonik R. Wagner's', 50–52, 67–9, 81–2, 97–100. On Wagner's music dramas, see Carl Dahlhaus, *Richard Wagner's Music Dramas*, Eng. trans. Mary Whittall (Cambridge: CUP, 1979; Ger. orig. 1971); and in the series *Studien zur Musikgeschichte des 19. Jahrhunderts* see vols. XXIII, *Das Drama Richard Wagners als musikalisches Kunstwerk*, ed. Carl Dahlhaus (1970), XXIV, *Studien zur Instrumentation Richard Wagners*, ed. Egon Voss (1970), and XXVI, *Richard Wagner: Werk und Wirkung*, ed. Carl Dahlhaus (1971).

Part III: The classification of personal style

For the text of Boethius, see *Fundamentals of Music: Anicius Manlius Severinus Boethius*, Eng. trans. Calvin M. Bower, ed. Claude V. Palisca (New Haven: Yale University Press, 1989), esp. pp. 9–10; also 'Boethius' "The Principles of Music": An Introduction and Translation', Eng. trans. Calvin Bower (PhD diss.: George Peabody College, 1967). For the text of Johannes de Grocheo, see *Der Musiktraktat des Johannes de Grocheo . . .*, ed. Ernst Rohloff (Leipzig: Reinecke, 1943), vol. II, pp. 41–67; and *Johannes de Grocheo: 'Concerning Music' (De Musica)*, Eng. trans. Albert Seay (Colorado Springs: Colorado College Music Press, 1967).

For the text of Marco Scacchi's *Breve discorso sopra la musica moderna*, see Claude V. Palisca, 'Marco Scacchi's Defense of Modern Music (1649)', in *Words and Music: . . . in Honor of A. Tillman Merritt*, ed. Laurence Berman (Cambridge, MA: Harvard University, 1972), pp. 189–235; see also Zygmunt M. Szweykowski, *Musica moderna w ujeciu Marka Scacchiego* (Krakow: Polskie Wydawnictwo Muzyczne, 1977). For the text of Christoph

Bernhard's three treatises, see Joseph Müller-Blattau, *Die Kompositionslehre Heinrich Schützens in der Fassung seines Schülers Christoph Bernhard* (Leipzig: B&H, 1926, 2/1963), esp. pp. 42–3, 63–90; and 'The Treatises of Christoph Bernhard', Eng. trans. Walter Hilse, *The Music Forum*, 3 (1973), 1–196, esp. 34–5, 76–123. The relevant treatise by Berardi is *Ragionamenti musicali* (Bologna: Monti, 1681), esp. pp. 133–6; and those by Mattheson *Das neu-eröffnete Orchestre; oder Universelle und gründliche Anleitung* . . . (Hamburg: Schiller, 1713), esp. 139–54, and *Der vollkommene Capellmeister* . . . (Hamburg: Herold, 1739), Part I, chap. 10, Eng. trans. E. C. Harriss (Ann Arbor: UMI Research Press, 1981).

For Quantz, see *Versuch einer Anweisung, die Flöte traversière zu spielen* . . . (Berlin: Voss, 1752); Eng. trans. E. R. Reilly (London: Faber, 1966, 1976; 2/1985); and his autobiography in F. W. Marpurg, *Historisch-kritische Beiträge zur Aufnahme der Musik*, vol. I (Berlin: Schütz, 1755; reprint edn Hildesheim: Olms, 1970), pp. 197–250; for C. P. E. Bach, see *Versuch über die wahre Art das Clavier zu spielen* (Berlin: Henning and Winter, 1753–62); Eng. trans. William Mitchell (London: Cassell, 1949); for Marpurg, see *Abhandlung von der Fuge* . . . (Berlin: Haude & Spener, 1753–4; reprint edn Hildesheim: Olms, 1970). On the operatic controversies, see Alfred R. Oliver, *The Encyclopedists as Critics of Music* (New York: Columbia University Press, 1947); Arnold Whittall, 'La querelle des bouffons' (PhD diss.: Cambridge University, 1963).

For early biographical dictionaries, consult James B. Coover's 'Dictionaries and Encyclopedias of Music', in *NGDM*. The two mentioned are Alexandre-Etienne Choron and F. J. M. Fayolle, *Dictionnaire historique des musiciens* (Paris: Valade & Lenormant, 1810–11; reprint edn Hildesheim: Olms, 1970), large portions of which were translated in J. H. Sainsbury, *A Dictionary of Musicians* (London: Sainsbury, 1824; reprint edn New York: Da Capo, 1966), and E. L. Gerber, *Neues historisch-biographisches Lexikon der Tonkünstler* (Leipzig: Kühnel, 1812–14; reprint edn Graz: Akademische Druck- und Verlagsanstalt, 1966–9). For Fétis, see §16, below. On composer-centred history, see W. D. Allen, *Philosophies of Music History: A Study of General Histories of Music 1600–1900* (New York: American Book Company, 1939, 2/1962), chap. 6. Of the early biographies cited, those not represented elsewhere in this volume are: Johann Nikolaus Forkel, *Über Johann Sebastian Bachs Leben, Kunst und Kunstwerke* (Leipzig: Hoffmeister und Kühnel, 1802, reprint edn Kassel: Bärenreiter, 1968), Eng. trans. Charles Sanford Terry (London: Constable, 1920; reprint edn New York: Johnson, 1970); Carl von Winterfeld, *Johannes Gabrieli und sein Zeitalter* (Berlin: Schlesinger, 1834; reprint edn Hildesheim: Olms, 1965); Anton Schindler, *Biographie von Ludwig van Beethoven* (Münster: Aschendorff, 1840, 2/1845, 3/1860, ed. D. W. McArdle as *Beethoven as I Knew Him* (New York: Norton, 1966)), Eng. trans. I. Moscheles (London: Colburn, 1841); Otto Jahn, *W. A. Mozart* (Leipzig: B&H, 1856–9, 2/1867), Eng. trans. Pauline D. Townsend (London: Novello, Ewer, 1882).

14 Baini/Palestrina

Baini's work is acknowledged, yet rarely read. See Andrea della Corte, *La critica musicale e i critici* (Turin: Unione tipographico, 1961); R. Meloncelli, 'Baini, Giuseppe Giacobbe Baldassarre', in *Dizionario biografico degli italiani* (Rome: Treccani, 1960–), vol. V (1963), pp. 288–91.

The literature on Palestrina, by contrast, is extensive. On his output in general, see Gustave Reese, *Music in the Renaissance* (New York: Norton, 1954), pp. 401–03 (secular music), 448–81 (Council of Trent, background, biography, style, motets, masses); Howard Mayer Brown, *Music in the Renaissance* (Englewood Cliffs: Prentice-Hall, 1976), pp. 284–

98. On his secular music, see Alfred Einstein, *The Italian Madrigal* (Princeton: Princeton University Press, 1940; reprint edn 1971), pp. 311–18. The article in *NGDM*, by Lewis Lockwood and Jessie Ann Owens, is outstanding. On his style, see Knud Jeppesen, *The Style of Palestrina and the Dissonance* (London: Cumberlege/OUP, 2/1946; Dan. orig. 1923); H. K. Andrews, *An Introduction to the Technique of Palestrina* (London: Novello, 1958). See specifically *Giovanni Pierluigi da Palestrina: Pope Marcellus Mass: An Authoritative Score, Backgrounds and Sources, History and Analysis, Views and Comments*, Norton Critical Score, ed. Lewis Lockwood (New York: Norton, 1975), with documentary evidence and seventeenth-, eighteenth- and nineteenth-century comment on Palestrina and the Council of Trent (pp. 10–36), important historical essays by Lockwood and Jeppesen (pp. 77–130), eighteenth- and nineteenth-century critiques (pp. 133–40) and bibliography (pp. 141–2).

15 *Ulïbïshev/Mozart*

There is no modern literature on Ulïbïshev other than the article in *NGDM* (Geoffrey Norris). On the mid-nineteenth-century controversy over Ulïbïshev's view on Beethoven, see §16, below.

On Mozart's string quartets, see Thomas F. Dunhill, *Mozart's String Quartets* (London: OUP, 1927, 2/1948); Alfred Einstein, 'Mozart's Ten Celebrated String Quartets', *Music Review*, 3 (1942), 159–69; A.-E. Cherbuliez, 'Bemerkungen zu den "Haydn"-Streichquartetten Mozarts und Haydns "Russischen" Streichquartetten', *Mozart-Jahrbuch 1959*, 28–45; Alan Tyson, 'New Light on Mozart's "Prussian" Quartets', *Musical Times*, 116 (1975), 126–30. Specifically on the C major Quartet K465 ('Dissonance'), see §10 above; and on Momigny's analysis of the D minor Quartet K417*b*, see vol. II, Analysis 8.

16 *Schlosser, Fétis, von Lenz, Ulïbïshev/Beethoven*

On the nineteenth-century stylistic classification of Beethoven's output, see Maynard Solomon, 'The Creative Periods of Beethoven', *Music Review*, 34 (1973), 30–38; reprinted in *Beethoven Essays* (Cambridge, MA: Harvard University Press, 1988), pp. 116–25, 323–6; Joseph Kerman and Alan Tyson, 'The "Three Periods"', in *NGDM*, 'Beethoven', reprinted in *The New Grove Beethoven* (London: Macmillan, 1983), pp. 89–91. On the Romantic reception of Beethoven, see Arnold Schmitz, *Das romantische Beethovenbild* (Berlin and Bonn: Dümmler, 1927; reprint edn 1978); Jean Boyer, *Le "romantisme" de Beethoven* (Paris: Didier, 1938); Leo Schrade, *Beethoven in France: The Growth of an Idea* (New Haven: Yale University Press, 1942); William S. Newman, 'Some nineteenth-century Consequences of Beethoven's "Hammerklavier" Sonata, Opus 106', *The Piano Quarterly*, no. 67 (Spring 1969), 12–18, and no. 68 (Summer 1969), 12–16; Hans Heinrich Eggebrecht, *Zur Geschichte der Beethoven-Rezeption – Beethoven 1970* (Wiesbaden: Steiner, 1972); William S. Newman, 'The Beethoven Mystique in Romantic Art, Literature, and Music', *The Musical Quarterly*, 69 (1983), 354–87.

There is no literature on Schlosser. On Fétis's music-theoretical output, see the bibliography to the General introduction, above. On von Lenz, see Joseph Kerman's fine Foreword to von Lenz's *Beethoven et ses trois styles*, new edition, ed. M. D. Calvocoressi (Paris: Legouix, 1909; reprint edn New York: Da Capo, 1980), pp. v–xiv; also Ernest Newman, 'Wilhelm von Lenz', *Music & Letters*, 8 (1927), 268–72. On Ulïbïshev, there is no modern literature. For controversy over Ulïbïshev's views in his own day, see Alexander

Seroff, 'Ulibischeff gegen Beethoven', *NZM*, 47 (1857), 173–5, 185–8, 197, and 'Der Status Quo der Beethoven-Literatur und die Betheilung Russlands derselben', 58 (1863), 4–6, 11–12, 20–21, 27–9, 37–40; H. von Bülow: Eine französische Stimme über Ulibischeff', *Anregung für Kunst, Leben und Wissenschaft*, 3 (1858), 16ff.

Index

Contents of Volume II